HONEY SPRINGS, OKLAHOMA

WILLIAMS-FORD
TEXAS A&M UNIVERSITY
MILITARY HISTORY SERIES

HONEY SPRINGS, OKLAHOMA

Historical Archaeology of a Civil War Battlefield

WILLIAM B. LEES

TEXAS A&M UNIVERSITY PRESS
COLLEGE STATION

First edition

♾ This paper meets the requirements of ANSI/NISO Z39.48-1992 (Permanence of Paper).
Binding materials have been chosen for durability.

Library of Congress Control Number: 2025009115
Identifiers: LCCN: 2025009115 | ISBN 9781648432934 (printed case) | ISBN 9781648432941 (ebook)
LC record available at https://lccn.loc.gov/2025009115

CONTENTS

PREFACE

My Road to Honey Springs

JUST AS THERE WAS a prelude to the July 1863 Battle of Honey Springs, there was a prelude for my involvement in Honey Springs, first as a student and then as a professional archaeologist. I became involved in Honey Springs through serendipity and converging opportunity. For me, then, Honey Springs is both Civil War history and personal history; some of the latter informs the archaeology that I did there in the 1990s and the perspective that I have subsequently brought to this book.

In 1972, as I was preparing to graduate from high school, my interest led to an opportunity to join an archaeological project at the Honey Springs Battlefield, not far from my home in Tulsa. I spent five weeks that summer working on a project fielded by University of Tulsa professor Dr. Charles D. Cheek. He had a contract from the Oklahoma Historical Society to investigate buildings thought to be part of the Confederate headquarters and supply depot during the 1863 Civil War battle. Participating in this project inspired me to pursue the study of anthropology, beginning at the University of Oklahoma that fall, and ultimately a lifelong career in archaeology focusing on the historic era and conflict archaeology.

In 1972, historical archaeology was itself a new thing. Many veteran archaeologists did not themselves understand the power of archaeology when applied to the recent past, primarily because they believed documents and memory already held the answers. The Society for Historical Archaeology, which now stands as one of the preeminent archaeological scholarly societies in the world, had been formed at Southern Methodist University in Dallas only a few years earlier.

After transferring to the University of Tulsa to study under Dr. Cheek, I had the good fortune to meet Dr. Douglas Scott who was then the archaeologist at the Fort Towson Historic Site. Doug's work in the 1980s at the Little Bighorn Battlefield National Monument ushered in the modern era of archaeological work on battlefields, now known as conflict archaeology. Doug assisted with my initial work at Honey Springs as well as at what is now the Washita Battlefield National Historic Site, also in Oklahoma.

The importance of Doug's work at Little Bighorn cannot be overstated. There he pioneered the systematic use of metal detectors, operated by volunteer metal detectorists, to scan large areas of this site, find artifacts, map their locations, and use this information to reconstruct the event's progression and the actions of individual combatants. Using this approach, Doug demonstrated how metal detectorists could be useful volunteers for archaeology. This method allowed archaeologists to examine large-scale sites as never before. In addition, this approach resulted in a dramatic new interpretation of how this event unfolded and, for the first time, used the archaeological record as the basis for reconciliation of Native American memory with the popular narrative of "Custer's last stand." It directly confronted a narrative that metal detectors had no practical use for scientific archaeology and that metal detector hobbyists were of no use because they were untrustworthy. The success of this project, rapid publication, and widespread publicity began to change this narrative among archaeologists.

In 1985, I took a permanent position with the Kansas State Historical Society. In 1989, colleague John Reynolds and I undertook a metal detector survey of state-owned lands at the Mine Creek Battlefield in anticipation of its development as a public history site. We used volunteers and the methods used by Scott at Little Bighorn and found that substantial archaeological evidence of the battle remained. Analysis of artifact locations revealed patterns related to the positioning of combatants during the fight. But we also found that the state land, purchased based on local understanding of where the battle was fought, was but a small part of a much larger battlefield (Buresh 1978). Our work led to the planning for acquisition of the entire battlefield and development of on-site interpretation with a series of trails (American Battlefield Trust, n.d.; Lees 1992, 1994, 1998).

In 1993, I left Kansas for a job as the historic sites director at the Oklahoma Historical Society. I supervised public history sites, including the Honey Springs and Cabin Creek Battlefields, the Murrell Home, and Forts Gibson, Towson, and Washita, all part of the Indian Territory's antebellum and Civil War story. Most of these sites had been open to the public for some time, but Honey Springs remained largely undeveloped. A small area south of the springs had a parking area that provided access to an interpretive pavilion and a series of monuments to the battle. The 1972 University of Tulsa excavation site had returned to pasture, and twenty years on I had returned to help manage this site's future.

The Oklahoma Historical Society (OHS) owned a considerable acreage at Honey Springs that was waiting for development. Local stakeholders and OHS deputy director Dr. Bob Blackburn were keen to see it become a premier public history site. I immediately began to lay plans for conducting battlefield archaeology at Honey Springs. Starting in 1994, we used the methods pioneered by Doug Scott and that I had used at Mine Creek to survey a swath of state and private land that stretched for almost two miles north to south along the route of the Texas Road.

Battlefield archaeology at Honey Springs in 1994, 1996, 1997, and 1999 resulted in the confident coverage of most Oklahoma Historical Society property north of the site of the Confederate headquarters at Honey Springs. We also surveyed private property adjacent to portions of the state property with landowner permission. Unlike my findings at Mine Creek, patterns of artifacts showed that the main fighting at Honey Springs did occur on state land. Surveys on adjacent land confirmed this, but we found significant evidence of the battle on private lands (since purchased by the state) between the main battlefield and Honey Springs. More details and the conclusions of this project are the subject of this book.

Although I completed the fieldwork more than thirty years ago, I never finished a comprehensive report, for which I accept full responsibility. However, I did use insights from these and other preliminary analyses during the development of the interpretive plan for the site that the OHS subsequently implemented. That is the basis for the current visitor experience (Lees 2002, 2004, 2016). In addition, the OHS has constructed an impressive new visitor center at the south end of the battlefield. In 2015 and 2019 I visited the OHS's Fort Towson Historic Site where the collections from Honey Springs were stored, to reanalyze artifacts as I was writing this book. After so many years it is time to put this project to rest.

ACKNOWLEDGMENTS

SUCCESSFUL COMPLETION of this book represents the culmination of research on the Honey Springs Battlefield that I began in 1994 while at the Oklahoma Historical Society. This project involved many people over thirty years. Most notable were the many volunteers, landowners, National Park Service staff, and OHS staff who came together to make the fieldwork at Honey Springs possible. Critical were grants in 1994 and 1995 from the National Park Service's American Battlefield Protection Program (ABBP) to the Oklahoma Historical Society that helped support fieldwork and initial analysis and reporting. My work on this book, including several research trips to Oklahoma, is based firmly on the archaeological data collected through these grants.

Landowners who graciously allowed us to survey their property were Mary Cochran, Willard Combs, Alvin Dearmore, Jerry Garner, Lovie Bates Morris, Elaine Perkins, Ruby Perkins, Bob Talley, Motha Wallace, Henry Whatley, and Sue Woodard. Their understanding and interest in this project are appreciated. In terms of the volunteers, I owe a particular debt of gratitude to Art Long, then of Midwest City, Oklahoma, and Wayne Donohoe, of Topeka, Kansas. Wayne first worked with me at the Mine Creek Battlefield in Kansas and then as crew foreman at Honey Springs in 1994 and 1996. Art Long's first project with me was in 1994 at Honey Springs, where he assembled most of the crew of metal detectors. He assisted Wayne in 1994 and 1996 and led the team in 1997 and 1999. Both were instrumental in the ultimate success of the project.

In addition to Wayne and Art, volunteers were Fred Armstrong ('96), Heather Atherton ('96), Ken Baltes ('94, '96), Mary Bange ('94), Carolyn Bernaski ('96), Charles and Doris Bohuslavicky ('94, '96), Russ Broxterman ('96), Ben Clemons ('99), John Davidson ('97), Ann Furr ('96), Jerry Garner ('94), Pete Goad ('94, '96, '97), Larry Grimes ('94, '96, '97, '99), Neal Hollingshead ('94, '96, '97), Laura Hollis ('96), Bill Howard ('96, '99), Rich Kilblane ('94), Traci Lees ('99), Don and Donna Lighty

('94, '96), Bill Lollis ('94), Roque Martinez ('94, '96, '97), Sheri McAllister ('96), Ken and Shelle McGee ('94), Howard McKinnis ('99), Gary Moore ('94, '96, '97), Larry Moore ('94), Dan Pierce ('96, '97), Jim Quinlan ('96, '97), Ken Rainbolt ('94), Joshua Ryan ('94), Bret Shropshire ('94), Dwight Streeter ('96), Eddie Tamplin ('94, '96), Tom Tudor ('94), and Verben Williams ('94). It is possible that I have inadvertently omitted someone from this list.

Of the volunteers, Gary Moore requires special recognition for sharing information that he had obtained about the battlefield from prior metal detecting of the site. In addition, Gary donated some of his collection and related records to the OHS. I also note that Gary's metal detecting on state land was with the permission of a former manager of Fort Gibson Historic Site.

At the Oklahoma Historical Society, J. Blake Wade and Dr. Bob L. Blackburn (during fieldwork, executive director and deputy director, respectively) were incredibly supportive of the research program. Dr. Blackburn, now retired from the OHS, remained supportive for a book that I should have completed years ago. But rather than consider this project long overdue, I have borrowed a phrase from Australian colleague Andy Viduka and call this a "legacy" project. It undoubtedly is a better contribution to Honey Springs now than it would have been a decade or more ago due to advances in conflict scholarship and the evolution of my own perspective.

On the OHS board of directors, Dr. LeRoy Fischer (1917–2014; Oppenheim Professor of History, Emeritus, Oklahoma State University) was most enthusiastic about our findings due to his abiding interest in the Indian Territory's Civil War and the preservation of the Honey Springs Battlefield. OHS staff John Davis, Ralph "Rocky" Jones, Lynita Langley-Ware, Howard McKinnis, Chris Morgan, Max Nichols, Bob Rea, Katie Rose, Richard Ryan, Lola Shropshire, Heather Spencer, and William Vandever assisted with the project. Lynita Langley-Ware worked over an extended period on the analysis of the artifacts. I would like to also acknowledge my then-young son Carter for accompanying me during fieldwork and helping with cleaning the hundreds of artifacts discovered on the battlefield.

Ralph Jones deserves special mention for making many of the logistical arrangements and managing the grants for the project. I appreciate his friendship and his thorough knowledge of the history of the battlefield and neighboring residents. He was always ready to tap his encyclopedic knowledge when fielding a question as I was writing, and he graciously reviewed an early draft of my manuscript. Bob Rea and Richard Ryan also deserve special mention for being present for the duration of the fieldwork, including some brutally raw winter days. Richard also arranged land access and cooked many excellent field lunches. In addition, both provided appropriately dry humor to counter the often-challenging weather and were vital parts of leadership in the field. John Davis has been a friend and a colleague since I first met him at Fort Towson in 1993. He worked tirelessly to facilitate my two research trips to Fort Towson to work with the collections from Honey Springs.

My acknowledgments would be grossly incomplete without singling out the Friends of the Honey Springs Battlefield for supporting the archaeological project. The Friends have been the driving force in the preservation and interpretation of this site since its founding. While there are way too many members who shared interest and support to acknowledge (and remember many years on), there is one person I would be remiss without mentioning by name: the late Emmy Scott Stidham. Her leadership, embodied by incredible goodwill and enthusiasm, was a driving force for Honey Springs. This leadership was one of many reasons the Oklahoma Historical Society inducted her into the Oklahoma Historians Hall of Fame in 2019. I will never forget stopping by Emmy's house for corn chowder after meetings in Checotah.

At the National Park Service (NPS), the American Battlefield Protection Program staff deserves credit for administering one of the most successful, focused, and proactive preservation programs in the history of historic preservation. First, I am most grateful for this program's support for archaeological research at Honey Springs. Neil Mangum, then of the NPS Santa Fe Regional Office, was instrumental in helping with our grant applications and, in the field, as a source of information and insight into the fight. Also of the Santa Fe office, Charlie Haecker provided assistance drawn from experience on the Palo Alto Battlefield National Historical Park. Dr. Douglas D. Scott, then of the NPS's Midwest Archeological Center, has my perpetual gratitude for assisting in the initial fieldwork in 1994. I first met Doug in 1974 when he was the archaeologist at Fort Towson, and, with his constant encouragement, he is in no small measure responsible for the completion of this book. I benefited from his thoughts on an early draft.

This book comes a long time after I left Oklahoma. It was a personal endeavor supported by the University of West Florida (UWF), where I was executive director of the Florida Public Archaeology Network (FPAN) from 2005 until my retirement in 2023. Dr. Steven Brown, then dean of the College of Arts, Social Sciences, and Humanities, and former provost Dr. George Ellenberg (a Civil War historian) supported my writing by granting my fall 2019 sabbatical.

At UWF, Katherine Sims helped me with GIS for this project while earning her master's GIS certificate and completing her master's degree in anthropology under my supervision. She continued to assist with GIS during the final writing; the maps in this book well represent her work. In addition, while helping me manage FPAN, administrative specialist Mari Thornton—with precision and diligent attention to detail—edited several drafts of this manuscript and in particular wrangled the references. Finally, subject specialist librarian Britt McGowan at UWF's John C. Pace Library assisted throughout this project, especially when this all became more difficult during the COVID-19 pandemic.

Katie Horstman, senior specialist in American historic ephemera and early photography at Hindman Auctions, helped me with questions about a historic photograph that was sold at auction in 2007, and said to be of a Cherokee killed at the Battle of Honey Springs. The existence of this important image was first brought to my attention by Steve Warren through his Cabin Creek Battlefield Facebook presence. In addition, Kevin Dyke of the Maps and Spatial Data Department at Oklahoma State University's Edmon Low Library, provided remote assistance with several map needs. At the Kansas Historical Society, head of reference Lauren Gray and numerous staff in the archives research room were amazing in planning for and during my visit in September 2021. Archivist Amy Edwards of the Cartographic Branch of the National Archives at College Park, Maryland, provided very efficient remote assistance. The reference staff at the Washington DC National Archives location were, without exception, amazing during my March 2022 visit, which began on the first day they reopened after shuttering for Covid.

My wife Monica not only survived my increasing focus on finishing this project and writing this book but also provided constant encouragement and support. I recognized my sabbatical in the fall of 2019 as the gift it was, and I know that my singular focus on this project through the end of that semester must have been at times almost unbearable. I continued working on the manuscript through the Covid-19 pandemic that began in earnest for us on March 16, 2020, with an order from the university to work remotely. Putting the final touches on this career-spanning project followed me into retirement in April 2023.

I especially thank the Texas A&M University Press and editor in chief Thom Lemmons for taking interest in my manuscript. Two peer reviews obtained by the press helped me to see ways to markedly improve the strength and readability of this book. Project editor Abagail Chartier oversaw transformation of my manuscript into a finished book. I appreciate freelance copyeditor Chris Dodge for his careful and thoughtful work.

To these individuals and those I may have overlooked, I offer my most sincere thanks.

LAND RECOGNITION

THE BATTLE OF HONEY SPRINGS took place in what has been home to Muscogee people since their forced removal from their eastern homelands in 1836 and 1837, joining others who had "voluntarily" relocated west as early as 1827. Honey Springs remains within the sovereign national boundaries of the Muscogee Nation, although since 1907 it has also been within Oklahoma's Muscogee and McIntosh Counties.

For thousands of years, Oklahoma was home to Native Americans whose presence is known from archaeological evidence but whose names remain for the most part unknown. Early written records tell us that many peoples lived or regularly hunted in Oklahoma before passage of the US Federal Indian Removal Act of 1830. These include the Arapaho, Caddo, Cheyenne, Chickasaw, Choctaw, Comanche, Delaware, Kickapoo, Kiowa, Osage, Pawnee, Plains Apache, Quapaw, Shawnee, and Wichita peoples. Increasingly through time, inhabitants included citizens of Spain, France, and the United States who, according to their worldview and attendant laws, believed they "owned" this land. Present also were enslaved African Americans taken there by people of European and Native American ancestry.

As one of the consequences of being allies to the Confederacy, the treaty-granted communally held land of the Muscogee Nation was divided into townships and sections by the US General Land Office. Tribal members who enrolled through the Dawes Act received an individual allotment, and what was not allotted was sold. Evidence of the Battle of Honey Springs is within Sections 2 and 11 of Township 12 North, Range 17 East, and Section 35 of Township 13 North Range 17 East. In the early twentieth century, land in these sections was allotted in parcels ranging in size from 40 to 160 acres to Anna Banks, Mary Brown, Robert Brown, Cora Colbert, Dicey Colbert, Fannie Colbert, Susie Drew, Henry Foreman, Amanda Freeman, Leona Harrison, Sarah Harrison, Jesse Keys, Pearl Keys, Fannie Love, and Lizzie Tanner. They ranged in age from seven months to sixty-five years. All but one enrolled under the Dawes Act as Creek (Muscogee) Freedmen (formerly enslaved or a descendant of enslaved people); the single exception was enrolled as Creek (Muscogee) (Hastain 1910, 263, 265). Although the State of Oklahoma now holds legal title to the Honey Springs Battlefield, it remains within the sovereign boundaries of the Muscogee Nation.

HONEY SPRINGS, OKLAHOMA

FIGURE 1. General James G. Blunt (seated, center) and staff. Courtesy of the Kansas State Historical Society.

INTRODUCTION

I have designated this engagement as the "Battle of Honey Springs," that being the headquarters of General Cooper, on Elk Creek, in the immediate vicinity of the battlefield.
—Major General James G. Blunt
In the Field, July 26, 1863

THIS BOOK IS ABOUT the Battle of Honey Springs, fought on July 17, 1863, in the Muscogee (Creek) Nation of today's eastern Oklahoma.[1] Here Indian, Black, and White Union troops under Major General James G. Blunt defeated rebel Indians and Texas troops commanded by Brigadier General Douglas H. Cooper. Historians have argued that this was the pivotal battle fought in the Indian Territory during the Civil War.

In the two years before this battle, sovereign Indian nations juxtaposed between two warring parts of the same fractured country reopened wounds never fully healed from the brutal Indian removals. Internecine warfare in the Cherokee and Muscogee Nations caused a humanitarian crisis, and refugees flooded Kansas. Unfortunately, the United States and its Confederate adversary seemingly cared little for this unfolding tragedy. In 1863 the question for the Indian nations became how best to survive a national civil war.

Although constantly preoccupied with needs elsewhere, the United States and the Confederacy increasingly focused on controlling the Indian Territory. The Confederacy relied on Indian troops and Texans in this struggle. The United States bolstered White troops from Kansas and other western states with Indian and Black regiments initially raised among refugees in Kansas. In the first two years of the war, these national antagonists led the most diverse armies of the Civil War in struggles over a sliver of land in the Indian Territory north of the Arkansas River, culminating in the Battle of Honey Springs. Fought on the sovereign land of

FIGURE 2. Brigadier General Douglas H. Cooper.
Library of Congress image LC-USZ62-134004.

the Muscogee Nation, with combatants who were primarily members of sovereign Indian Nations and the formerly enslaved who were citizens of no nation, this battle and others in the Indian Territory are unique. Yet, while recognizing the human diversity of the participants, Honey Springs and other conflicts in Civil War Indian Territory have been treated by scholars as just another Civil War battle. Until recently, it was seen by many as a colorful expression of the "brother against brother" war, with few strategic consequences.

Twenty-first-century scholarship and the embrace by historians and anthropologists of a more inclusive interpretation of the past require that what happened in the Indian Territory receive new scrutiny. As a result, they are casting aside the mantle of sameness that has relegated Honey Springs and the entire West to the sidelines of Civil War history.

The importance of Honey Springs is evident when we look beyond the struggle over national unity and seek to engage with the agency of all participants. Seeing the Indian Territory not as the periphery to a war centered on the eastern seaboard but instead as related to a larger struggle of a nation rapidly expanding to the Far West serves to bridge the Civil War and a "Greater Reconstruction" that enveloped the West into the twentieth century.

This book is the first that focuses solely on the Battle of Honey Springs. Unlike most works on the Civil War, I have built it by analyzing the historical record (memory), the landscape, and the physical, archaeological remains of the fighting. Archaeology introduces new information on this conflict that has previously been unavailable to scholars and the interested public. Because this information is being introduced in print for the first time, the presentation may be unfamiliar for readers of history because of the attention to artifacts and the analysis of their placement on the landscape. Through this process, the location of fighting on July 17, 1863, is anchored to the modern landscape and precisely delimited for the first time. Within these boundaries of the conflict, patterns in the location of found artifacts provide new information and insight on the participants and the tragic events in which they were involved. With archaeology's ability to fix events to the land, the landscape itself becomes a critical factor facilitating "triangulation" with memory and the archaeological remains of the battle.

Considering landscape is essential for thinking about not only Honey Springs but also any battle. Still, all places are surely not the same. In a physical sense, some places are broad prairies, and others are mountainous. Some are an ocean or span a shoreline. Some are wooded, others grassland or wetland, and some are mixed. All can be covered with rocks or fragmented and delimited by ravines, bluffs, or cliffs. Some incorporate roads, houses, or towns, and some have rivers passing through. A landscape also may have cultural or emotional value. A battle may change the land dramatically for a time (with earthworks built, trees felled and damaged by shells, graves dug, and debris of war strewn). Some would say the very occurrence of conflict forever adds a character or value we call "hallowed." Human struggle and sacrifice consecrate the hallowed ground, and many believe it is an immutable quality of place. As Peter Svenson (1992, 39) wrote of his experience on Virginia's Cross Keys

Battlefield, "The very first time I walked on the battlefield, there seemed to be a faint emanation [that] was nothing I could put my finger on. . . . I dismissed it as a product of my imagination. I soon realized, however, that it had nothing to do with me, no matter how susceptible my brain was to the power of suggestion." Svenson goes on to say, "After that length of time, I would not have thought it possible to stand at the heart of a battlefield and pick up its living pulse." I have heard some say they feel this on the Honey Springs Battlefield.

It is possible to read an eyewitness account of a battle and form a vivid mental image of what happened and where. But invariably a mental image is challenged on a visit, if not discarded altogether. When there, you must reimagine the battle with the actual landscape before your eyes. Reading multiple accounts of the same event or place becomes even more confusing. It becomes clear that written statements are fragments of memories that only contain what an author thought useful for chronicling their experience. A witness may describe a seemingly prominent feature of the landscape. At the same time, another may ignore it entirely, and you may find that viewing the landscape today provides no solution to this discrepancy. The last Civil War veterans died in the 1950s and can no longer clarify missing or confusing details; unconscious memories that combine to form a flawed and sometimes confusing or contradictory record remain.

A historian's summary of a conflict may be compelling and may seem to have resolved all the conflicting and vague accounts and "properly" filled in the parts that are entirely missing. Still, these summaries are imperfect; historians often rise to challenge the narratives of others. The landscape contested in battle thus becomes contested by historians and the interested public who favor different ways of seeing the same past. In this era of post-colonial aspirations, culture-bound assumptions about history also require reevaluation.

Of course, long-standing debates over a historical event can be advanced and sometimes solved by discoveries of additional documents that shed light on contested or poorly understood narratives. Significant sources still come to light. A perfect example is the map of Union and Confederate graves on the Antietam battlefield drawn in 1864 and rediscovered in 2020 in the New York Public Library (Ruane 2020). However, increasingly archaeology brings to light a new set of information that, while imperfect, is not skewed by memory (but perhaps is skewed in other ways) and is tied literally to the battlefield landscape.

Because of the centrality of landscape, I use the concept of "battlespace" and KOCOA military terrain analysis to reconcile the two main sources of historical information about the battle: 1) the archaeological remains of the fight consisting of found artifacts and their location on the modern landscape, and 2) the memory of the battle, consisting primarily of reports and accounts written near the time of the event and stories transcribed years later. Battlespace and KOCOA analysis are forward-looking tools developed to help military strategists evaluate landscape for tactical or defensive advantage and risk. These have been adapted by historians and archaeologists as tools to consider the record of a historical event in a sort of reverse engineering approach. Where only memory is available, these approaches can help us understand the link between events and the landscape and also suggest the best fit between vague or seemingly contradictory memory and a landscape where conflicting interpretations are possible. Archaeology adds greater certainty to the question of where, and these tools then provide a useful lens through which to see the battle in terms that I believe would be familiar to participants. They do so by exposing the landscape as a set of complex variables that commanders and soldiers reacted to leading up to, during, and after the battle.

Understanding artifacts and their placement on the landscape and juxtaposing this with the recorded history of the battle brings new information, questions, and conclusions to the study of the Battle of Honey Springs. Because this archaeological information results from new scientific inquiry, I necessarily expose the reader to the process that gives this information validity and value. Thus, this book will not read the same as the typical narrative of an event penned by a historian. Many types of artifacts are described, and their use and importance are established. Maps of the distribution of artifacts on the fields of conflict are analyzed to consider what they have to say about what transpired the day of the battle. This process releases and validates new information on the Battle of Honey Springs. Still, I strive to stay out of the literary weeds that archaeologists are known to let grow very tall and keep the narrative moving forward to conclusions that I believe are new and important.

Above all, I think the physical evidence has helped to balance the story of the Battle of Honey Springs. There is no way to read this event's historical accounts and transcribed memories and not conclude that witnesses left much unsaid or shrouded in uncertainty. Imbalance also results from fewer rebel reports and more focus on the initial fighting than what followed. Furthermore, most participants were Indians and African Americans, who are consistently not well represented in the historical record of the Civil War (Yarbrough 2021, 7).

Thus, this first book on the Battle of Honey Springs stands on the convergence of three complementary lines of evidence: historical, landscape, and archaeology. Physical evidence anchors the historical record to the landscape in previously impossible ways, resolving questions born of uncertainty while invariably leading to new questions. Some of these questions come into focus when the physical remains of the battle are inconsistent with expectations flowing from the historical accounts. For example, a skirmish referred to in passing attains an unexpected physical reality, and exceedingly vague descriptions of the final action of the day become visible in time and space. Others require a reexamination of the history and sometimes the search elsewhere for explanations. Considering the historical references, the physical footprint of fighting, and different cultural concepts of warfare offers an interpretation of physical reality that I believe helps restore voice to the Native American combatants.

The Battle of Honey Springs spanned only a moment in time. The battlefield that we know today is defined on the one hand by a physical landscape long established in the region and by cultural events (particularly in the nineteenth and twentieth centuries). With the acquisition of Louisiana by the United States in 1803, land became available that would soon become a new home for many members of the Cherokee, Choctaw, Muscogee, Chickasaw, and Seminole Nations (the "Five Civilized Tribes" or "Five Tribes"). These people were forced from their eastern homelands by increasing encroachment and pressure by neighboring White settlers and ultimately by provisions of the Indian Removal Act of 1830. In relocating from their eastern homelands in a process that by itself was tragic, many members of these tribes moved into lands long used by others, such as Osage, Wichita, Comanche, Kiowa, and Plains Apache people (Warde 2013, 5). Inevitable conflicts affected the settlement of the immigrant tribes and ultimately the canvas on which the Civil War would unfold.

In 1860, the US government considered the Indian Territory to belong to the Five Tribes.[2] They represented only about half of the one

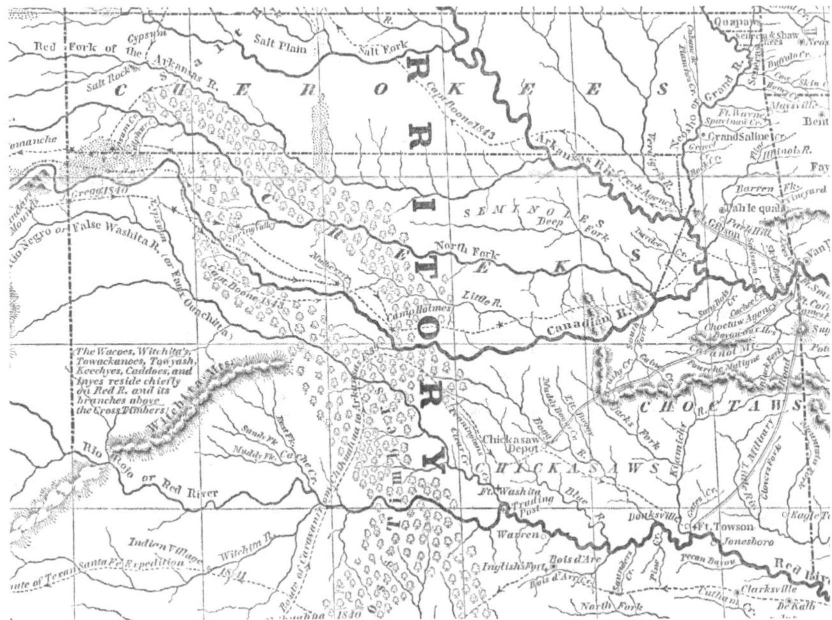

FIGURE 3. Detail of 1844 Josiah Gregg map showing the eastern Indian Territory (Gregg 1844). Courtesy of the Oklahoma State University Library Digital Map Collection.

hundred thousand people who Oklahoma Historical Society historian Mary Jane Warde (2013) believes should be counted as residents at that time. Other residents included the "indigenous" tribes mentioned above; small groups of Quapaw, Seneca, and Shawnee people relocated from Kansas; plains tribes relocated from Texas; US military personnel occupying forts in the southwestern part of the territory; along with authorized missionaries, traders, and contractors. It is, nonetheless, the Five Tribes, inhabiting the eastern half of the territory, that are central to the story of Honey Springs.

Enrollment figures of the Five Tribes at their removal, which varied by their respective negotiated treaty agreements, provide an estimate of population, which Doran places at 47,927 individuals (Doran 1975, 496). By 1860, due to the hardship of removal itself and rampant disease on arrival in the West, populations had declined sharply by about one-third overall, with ranges from 18 to 53 percent by tribe (Doran 1975,

498). There were also in 1860 some 2,299 Whites and an estimated 8,376 enslaved African Americans in the territory (Doran 1975, 501). This adds up to 58,602, a number measurably below the 1860 populations for the states and US territory sharing a border with the Indian Territory (Kennedy 1864, iv).

This small population was not distributed evenly across the treaty lands. This unevenness was undoubtedly partly due to a preference for the eastern part of the territory because it closely resembled the new residents' former eastern homelands (Confer 2007, 37). This area also more easily supported "traditional" agricultural and hunting economies and the market-driven agriculture common in the southeastern states at the time (Warde 2013, 26). Another factor affecting settlement was the conflict with plains tribes, who refused to recognize the territorial claims of the new residents. The Chickasaws, for example, did not settle in their treaty lands until the United States established military posts along the Washita River for their protection, choosing instead to live temporarily among the Choctaws. Earlier, clashes between Cherokees in northwestern Arkansas, who had moved there during the second decade of the nineteenth century in anticipation of removal, and Osages living on the Verdigris River prompted the establishment of Fort Gibson to stop their violent reciprocity.

Settlement of tribal members and the relatively small number of Whites and a more significant number of enslaved people has been reconstructed by Doran using several unfortunately uneven and scarce sources. Doran used the 1852 Drennan Payroll to show that Cherokees had settled primarily in the eastern part of their treaty lands bounded on the west by the Arkansas and Grand Rivers; important Cherokee towns of Tahlequah and Park Hill are central to this region (Doran 1975, 499–500). Other sources, including the 1860 US Census, which did not record tribal citizens but did record Whites and enslaved African Americans, led Doran to show:

- a band of settlement in the Choctaw and Chickasaw Nations stretching west along the Red River to slightly past the Washita River (and protection of its US forts);
- a concentration of settlement in the northern Choctaw Nation along and south of the Canadian and Arkansas Rivers;

- a corresponding concentration in the eastern Muscogee Nation on the opposite side of the North Canadian;
- and a broad area of settlement in the northeastern part of the Muscogee Nation, including the towns of Tulsa and Muskogee.

Based on demographic data for Whites and enslaved people in the 1860 census, which excludes most of the population, Doran suggests that most of the settlement in the Indian Territory around 1860 was on small farms typical of most of the Southeast. Also, certain areas showed concentrations of enslaved African Americans. One was in the band of settlements along the Red River in the Choctaw and Chickasaw Nations. Doran associates this band with large-scale plantation agriculture focused on crops such as cotton. In other areas in the southern Muscogee Nation and the Muscogee and Cherokee Nations at the juncture of the Verdigris and Grand Rivers, he argues, enslaved people were made to toil in the production of corn, cattle, and salt (Doran 1975, 505–6).

The Honey Springs Battlefield straddles present-day Muskogee and McIntosh Counties in east-central Oklahoma, on the eastern side of the Muscogee Nation. It lies between the present-day communities of Oktaha to the north and Rentiesville and Checotah to the south. To the southeast are the Ouachita Mountains, with a cover mostly of oak-pine forest. Northeast lies the "foothills" of the Ozark Plateau (known locally as "mountains"), with a cover mostly of oak-hickory forest. The battlefield lies to the west, somewhere in the transition zone between the southeastern woodlands and the Great Plains (Hoagland 2008). Rainfall and elevation are the critical variables in defining this transition, with precipitation falling by half in a relatively even continuum from east to west (H. L. Johnson 2008) and elevation increasing progressively toward the west (K. S. Johnson 2008). In defining the extent of the Great Plains, Wishart (2011, para. 24) concludes, without saying where he would draw the line, "Eastern Oklahoma and eastern Texas are . . . excluded from the Plains because of overwhelming evidence that historically, environmentally, and culturally their orientation is to the South." In discussing the Choctaws and Chickasaws in the Indian Territory, Yarbrough (2021, 75–113) would wholeheartedly agree with Wishart.

Many factors, such as land abandonment and fire suppression, have since conspired to mask what earth scientists call the "potential" native vegetation (before human intervention). In the mid-nineteenth century, the area from Honey Springs stretching north to Fort Gibson, Cabin Creek, and eventually to Fort Scott, Kansas—all places familiar to the US soldiers who fought at Honey Springs—was a swath of tallgrass prairie (Hoagland 2008). This swath was in a wide band of tallgrass prairie intermixed with old-growth post oak–blackjack oak forest known as the Cross Timbers that stretched from Texas to Kansas and the Ozark and Ouachita uplifts to far western Custer County (Hoagland 2008).

Most of this area, and most of Oklahoma, is in the Arkansas River drainage, which flows to the Mississippi River through Arkansas past historical places such as Fort Smith, Little Rock, and Arkansas Post. The southern part of the state, familiar to the Confederate-allied Indians who fought at Honey Springs, is drained by the Red River. The Red River was an international boundary between the United States and Mexico and then, after the Texas Revolution, the Republic of Texas. In 1845, it became the border with the new state of Texas. The Red flows east through Arkansas and into Louisiana past Shreveport (until the 1830s the head of navigation), past fertile antebellum plantation lands around Natchitoches, Louisiana, then through Alexandria, Louisiana, and eventually connecting to the Mississippi and the Atchafalaya Rivers. Both the Arkansas and the Red Rivers tied the Indian Territory to places such as New Orleans, Vicksburg, St. Louis, and Cincinnati.

Although imported goods could come overland, the rapid expansion of steam power to the western rivers in the second and third decades of the nineteenth century make it likely that they were shipped via steamboats on the Arkansas and Red Rivers. Steamboats could not reach beyond Shreveport on the Red River until 1838 after the US government had spent years and considerable treasure driving a channel through the "Great Raft," a log jam that had blocked the river seemingly forever. This herculean government program spoke to the importance of the young nation's economic interests of gaining reliable access for steamboats to the new Republic of Texas and the Indian Territory. Here newly relocated Choctaws and Chickasaws were rebuilding their lives, with an economy partly focused on large-scale agricultural production for export (Crisman, Lees, and Davis 2013).

The landscape also defined overland transportation in the Indian Territory. For example, the Osage Trace was used by Osage people to travel southwest from their western Missouri villages to hunting grounds in Oklahoma and Arkansas. It followed the Grand or Neosho River and skirted the dense oak-hickory forests and foothills of the Ozark Plateau in northeastern Oklahoma and eventually merged with the Arkansas River. There, the Osages could follow the Arkansas upstream to the Great Plains or downstream to traditional hunting grounds in what is today the state of Arkansas (Weaver n.d.).

Beginning in the 1780s, some Cherokee began a voluntary migration from ancestral homelands east of the Appalachians to the eastern Arkansas Territory. By the second decade of the nineteenth century, they had started to relocate to the Arkansas River valley of western Arkansas (Warde 2013, 13–14). Here these Cherokee "Old Settlers" clashed with the Osages, then living in what is now west-central Missouri, who had long claimed this land as hunting territory. Clashes were fierce with Clermont's village, an Osage outlier located on the Verdigris River along the Osage Trace from about 1802 to 1840 (Lees 1975). As a result, the United States established Fort Smith in 1817 and Fort Gibson in 1824 to prevent the brutal reciprocal attacks that resulted from this conflict (Agnew 1980, 7–28; Stewart-Abernathy 2019).

Similar in route to the Osage Trace, at least as far south as Fort Gibson, was the Texas Road, which early in the nineteenth century became the major north–south route through the Indian Territory. Much like the Osage Trace, the Texas Road took the path of least resistance in the relatively open prairies just west of the Ozarks and Ouachitas. After the Confederacy denied federal use of the Arkansas River, supplies to US-held Fort Gibson came from Fort Scott, Kansas, via Cabin Creek along the Texas Road. To the south were Honey Springs, North Fork Town, Perryville, Boggy Depot, Fort Washita, and finally Colbert's Ferry on the Red River (just down the Washita River from Forts Cobb, Arbuckle, and Washita) (Foreman 1936).

Following the Civil War, the Missouri, Kansas, and Texas Railroad (MK&T) gained the right to build a line through the Indian Territory (Veenendall n.d.). The line was built in the territory between 1871 and 1872 and roughly followed the Texas Road. The line runs a little over one-half mile west of the course of the Texas Road at Honey Springs. Speculators established the towns mentioned earlier—Oktaha, Rentiesville, and Checotah—along the MK&T shortly after its construction. On

FIGURE 4. Swales of the Texas Road near Honey Springs. Photo taken before 1934 by Alvin Rucker. Courtesy of the Oklahoma Historical Society.

his way to Texas in 1874, Albert Rust (1874, 2) noted, "In passing over this road [the MK&T] we are in sight of the battlefield of . . . Honey Springs, as the confederates called it. I am told there are many human bones unburried on the spot."

In the early twentieth century, the Jefferson Highway Association marked an automobile route, known as the Jefferson Highway, along existing roads that very roughly followed the Texas Road, and it passed by Honey Springs. This route evolved into a highway labeled State Road 6, US 73, and ultimately US 69. It passes about one and one-quarter miles west of Honey Springs. While the Civil War was the first blow to the Texas Road, the next—and having a more lasting impact—was the railroad. The final blow was section-line roads for local travel and state and national highways for wider automobile travel (Corbett n.d.).

Honey Springs

Honey Springs is a natural freshwater spring that became a landmark destination on the Texas Road and gained lasting recognition as the namesake of the most consequential Civil War battle in the Indian Territory.

FIGURE 5. Rock walls of Honey Springs. Photo taken before 1934 by Alvin Rucker. Courtesy of the Oklahoma Historical Society.

Lucinda Davis, an often-quoted source about the Battle of Honey Springs, lived about two miles south of Elk Creek on the Texas Road.[3] In 1937, Works Progress Administration interviewers recorded Ms. Davis.[4] She was about eighty-nine years old (born about 1848). In 1863, she would have been fifteen and one of about ten enslaved people belonging to full-blood Muscogee Tuskaya-hiniha. Her narrative provides a more helpful picture of life in the vicinity of Honey Springs Depot at the time of the battle than it does of the battle itself (Baker and Baker 1996, 107–17).

Ms. Davis said her master bought her to take care of his young child, and she described his residence: "A good log house and a bresch shelter [brush arbor] out in front like all de houses had. Like a gallery, only it had de dirt for de flo' and bresh on de roof. Dey cook everything out in de yard in big pots, and dey eat out in de yard too" (Baker and Baker 1996, 109). She said that the house was "set in a little patch of woods wid de field in de back, but all out on de north side was a little open space, like a kind of prairie" (112).

Ms. Davis also described what slavery looked like from her family's perspective, "My mammy and pappy belong to two masters, but dey live together on a place. Dat de way de Creek slaves do lots of times. Dey work patches and give de masters most all dey make, but dey have some for demselves. Dey didn't have to stay on de master's place and work like I hear de slaves of de white people and de Cherokee and Choctaw people say dey had to do" (Baker and Baker 1996, 109). Although what slavery looked like differed by nation and region of the Indian Territory, this, as well as the details of the daily lifestyle she described, was probably typical of the Muscogee Nation for some distance around Honey Springs (Krauthamer n.d.; Warde 2013, 31).

According to Warde (2013, 26–7),

> Some of the more traditional Muscogee people kept their communities intact as they moved to their new homeland. They cleared and planted large common fields in the river valleys and reestablished their ceremonial grounds. Others chose to live on individual ranches and plantations. By the 1840s Indian farmers were raising crops of corn, beans, and squash along with peas, sweet and Irish potatoes, melons, peaches, apples, pears, plums, cherries, oats, rice, and cotton. Indian farmers raised turkeys, ducks, and geese and turned their hogs loose to multiply and graze on acorns in the eastern Indian Territory forests. Ranchers, though, sometimes resettled on the prairies to graze their cattle and horses on the abundant, head-high bluestem grass. Livestock, in fact, became the wealth of the Indian Territory by 1860.

It is challenging to describe the mid-nineteenth-century appearance of Honey Springs and the cultural landscape along the Texas Road near the battlefield. Communal ownership in the Muscogee Nation did not produce records that historians use to track residents and their locations through time. Also, the status of the Muscogee people as members of their nation but not citizens of the United States meant there were no antebellum census records. Nevertheless, in the report on an archaeological study of two buildings excavated at Honey Springs in 1972, Drs. Garrick Bailey and Charles Cheek of the University of Tulsa spent considerable effort reconstructing this landscape (Bailey 1976; Cheek 1976, 27–32). Although the accompanying map has accuracy issues, the James S. Buchanan and Carl Plischke Honey Springs Battlefield Survey of 1938 (Buchanan and Plischke 1976, 4, 129–34) documented the location of the Shaw Place, the McIntosh Toll Bridge over Elk Creek, two soldier burial grounds south of Elk Creek on either side of the Texas Road, and several features around Honey Springs itself.

FIGURE 6. Ruin of stone building at Honey Springs. Photo taken before 1934 by Alvin Rucker. Courtesy of the Oklahoma Historical Society.

FIGURE 7. Foundation of the stone building uncovered by the University of Tulsa in 1972. Photo by William Lees.

In 1964, Jess C. Epple published a description of the Confederate headquarters at Honey Springs, apparently informed by interviews with locals and battle veterans. Epple described the stone-walled springs, which are still visible, and a stone "Trading Post built in the early 1850's, used as a Commissary building by Confederates" (Epple 1964, 25). Buildings constructed by Confederates were a stone powder magazine and log warehouse, hospital, and officer quarters. Epple says Confederate troops camped in tents around the springs and to the north and that the stone powder magazine was the last building standing on the site (Epple 1964, 25). However, what Epple called the powder magazine was one of the buildings excavated by Cheek in 1972 that he believes was built after the Civil War (Cheek 1976, 128).

In an 1875 account of traveling through the Indian Territory on the Texas Road in the vicinity of Honey Springs, C. C. Poole (1875) noted that the Creeks operated toll bridges across even dry branches of streams and harvested hay from the abundant prairie lands. Along the Texas Road in the vicinity of Honey Springs, the modern vegetation is a mixture of reasonably mature woods and grasslands. However, except for extreme slopes, this setting has been changed by preparing fields for cultivation or grazing. This alteration is readily apparent from modern aerial photography, which reveals a patchwork of sections divided and subdivided, most commonly down to forty-acre blocks. The "rectangular" system that created this patchwork was not present until the US General Land Office divided the future state of Oklahoma into "townships." Each township contained thirty-six "sections" that were one-mile square each (640 acres), which were then commonly subdivided into quarter sections (160 acres) and quarter-quarter sections (40 acres).

In Muskogee County, R. L. McAlpine and J. W. Riley established this grid by survey in March 1896. In McIntosh County, C. H. Dana and J. P. Thayer completed a similar survey in June 1897. Although they observed the landscape over thirty years after the battle, their general description probably comes close to mirroring what participants would have seen in 1863. For the area lying north of Elk Creek in Muskogee County, they noted an abundance of prairie except along the streams and that farming was done along the creek bottoms, with haying and grazing in the uplands (McAlpine and Riley 1896, 38). To the south in McIntosh

FIGURE 8. Volunteers during the 1994 survey at Honey Springs. Photo by William Lees.

County, the surveyors noted rolling prairie with timber along the creeks in the bottomlands (Dana and Thayer 1897, 45).

Archaeology at Honey Springs

During the late 1990s, I led a team of professional archaeologists, Oklahoma Historical Society (OHS) staff, and volunteers, some armed with metal detectors, on repeated visits to the Honey Springs Battlefield to find artifacts left from the conflict of July 17, 1863. Our project expeditions were made during the fall and winter when temperatures were cool, if not cold, and vegetation (leaves and vines) and insects (ticks and mosquitoes) were less of a problem. Insects and heat are an annoyance, but woods in the summer impeded visual coordination and use of optical surveying instruments that required a clear line of sight. The focus of these visits was land owned by the OHS, but through the kind permission of some adjacent landowners, the search extended beyond.

Our work stretched along the old Texas Road for over three miles, running roughly north to south. We determined the width of our survey by artifact finds and access to private land, but in general this was about one-half mile or less. We spent thirty-nine days in the field between 1994 and 1999.[5] We recovered 736 artifacts that I consider likely to be related to the battle and are the central foundation of this book. These artifacts include conical and spherical ammunition and a few cartridge cases, parts of firearms, artillery projectiles, military equipment, buttons, personal possessions, and arrowheads (that I argue do relate to the battle). Other found objects not discussed here may relate to the period of the battle, but it is these 736 that I use with relative confidence to reconstruct the conflict and place it in the modern landscape. However, correlating individual artifacts with the battle cannot be done without some caution because the Texas Road was used long before and after. Travelers or residents may have left some of the discovered items at another time. I will show, however, why this is generally an unlikely concern.

The 736 found artifacts may seem an insignificant number to study a battle of the Civil War. Nevertheless, using standard methods of battlefield archaeology, this number is sufficient. Our intention was never to recover all the artifacts remaining on the battlefield but rather to retrieve a consistently representative sample of those within the study area. By careful analysis of material and form, the function, age, and cultural associations of artifacts can often be determined. Artifacts deriving from the battle can be sorted from those of a more recent age. This and the precise location where each was found are central to this study. Mapping the physical residue of the battle on the modern landscape makes it possible to anchor historical places and events and set the stage for comparing the archaeological and the historical.

We employed methods at Honey Springs designed to achieve consistent and even coverage of the landscape as our project progressed. This consistency made us confident that the observed and documented distribution of artifacts on the landscape mimics the location of areas of fighting in the summer of 1863. Modern terrain and vegetation in the study varied from open fields to thick brush. Achieving consistent coverage was a challenge, but I am comfortable with the results.

The method used at Honey Springs was the same that I used in the late 1980s to study the 1864 Battle of Mine Creek in Kansas (Lees 1998). I based this directly on the methods developed by National Park Service archaeologist Dr. Douglas D. Scott and others during pioneering work at the Little Bighorn Battlefield National Monument earlier in that decade (D. Scott and Fox 1987; D. Scott et al. 1989). Scott divided the battlefield into manageable units; a crew of professionals and volunteers used metal detectors to scan each unit and mark finds systematically; and artifacts were excavated, recorded, and collected. Metal detectorists were spaced at set intervals along one edge of a study unit and walked and swept the ground in front of them as a team, progressing slowly across the field and marking "hits" with pin flags. A crew followed behind, excavated the hits carefully, and recorded and collected the finds. Yet another team mapped the findspot with electronic surveying instruments, preserving the artifact's precise depth below the surface and its exact horizontal location: being systematic and recording comparable data was key.

Earlier, a few others had done successful archaeological projects on battlefields—for example, Robert Bray's 1958 work at the Reno-Benteen defense site at the Little Bighorn Battlefield and Dean Snow's 1972 work at Saratoga Battlefield (Bray 1958; Snow 1972). Still, Scott's Little Bighorn project went viral, and both the public and the archaeology profession took note, leading to a rapidly growing number of studies in conflict archaeology (Lees and Noble 2015, 3). In many ways, this project was transformational, not only because of its pioneering methods but also because the technique allowed the systematic archaeological study of large-scale events like battles. These had before been considered unapproachable through traditional archaeological methods. Likewise, it was pioneering because archaeologists had long seen hobbyist–metal detectorists as the bane of their profession. Many archaeologists believed (and some still do) that working alongside them is unacceptable (Longo 1988). Today the use of metal detectors in conflict archaeology has become normalized, and archaeologists are finding more and more applications of metal detection to address problems beyond conflict studies (see, for example, Reeves and Schweickart 2019).

Honey Springs was challenging ground for this method, partly because of the size of the study area and partly because the land was a mixture of parcels of pasture and woods divided along current and former property lines and long-established agricultural fields used for crops or pasture. Although some areas proved more difficult to survey and record (trees and brush are a problem for both, even without leaves), we employed a consistent single-pass approach. The field crew recorded location information with electronic and optical transits, with parcel surveys referenced to known points such as section corners, cemetery fences, and buildings. This ability to correlate all finds with known landmarks allowed the correlation of data into one AutoCAD map in the 1990s that was in turn migrated into a geographic information systems (GIS) platform a few years ago. While certainly not as accurate as it would have been with the aid of current Global Positioning System (GPS) technology, the resulting maps are sufficiently precise for the questions at hand, focusing on landscape-level analysis.

Private Collecting and the Battlefield

Our job as archaeologists would be easier if all the battle-related artifacts that once lay scattered across the battlefield had remained in 1994 for us to find, record, and map. That was not to be, however. Many natural processes (decay and erosion) and cultural processes (salvage, clearing, and collecting) have removed many of these artifacts from Honey Springs and most other Civil War sites. Decay was undoubtedly a factor, with artifacts made from cloth and leather, for example, disintegrating over time. Salvage of military goods from Honey Springs also is known to have happened. Major General Blunt reported "1 piece of artillery, 1 stand of colors, 200 stand of arms, and 15 wagons" collected from the battlefield by his troops following the battle (Blunt 1888g, 448). Lyman A. Darling, who lived in Oktaha between 1902 and 1918, remembered: "[Uncle Charley Foreman brought] cannon balls and shell fragments and minnie balls from the battlefield, some of which are still in our family" (Darling 1976, 137). In addition, changing landscapes following subdivision and allotment resulted in profound changes in the appearance of the battlefield since 1863. There is, however, no question that private collecting of artifacts—more than decay or post-battle military gathering—has had the most significant impact on the archaeological landscape of the battle.

Collecting artifacts from Civil War battlefields is known to have started as soon as the smoke cleared. Although there is no report of this, the US soldiers encamped on the battlefield at Honey Springs probably collected souvenirs of the fight in which they had just engaged. Wiley Britton (1890, 366) describes the soldiers under Blunt, then a brigadier general, collecting souvenirs at the Pea Ridge Battlefield when encamped there before the Battle of Old Fort Wayne in October 1862: "The signs of the great battle fought in March, between the Federal forces under General Samuel R. Curtis and the Confederate forces under Generals Earl Van Dorn, Sterling Price, and Benjamin McCulloch, were still visible on every hand, and many of the soldiers availed themselves of the opportunity of going over the field which had recently been the scene of blood and strife, for the purpose of picking up something, such as a piece of shell, or bullet, or buckle, as a souvenir to be sent north to relatives or friends."

Museums ranging from the Smithsonian Institution's Museum of American History in Washington, DC, to the Confederate Memorial Hall Museum in New Orleans display long-ago-collected relic tree stumps laden with embedded bullets and shrapnel speaking of the ferocity of battle. Alongside these are memorial "relic boards" made by veterans within a decade or so of an epic struggle, often presented to their officers as remembrances of fighting in which they were engaged. I know of no similar examples from the Battle of Honey Springs.

Untold artifacts also found their way onto the mantles of early battlefield tourists or landowners as casual souvenirs or were picked up, literally bucketsful, by farmers working fields behind mule-drawn plows. Some of these found their way into antique and souvenir shops near significant battlefields; most have an unknown fate and are probably lost forever (see, for example, Svenson 1992, 17). Finally, a pitiful few have found their way into museums cataloged as to who found them and sometimes a vague notation of where. Claims of precise provenance that come from some of these old collector donations require scrutiny (Bonsall 2019).

Interest in making Honey Springs a battlefield park grew during the Civil War centennial. In 1965, a reporter with the *Checotah News* wrote, "A collection of civil war relics to be exhibited at a museum to be erected at Honey Springs battle field, has been started by Charley Little, local real estate operator" (*Checotah News* 1965). Little was seeking loans from other private collections from the battlefield. Unfortunately, I know not of Mr. Little's success in this endeavor or his collection and its disposition today.

Following World War II and the Korean conflict, surplus military mine detectors became available for public purchase. These devices began to be used by individuals looking for everything from Spanish coins washed up on Florida and Texas beaches to relics of the Civil War. By the 1960s, a growing number of private manufacturers commercialized this technology for civilian use (Von Mueller 1966, 122, 313). Aggressive advertising touted the ease of finding coins, treasure, and relics. As a result, a favorite genre of metal detecting became "relics," and hobbyists increasingly ventured to publicly and privately owned heritage sites such as forts and battlefields, including Honey Springs.

Private individuals using metal detectors have, with certainty, extracted artifacts from Honey Springs in large numbers. Some of these individuals detected on private land, perhaps with permission, and much was undoubtedly done on state-owned land, occasionally with permission. Unfortunately, most artifacts acquired in this fashion have vanished along with the information on their locations. An unusual and fortunate exception is the work of Fort Gibson resident Gary Moore in the early 1980s. With the permission of Fort Gibson Historic Site manager David Robertson, Moore conducted metal detecting in 1982 and 1983 in an area known locally, or at least by him, as the "Wooded Forty." This land is located north of Elk Creek and contains visible swales of the Texas Road. The Oklahoma Historical Society purchased this land in about 1980 because they correctly believed it to be central to the Battle of Honey Springs.

Moore was also a key member of our project team in 1994, 1996, and 1997. In 1994, we surveyed the Wooded Forty, and Moore's insights into this area from his previous work proved essential. From Moore and other informants we know that many individuals were working the state land, most without permission. What is different and important about Moore is that he kept records of his findings, worked closely with us, and shared his insights on what we found. Insights from comparing his work with ours provide a rare window into a significant process of site formation: private removal of artifacts from the site. Moore recorded his finds in a "Search & Recovery Log" that included a list of finds and a map of locations. His maps of his finds are vague sketches but show most were from the western edge of the Wooded Forty in the vicinity of the Texas Road swales. He was with us as we systematically covered this Wooded Forty, working from east to west. As we moved into the western edge of the parcel, Moore was disheartened because the location where he had found most artifacts was an area where fewer artifacts remained (Lees 1996). He also noted that while we were finding only bullets and exploded cannonballs, his finds had been more diverse and included items such as buttons and gun parts. As collecting had diminished the overall numbers, these items had become exceedingly rare.

In earlier work at the Mine Creek Battlefield in Kansas, I surveyed land owned by the Kansas State Historical Society and adjacent private land. I noted that the density of artifacts increased when we crossed the fence and passed from state onto private land. Private landowners that had granted the society permission to extend our archaeological survey onto their land told us they had not previously allowed private access to search for artifacts. The conclusion that I reached is that private individuals chose to use their metal detectors on what was then unsupervised state land because they were denied access elsewhere or just because it was easier. The bottom line at Mine Creek is that our study showed private metal detecting had concentrated on state land and had affected the preservation of scientific information across the larger battlefield (Lees 1996, 1998).

The Mine Creek example shows the impact of land ownership on archaeological preservation. Honey Springs is a patchwork of public and private lands, and it can be inferred, by extension, that this has resulted in some grounds being searched more intensively by private collectors. Although we have reliable information on what happened in the Wooded Forty, we can only speculate about the history of collecting elsewhere and its impact on our ability to see the residues of battle as an accurate reflection of actions on July 17, 1863.

In my research, I have run across two accounts of private collecting at Honey Springs published in magazines geared to metal detector hobbyists. The first is by Boyd McFadden, who, in his opening lines, claims, "I have spent years on the site recovering relics," but, rather than discuss these, he addresses the battle as a historical mystery of missed Confederate opportunity (McFadden 1989). The other article, by Charles Harris, was published a few years before McFadden's and recounts a metal detecting trip to the battlefield in about 1985 on private land with landowner permission. By this account, Harris made his first trip to the site with an acquaintance who had detected Honey Springs for years (Harris 1987).

Harris detected in two places along Elk Creek: the “back 40” (Harris’s term), which may be the same as Gary Moore’s Wooded Forty, and another area south of Elk Creek. In the former Harris described finding a variety of bullets. South of Elk Creek, which he believed to be the site of a Confederate camp, he reported finding almost nothing. Harris attributed the lack of finds to his acquaintance having “already cleaned out” the campsite.

These articles provide limited information, but they substantiate Gary Moore’s claim that private metal detecting at Honey Springs, possibly including state-owned land, was common in the 1980s. Also, artifacts described by Harris mirror my conclusions in comparing our finds with Moore’s in that they include items that we found in low numbers. If Harris’s “back 40” and Moore’s “Wooded Forty” are indeed the same, part of the answer to Moore’s puzzlement about our finds in 1994 is that others continued to hunt this area and other areas of the battlefield in the intervening years.

Does prior private collecting invalidate the archaeology that we undertook at Honey Springs? Certainly not! Still, private collecting has damaged the archaeological record, and we must use our findings with this in mind. Musing on the Cross Keys Battlefield, Svenson (1992, 16) concluded, “Stripping artifacts from a battlefield is a strange hobby—a plunderer’s pastime, like robbing graves. Morally, it is indefensible. As insignificant as these artifacts may be, surely they lose their final iota of meaning as soon as they’re lifted from the soil.” Looting of Civil War battlefields requires us to be mindful of how this might bias archaeological data and inferences we draw from them. However, we cannot ignore this information as it brings a strikingly different perspective on that part of history previously only known from written bits of memory.

As has already been mentioned, we must also be conscious of the shortcomings of other lines of evidence, such as written documents and recorded reminiscences; both are forms of memory. Written documents such as reports, letters, and diaries tell a story from the author’s point of view and include only those things that were deemed worthy of note. For many segments of the mid-nineteenth-century population, written records were rarely prepared (for example, by enslaved people or Native Americans). Also, many of the documents, such as reports of most of Confederate general Douglas H. Cooper’s subordinate officers, have not been preserved for us to read today. Memory, which is the stuff written documents are made of, is likewise biased by the teller's perspective, and these individual stories can combine to become a collective memory of an event through time. As compelling as a bit of evidence may be, the past is best understood by looking for convergences (triangulation) of multiple lines of information. These lines of evidence now include archaeology.

CHAPTER ONE

History Remembered

WHEN TALKING ABOUT the Civil War, I often tell an abbreviated tale of the conflict in the West and conclude with something like this: "The Civil War started in the West, ended in the West, and everything in between (Fort Sumter, Manassas, Gettysburg, etc.) was inconsequential." This statement engenders instant indignation from those even a little steeped in the war's history, but it does contain more than a single grain of truth.

Violent conflict broke out with the establishment of the Kansas Territory in 1854, in what became known as Bleeding Kansas. The fighting that erupted along the border between Kansas and Missouri was a civil war inseparable from the conflict between "nations" that is said to have begun in 1861 at Fort Sumter. Americans along the border died fighting one another over the same issue—slavery—that ultimately caused the South to attempt to leave the Union after Abraham Lincoln won the 1860 election. At that moment, Southerners believed that the decades of compromise (Missouri Compromise of 1820, Compromise of 1850, and Kansas-Nebraska Act of 1854, to name just a few), which had kept alive a Southern economy based on the enslavement of human beings, were over.

General Robert E. Lee's surrender on April 9, 1865, at Appomattox Court House was the knockout blow to the Confederacy. However, Confederate armies under General Joseph E. Johnston, Lieutenant General Richard Taylor, and General E. Kirby Smith remained in the field and posed a continuing threat. The last land battle, the Battle of Palmito Ranch, was fought along the Rio Grande on May 13, 1865, near Brownsville, Texas (Hunt 2018). The Confederate Army of the Trans-Mississippi under Smith was the last to surrender, which happened formally on June 2, 1865, at Galveston, Texas, not quite two months after Lee's surrender (Sesser 2018).

The last Confederate general to surrender served under Smith and was a Cherokee chief: Brigadier General Stand Watie. He fought in the Indian Territory and laid down his sword at Doaksville, Choctaw Nation, on June 23, 1865 (Franks n.d.).

Of course, a lot did happen between the eruption of violence in Kansas in 1854 and the surrender of Stand Watie. Confederate brigadier general Pierre Gustave Toutant Beauregard ordered the bombardment of Fort Sumter on April 12, 1861, starting four years of a broader civil war stretching from the Atlantic to the Far West. The Battle of Honey Springs is part of what followed, but it, and most of what happened west of the Mississippi, has long been overshadowed by epic events to the east. Still, many believe the human tragedy that occurred in the Indian Territory during the Civil War equaled or even surpassed that felt in other areas (Confer 2007; Warde 1993, 2013).

In her 1919 book *The American Indian as Participant in the Civil War*, Smith College professor Annie Heloise Abel wrote, "It has been most truthfully said that never, throughout the period of the entire war, did the southern government fully realize the surpassingly great importance of its Trans-Mississippi District [the theater of war west of the Mississippi River]" (Abel 1919, 14). Ironically, this neglect extended to scholarship on the Civil War that, until recently, focused east of the Mississippi except for almost anecdotal references to faraway and remote western places. In this context, the Indian Territory, present-day Oklahoma, has been even further overlooked, despite some pioneering treatments, including that written by Abel.

Fortunately, federal and state bureaucrats charged with the results of the war were diligent in preserving the records that scholars have used to study this conflict. They excelled in two areas: 1) official correspondence, reports, maps, and returns of the war, and 2) soldier service and pension records. Attention to preservation was uneven between US and Confederate records; many of the latter are housed at the state level and vary accordingly in nature and availability. The United States, via the National Archives, preserves the US and captured Confederate military records and the service and pension records compiled by the US Pension Office for decades after the conflict. Many other records are found in local libraries, museums, and historical societies and are owned privately.

The US government published 128 volumes of *The War of the Rebellion: A Compilation of the Official Records of the Union and Confederate Armies* (hereafter *Official Records*) between 1880 and 1901. Also contained in the National Archives are other records such as regimental records, quartermaster records, maps, compiled service records, and pension records. These are without a doubt the foundation for most Civil War scholarship of the past century and a half, and their imprint on scholarship in the Trans-Mississippi West is evident. Fortunately, the bureaucrats of the past were not myopic with regard to the importance of collecting and preserving records of the conflict.

These records become even more critical for understanding the war in the Indian Territory due to the relative absence of civil and personal records documenting the lives and experience of the residents—mainly Native American—most affected by the conflict. The tribes held land communally, and their members were neither US nor Confederate citizens. Tribal people were therefore not enumerated in the same fashion as in states and congressionally organized territories. Tribal members often did not speak English and generally left a sparse written record of letters, diaries, and other personal accounting (Yarbrough 2021, 149). Further, much of the conflict was asymmetrical (guerrilla warfare, bushwhacking), which did not always or even often find its way into formal records of the Union or Confederacy. Some conflict was outside of the "formal" structure of the Civil War as a war between the United States and the states in rebellion (the Confederacy) and was instead intra-tribal conflict held over from fault lines developed during a contested removal reignited on occasion of Southern secession.

An early and essential author on the war in the Trans-Mississippi West, including the Indian Territory, was Wiley Britton, who in 1882 published *Memoirs of the Rebellion on the Border, 1863*; two volumes of *The Civil War on the Border*, in 1890 and 1899; and *The Union Indian Brigade in the Civil War* in 1922. When Britton published the first volume of *The Civil War on the Border* in 1890, *The Literary World* welcomed it as satisfying "a deficiency in the existing literature of the Civil War" that by then was rapidly growing in extent (*The Literary World* 1890, 282–83). As Britton himself wrote in his first preface, "While much has been written on the late war, no one that I am aware of has hitherto undertaken to give an account of the operations extending over that section during the period covered by this volume" (Britton 1890, v).

Britton was a Union veteran who had witnessed the war as it transpired in western Missouri, western Arkansas, eastern Kansas, and eastern Indian Territory. Britton served with the Sixth Kansas Cavalry and was at the Battle of Honey Springs (Britton 1882). After the war, he worked for the War Department investigating property and pension claims from this area and gained insight from individual interviews (Britton 1890, 1899). Officer correspondence and reports printed in *Official Records* support his narrative. Britton used his wisdom from firsthand experience and interviews (although his books lack source citations). He wrote, "Having participated in the operations described, and having subsequently for years traveled over that section sifting the testimony of witnesses relating to the war, I may perhaps justly claim special advantages for doing the work which I have undertaken" (Britton 1899, iv). For the reader armed with a familiarity of the official reports of events, Britton reveals details that, while their sources may be unknown, are likely insights gained from witness testimony.

Later Abel published three books of relevance as groundbreaking in Native American history. Her three volumes are collectively known as The Slaveholding Indians and include *The American Indian as Slaveholder and Secessionist* (1915), *The American Indian as Participant in the Civil War* (1919), and *The American Indian Under Reconstruction* (1925). Abel's second book was a thoroughly researched and documented work that, despite its seemingly broader title, focuses on the Indian as a participant in the Civil War in the Indian Territory (and to some degree the borders also covered by Wiley Britton). Her focus is the March 1862 Battle of Pea Ridge, Arkansas, through the end of 1863. She provides a brief treatment of events in 1864 and 1865. Researched and written at the height of de jure Jim Crow racial segregation, Abel's treatment of Native Americans in this book carries an unsurprising negative racial bias. Her historiography is—despite this—credible, and she did bring a pioneering focus on the West in the Civil War, the Indian Territory, and Native Americans.

Subsequently, others have worked in the region covered by Britton and Abel, resulting in books such as *Civil War on the Western Border, 1854–1865*, by Jay Monaghan (1955). In 1991, author Alvin M. Josephy Jr., in his book

The Civil War in the American West tapped a rebirth of interest in the Civil War, benchmarked a year earlier by the release of Ken Burns's television documentary miniseries *The Civil War* (Ward, Burns, and Burns 1990, xxvi). Writing for a general audience, Josephy treats the same eastern Kansas, western Missouri, western Arkansas, and Indian Territory borders but also other Civil War–era conflict in New Mexico, Minnesota, along the Red River, and along the western trails. Laurence Hauptman's 1995 *Between Two Fires* addresses the broad participation of Native Americans in the Civil War through select regional cases including the Trans-Mississippi West. With a focus on Cherokees in the Indian Territory, Clarissa Confer's *The Cherokee Nation in the Civil War* does much to further a discussion of not only the conflict but also how Cherokee culture affected and was affected by its course and outcome. Confer's insight is relevant to the other sovereign nations of the Indian Territory (Confer 2007).

Important regimental histories have added to a growing body of scholarship on the Civil War in the Indian Territory. John P. Ringquist's dissertation on the First Kansas Colored Infantry considered the history of this unit but also focused on issues of race and identity in the process (Ringquist 2011). In 2014, Ian Michael Spurgeon published a public-facing account of the First Kansas (Spurgeon 2014). Together these works focused much-needed attention on the active participation in the conflict of those most affected by its underlying causes. Work of similar importance includes Chris Rein's 2013 article on the first-in-history authorization of a regular US regiment recruited from American Indians, in this case refugees from the Indian Territory who filled the ranks of the First Indian Home Guard.

About this same time, Mary Jane Warde published what is in my opinion one of the most important books on the Civil War in the Indian Territory. It would be easy to confuse *When the Wolf Came: The Civil War and the Indian Territory* with Abel's book published almost a century earlier. That confusion evaporates with the reading. Warde presents a thoroughly contextualized account of the Indian Territory during the Civil War using a decolonizing approach that values Native Americans (and others) who called their sovereign nations home. This book continues her work on the effect of the Civil War on the civilian residents of the Indian Territory (Warde 1993). Although she covers well the military strategy and operations in and affecting the Indian Territory, this is a context for an essential and unprecedented discussion of the effect of the war on the Indian nations themselves and their civilian residents.

In 2021, Fay A. Yarbrough published an important book, *Choctaw Confederates: The American Civil War in the Indian Country*. This book confronts issues of consequence for the Choctaws in the West in terms of understanding the relationship of this sovereign people to the "American" Civil War and addresses the general lack of Native voices in Civil War history. Of particular importance for my book are two chapters that examine the Choctaw soldiers in the conflict and the changing relationship between warfare and masculinity. As much as any prior work, this book addresses the importance of Native American culture in defining the Indian soldier (warrior) and how that in turn affected the warfare in which they were engaged.

Although traditionally focused on military conflict between the North and the South, Civil War–era scholarship since the last decades of the twentieth century has slowly but increasingly included the West in a national narrative about resistance to and extension of federal power, of which the South was but a part (S. J. Smith 2016). S. J. Smith sees the focus of traditional scholarship of the Civil War as a conflict between regional cultures (North vs. South) as ironic. According to Smith (567), this was only one of the numerous regional conflicts between "local sovereignty and federal power" in the nation that were apparent before Fort Sumter and lasted through and well beyond Reconstruction. The label "Greater Reconstruction" is used to bring western conflicts, which the US government dealt with following the subjugation of the South, into discussions of the Civil War era, through and beyond 1877. According to Smith (583), "Slowly, the narrative of the Civil War as the triumph of the United States over the Confederacy, the North over the South, has given way to a national story in which the consolidation of federal power happened over multiple landscapes across the continent and over multiple and divergent peoples."

The Indian Territory is profoundly part of this Greater Reconstruction narrative. The Civil War and its aftermath materially affected the relationship between the Cherokees, Chickasaws, Choctaws, Muscogees, and Seminoles and the US government. The US rationalized this changed relationship partly by referencing the existence of alliances with the Confederacy and the fielding of Indian soldiers against US troops during the conflict. A significant result, though not the only one, was the eventual allotment of communally held tribal land to individual tribal members, and sale of the rest (Dawes Severalty Act of 1887), and curtailment of the power of tribal governments (Curtis Act of 1897). In considering the South and the West during Reconstruction, S. J. Smith (2016, 575) concludes that "the Civil War was more effective in suppressing the independence of Native nations in the West than white secessionists in the South." The narrative of the Civil War and Reconstruction in the Indian Territory continues to the present day, recently surfacing in the US Supreme Court's 2020 decision in *McGirt v. Oklahoma*. In *McGirt*, the court decided, "land reserved for the Creek [Muscogee] Nation since the 19th century remains 'Indian country'" despite the Dawes and Curtis Acts. Tribal sovereignty as confirmed by *McGirt* was subsequently diminished in a Supreme Court decision regarding state criminal jurisdiction in the Muskogee Nation (*Oklahoma v. Castro-Huerta* 2022), signaling that the struggle over tribal sovereignty remains as an ongoing legacy of the Civil War.

The Battle of Honey Springs is, of course, a small piece of this evolving understanding of the Civil War and especially how this conflict affected the West. You can, by taking a landscape approach to this event, see the conflict from different perspectives. On the one hand, for example, you can see the battle in a landscape familiar to mid-nineteenth-century Muscogee residents and travelers on the Texas Road. But you can also understand the landscape as it was at the time of the archaeological study and today, bearing the "scars" of Dawes Act land allotment. In taking a landscape perspective, it becomes impossible to uncouple from the Civil War the ironic reality that this site is preserved today because of ownership by the State of Oklahoma rather than the Muscogee Nation.

Federal Withdrawal and Prelude to Honey Springs

With the election of Abraham Lincoln as president on November 6, 1860, the South took the road leading to secession, beginning with South Carolina on December 20, the convening of a secession convention on February 4, 1861, and the beginning of the armed conflict with the bombardment of Fort Sumter on April 12 (Randall and Donald 1969). During this period, the US military prepared for a war that seemed increasingly likely. These preparations included the Trans-Mississippi and Far West. The preponderance of US troops had, in fact, been stationed in frontier garrisons guarding White settlement on the frontier, the roads used for commerce and immigrants, and the resettled Indian nations in the Indian Territory and Kansas Territory.

The US military presence in the Indian Territory during this period was at Fort Washita (established in 1842) along the Washita River on the southern border of the Chickasaw Nation, Fort Arbuckle (1850) along the Washita River northwest of Fort Washita, and Fort Cobb (1859), even farther northwest along the Washita. Although it was placed in 1842 along the southern border with Mexico and later Texas, Fort Washita's primary purpose was to protect the Chickasaws from western Indians and the unwanted actions of other outsiders (Gibson 1971, 222). This harassment had at first prevented the Chickasaws from occupying most of their western lands. With Texas's annexation as a state in 1845, this charge increasingly became to protect Texans from attacks from Plains Indians (Comanches, Kiowas, Kiowa-Apaches, and Cheyennes) living in the western Indian Territory (Norris, Milligan, and Faulk 1998, 173). Fort Arbuckle was established in 1850 to assist in this endeavor. In 1859, Major William H. Emory of the First Cavalry constructed Fort Cobb in the Leased District near the new Wichita Agency. The Leased District was west of the lands occupied by the Choctaws and Chickasaws; troops at Fort Cobb protected peaceful tribes, including the Wichitas and others relocated from reservations in Texas, from Comanches and Kiowas (Gibson 1971, 262; Norris, Milligan, and Faulk 1998, 175; Warde 2013, 46–47).

Also crucial for the Indian Territory was Fort Smith (established in 1817), located on the Arkansas River just across the territory's eastern border. Long-important military posts of Fort Towson (1824) along the Red River in southeastern Oklahoma's Choctaw Nation and Fort Gibson (1824) on the Arkansas River in northeastern Oklahoma's Cherokee Nation, which had been crucial during tribal relocations, had been abandoned in 1854 and 1857, respectively (Gibson 1965, 185–86).

The tribes in the eastern Indian Territory were keenly aware of what was happening in early 1861. They had experienced a traumatic removal from their eastern homelands only recently, in which tribal fractures that would last into the next century were created. Still, they had successfully reestablished their lives and national governments in the West. They recognized the importance of ties to the United States through treaties and realized they were bordered on the east, southeast, and south by states increasingly belligerent to the federal government. Their ties to the South, where many members of their tribes—and family—remained, were close. They relied on transportation and commerce on southern rivers. Some tribes had ties to the South because of a reliance on a market-driven agricultural economy, depending on the labor of enslaved African Americans. The tribes correctly perceived themselves to be independent, sovereign nations requiring protection from outside interference and caught between increasingly estranged parts of the United States (Warde 2013, 44; Yarbrough 2021, 5–6).

Louisiana, on January 26, became the sixth state to secede (Randall and Donald 1969, 139–41). While not sharing a border with the Indian Territory, the Red River, vital for the southern third of the territory and especially the Choctaw and Chickasaw Nations, runs for much of its course through that state. On February 1, 1861, Texas, across the Red River from the Choctaw and Chickasaw Nations, passed an ordinance of secession from the United States (Texas State Library and Archives Commission n.d.). The geographic predicament of the tribes in the Indian Territory was quickly becoming crystal clear, and there was little question that Arkansas would eventually follow others out of the Union.

As the nation appeared headed to war, US lieutenant colonel William H. Emory of the First Cavalry, stationed at Fort Arbuckle since 1858, was on detached duty from January 1860 and was in Washington, DC, in early 1861. In recognition of the US military's precarious position in the Indian Territory, Emory received orders to return west to concentrate US troops at Fort Washita, including those at Fort Smith, Arkansas (Norris, Milligan, and Faulk 1998, 196–97; Townsend 1880a, 656). On April 17, a few days after Confederate artillery had fired on Fort Sumter, Emory received new orders to withdraw all troops in the territory to Fort Leavenworth, Kansas (Norris, Milligan, and Faulk, 1998, 199–201; Townsend 1880b, 667). Anticipating this order, Emory had abandoned Washita on April 16 and headed north toward Kansas. Major Samuel D. Sturgis left Fort Smith on April 23 and made rendezvous with Emory. The combined forces, along with dependents, teamsters, and other noncombatants, arrived at Leavenworth on May 31 (Emory 1880, 649).

During the US withdrawal, on May 6, Arkansas passed an ordinance of secession (Randall and Donald 1969, 183–84). The Indian Territory found itself awkwardly bounded to the North, South, and East by sections of the country engaging each other in war. Long-established commercial, economic, and social connections along the Arkansas and Red Rivers now ran through a young Confederacy involved in armed rebellion with the United States.

The Confederacy wasted no time moving to fill the vacuum in the Indian Territory created by the total US withdrawal. The territory held potential soldiers and resources ranging from lead to salt to livestock that would be of importance to whomever had the upper hand there through military occupation or alliance with the resident Indians (Warde 2013, 42–43). On May 13, 1861, Confederate brigadier general Benjamin McCulloch was assigned to the Indian Territory "to guard that Territory against invasion from Kansas or elsewhere." McCulloch made his headquarters at Fort Smith (S. Cooper 1881, 575–76). At the same time, Albert Pike, who had been appointed Confederate commissioner of Indian affairs in March, was hard at work negotiating with tribes residing in the territory to forsake their long alliances with the United States in favor of new ones with the fledgling Confederacy. His work was made easier by the total abandonment of the territory by the United States, its concurrent failure to provide protection and support guaranteed by treaty, and a string of Union defeats that cast doubt on their ability to bring the rebellion to an end (Abel 1919, 49–63; Johansson 2016, 10). Pike's negotiations ultimately resulted in treaties of alliance signed by the Muscogees on July 9, 1861, Choctaws and Chickasaws on July 12, Seminoles on August 1, and finally by the Cherokees on October 7 (Matthews 1864).

The signing of these treaties showed no more solidarity with the Confederate cause among the general population than did the secession ordinances in many southern states. The Choctaws and Chickasaws were more solidly aligned with the South and maintained that stance throughout the Civil War. The Cherokees and Muscogees, however, were divided from the start. These divisions tended to mirror cracks in the nations resulting from disagreements over removal. Traditional, full-blood communities relying mainly on subsistence agriculture and hunting tended to favor retaining alliance with the United States. Those practicing small farm and market-driven plantation agriculture (some using enslaved African Americans), and whose numbers included intermarried Whites, were more open to establishing alliances with the South for mostly economic reasons.

For different reasons, Missourians were also divided over alignment with North or South, which for a state was a question of secession. Although Missouri did not secede, pro-Union and pro-Confederate factions contested control of the government with violent consequences, especially in the western third of the state, with significant effects on the Indian Territory through the end of 1862 (Randall and Donald 1969, 234–36). In simple terms, the struggle in Missouri drew troops and resources from both the United States and the Confederacy that could have been used in the Indian Territory to provide stability and protection from external and internal strife. Residents living north of the Choctaw and Chickasaw Nations were in particular need of protection as this area devolved into intra-tribal conflict during 1861 (Agnew 2015, 70–71).

Shortly after the treaty with the Cherokees was finalized, in October, Albert Pike was appointed brigadier general of the Provisional Army of the Confederate States of America, Department of Indian Territory. He immediately ordered the construction of Fort Davis in the northern Indian Territory to serve as his headquarters. Fort Davis was an unfortified collection of log buildings located along the Texas Road across the Arkansas River from Fort Gibson, then in use by the Cherokee Nation after having been abandoned by the US War Department in 1857.

The Choctaws carefully protected their sovereignty during negotiations with the Confederacy and were the first to raise troops for its protection. They saw their relationship with the Confederacy as an alliance, and any troops formed would be home guards for the defense of their treaty lands. Choctaws and Chickasaws quickly filled the First and Second Choctaw and Chickasaw Regiments. The First Regiment, commanded by Colonel Tandy Walker, was at Honey Springs and was one of the more effective units operating in the Indian Territory. Successful Choctaw plantation owner and businessman Robert M. Jones was an early supporter of an alliance with the Confederacy and recruitment of Indian troops. It is impossible to separate Jones's motives for so doing from his operation of several plantations along the Red River, where he enslaved hundreds of African Americans. Jones was instrumental in supplying recruits with provisions and equipment from his stores and using his blacksmiths, wagons, and enslaved people as needed, for all of which he received reimbursement by the Confederate government. Although Jones may have provided some firearms from his stores, the lack of weapons was a problem for the Choctaws and Chickasaws and for regiments forming to the south in Texas (Fortney 2016, 220–24).

The Cherokees, Muscogees, and Seminoles followed by forming regiments. Major John Jumper formed the First Battalion of Seminole Mounted Rifles. No Seminole regiment was present for the Confederacy at Honey Springs, but Seminole warriors were there in the ranks of the US Indian Home Guard. Planter Daniel N. McIntosh, son of Muscogee chief William McIntosh, formed the First Regiment of Creek Mounted Volunteers. Daniel's half-brother Chilly commanded the First Battalion of Creek Cavalry, which in 1862 was reorganized as the Second Regiment of Creek Mounted Volunteers. Both the First and Second Regiments, under the overall command of Daniel McIntosh, were present at Honey Springs (May n.d.; Warde 2013, 60).

Against the wishes of Cherokee principal chief John Ross, Chief Stand Watie formed the First Regiment of Cherokee Mounted Volunteers after receiving a commission as colonel in the Confederate army in July 1861. When Ross signed a treaty of alliance between the Cherokees and the Confederacy in October 1861, he raised from his loyalists the First Regiment of Cherokee Mounted Rifles and appointed John T. Drew as its colonel, at which time Watie's regiment became the Second Regiment. Due to disenchantment with the Confederacy, Drew's regiment dissolved during the federal Indian Expedition of 1862 and Watie's once again became the First Regiment. Many former members of Drew's command went on to fill the ranks of the US Second and Third Indian Home Guard. In early 1863, Colonel William Penn Adair formed the Second Regiment of Cherokee Mounted Rifles with new recruits and some veterans from Watie's regiment. Both Watie's and Adair's regiments were at Honey Springs, although neither of their commanders were present (Dale and Litton 1995, 140–41; Franks n.d.).

Of the growing intra-tribal conflict, none had worse consequences than among the Muscogees. In November, pro-Union Muscogees under Opothle Yahola (Opothleyahola), facing armed opposition from the Confederacy, gathered and prepared to seek refuge in southern Kansas (Abel 1919, 79–82; Warde 2013, 53–70). Members of other tribes who

FIGURE 9. Stand Watie.
Courtesy of the Wilson's Creek National Battlefield.

favored maintaining ties with the United States joined Opothle Yahola in increasing numbers, along with self-emancipating enslaved people from the Muscogee and Cherokee Nations (Warde 2013, 66–68). Opothle Yahola soon realized his fears of aggression. His loyal families included as many as seven or eight thousand individuals accompanied by a wagon train of possessions and provisions. Opothle Yahola's warriors fought a series of battles with Confederate and Confederate-allied Indian forces in November and December 1861. The first, at Round Mountains and Chusto-Talasah, were against troops under Colonel Douglas H. Cooper, including a battalion of the First Choctaw and Chickasaw Mounted Rifles,

First Creek Regiment, the Creek and Seminole Battalion, and a detachment of the Ninth Texas Cavalry (Warde 2013, 72). Cooper had served as agent to the Choctaw Nation since 1853 when Secretary of War Jefferson Davis recommended him for the post. He retained that post for the Confederacy and raised the Choctaw and Chickasaw Regiment of Mounted Rifles in 1861 (Delashaw n.d.).

After Opothle Yahola proved he could offer a successful defense of his people, Cooper called for reinforcements from Colonel James McIntosh (no relation to the Muscogee family of that name) with Texas and Arkansas troops for a final attack. On December 26, however, McIntosh acted alone when he found Opothle Yahola in camp and routed his warriors at a battle called Achustenalah (Chustenahlah). Afterward, those who had not been killed by combat or exposure to harsh winter conditions headed as rapidly as possible to Kansas, mainly without possessions or provisions, under harassment from pursuing Confederates. When they arrived in the relative safety of southern Kansas, the support they had hoped for from the United States did not materialize. The refugees' destitute condition only worsened when they were joined by more refugees from the northern Indian Territory in part due to harassment by Confederate-allied Cherokees serving under Stand Watie (Abel 1919, 29–89; Warde 2013, 91). Warde says that in late January, there were in Kansas "3,168 Muscogees with fifty-three slaves and thirty-eight freedmen, 777 Seminoles, 136 Quapaws, fifty-nine Cherokees, thirty-one Chickasaws, and members of a few other tribes. The total was about 4,500, but that number continued to grow as more arrived—from twenty to sixty per day" (Warde 2013, 93). The Indian refugees had arrived with little in the way of provisions, clothing, or tools, and, without assistance from the government, conditions among them only worsened.

The battles with Opothle Yahola were the first organized conflict in the Indian Territory. Soon, small-scale, asymmetrical warfare, generally referred to as "bushwhacking," became increasingly common. More and more refugees were heading either north to Kansas or to Arkansas or Texas. Concurrent with events in the Indian Territory, the tug of war over Missouri, however, had garnered the most attention in the region, with a significant Union defeat in the southwest corner of the state at Wilson's Creek on August 10 at the hands of Confederate troops from Arkansas under McCulloch and Missouri State Guard under Major General

Sterling Price. Following this battle, US troops retreated to Rolla, Missouri, and McCulloch returned to Arkansas. Price, however, moved north and defeated a federal garrison at Lexington, Missouri, before eventually falling back south of Wilson's Creek Battlefield to wait out the rest of the year (Castel 1968, 25–65).

The new year saw renewed efforts by federal command to rid Missouri of the threat represented by Price and his Missouri State Guard and Confederate forces in northeastern Arkansas. Price hoped to combine rebel forces and move on St. Louis. A federal campaign was launched on February 10 and moved rapidly southwest toward Springfield, driving Price's Missouri State Guard into Arkansas. The new Confederate commander in Arkansas, Major General Earl Van Dorn, had earlier called on Pike to bring Cooper's Indian regiments and join his planned offensive, but he instead found himself needing them to defend against the federal advance. The ultimate result was the collision of opposing forces, including late-arriving Confederate-allied Cherokees from the Indian Territory, at the Battle of Pea Ridge on March 7 and 8. The battle was a disaster for Van Dorn, and he subsequently moved his forces east of the Mississippi, leaving Arkansas mostly undefended. Responding immediately to his precarious position after the catastrophe at Pea Ridge, Pike abandoned Fort Davis and relocated south along the Red River, where he built Fort McCulloch as his headquarters. Cherokees under Watie and Colonel John Drew stayed in the Cherokee Nation at Cowskin Prairie and Webbers Falls, respectively. Small bands of bushwhackers, some who considered themselves partisans, operated freely in the northern Indian Territory. This asymmetrical warfare was especially common in the Cherokee Nation, where divided loyalties "justified" their actions (Castel 1968, 66–83; Warde 2013, 100–101).

On April 18, 1862, Lieutenant Colonel James G. Blunt received a promotion to brigadier general. Blunt had moved to Kansas Territory, was an active abolitionist, and was a delegate to the free-state constitutional convention in 1859. In July 1861, he was appointed a lieutenant colonel of the Third Kansas Volunteer Infantry, where he served until promoted in April 1862. As brigadier general, Blunt was soon in command of the newly created Department of Kansas. The organization of the federal army on the border of Missouri and Kansas went through many changes in the following year, and, with those, so did Blunt's assignment. He became major general in March 1863 and was a crucial figure in the region through and beyond the Honey Springs campaign (Blunt 1932).

On April 2, 1862, the US secretary of war had authorized the raising of two regiments from refugee Indians in Kansas with a specific goal of securing Indian Territory north of the Arkansas River. Recruitment of these regiments, called the Indian Home Guard, began in southern Kansas in April with the First Regiment formed by the end of the month and mustered into service on May 22 (Rein 2013, 6–7). Recruitment of the Second Regiment also began in the refugee camps of southern Kansas in June and was completed during the "Indian Expedition" to the Cherokee Nation. These regiments also enlisted free and self-emancipated Blacks who had come into the camps with Opothle Yahola or in the following months. A third regiment was organized and filled in the Cherokee Nation during the expedition. It included many Cherokee who had previously allied with the Confederacy under Watie and Drew (Britton 1922, 73; Warde 2013, 102–3).

The Indian Expedition was an effort to escort refugee Indians back to their homes in the Indian Territory and provide them protection. It was inspired by the refugees' desire to return home (and escape the deplorable conditions in the refugee camps), by the federal government's desire to solve the "refugee problem" made in part by their inability to provide proper housing and provisions, and by growing concern about Confederate intentions (Abel 1919, 91–123; Britton 1922, 61; Rein 2013, 6). Suppression of "guerrilla" warfare waged by Colonel Watie out of his camps at Cowskin Prairie and elsewhere in the northern part of the Indian Territory was necessary for the expedition to succeed (Warde 2013, 103).

The expedition assembled in late June 1862 under the command of Colonel William Weer in camp at Baxter Springs, Kansas, on the border of the Indian Territory. Present in two brigades were the First and Second (partially recruited) Indian Home Guard and a larger contingent of state volunteers of the Tenth Kansas Infantry, Ninth and Twelfth Wisconsin Infantry, Second Ohio Cavalry, Sixth Kansas Cavalry, Ninth Kansas Cavalry, Second Indiana Battery, and First Kansas Battery. The expedition began to move south into the Indian Territory on June 28, with the brigades following slightly diverging routes along the Grand (Neosho) River. Refugee families with their possessions followed the expedition as it moved into the Indian Territory (Abel 1919, 125–27; Britton 1890, 297).

The expedition moved quickly down the Grand River toward Fort Gibson, and elements, including three hundred men from the Ninth and Tenth Kansas and the First Indian Home Guard, engaged and routed a small detachment of Confederates under Colonel James J. Clarkson at Locust Grove on July 3. This skirmish resulted in the capture of Clarkson and a large portion of his battalion. Spread by those who escaped, word of this decisive Union victory caused many Cherokees to reconsider their alliance to the Confederacy, and by July 5 three hundred had joined the Second Indian Home Guard at Cabin Creek (Britton 1922, 68; Ritchie 1885, 463–64).

The expedition proceeded to a camp at Flat Rock on the Grand River about fifteen miles north of Fort Gibson, from which point refugees began to return to their homes, and detachments of soldiers scouted the countryside and drove a small Confederate force out of Fort Gibson (Britton 1922, 67–68). A company of Sixth Kansas Cavalry and fifty Cherokees under Captain Harris S. Greeno went to Tahlequah and Park Hill on July 15, encountered numerous disenchanted Confederate Cherokees of Drew's regiment in town, and met officers of this regiment at the house of Chief John Ross. Some two hundred Cherokee soldiers followed Greeno on his departure and ultimately enlisted in the Second Regiment of Indian Home Guard at Flat Rock. Continued US recruitment of Confederate Cherokees required creating and filling the Third Indian Home Guard during the expedition (Greeno 1885, 161–62).

At its camp on the Grand River, the expedition suffered from lack of supplies and communication from Fort Scott and depletion of forage. The bulk of the expedition subsequently moved back to Baxter Springs, arriving on July 19, leaving the Indian Home Guard in camp on the Verdigris as a "corps of observation" (Blocki 1885, 477). After briefly patrolling and a skirmish with rebels at Bayou Menard, the Indian Home Guard withdrew to Baxter Springs, and the northern Indian Territory again became insecure for Unionist Indians. Most soon returned to the refugee camps in Kansas (Wyant 1967, 14–16). As conditions continued to deteriorate in the fall, especially in the Cherokee Nation, the stream of refugees to Kansas or south towards Texas increased, with destinations based on loyalties to the US or the southern states in rebellion (Warde 2013, 111).

In late September 1862, a new incursion of Confederate troops into Missouri, including Indian troops under Cooper, threatened Fort Scott and southeastern Kansas and diverted attention from the Indian Territory. As Confederate troops moved into Missouri, Colonel Cooper occupied the town of Newtonia, and Confederate general Thomas Hindman threatened Springfield. Cooper repulsed a Union attack at Newtonia on September 30. Still, Brigadier General Blunt returned with a superior force, including the Indian Home Guard, forcing the Confederates under Cooper and Hindman to begin a retreat to Arkansas on October 4. However, Cooper took his troops into the Indian Territory with the intent of attacking Kansas and went into camp near Maysville at old Fort Wayne. While the rest of the federals pursued Hindman south of the old Pea Ridge Battlefield, Blunt pursued Cooper. On October 22, at the Battle of Old Fort Wayne, Blunt surprised and overwhelmed Cooper and captured two sections (four guns) of artillery (W. Edwards n.d. a; Rein 2013, 11). Because this show of force caused rebel troops to retreat to Fort Davis, historian Mary Jane Warde sees this decisive victory as a turning point in the federal army's control of the Indian Territory north of the Arkansas River (Warde 2013, 129).

On October 12, Major General Samuel R. Curtis had created the Army of the Frontier to include Union forces in Missouri and Kansas and the army corps in the field (H. Curtis 1885, 730). As part of this reorganization, Colonel William A. Phillips, commanding the Third Indian Home Guard, was assigned command of the Third (or "Indian") Brigade in Brigadier General Blunt's First Division. This new brigade was the First, Second, and Third Indian Home Guard, and Second Indiana Battery and Captain Henry Hopkins's Kansas Battery (Wyant 1967, 18).

On December 26, the First Indian Home Guard left their camp in Arkansas and entered the Indian Territory to conduct reconnaissance to the vicinity of Fort Gibson and the Creek Agency, and on December 27 they burned Fort Davis. They returned to Arkansas and went into camp near Maysville with their brigade, arriving there on January 11, 1863 (Rein 2013, 13). Despite these successes, the earlier failure of the Indian Expedition left the refugee crisis and the related lack of federal control in the Indian Territory as a central problem facing the new year.

FIGURE 10. Colonel W. A. Phillips.
Courtesy of the Kansas State Historical Society.

These problems were felt most directly by the Indian occupants of the Indian Territory, none more severely than the Cherokees, who had suffered internecine conflict between factions in the tribe. The result was destruction and abandonment of personal property and a steady flow of refugees to the north and south (Warde 2013, 133).

1863 and the Battle of Honey Springs

The end of 1862 had seen the gradual withdrawal of US troops from the Indian Territory following the failed federal Indian Expedition. The Confederate-allied Choctaw and Chickasaw regiment withdrew to the southern Indian Territory, and the ranks of rebel Cherokee, Muskogee, and Seminole troops that remained above the Canadian River were demoralized. Many went home or deserted (Warde 2013, 135).

After a successful campaign in southwestern Missouri and northwestern Arkansas during 1862, the US Department of the Missouri began to eye the Indian Territory. In early January 1863, Brigadier General James M. Schofield, commanding the Army of the Frontier with headquarters in Fayetteville, Arkansas, detached Colonel William A. Phillips's Third Brigade for service primarily in the Indian Territory. In January 11 orders, Schofield instructed Phillips to occupy the line of the Arkansas River and the territory to the north, protect and allow resettlement of refugees, and assist in providing provisions for the refugees and other Indians in northeastern Indian Territory (Schofield 1888a, 33). On January 13, Schofield placed Colonel Phillips in command of the Eighth and Ninth Districts of the Department of the Missouri (western Arkansas and the Indian Territory) (H. Curtis 1888b, 40). Phillips's brigade consisted mostly of the First, Second, and Third Indian Regiments. They were all mounted regiments but had supplied their own mounts, which were in poor condition by January. Of his Indian troops, Phillips noted, "[They] are brave as death . . . [and] make poor infantry, but first-class mounted riflemen" (W. A. Phillips 1888b, 56–58).

Phillips initially took on his new charge while at headquarters at Camp Curtis, near Maysville, Arkansas. From there, he operated several mills, including Hildebrand in the Indian Territory, to produce flour and meal to supplement his supplies and "feed the destitute and starving people of an overrun and war-ridden country" (W. A. Phillips 1888g, 100–101). In

February, he moved his troops into the Indian Territory to Camp John Ross at Cowskin Prairie to avail of fresh forage and protect the "national legislature of the Cherokee Nation" (the Cowskin Prairie Council) convened to consider repeal of their "ordinance of secession" (W. A. Phillips 1888a, 96–97). In a mostly symbolic action, this council repealed the Cherokee "Treaty of Friendship and Alliance" of October 7, 1861, and effectively split the nation into factions aligned with the Union, under Thomas Pegg as acting chief, and the Confederacy, under Chief Stand Watie (Huston n.d.; Matthews 1864, 394–411; Warde 2013, 137).

Phillips stationed details from his command at various places in northwestern Arkansas and the Indian Territory so they could continuously patrol and confront small bands of rebel bushwhackers. He monitored Confederate action below the Arkansas River through patrols and informants and determined that they were poorly organized, equipped, and provisioned. He made frequent reports to his superiors of the destitute condition of the Indian Territory. A growing number of refugees headed to the safety of the Union lines.

In January 1863, the US Senate approved Brigadier General Blunt's promotion to major general. Blunt assumed command of the District of Kansas (including the Indian Territory), with headquarters at Fort Leavenworth. In correspondence dated February 17, Phillips was instructed by Major General Curtis that he should also report to Blunt, in command of the District of Kansas, at his headquarters at Fort Leavenworth (S. Curtis 1888b, 113–14). Blunt soon afterward instructed Phillips to prepare for a spring offensive in the Indian Territory and until then sweep guerrillas from the region (Blunt 1888a, 121–22).

An increasingly frustrated Phillips counseled anyone who would listen that, due to rebel disorganization and their lack of troops in readiness, the US army could quickly occupy Fort Smith and the Indian Territory south of the Arkansas River—and that he was ready to do so. In correspondence dated April 11, as Phillips extended his control of Indian Territory to Fort Gibson, Blunt directed Phillips to stay north of the Arkansas except for occasional opportunistic incursions to the south (Blunt 1888b, 210). On April 24 and 25, Phillips did just that by dispatching a force of some six hundred mounted troops across the Arkansas to attack and defeat Stand Watie's rebels at Webbers Falls (Britton 1899, 41).

By early April, Phillips had concentrated a large portion of his brigade at Fort Gibson, driving "a force of 200 rebels out of Gibson," he reported, and was himself at the fort by mid-April (W. A. Phillips 1888c, 224–25; W. A. Phillips 1888d, 213). Major General Samuel R. Curtis, however, admonished Phillips on April 20 for moving his small command so far west that he was not able to support Colonel M. La Rue Harrison (S. Curtis 1888c, 230). Nevertheless, Blunt was becoming convinced that the Confederates were intent on securing the Indian Territory north of the Arkansas River if not venturing into Kansas.[1]

Phillips continued operations north of the Arkansas River to maintain Union control of the line of that river. He immediately began to strengthen Fort Gibson with earthwork fortifications (W. A. Phillips 1888f, 266).[2] In late April, Major General J. M. Schofield replaced Curtis, who instructed Blunt, "Maintain Colonel Phillips' present line, if possible" (Schofield 1888c, 296). In early June, Blunt reported continual rebel harassment of Phillips's brigade and attacks on the Union supply train from Fort Scott (Blunt 1888f, 341).

When Confederate brigadier general William Steele assumed command of the Indian Territory in January 1863, he found both the condition of troops under his command and the Indian Territory north of the Arkansas River in a deplorable state. Equipment was in poor condition or nonexistent, and supplies and forage were very scarce. Desertion, sickness, and furlough had depleted regiments. He was forced to send most of his troops, including Cooper's Indian Regiments, to the southern Indian Territory and North Texas, where supplies and forage were more readily available (Steele 1888a). Steele and Cooper's mutual animosity aside, the Confederates and their Indian allies were poorly poised to defend the territory against US intentions (Abel 1919, 243–48).

Steele had sought to challenge US control of the Indian Territory north of the Arkansas River before the federals could mount a spring offensive, which he ultimately knew would contest his headquarters at Fort Smith. Having instead been forced to move his troops south, he was unable to act before Phillips had occupied Fort Gibson and began constructing earthwork fortifications. In response to the growing federal strength at Fort Gibson, Steele ordered Cooper to Honey Springs and Brigadier General W. L. Cabell to Fayetteville, Arkansas. Cooper's force consisted of "two regiments of Texas Cavalry (DeMorse's and Martin's), with the bulk of the Indian troops, and a battery of three mountain howitzers and one small prairie rifle gun" (Steele 1888a, 28–36). Working together, they were to prevent continued reinforcement and resupply of Fort Gibson from Kansas by keeping pressure on that place and by harassing the federal line of supply from Fort Scott along the Texas Road.

In April, Steele's directive, coupled with the concern of the Confederate-allied Indian nations, saw the congregation of Confederate and Indian troops in the vicinity of Honey Springs in the Muscogee Nation, south along the Texas Road from Fort Gibson (Warde 2013, 148). Military posturing by the United States and the Confederacy and its Indian allies did nothing to make the Indian Territory secure for refugees seeking to reestablish their lives there or those who had never left. In reality, the posturing of two belligerent forces in the territory brought new insecurities as the year progressed (Warde 2013, 154).

On June 9, 1863, Schofield divided the District of Kansas, which included the Indian Territory, into the District of the Border and the District of the Frontier. He placed Blunt in charge of the District of the Frontier, which included the Indian Territory and adjacent portions of Kansas, Missouri, and Arkansas. The next day, Schofield advised Blunt that he could not fulfill his frequent request for more troops for the Indian Territory because of their need at Vicksburg (Schofield 1888b, 315). Regardless, Blunt moved his headquarters from Fort Leavenworth to Fort Scott, or "in the field" (Colburn 1888, 315).

In early July, Brigadier General Steele ordered Colonel Watie and cavalry from Brigadier General Cabell to harass a scheduled supply train from Fort Scott to Fort Gibson. On July 1 and 2, the US escort battled Watie at Cabin Creek and foiled his attempt to prevent resupply of Fort Gibson. High river levels prevented Cabell's troops from joining forces with Watie. Federal forces, including the Second Colorado Infantry, Third Wisconsin Cavalry, Sixth and Ninth Kansas Cavalry, Third Indian Home Guard, First Kansas Colored Infantry, and a section of the Second Kansas Battery drove off Watie's forces on July 2. The federal supply train continued to Fort Gibson (Steele 1888b, 906; Warren n.d.; Williams 1888). Unknown to the Confederates, the US escort had included reinforcements for Fort Gibson and was more formidable than anticipated.

Major General Blunt foresaw a battle with Confederates congregating across the Arkansas River to the south of Fort Gibson. He departed Fort Scott for Fort Gibson on July 5, 1863, with "four companies of the Sixth

Kansas Cavalry, one section of the Second Kansas Battery, one company of the Fourteenth Kansas Cavalry, and one company of the Third Wisconsin Cavalry" (H. Curtis 1888a, 354). While Blunt was en route to the Indian Territory, Phillips sent a dispatch in which he reported, "The enemy are now camped on Elk Creek, 15 miles south of the Arkansas River. They keep heavy stations on picket at every ford of the [Arkansas] river. They have dug rifle-pits at the fords" (W. A. Phillips 1888e, 355). Major General Blunt arrived at and assumed command of the garrison at Fort Gibson on the morning of July 11 and reported plans to move on Cooper's headquarters as soon as practical (Blunt 1888d, 367–68).

The failure of the recent attack on the federal column at Cabin Creek, the subsequent reinforcement of Fort Gibson, and news that Blunt was himself moving to that post caused Steele great concern. In response, he ordered Cabell to move his brigade to reinforce Cooper at Honey Springs. On July 10, he reported that Cabell was departing Fort Smith, but that "his command [was] much broken down and weakened by his recent expedition [to Cabin Creek]" (Steele 1888d, 917). In fact, it was greatly demoralized by the long and failed march to Cabin Creek and certainly by news of recent Confederate setbacks around the country (Dale and Litton 1995, 136–37).

Preparing for a possible attack by forces from Fort Gibson, on July 14 Cooper issued General Orders No. 25 from his headquarters at Honey Springs that described the establishment of a defensive line north of Elk Creek (Heiston 1888, 461–62). The center of the Confederate line was to be commanded by Colonel Thomas C. Bass and consist of Twentieth Texas Cavalry (dismounted), Twenty-Ninth Texas Cavalry, Fifth Texas Partisan Rangers, and Captain Roswell W. Lee's Light Battery. These were to camp near the middle ford of Elk Creek, which was the Texas Road's main crossing. A bridge also spanned the creek at this location. The right wing was to be commanded by Colonel Stand Watie and include the First and Second Cherokee Regiments.[3] They were to camp along Elk Creek near the lower ford. The left wing comprised the First and Second Creek Regiments, Colonel Daniel N. McIntosh commanding. They were to camp near the upper ford of Elk Creek. Colonel Tandy Walker commanded the reserve, consisting of his own First Choctaw and Chickasaw Regiment (mounted) and two independent Texas mounted squadrons under John C. Scanland and Captain Levi Elliott Gillette. They were to camp near the Confederate headquarters at Honey Springs.

In his official report of the battle, written on July 26, Major General Blunt stated that Cooper's Confederates numbered 6,000 and that Cabell's force coming up was about 3,000 strong (Blunt 1888g, 447). In a "private" letter to a friend, first published in the *Leavenworth Commercial*, Blunt describes capturing Cooper's morning report of July 17, which is a report of the soldiers present for duty at that time. The number of enlisted men available, according to Blunt, was 5,700 (Blunt 1863). Unfortunately, this captured report does not seem to have survived, and the number of soldiers available in the individual Confederate units during the battle remains unknown.

Cooper stressed the importance of becoming familiar with the potential battlefield to prepare passages through the wooded terrain, for troops to move up quickly from their camps and from point to point along the front. If attacked, the front was to be "along the skirt of the prairie in front (north side of the creek), with adequate support formed near the creek." He further cautioned,

> The enemy must, if possible, be prevented from gaining the cover of the timber on the north side. Commandants will examine the ground in front of them, and especially creeks, bayous, or wooded ways leading from the prairie north and west of camp down southward and connecting with the main bottom of Elk Creek. These smaller creeks will be used in case of attack by the enemy to penetrate to Elk Creek, and thus flank the different positions near the fords. These can be used by our troops to advantage in gaining a position in advance of the general line of the prairie to flank the columns of the enemy while advancing on the roads leading to the fords. It is necessary that commanding officers should examine and understand the ground in front of their positions, and also those occupied by other corps. (Heiston 1888, 462)

Cooper's advice to his officers showed he had a full appreciation of the importance of landscape in gaining victory and preventing defeat. While Cooper's order reflected a defensive posture, his preparations still reached north from headquarters at Honey Springs up the Texas Road to the Arkansas River where he had established picket posts overlooking fords.

On July 15, Blunt sent a small force across the Arkansas River to clear Confederate pickets from crossings near Fort Gibson and found the pickets had withdrawn. On July 16, he crossed his main body of troops at the confluence of the Neosho (Grand) River and Arkansas River opposite the fort. From there, he marched through the night, in the rain, pausing for a few hours to rest. His route was along the Texas Road in a roughly south-southeast direction through generally rolling, open prairie covered with grasses and some timber (Johnson and Hickman 1896).

Along this route, small groups of rebels pressed Blunt, but about five miles north of Elk Creek he encountered a challenge to his advance. He reported that, in response, his cavalry "drove them in rapidly upon their main force" in position north of Elk Creek. After marching all night, most of his troops arrived around 8:00 a.m. on July 17 on the prairie north of Elk Creek, on the north edge of what is now the Honey Springs Battlefield Historic Site and the north edge of our study area.

Brigadier General Cooper penned one of two surviving Confederate after-action reports of the Battle of Honey Springs (D. Cooper 1888, 457–61).[4] He acknowledged the Union army's activity at Fort Gibson on July 15 and that enemy troops were crossing the Arkansas at the Creek Agency on the next day. In response, Cooper had withdrawn his pickets. He sent Colonel Tandy Walker's First Choctaw and Chickasaw Regiment and Captain Gillette's squadron of Texas cavalry north along the Texas Road toward Chimney Mountain (near present-day Summit, Oklahoma). Well before reaching Chimney Mountain, these rebels made contact with Blunt's advance at daylight on the morning of July 17 and exchanged fire, "followed by a charge, which drove the enemy back upon the main column" (D. Cooper 1888, 458). After this clash, Cooper reported that Walker's and Gillette's troops returned to Honey Springs as heavy rain had made their weapons useless due to low-quality gunpowder. A small force under Cooper's aide-de-camp Lieutenant T. B. Heiston remained and positioned themselves on the Texas Road at Prairie Mountain about three miles north of the main crossing of Elk Creek (D. Cooper 1888).

From his vantage point, Heiston observed (and overestimated) the size of Blunt's army, then only a short distance from Cooper's Confederates. According to Cooper, it was after he had received Heiston's report from

FIGURE 11. Chimney Mountain. Photograph by Alphia O. Hart, 1936. Courtesy of the Oklahoma Historical Society.

Prairie Mountain that he ordered his troops into position as outlined in his July 14 general orders. However, Cooper's after-action report reveals that a slightly modified deployment occurred at the start of July 17, as would be expected as events unfolded (D. Cooper 1888).

As Cooper initially ordered, the First and Second Creek regiments were on the left, but he moved Scanland and Gillette from the reserve at Honey Springs to support the Creeks. Cooper reports that when he rode to the center he found Lee's Light Battery, Colonel Thomas C. Bass's Twentieth Texas Cavalry (dismounted), and a portion of the Second Cherokee Regiment commanded by Colonel William P. Adair. Adair was, however, not present due to illness and instead Lieutenant Colonel James M. Bell was in command (Dale and Litton 1995, 140–41).

TABLE 1. Deployment of rebel troops during fighting north of Elk Creek based on Cooper's General Orders No. 25 and report of August 12

Order No. 25	Regiment	July 17 initial deployment	Redeployment July 17
Right wing, Lt. Col. James M. Bell commanding[1]	First Cherokee Regiment, Capt. Hugh Tinnin	As skirmishers on right (remainder in camp)	Those in camp ordered to right
	Second Cherokee, Maj. Joseph F. Thompson[2]	Some at center, remainder at creek and camp	Those in camp ordered to right
Center, Col. Thomas C. Bass commanding	Twentieth Texas Cavalry (dismounted), Col. Thomas C. Bass	At center to support Lee's Battery	One half under Capt. J. R. Johnson sent to right to support skirmishers
	Twenty-Ninth Texas Cavalry, Col. Charles DeMorse	At center to support Lee's Light Battery	
	Fifth Texas Partisan Rangers, Col. Leonidas M. Martin	At center to support Lee's Light Battery	
Center at Texas Road	Lee's Light Battery, Capt. Roswell W. Lee	Center of rebel line at Texas Road	
Left wing, Col. Daniel N. McIntosh commanding	First Regiment of Creek Mounted Volunteers, Col. Daniel N. McIntosh	Upper crossing (third above bridge)	Ordered to left flank to support DeMorse and Martin
	Second Regiment of Creek Mounted Volunteers, Chilly McIntosh	Upper crossing (third above bridge)	Ordered to left flank to support DeMorse and Martin
Reserve at Honey Springs, Col. Tandy Walker commanding	Scanland's squadron, Capt. John Scanland	Deployed into line (center with other Texans?)	Moved to center?
	Gillette's squadron, Capt. Levi E. Gillette	Scout toward Chimney Mountain; upper crossing; deployed at center?	During retreat, formed on Texas Road
	First Choctaw and Chickasaw Regiment, Col. Tandy Walker	Scout toward Chimney Mountain; reserve at Honey Springs	Entire regiment on scout on Prairie Road by error; on return and during retreat joined Gillette on Texas Road

[1] Bell was in command on the day of the battle due to Watie's absence on detached duty to Webbers Falls.

[2] Thompson took the place of Colonel Adair due to his illness during the battle.

Britton (1899, 119) noted that Lee's battery was "posted in front of the twentieth Texas, and supported by that regiment." Cooper ordered Colonel Charles DeMorse's Twenty-Ninth Texas Cavalry and Colonel Leonidas M. Martin's Fifth Texas Partisan Rangers to the left of center, and he ordered the First and Second Creek regiments, under Daniel and Chilly McIntosh, respectively, to move toward the center in their support. Cooper had initially ordered Walker to send pickets "across the mountain in the direction of Prairie Springs" and hold the rest of the regiment in reserve, and he later ordered the remainder to the center. Possibly misunderstanding these orders, Walker led his entire regiment across the "mountain" and could not be recalled in time to help in the initial engagement north of Elk Creek. On the right were Captain Hugh Tinnin's skirmishers from the First Cherokee Regiment. On assessing the approaching federal troops, Cooper ordered half of Bass's regiment and the remainder of the Second Cherokee Regiment, who were then in camp, to their support (D. Cooper 1888).

Cooper says very little about the actual fighting north of Elk Creek. He did note that the troops at the center, notably Bass's Twentieth Texas and Lee's battery, performed valiantly. "Riding back near the creek, I discovered our men in small parties giving way. These increased until the retreat became general. Colonel Bass' regiment and Captain Lee's battery, after a most gallant defense of their positions, were compelled to fall back" (D. Cooper 1888, 459). Cooper added praise for Bass's protection of the battery to the point of engaging in hand-to-hand fighting (460).

Cooper wrote very little in his report regarding what happened between Elk Creek and Honey Springs. Of fighting along Elk Creek, he noted only that attempts to hold the crossings failed and that a full retreat began (D. Cooper 1888, 459). Cooper ordered regiments to fall back to Honey Springs to guard and join the Confederate wagon train's retreat from that place, but Gillette's squadron formed on the Texas Road until Colonel Walker's regiment came up and under Cooper's personal direction charged the enemy. Walker held his position until forced to retire by the concentration of US troops in their front and due to "worthless ammunition" (D. Cooper 1888, 460)

Cooper reported one hundred thirty-four killed and wounded and forty-seven taken prisoner, minimized loss of supplies at Honey Springs, and blamed his defeat on worthless gunpowder and superior federal

TABLE 2. Rebel casualties listed in the *Standard*, Clarksville, Texas

First Cherokee Regiment, Col. James M. Bell (Col. Stand Watie was on detached service)		
Killed	Ned Cramp, Co. B	Andy Ross, Co. H
Wounded	Tom Thomas, Co. G Lock Tiner, Co. G	Lt. L. Sweeny, Co. K E. J. Lindsay, Co. K.
Second Cherokee Regiment, Maj. Joseph F. Thompson (Col. W. P. Adair was ill)		
Killed	2nd Lt. A. B. Ballinger, Co. C John Berry, Co. I	Wm. Jones, Co. K
Wounded	John Ragdsdale, Co B S. W. Colbey, Co. B Pigeon, Co. B Logan Burgen, Co. C T. W. Lester, Co. C	C. W. Nail, Co. C John Gordon, Co. F Wm. Hays, Co. F Benj. F. Bigby, Co. K
First Choctaw and Chickasaw Regiment, Col. Tandy Walker		
Killed	Ahi-Ka-Tam-Ba, Co. D	Jackson, Co. D
Wounded	Wm. Hunter, Co. D Akin Wakaya, Co. D Carson, Co. D	Long John, Co. D Lewis Cass, Co. F Elonubbie, Co. F
Twentieth Texas Cavalry (dismounted), Col. T. C. Bass		
Killed	W. M. Glover, Co. B J. H. Callaway, Co. B O. H. P. Ellis, Co. B Corporal Huddleston, Co. C Jno. H. Hamilton, Co. D 1st Sgt. I. T. Grisham, Co. E Corp. Jno. Huff, Co. E 5th Sgt. G. W. Nicholls, Co. F Jas. Street, Co. F J. W. Jackson, Co. F	Jas. Sanders, Co. F I. H. Rhodes, Co. F H. L. Hanks, Co. F J. J. Edwards, Co. H M. F. Odom, Co. H G. M. Pierce, Co. H F. M. Richardson, Co. H John W. Alford, Co. K J. F. Kinley, Co. K
Wounded	Capt. F. M. Hanks Capt. H. Molly, Co. B* Lt. J. A. Story, Co. B Lt. G. T. Davis, Co. B* J. P. Robinson, Co. B* D. S. Bates, Co. B* J. M. Doolen, Co. B Solon Raseo, Co. B M. S. Phillips, Co. B Nathaniel York, Co. B J. A. Andrews, Co. C Lt. M. M. Stover, Co. C N. K. Crow, Co. C I. I. Spikes, Co. C	1st Sgt. T. A. McSpadden, Co. D 3rd Sgt. H. H. Campbell, Co. D 5th Sgt. Martin Simmons, Co. D Lt. J. N. Degaive, Co. E 3rd Sgt. I. K. Humphrey, Co. E 4th Sgt. A. T. McDonald, Co. E L. G. Whiteman, Co. E T. J. Murray, Co. E R. B. Louri, Co. E Levi Pickery, Co. E 1st Lt. I. C. Durm, Co. F* 2nd Sgt. Wm. Davis, Co. F Wm. Slamper, Co. F Jas. Turner, Co. F

TABLE 2. (*continued*)

Wounded	F. M. Hines, Co. F J. W. Deatheridge, Co. F R. M. Carmichael, Co. F Lieutenant Addington, Co. G S. F. Dellis, Co. G John Wright, Co. G M. F. Richards, Co. G John Golihar, Co. G 3rd Sgt. W. L. Harrell, Co. H 1st Corp. M. M. Chaney, Co. H W. B. Griggs, Co. H	L. M. Head, Co. H J. P. Kirkland, Co. H J. W. Saunders, Co. H J. O. Thompson, Co. H 2nd Lt. J. C. Roberts, Co. I Corporal Donohoo, Co. I Nelson Owens, Co. I Thos. Poientine, Co. K W. M. Brewer, Co. K Jonathan Whitfield, Co. K W. T. Fry, Co. K
Twenty-Ninth Texas Cavalry, Col. Charles DeMorse		
Killed	W. R. Bailey, Co. A J. M. Tatum, Co. B B. F. Short, Co. B J. F. Proctor, Co. B Sgt. E. W. McBride, Co. D** J. Walker, Co. D Enon Lany, Co. D	W. C. Blount, Co. E Wm. Wilson, Co. E Hugh Hightower, Co. E J. F. Cook, Co. E Sgt. J. E. Garner, Co. G E. M. Rumsour, Co. G J. H. Henderson, Co. K
Wounded	Col. Charles DeMorse M. D. Lynch, Co. A C. Saunders, Co. B W. C. Patrick, Co. B W. D. Blankenship, Co. B T. A. Palmer, Co. B E. J. Birmingham, Co. C B. F. Blount, Co. C I. N. Thompson, Co. C G. W. Davis, Co. C 1st Sgt. G. A. Andrews, Co. D P. H. Igo, Co. D W. R. Wilson, Co. D Thos. Waddell, Co. D	Wm. Cook, Co. D T. Hodges, Co. E G. W. King, Co. E W. W. Lovejoy, Co. E David Rogers, Co. F J. Erwin, Co. F C. W. DeWitt, Co G Capt. W. A. Brown, Co. H Eli Murphey, Co. H Corp. M. O. Lofton, Co. I J. J. McClosky, Co. I C. W. Hollond, Co. K Wm. Croley, Co. K J. Barnes, Co. K
Wells's Battalion, Lt. Col. J. W. Wells		
Killed	Jesse Merrill, Co. D.	
Wounded	W. Frank Jackson, Co. B	
Lee's Battery, Captain R. W. Lee		
Wounded	Jno. Cornelius W. B. Baker	L. B. Brown

* Mortally wounded
** Regimental color bearer

numbers and artillery (D. Cooper 1888, 460). The September 12, 1863, issue of the *Standard*, published in Clarksville, Texas, carried a list of the rebel killed and wounded of the battle (*Standard* 1863c). Listed were forty-one killed and one hundred one wounded (five mortally): First Cherokee Regiment, two killed and four wounded; Second Cherokee Regiment, three killed and nine wounded; First Choctaw and Chickasaw Regiment, two killed and six wounded; Twentieth Texas Cavalry (dismounted), nineteen killed and fifty wounded; Twenty-Ninth Texas Cavalry, fourteen killed and twenty-eight wounded; Wells's Battalion (Gillette's and Scanland's Texans), one killed and one wounded; and Lee's battery, no killed and three wounded.[5] While this is similar to Cooper's assessment of his casualties, Blunt claims to have buried one hundred fifty rebels on the field. The difference probably relates to the certainty that many of the wounded left on the field later died and the difficulty of making a thorough assessment of dead and wounded during a heated fight and hasty retreat. While the numbers may be underreported, they likely show the relative impact of the day's fighting on the rebel regiments engaged.

Lieutenant Colonel Otis G. Welch took over command of the Twenty-Ninth Texas Cavalry when Colonel DeMorse was severely wounded, and his is the only surviving rebel regimental after-action report. Welch directed his comments and report to Colonel Bass of the Twentieth Texas whom he referred to as commander of the center. He described deployment of his troops on the battlefield: "This regiment was promptly mounted and marched across Elk Creek to its north fork, when it was dismounted under cover of the timber, and proceeded rapidly on foot across the skirt of timber into the prairie, where we were under your directions posted in line of battle" (Welch 1863).[6] He says that after half an hour he was ordered to move three hundred yards to the east and close on the left of the Twenty-Ninth Texas, and that two companies were deployed in advance as skirmishers. He described his position as being concealed by small bushes.

Welch provided very useful details of the fighting north of Elk Creek (Welch 1863, 2). He noted that the US troops were four deep along the entire rebel front and fired while advancing. His regiment, however, "reserved . . . fire until the enemy had approached within twenty yards." Welch reported that the rebel right was "swept" by a heavy column of US infantry and that the Twentieth and Twenty-Ninth Texas were being pressed on the right and left. Welch's right joined the Twentieth Texas when they were ordered to retreat. DeMorse later noted that Welch and his left wing were the last to leave their positions north of Elk Creek (DeMorse 1863). As mentioned earlier, Cooper (1888, 460) said this honor belonged to Bass and his Twentieth Texas Cavalry (dismounted).

Welch provided an illuminating description of what he encountered when he withdrew his left wing from the initial fighting to a position certainly in the Elk Creek valley: "We fell back to a small branch directly in our rear [Elk Creek?], where I ordered a halt, and made a stand, supposing that I was supported by the whole brigade" (Welch 1863). He soon found that the other parts of the brigade had continued their retreat. "[US troops were] passing rapidly to our rear, on the right." Being at that point cut off, he led his command up Elk Creek and made his way independently to North Fork, where they went into camp.

In his summary report for 1863, Confederate brigadier general William Steele noted with criticism, "General Cooper, then encamped at Honey Springs, who, with twenty-four hours' notice of the enemy's approach, and with the knowledge that re-enforcements were *en route* to join him, gave battle upon the ground he occupied, and, having taken no steps to strengthen his position, was driven from it, after a short contest, with the loss of one howitzer and about 200 men in killed, wounded, and captured" (Steele 1888a, 32). Steele's description that the battle was short differed from most accounts, but Cooper's report seems to suggest that the retreat of small groups probably began soon after the fighting commenced in earnest. Steele is also obviously critical of Cooper's failure to construct entrenchments or other fortifications even with plenty of warning and topography that he apparently presumed was well suited for defensive works.

Lieutenant George W. Grayson's (Second Creek Mounted Infantry) memory of the battle supports Steele's criticism: "By what I have always confidently believed to be bad management, we lost the day here when the enemy came up and engaged us, for Gen. Cooper did not even get all his men out on the firing line, or into any engagement with his adversary before he ordered his forces to retire." Instead, the Second Creek remained under cover at a position along Elk Creek. While in earshot of fighting, they never received orders to advance (Grayson and Baird 1988, 61–62).

In his relatively brief report, Major General Blunt provides a concise recap of the action,

> After two hours' rest, and at about 10 a.m., I formed them in two columns, one on the right of the road, under Colonel [William R.] Judson, the other on the left, under Colonel [William A.] Phillips. The infantry was in column by companies, the cavalry by platoons and artillery by sections, and all closed in mass so as to deceive the enemy in regard to the strength of my force. In this order I moved up rapidly to within one-fourth of a mile of their line, when both columns were suddenly deployed to the right and left, and in less than five minutes my whole force was in line of battle, covering the enemy's entire front. Without halting, I moved them forward in line of battle, throwing out skirmishers in advance, and soon drew their fire, which revealed the location of their artillery. The cavalry, which was on two flanks, was dismounted, and fought on foot with their carbines. In a few moments the entire force was engaged. My men steadily advanced into the edge of the timber, and the fighting was unremitting and terrific for two hours, when the center of the rebel lines, where they had massed their heaviest force, became broken, and they commenced a retreat. In their rout I pushed them vigorously, they making several determined stands, especially at the bridge over Elk Creek, but were each time repulsed. In their retreat they set fire to their commissary buildings, which were 2 miles south of where the battle commenced, destroying all their supplies. (Blunt 1888g, 447–48)

Major General Blunt was very ill before and during the battle and, in fact, for some time afterward. Fortunately, reports from his subordinate officers fill in more details of the action at Honey Springs.

Reports from all federal units listed as engaged by Blunt, except for the Third Indian Home Guard, are reprinted in *Official Records*. No mention of the Third Regiment appears in reports of other subordinate officers, and the role of this regiment at Honey Springs remains uncertain. They appear to have not participated in the main engagement.[7] Reports of subordinate officers vary in detail. These unit reports are useful in building a more nuanced narrative of what happened, although they remain difficult to reconcile with the modern landscape because the landscape is so vaguely described. They also provide more detail about actions north of

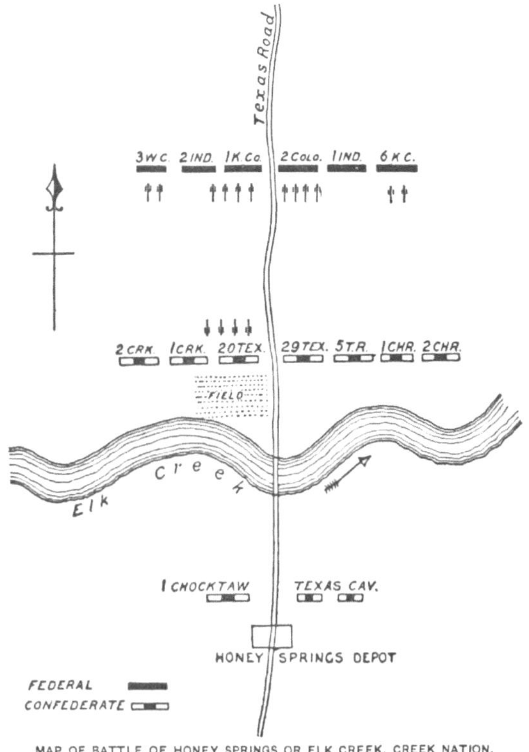

FIGURE 12. Battle of Honey Springs map published in 1899 by Wiley Britton (1899, 113).

Elk Creek than about what happened to the south. Unfortunately, no contemporary maps of the battle or battlefield are known to exist, although the Golden, Colorado, newspaper, the *Colorado Transcript,* mentions papers in their possession that included an account by Edward Palmer and a map of the battlefield and troop disposition by Private George Putman, Company C, Second Colorado Volunteers (Burrell 1877b, 3). It is most unfortunate that the whereabouts of Private Putman's map or Dr. Palmer's description are unknown. Both are likely lost to history. Britton did publish a map in his second volume, although it is not to scale. This map is slightly misleading because it appears to depict the Confederate deployment planned by Cooper before the battle and does not reflect some minor changes in deployment described in after-action reports (Britton

1899, 113). It is also one more item that does not show the presence of the Third Regiment Indian Home Guard.

Blunt writes of the first significant contact with the enemy coming about five miles north of Elk Creek, "[There] with my cavalry [I] drove them in rapidly on their main force [at Elk Creek]" (Blunt 1888g, 447). Lieutenant William T. Campbell of the Sixth Kansas Cavalry (four companies) says his advance was repulsed by an enemy posted on high ground but that the rebels fell back when the rest of his battalion came up (Campbell 1888, 452). Captain Henry Hopkins noted that his Kansas Battery was then deployed into line of battle but found the "enemy had fled" (Hopkins 1888, 456). None of the other reports, including that of the Third Wisconsin Cavalry, mention this brief engagement.

Blunt noted what transpired after this skirmish: "While the column was closing up, I went forward with a small party to examine the enemy's position [at Elk Creek]." He noted that a Confederate shot one of his escorts. A letter reprinted in the *Delphi (IN) Journal* reported, "Our advance proceeded to feel the enemy, whom they found very strongly posted in the brush and cornfields, behind rocks and fences" (W. H. S. 1863). In a personal letter by Blunt published in the *Burlington Weekly Hawk Eye*, he noted, "They were formed on the north side of the timber of Elk Creek, which formed a partial semi circle, the road running through the center. The timber here was quite brushy and formed a complete cover for them, but I had watched them take their position, and knew the 'game' was there" (Blunt 1863).

Blunt's bodyguard or escort units were the Sixth Kansas Cavalry and the Third Wisconsin Cavalry (National Archives 1863). Lieutenant Colonel Campbell of the Sixth Kansas described moving forward after the initial skirmish until he found the main body of the enemy "posted in force under cover of timber" at Elk Creek. "Here I came to a halt, and sent a company forward to reconnoiter; found the enemy strongly posted in the woods, their line extending on the right and left of the road. I kept up a brisk fire on them; they, however, kept under cover" (Campbell 1888, 452). Britton writes that the Confederate line was "formed in the timber about half a mile in length on each side of the Texas Road" (Britton 1922, 275).

Private Thomas White of the Sixth Kansas was shot through the shoulder during this action and was undoubtedly the soldier referred to in

Blunt's account of this reconnaissance.[8] White may have been the first federal casualty, if not the first casualty, in the study area. All of this happened before 7:00 a.m., when Campbell says Major General Blunt transferred his battalion from Judson's to Phillips's command (Campbell 1888, 452). Judson, however, retained Campbell's section of mountain howitzers. Britton wrote that the Sixth Kansas's reassignment to Phillips and their placement on the federal left flank was because "General Blunt wished to have white troops on his extreme flanks" (Britton 1899, 118). It seems as likely that he wanted his flanks protected by cavalry.

Britton notes that as Blunt's column was coming up, a heavy rain had begun (Britton 1899, 118). Blunt describes bringing his troops to rest behind a ridge after the reconnaissance mentioned above. This was apparently around 8:00 a.m. Here they were out of sight of the enemy, who, by Blunt's account, were then one-half mile forward. In the aforementioned private letter, Blunt remembered, "I had them halted behind a little rise of ground to rest and take lunch from their haversacks. After they had rested, I went back among the officers and men of the different commands and told them what I expected of them. They were now about one-half mile from the rebel line" (Blunt 1863).

Blunt says he moved his men to action at about 10:00 a.m., advanced them forward in two columns by company, cavalry in front, on either side of the Texas Road, and deployed them to the right and left. The right was commanded by Colonel Judson and included the First Kansas Colored Infantry, the Second Indian Home Guard, the Third Wisconsin Cavalry, two sections of mountain howitzers, and the Second Kansas Battery. The left was commanded by Colonel Phillips and included the Second Colorado Infantry, the First Indian Home Guard, the Sixth Kansas Cavalry, and Hopkins's Kansas Battery. Blunt deployed his troops into line of battle and advanced toward the enemy (Blunt 1888g, 448). Britton said, "Captain [Edward A.] Smith's guns came into battery in front of the colored infantry, and Captain Hopkins' guns came into battery just in front of the Colorado infantry" (Britton 1899, 119). Lieutenant Colonel John Bowles of the First Kansas Colored Infantry reported that they formed to the right of a section of Smith's Second Kansas Battery that was already in position three hundred yards from the Confederate line. He did not advance until the guns had ceased firing shell and canister at the enemy (Bowles 1888). Lieutenant Colonel Frederick W. Schaurte of the Second

Indian, lined up to the right of the First Kansas, would imply in his report that the engagement opened when Smith's Battery commenced fire at about 10:20 a.m. (although a newspaper account says it was opened by Hopkins's battery [W. H. S. 1863]). Schaurte then advanced his command after the artillery barrage ceased (Schaurte 1888). On the far right, Captain Edward R. Stevens of the Third Wisconsin Cavalry (Companies B, G, H, I, and M) moved part of his command farther right in a flanking action at the same time that his section of mountain howitzers was going into action (Stevens 1888; Quiner 1866, 913).

Captain Smith would report that his battery deployed to the right of the Texas Road and "opened with spherical-case shot, shell, and solid shot on the rebel batteries, which were soon silenced." He then moved his twelve-pounder guns to the left of the Texas Road and into battery one hundred yards in front of the Second Colorado Infantry. "[Then,] almost at the edge of the brush, I fired 3 or 4 rounds of canister and 10 or 12 of shell at the rebel position on the hill" (it is unclear what Captain Smith was referring to by "the hill") (E. Smith 1888, 454). Smith then ordered his battery to cease firing to allow the general advance on the federal line.

Captain Hopkins noted that his Kansas Battery went into position three hundred yards from the Confederate line and that they shelled the woods to their front for about one and one-quarter hours. He directed one section of his battery at the Confederate artillery to their right and front. Hopkins's report says his battery dismounted one Confederate gun and killed the crew (Hopkins 1888).[9] However, immediately upon firing his battery at the rebels, they returned fire and inflicted substantial casualties, "wounding 1 sergeant, mortally (left leg shot off above the knee), killing 1 private, killing 4 horses, and wounding 4 others, totally unfitting them for service" (Hopkins 1888, 456).

After deploying his troops in line of battle, Blunt thus seems to have loosed his artillery for possibly a little over one hour and deployed part of the Third Wisconsin Cavalry to flank the enemy's left. Captain Stevens of the Third Wisconsin Cavalry noted that his flanking action and fire of his battery of mountain howitzers toward the Confederate left "forced the enemy to fall back upon their center." There Blunt, separately noted, the rebels "had massed their heaviest force" (Blunt 1888g, 448; Stevens 1888, 453). After federal artillery had silenced the Confederate guns, Blunt engaged his infantry and dismounted cavalry against the enemy.

Fighting north of Elk Creek would, in probably another hour or so, close with the rout of the enemy.

At this time, the dismounted Third Wisconsin Cavalry on the right flank continued their work by moving into the woods as skirmishers, capturing eight prisoners in the process. On the left flank, three dismounted companies of the Sixth Kansas Cavalry moved into the woods as skirmishers to stop a Confederate flanking action. They were ultimately assisted by a charge from the First Indian Home Guard driving "the enemy from his position" and eventually across Elk Creek (Campbell 1888, 453). Initially commanded by Colonel Theodore H. Dodd, the Second Colorado Infantry was to the left of the Texas Road. In his report, Major J. Nelson Smith noted that Colonel Dodd had placed him in command. This was apparently after the fighting ended north of Elk Creek (J. N. Smith 1888). Neither Dodd nor Smith describes the fighting in this area.

In a letter to the *Rocky Mountain News*, George West of Company H of the Second Colorado Volunteers told of their position between the First Kansas and the First Indian Home Guard, and their fight with the Texans in which the Coloradans lost four killed and four wounded (West 1877). West further reported, "About eighty prisoners were captured by us, most of them belonging to the Twentieth Texas Infantry. The prisoners captured were armed with new Enfield muskets."

Britton provided additional information:

> Early in the action, before the Confederate line had commenced to yield, three companies of the right wing of the Second Colorado Infantry, on the left of the colored infantry, came near being cut off and captured. While the Federal line was advancing through the brush, which was thick enough in places with the leaves and heavy foliage to hide from view a foe a few yards in advance, these companies had got out of alignment—had got as much, perhaps, as twenty paces in advance of the left of the line of the colored infantry—and coming to an impassable ditch or washout directly in their front, filed to the right and crossed it just in front of the left of the line of the colored infantry. When the Colorado men got over the ditch, they filed to the left again and came into line, but still in advance of the colored infantry on their right. At this moment a confederate force which had been lying down concealed in the

> brush behind the ditch or gully, but now between the Colorado men and ditch, rose up to cut them off. The colored regiment was almost instantly ordered to oblique to the left, and coming up within less than fifty yards of the Confederates poured several well-directed volleys of musketry into them, which caused them to break, and they ran back in the direction of the Colorado men, who, now realizing the situation and seeing the enemy in confusion, turned and opened fire upon them only a few yards distant, killing and wounding a good many and capturing a few. (Britton 1899, 121–22)

On the US right, the Second Indian Home Guard, between the Third Wisconsin and the First Kansas Colored, was ordered to deploy as skirmishers and enter the woods. Lieutenant Colonel Schaurte reported no more about the action north of Elk Creek. He commended the officers and men of his command and noted that they were the first to establish a position across Elk Creek (Schaurte 1888, 452). Lieutenant Colonel John Bowles of the First Kansas Colored Infantry, in describing his actions, also mentioned those of the Second Indian (Bowles 1888).

The First Kansas had almost five hundred men on the field, and Blunt singled them out in his report for outstanding performance: "The First Kansas (colored) particularly distinguished itself; they fought like veterans [which they were], and preserved their line unbroken throughout the engagement. Their coolness and bravery I have never seen surpassed; they were in the hottest of the fight, and opposed to Texas troops twice their number, whom they completely routed. One Texas regiment (the Twentieth Cavalry) that fought against them went into the fight with 300 men and came out with only 60" (Blunt 1888g, 448). Blunt concluded, "The question that negroes will fight is settled" (Blunt 1863).

As soon as the batteries fell silent, Colonel James M. Williams moved the First Kansas forward, stopping at the right of the Second Colorado, about "forty paces [from] the concealed foe." Williams ordered the regiment to fire, which was met simultaneously with a volley from the Confederate line, wounding Williams severely (Bowles 1888). Lieutenant Colonel Bowles then assumed command of the regiment and ordered his men to fall to the ground and fire from the prone position "until the enemy's line yielded" (Britton 1922, 279).

Bowles reported that, as the firing continued, soldiers of the Second

Indian moved in front of his right. He ordered them to fall back and to the right. Possibly mistaking this as a call for a general retreat, the Twenty-Ninth Texas advanced to within twenty-five yards when the First Kansas fired a second volley and then a third, decimating the Texans and felling their flag for a second and third time. The flag was left on the ground but was picked up by the Second Indian Home Guard, much to the protest of the ranks and officers of the First Kansas who felt it was a prize they had earned. The right of the First Kansas then pressed the Texans to a cornfield where they broke and fled, and the First reformed on their original line (Bowles 1888).

Correspondence in the *Delphi Journal* united the actions of the First Kansas and Second Colorado:

> The 2d Colorado and the 1st Kansas (colored) regiments were brought up to face the deadly fire of the 20th and 29th Texas. And here was the hottest part of the battle. The 2d Colorado, led by their cool and daring Lieutenant Colonel, pressed into the thickest of the fight; regardless of the deadly havoc, which increased with every step. This regiment lost more in killed than any other. But in this connection I cannot forbear noticing the conduct of both the officers and men of the 1st Kansas, colored. This regiment, under their fighting Colonel, came up nobly to the work. They advanced to within about forty paces of the enemy, who then opened upon them a terrible fire of buckshot. This volley mostly passed over their heads, and their brave Colonel was felled from his horse by three different shots, just after he had given the command to fire, and while he was in the act of commanding a "charge bayonet." Now the hottest part of the work commenced; the blacks fought with a courage rarely equaled. The whole of our forces pressed upon the enemy, who was finally compelled to retire in great disorder. (W. H. S. 1863)

A report in the *Cincinnati Daily Commercial*, attributed to a correspondent of the *New York Tribune*, noted the Colorado volunteers' reaction to the First Kansas: "Much distrust and dissatisfaction were openly expressed by many of our Colorado troops at being put into the same brigade with the 'niggers,' but the man is yet to be found, since this fight, who does not speak in the highest terms of this regiment" (*Cincinnati Daily Commercial* 1863, 4).

Of the action following the defeat of the Confederates north of Elk Creek, Blunt said only, "In their rout I pushed them vigorously, they making several determined stands, especially at the bridge over Elk Creek, but were each time repulsed." He also noted that they burned supplies at Honey Springs and that he pursued them for a total of about three miles beyond Elk Creek (about one mile beyond Honey Springs) (Blunt 1888g, 449). Once again, the *Delphi Journal* letter provides insight: "The rebels made another stand in a cornfield, about half a mile distant, but were soon driven from this position by the Indians, who always kept up close to their rear. After some severe fighting here for a few moments, they again fled in the greatest confusion, and only kept back a small party to cover the retreat of their main body, which was now fairly begun" (W. H. S. 1863). This suggests that there was a cornfield in the Elk Creek bottoms, possibly near the main crossing, which was about one-half mile from where the Indian troops initially breached the rebel line. This may be the same cornfield referred to by Lieutenant Colonel Bowles of the First Kansas.

Captain Smith's report clearly states that the Second Kansas Battery did not cross Elk Creek. Smith's orders to advance were countermanded, and he moved the battery "back and encamped on the prairie, north of the creek." From Captain Stevens's report, it is difficult to determine if the Third Wisconsin Cavalry and their mountain howitzers crossed south of Elk Creek, but this seems unlikely. The Sixth Kansas Cavalry and Captain Henry Hopkins's Kansas Battery did join the fight south of Elk Creek, along with the First and Second Indian, First Kansas Colored, and Second Colorado Infantry regiments. The battery of mountain howitzers assigned to the Sixth Kansas was retained in Judson's brigade on the US right when the Sixth was moved to Phillips's brigade on the left flank but may have joined the Sixth as they crossed Elk Creek.

Lieutenant Colonel Campbell of the Sixth Kansas Cavalry provided one of two regimental accounts that describe fighting along Elk Creek, although he did not mention the bridge (Campbell 1888). Being posted on the federal left flank, the Sixth may have crossed at the lower ford. According to Campbell, "Shortly after crossing the creek, I charged into a large body of rebels, whom I took to be Stand Watie's Indians and Texans [Watie was not present during the battle]. They retreated to the woods, where they made a stand. My men dismounted and opened a vigorous fire, which together with a section of Hopkins' Battery and the mountain howitzers, soon put them to flight" (Campbell 1888, 453). Campbell described continuing until pursuit ceased but mentioned no other fighting. Colonel Stephen H. Wattles of the First Indian briefly noted fighting at the creek, saying, "[We] drove the enemy across the stream [Elk Creek], on the left of the bridge, the enemy forming several times, and desperately contesting every foot of ground" (Wattles 1888, 456). In the opening engagement, the Sixth Kansas was to the left of the First Indian, so these accounts do seem to describe a parallel movement across the creek to engage the enemy on the other side, to the left (east) of the Elk Creek bridge.

Britton remembered that the First Indian and Sixth Kansas Cavalry drove the rebel Indians and Texans across Elk Creek at the lower ford "in a good deal of confusion" (Britton 1899, 122). Speaking of the Confederate resistance at Elk Creek, Britton went on to say, "A feeble effort, however, was made to hold the bridge over Elk Creek and some of the fords, but the troops defending them were speedily driven from these positions by the Federal infantry and the guns of Captain Hopkins' battery, which had moved forward and taken up the position which had just been occupied by the guns of the Confederate battery" (Britton 1899, 122).

William Howland remembered his father's story of the action at the creek in a 1937 interview,

> It was at the Elk Creek toll bridge that the Federals met with the most stubborn resistance by the Confederates and paid the greatest price for victory, for it was there they found Major [Erastus J.] Howland with his loyal Indian Command well fortified at the south approach of the bridge, many of his men hidden in a ravine just west of the south approach, a cannon [barricaded] in the roadway near the south approach commanding the passage of the bridge. It was there where the most severe fighting of the battle of Honey springs took place, as the Federals made several attempts to take the bridge, each time meeting the deadly fire of Major Howland's Indian riflemen which blocked the bridge with Federal dead and made Elk Creek run red with their blood. The Confederates held the bridge against superior numbers until the Federals almost enveloped his command by crossing Elk Creek, both east and west of the bridge. (Foreman 1937e)

Major Howland was with the First Regiment, Cherokee Mounted Rifles (Foreman 1937e; Oates 1961, 167–68). Still, no other account describes an action of this ferocity at the bridge or along Elk Creek.

Captain Hopkins provided the most detailed account of what happened after the engagement north of Elk Creek, but the account does not seem to mention the fight at the creek that Campbell says involved his section of artillery. According to Hopkins, "Orders were received to move forward . . . and occupy a position on the prairie beyond the ravine. Lieutenant [John F.] Aduddell moving to the left of the road with one section, opened upon the enemy's cavalry, upon a hill beyond, causing them to fall back quite precipitately, the shell bursting in their immediate vicinity. Again, moving forward one-quarter of a mile, a line of the enemy's cavalry was discovered and driven back after the firing of a few rounds of shell" (Hopkins 1888, 457). From this point, the battery continued to move forward but fired only rarely, for a distance stated as one and one-half miles, where federal pursuit halted.

Major Smith's report on the Second Colorado Infantry's action described only activity south of Elk Creek since he was in command only after the fight north of the creek had ended. Initially two of the six companies were detailed to support Hopkins's battery as it crossed Elk Creek and pursued the retreating enemy. According to Smith, "After rallying my companies, we crossed the stream, and discovered the enemy on a hill, or rise of ground in the advance. Here Hopkins' battery, supported by my infantry, opened upon the enemy, who fled in confusion after the second fire. I was here ordered by Colonel [William A.] Phillips, commanding brigade, to have the rest of my command brought forward, which order was promptly obeyed, I at the same time moving my two companies forward in support of the battery, until we occupied the enemy's former position. Here the remainder of my company came up" (J. N. Smith 1888, 455).

On the federal right, the First Kansas and the Second Indian both fought through the initial Confederate lines and crossed Elk Creek in pursuit of the enemy. Lieutenant Colonel Schaurte said of the First Indian only this: "My command continued to act as skirmishers during the entire engagement, which lasted about four hours. The enemy were repulsed from the field, and pursued till pursuing became useless" (Schaurte 1888, 451). Although providing great detail of the initial engagement north of Elk Creek, Lieutenant Colonel Bowles of the First Kansas reported, "[After that engagement,] we advanced in line for a distance of 3 miles, skirmishing occasionally with the enemy from the high bluffs in front and to the left" (Bowles 1888, 450).

About one mile south of Honey Springs, Blunt noted, he halted pursuit due to exhaustion of his horses and infantry. He reported that rebel cavalry "hovered" in his front and that Cabell's reinforcements arrived around 4:00 p.m. (Blunt 1888g, 448). The enemy cavalry in his front may have been the Creek regiments that Cooper says moved down the North Fork Road (the Texas Road) and that Blunt may have mistaken for Cooper's main force. Cooper noted that his troops remained formed along the Briartown Road for hours as his supply train escaped and does not mention the arrival of Cabell (Cooper 1888). Writing to his wife after the battle, Lieutenant Colonel Bell, who commanded the Second Regiment Cherokee Mounted Rifles, noted, "Gen'l Cabal reinforced us soon after the Honey Springs fight, his Brigade becoming dissatisfied Commenced deserting and all left him but about three hundred, he of course had to follow them back to Fort Smith & elsewhere to reorganize" (Dale and Litton 1995, 136–37).

As they retreated, the rebels destroyed stores at Honey Springs that they could not manage to take along. Brigadier General Cooper minimized the loss, saying, "A quantity of flour, some salt, and sugar were necessarily burned at Honey Springs, there being no transportation for it" (D. Cooper 1888, 460). Blunt noted only, "In their retreat they set fire to their commissary buildings, which were 2 miles south of where the battle commenced, destroying all their supplies" (Blunt 1888g, 448). Citing a participant account, Warde (2013, 172) says that the Union troops were so close behind the Rebel retreat that they "did not have time to destroy the supplies before Union troops put [the fire] out, saving much of the stored bacon, flour, and preserved beef." A report in the August 10, 1863, *Cincinnati Daily Commercial* valued the supplies destroyed by the rebels at $250,000. This account also says, "There were found in store about 600 hand-cuffs, which they had just manufactured to have ready when the 'niggers and their cowardly officers surrendered to their forces'" (*Cincinnati Daily Commercial* 1863). Britton corroborated this account but put the number of handcuffs at three to four hundred (Britton 1899, 123). Colonel Thomas Moonlight, chief of staff for Major General

Blunt, recalled in his memoirs written shortly after the war that the number was five hundred (Lindberg, Matthews, and Moonlight 2003, 32).

That evening, the federal army camped on the battlefield, and a few officers described their locations in their report: First Kansas, near the ford on Elk Creek; Second Indian Home Guard, on Elk Creek; and the Second Kansas Battery, on the prairie north of Elk Creek. The Second Colorado Infantry were "ordered into camp" at the location of their last position. Hopkins does not explicitly say where his battery went into camp. Still, he does say he moved his battery back to Elk Creek. "[There,] immediately after fighting had ceased, and we were selecting a camp-ground, we discovered at the edge of the woods, in their old camp, nearly the entire camp-equipage of one regiment, cooking utensils, tents, &c., which we destroyed" (Hopkins 1888, 457). According to Lieutenant Colonel Schaurte, the federal army remained on the battlefield until 5:00 p.m. on July 18, when they marched toward Fort Gibson and went into camp for the night two miles south of the Arkansas River. They arrived at Fort Gibson midday on July 19 (Schaurte 1888, 451).

Blunt reported one officer and thirteen enlisted men killed and sixty-one enlisted men wounded: First Kansas Colored Infantry, two killed and thirty wounded; Second Colorado Infantry, five killed and fourteen wounded; First Indian Home Guard, two killed and six wounded; Second Indian Home Guard, three killed (drowned) and three wounded; Third Indian Home Guard, two wounded; Sixth Kansas Cavalry, five wounded; Third Wisconsin Cavalry, no casualties; Hopkins's Kansas Battery, one killed and one wounded; and Second Kansas Battery, one wounded (Return of Casualties, 1888, 449). The *Daily Conservative* published casualties that differed slightly from this, listing an additional three wounded for the First Kansas and one additional killed for the First Indian Home Guard (*Daily Conservative* 1863b, 2). Table 3 provides names of the killed and wounded and uneven information on rank, company, and wounds.

One of the victor's duties was to bury the dead, but they also gathered and destroyed or transported military equipment left on the field by their enemy. Blunt says they buried 150 Confederates, but there is no specific mention of these burials or those of the federal dead in any of the reports. In the personal letter previously mentioned, Blunt commented, "Cooper sent me a very warm letter of thanks for the care I had taken of his wounded and the burial of his dead" (Blunt 1863). In a

TABLE 3. US casualties listed in the *Daily Conservative*, Leavenworth, Kansas

First Kansas Colored Infantry		
Killed	Joseph Long, Co. C	Thomas Mitchell, Co. F.
Wounded	Col. J. M. Williams, severely	John Maddox, Co. F, severely
	Jno. Gregg, Co. A	George Dellum, Co. H
	Sanford Strawley, Co. C	Charles Clark, Co. H
	Jos. Reynolds, Co. C, severely	C. Williams, Co. I, severely
	Isaac Reed, Co. C.	Charles Buckner, Co. I
	Louis Linn, Co. D	Hamber Childs, Co. I, badly
	J. H. Nelson, Co. E, severely	Cunnell, Co I
	Chas. Smith, Co. E, severely	Richard Hawking, Co. I
	Thos. M. Orison, Co. E	Joseph McIntosh, Co. I, severely
	Dennis Merrill, Co. E	Lafayette Shelby, Co. I, severely
	H. Deall, Co. E	George Jonah, Co. I
	W. Gordon, Co. E	J. Thomas, Co. K, severely
	Allen Lynch, Co. E	Clit Jackson, Co. K
	L. Mervin, Co. E., severely	Perry Jackson, Co. K
	D. Saunders, Co E., severely	Richmond Floe, unassigned*
	Jesse Warren, Co. E	Henry Thompson, unassigned*
	Wesley Warren, Co. E	
Second Colorado Infantry		
Killed	Sgt. David C. Prickett	Wm. M. McDougall, private
	David W. Butts, private	Crispin Treadway, private
	James W. Clem, private	
Wounded	Sgt. Wm. Cook, arm	Edward P. Robinson, private, face
	Sgt. Jacob Sieux, cheek	Patrick Dawson, private, mortally,
	Corp. Jas. B. Folsom, severely	Wm. Cummings, private, slightly
	Thos. M. Mcfadden, private, arm	G. Spencer, private, slightly
	Wm. Cox, private, arm	Charles Withrow, private, slightly
	James H. Hix, private, dangerously	Mareus D. Sailsbury, private, slightly
	Reuben Dawson, private, foot	J. Braithwaith, slightly
First Indian Home Guard		
Killed	So ha you, private	
Wounded	Ki hi mastle, private, slight	Ah has la ge mart le, private, in leg
	No kas fin se ko, private, slight	Geo. Bayou, private, in arm
	No kas ko chuck ko re, private, slight	Lui I lo chee, private, in thigh
Second Indian Home Guard		
Drowned	Husk Mayfield, Co. F, crossing Arkansas River	
	Ky Dougherty, Co. F, crossing Arkansas River	
	Te-cah-le-gesekie, Co. F, crossing Arkansas River	
Wounded	Backwater, Co. A, severely	Grass, Co. A
	Leander Rice, Co. A	

* New recruit

(*continued*)

TABLE 3. (*continued*)

Third Indian Home Guard		
Wounded	Corp. Was so ty Hop, slight, in arm Elijah Banks, slight	
Sixth Kansas Cavalry		
Wounded	G. Holderman, hospital steward, severely Thomas White, Co. A	Josiah Rohrer, Co. F, severely Jas. Allingham, Co. F Jacoe Banks, Co. C.
Hopkins's Battery		
Killed	Booth, private	
Wounded	Sergeant Daniel Sayre, mortally	
Second Kansas Battery		
Wounded	Wm. C. Caskey, severely	

* New recruit

FIGURE 13. "Honey Springs Battlefield 140 Confederate Graves." Photo by Joseph Thoburn. Courtesy of the Oklahoma Historical Society.

1937 interview, Cherokee Freedman Dennis Vann (born 1849) remembered the dead being buried: "After the battle was over, the Union forces worked for 2 or 3 days, digging trenches and burying the dead, General Blunt then went back to Ft. Gibson" (Foreman 1937f). Colonel Thomas Moonlight noted, "The day was spent in caring for the wounded and burying the dead, and be it said to the memory of the 1st Kansas Colored they behaved with marked humanity and kindness to the wounded, who but a few hours before had worry to place the yoke of slavery forever on their necks if within their power" (Lindberg, Matthews, and Moonlight 2003, 32). William K. Makemson of the Fifth Texas Partisan Rangers says in a letter that the rebel dead were buried in the "bottom on the North Side of Elk Creek" and the federal dead "in a corner of the garden at the McIntosh Place" (quoted in Warde 2013, 174).

In 1938 Buchanan and Plischke described the post-battle burial ground: "Mr. A. J. Berryhill located this old burial ground and was very positive in his statements. He states that in 1867 he saw Federal soldiers at this place removing the Federal soldiers that fell in the battle of Honey Springs from this place to the National Cemetery at Fort Gibson." The location shown on the Buchanan and Plischke map shows a location well south of Elk Creek, which is problematic since most of the federal casualties certainly occurred well to the north (Buchanan and Plischke 1976, 131). An advertisement published in the Washington, DC, *Evening Star* on May 26, 1868, listed twenty-five federal bodies at "Honey Springs and south side Arkansas river, opposite Fort Gibson" to be disinterred and moved to the Fort Gibson National Cemetery. The ledger of the National Cemetery lists only fourteen interments from Honey Springs, all unknown (markers 584 through 597).

While not exhaustive, this historical narrative portrays the Battle of Honey Springs based on the written record (recorded memory). Questions remain, however, because written accounts are both imperfect and incomplete. Questions concern precise locations of events, the nature of conflict, and the actions of regiments. Ultimately, they also consider the cause of victory or defeat. While we were in the field, our view of the conflict changed as we incrementally documented the archaeological findings. Field insights are very useful but must ultimately be confirmed through rigorous analysis of the archaeological finds and their locations on the landscape. The first step is the confirmation of which of the artifacts found through our archaeological survey are confidently associated with the battle, and how these define the boundaries of conflict on the modern landscape.

CHAPTER TWO

The Battlefield

THE NARRATIVE OF the preceding chapter presents the battle and battlefield based on recorded memory. In introducing archaeological interpretation in this chapter, I begin by envisioning the fields of conflict of the Battle of Honey Springs based on found artifacts at the most general level. Being able to resolutely place and bound a battle on the modern landscape using the found artifacts is one of the fundamental strengths that archaeology brings to the study of conflict. After reviewing what was found, I address two fundamental questions. First, where are the places on the investigated landscape that show evidence of conflict, and how are they delimited or bounded? Second, what natural or cultural aspects of the landscape relate to how these places are defined?

The basic building blocks of conflict archaeology are the artifacts themselves, and the connective tissue is their individual location on the landscape as recorded as they were discovered. Only by using archaeological science to consider the collective whole through knowledge of placement on the battlefield do artifacts become a voice supplementing the memory-based narratives of the battle. Unlike memory, artifacts are a direct link to events and the landscape in which they occurred. As the direct result of historical action, the placement of artifacts thus allows us to reconcile a remembered event with the modern landscape and expand what is possible only with memory.

Battles and the landscapes on which they occur are inseparable; the battle cannot be fully understood without also understanding the landscape as it was during the conflict (Carman and Carman 2019; King 2019). Honey Springs and vicinity has been a lived landscape for many thousands of years—dating well into prehistory. While it includes many "natural" things such as waterways, hills, trees, and wildlife, it is best conceived as an evolved cultural or anthropogenic landscape that both affected and was affected by the events of July 1863.

Even the most remote parts of the United States and the world are to some degree cultural landscapes. The Cultural Landscape Foundation defines cultural landscapes as "landscapes that have been affected, influenced, or shaped by human involvement" (TCLF n.d.). The US National Park Service defines a cultural landscape as "a geographic area, including both cultural and natural resources and the wildlife or domestic animals therein, associated with a historic event, activity, or person, or exhibiting other cultural or aesthetic values" (NPS n.d.). The National Park Service explicitly defines battlefields as cultural landscapes (NPS 2015).

Union and rebel troops encountered landscapes founded on a geologic topography that supported a natural environment long influenced by cultural activities such as hunting, clearing land for agriculture, constructing dwellings, developing transportation routes, and using (and later suppressing) fire. Battles of the Civil War typically affected a cultural landscape by deposit of artifacts, the burial of the dead, destruction of buildings and vegetation, and sometimes construction of fortifications. Importantly, battles can also add cultural meaning and value to the landscape for participants, for those who lived nearby, and sometimes for others far away (the concept of "hallowed ground," for example). Cultural landscapes affected by conflict typically gain diverse and sometimes conflicting meanings that, like culture, are not static (Carman and Carman 2019; Linenthal 1991; T. B. Smith 2017).

While this is not a cultural landscape study per se, understanding key elements of the "natural" and cultural landscape is essential work of this book. I will use two methods to talk about landscape that I, along with other archaeologists and historians, find useful in battlefield studies. "Battlespace" and "KOCOA terrain analysis" both derive from military use, where they help envision how to plan for a future military situation. Archaeologists who use these methods employ them instead as a structure through which memory, archaeology, and landscape can be triangulated, or reconciled, to forge an explanation of a past battle that would make sense to participating military leaders and their soldiers. This is in essence a form of reverse engineering with which we look back on what happened rather than plan for what may.

The US military defines "battlespace" as "the environment, factors, and conditions commanders must understand to successfully apply combat power, protect the force, or complete the mission" (quoted in Bleed, Scott, and Renner 2014, 1). Battlespace is further conceived through several values, including the area of operations (location of forces), area of influence (where force can be effectively projected), and area of interest (including potential objectives, which might include the presence of an enemy) (Bleed, Scott, and Renner 2014).

Battlespace is a beneficial concept for looking at the rebel headquarters at Honey Springs. Here Confederate brigadier general Cooper made decisions regarding his defense against a potential adversary from Fort Gibson. But it is crucial to extend the view more broadly to include at least Fort Gibson and the Texas Road from Honey Springs to Kansas to visualize the battlespace from both a rebel and Union perspective. Between Honey Springs and Fort Gibson, the Texas Road was an avenue of attack for both Union and rebel commanders; from Fort Gibson to Fort Scott, it was an essential Union supply umbilical. From Honey Springs to the south, the Texas Road and the Briartown Road were avenues of rebel supply and reinforcement.

Along with battlespace, the conflict archaeologist's tool kit also contains KOCOA analysis. KOCOA is a military terrain analysis tool and is an acronym for "Key Terrain, Observation and Fields of Fire, Concealment and Cover, Obstacles, and Avenues of Approach" (Department of the Navy 1990, 2.1–5). Key terrain is any landscape feature necessary to gain an advantage over the enemy. Observations and fields of fire often entail the same features as key terrain, places allowing observations of the enemy and an unobstructed landscape for firing toward them. Cover and concealment are landscape features that cover or conceal maneuvers from the opponent, and avenues of approach are the likely features (such as roads) that allow or accelerate movement to and from the battlefield (S. D. Smith 2019, 9). S. D. Smith says of KOCOA, "It is a systematic method of looking at the battlefield landscape from the perspective of the soldier on the ground attempting to achieve a military objective" (2019, 9).

KOCOA is a recommended analytical approach of the National Park Service's American Battlefield Protection Program for battlefield studies, whether or not they involve archaeology (NPS 2015). Military strategists developed KOCOA terrain analysis to plan for potential future engagement with an enemy. Archaeologists are instead looking at the aftermath of a conflict and use this method to help deconstruct what happened from a strategic landscape perspective.

I use battlespace in this chapter because it presents a better framework to understand the challenges—and responses to those challenges—of Union and rebel antagonists at Honey Springs. I will reserve KOCOA analysis for later in this book, after I have defined in this chapter the "fields of conflict," or engagements that make up the Battle of Honey Springs. There I will use KOCOA to critically examine the landscape and frame a nuanced interpretation of the battle using insight from archaeology, history, and the landscape itself.

A Narrowing Battlespace

From the occupation of Fort Gibson in late 1862 until its reinforcement in early July 1863, US colonel William A. Phillips's battlespace was firmly within the Indian Territory north of the Arkansas River. This fact was confirmed when, in orders dated January 11, 1863, the commander of the Army of the Frontier, Brigadier General Schofield, detached Phillips's brigade from the First Division and ordered Phillips "to occupy, if practicable, the line of the Arkansas River and the Indian Territory northeast of it" (Schofield 1888a, 33).

From Fort Gibson, Phillips sent troops to the east and southeast and routinely engaged small groups of rebels and "bushwhackers" to protect his primary interest: preventing enemy control of the Arkansas River and the region to the north. In April, May, and June, US troops engaged Confederates threatening Fort Gibson and downstream as far as Webbers Falls. These conflicts reflected constant rebel incursions north of the Arkansas River. Rebels were clearly focusing their efforts on this same area with the hope of driving federals out of the Indian Territory altogether. They were increasingly focused on the relatively small garrison at Fort Gibson as the main obstacle to achieving that goal.

In the face of the federal occupation of Fort Gibson and its ever-improving fortification with well-engineered earthworks, the new Confederate Department of the Indian Territory commander Brigadier General William Steele, headquartered at Fort Smith, rightly perceived a growing threat. This threat was not only to the territory north of the

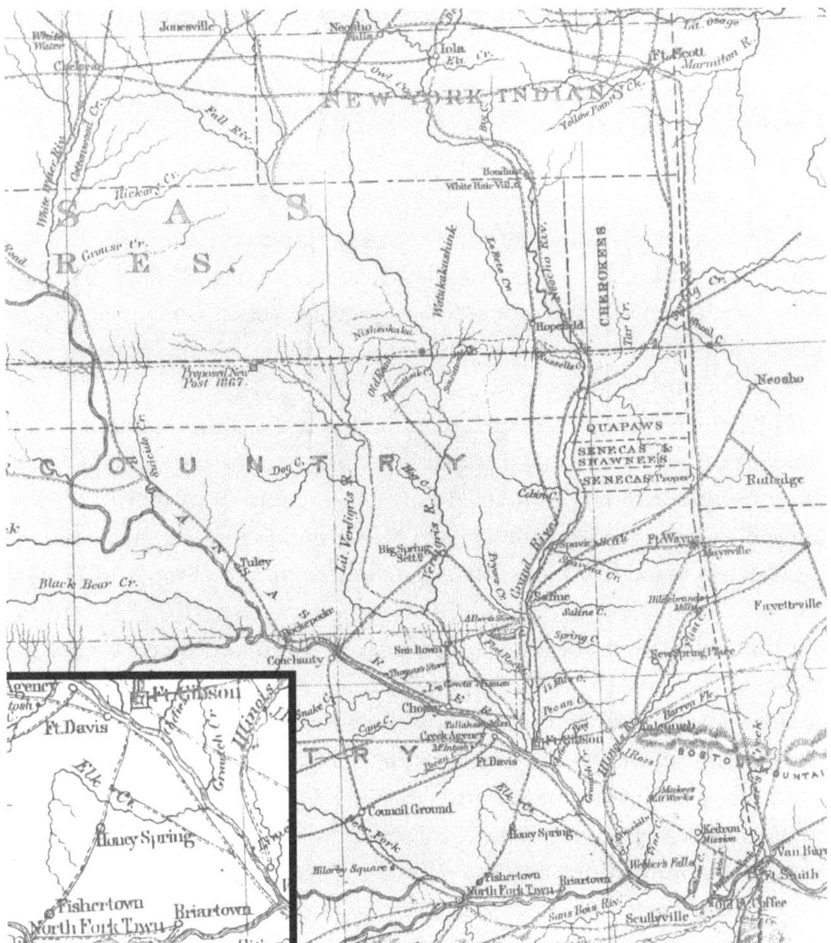

FIGURE 14. Indian Territory north of the Arkansas River. Detail shows Honey Springs vicinity. US Army, 1866. Courtesy of the Oklahoma State University Library Digital Map Collection.

Arkansas River but also to the region lying to the south and to Fort Smith itself and thus western Arkansas. He saw a broadening federal battlespace (Ashcraft 1963, 279). In reaction, Steele was narrowing his battlespace to encircle the federal garrison at Fort Gibson and the federal supply route—essentially the Texas Road from Fort Gibson northeast to where it entered Kansas. Steele ordered his brigade under Brigadier General Cabell to Fayetteville and that under Cooper to Honey Springs with orders to apply pressure on the federal supply line, with the hope of forcing the abandonment of Fort Gibson (Steele 1888a, 28–36). Rebel forces attacked supply trains at Cabin Creek on May 8 and again on July 1 and 2. The second attack was by Stand Watie's cavalry, with intended support by Cabell's brigade from Fayetteville. It was repulsed by a strong federal force that included reinforcements for Fort Gibson, which increased significantly that garrison's strength upon arrival. With Blunt's relocation to Fort Gibson shortly after, accompanied by additional troops and carrying news of the recent federal victory against Lee at Gettysburg and Pemberton's surrender of Vicksburg, the federal battlespace pivoted to south of the Arkansas (Britton 1922, 270).

The failure of the recent attack on the federal column at Cabin Creek (due in part to Cabell's inability to reach Watie because of flooded rivers), the subsequent reinforcement of Fort Gibson, and news that Blunt was himself moving to that post, caused Steele great concern. In response, he ordered Cabell to move his brigade to reinforce Cooper at Honey Springs. On July 10, he reported that Cabell was departing Fort Smith, but that "his command [was] much broken down and weakened by his recent expedition [to Cabin Creek]" (Steele 1888d, 917). In fact, it was greatly demoralized by the long and failed march to Cabin Creek and certainly by news of recent Confederate setbacks around the country.

As this situation unfolded after the failed July raid at Cabin Creek, Steele's and Cooper's battlespace increasingly focused on a circle around Fort Gibson and Honey Springs. Although Steele ordered Cabell to join forces with Cooper, Cooper realized Blunt could strike his headquarters before these reinforcements arrived. Still, he was determined to attack the US garrison before Blunt could put any of his strategic plans into action. Cooper strengthened his reconnaissance toward Fort Gibson and established picket posts fortified with rifle pits at Arkansas River crossings. With the arrival of Cabell's brigade, forces fielded by Cooper would be vastly superior to those available to Blunt. Learning of Cabell's movement toward Honey Springs, and rightfully fearing his brigade's concentration with Cooper's, Blunt certainly knew his only chance of offensive success relied on acting before that eventuality. His battlespace also quickly narrowed to a line drawn around Fort Gibson and Honey Springs, and the Texas Road in between, and the clock began ticking down to July 17 when the precise fields of conflict of the Battle of Honey Springs would be forever imprinted on the landscape. This imprint is, of course, the archaeological footprint of conflict revealed by the mapping of the locations of the artifacts discovered during our fieldwork.

The Artifacts of Conflict

Analysis of artifacts is tedious and repetitive. It involves searches for and documentation of seemingly esoteric clues that allow categorization of finds, which is the basis for generalizations that have a broader meaning for our understanding of events such as Civil War conflict. Determining which artifacts found at Honey Springs relate to the battle requires general information about the arms, clothing, and equipment used during the Civil War garnered from historical and archaeological studies. Some items are easier to identify than others; a button stamped with an eagle on the front and the manufacturer's name on the back provides clear clues to when it was manufactured and its use by the military. Fragments of exploded cannonballs are impossible to explain except as residue of battle.

TABLE 4. All artifacts

Description	Number
Artillery ammunition	60
Firearm parts	6
Conical bullets for rifle-musket	85
Conical bullets: Pickett	3
Breech-loading and magazine bullets and cartridge cases	25
Conical sidearm ammunition	20
Spherical (round) ball ammunition	480
Arrowheads	8
Civilian and military buttons	17
Other military equipment	12
Padlocks	2
Personal Items	18
TOTAL	736

Other artifacts were not necessarily so clearly associated with the battle, and scrutiny was required before including any in this study. The first vetting happened in the field. We did not collect artifacts that obviously postdated the battle, in a modified catch-and-release approach. Still, artifacts that were collected included some that we thought might date to the time of the battle but on closer examination in the laboratory were excluded. For those so excluded, I had determined they were of later manufacture or simply too undiagnostic for inclusion. An example of the former are conical bullets that, after cleaning, were found to have knurling in cannelures (grooves) around their circumference. This knurling did not occur until after the Civil War. In the following discussion are those I am confident resulted from fighting during the Battle of Honey Springs. I also sometimes include artifacts collected in the 1980s by Gary Moore that are now part of the OHS's Honey Springs research collection. While these are not routinely included in my detailed analysis of the battlefield because we know only their general location (in a forty-acre parcel), a few are unusual enough to contribute to this discussion.

The Civil War was affected by many innovations in armaments. These innovations, for better or worse, influenced things such as tactics and medicine. Rifled artillery increased accuracy and allowed for impact-detonation of projectiles. The April 1862 breaching of the walls of Confederate Fort Pulaski at the mouth of the Savannah River by the concentrated fire of federal rifled guns instantly and famously signaled the obsolescence of masonry fortification (Bell 2003, 22–24; McGee 2017). However, except for one small, rifled cannon in Roswell Lee's Confederate battery, rifled artillery was not used at Honey Springs. Other guns on the field were not much different than those used in the War of 1812 (1812–15) and the War with Mexico (1846–48). The small arms, however, are a different story.

The Crimean War (1853–55), where Britain, France, Turkey, and Sardinia fought against Russia, saw large-scale use of the rifle-musket for the first time. This weapon fired a large-caliber compression bullet invented by French army captain Claude-Ètienne Minié in 1849 (D. Thomas 1997, 3). As designed by Captain Minié, this bullet has a basal cavity, conical head, and cannelures around its base. Minié intended the bullet to expand when the powder charge ignited, pressing the soft lead of the bullet's sides ("skirt") into the twisting grooves ("rifles") cut into the barrel, causing the bullet to spin to increase accuracy. The Minié ball was smaller than the rifle's bore diameter and thus loaded more quickly than the patched balls used in martial rifles such as the US Model 1841 (known as the Mississippi rifle). The rifle-musket firing a Minié ball was more accurate at extended range than the formerly standard smoothbore musket and caused more severe and life-threatening wounds. Also new were innovations in the form of breech-loading carbines and rifles such as the Sharps rifles and carbines, the Smith carbine, and the Gallagher, and magazine carbines and rifles such as the Spencer and the Henry using self-contained metallic cartridges. These new weapons were used at Honey Springs but stood out from others that by 1863 had become increasingly rare due to their obsolescence.

Of all the found artifacts, the association of artillery ammunition with the Battle of Honey Springs is the most certain. Artillery was, of course, rarely discharged except in warfare or during military training. During our survey, the sixty artillery artifacts discovered are twelve-pound spherical explosive shell, six- and twelve-pound explosive case, iron canister fired in six- and twelve-pound guns, and fuses. Guns in use at Honey Springs had bore diameters of 3.67 inches for six-pounders and 4.62 inches for twelve-pounders.

Canister was widely used during the Civil War against massed troops and artillery at close range of around three hundred to six hundred yards, with less than three hundred yards probably being optimal (Ripley 1970, 267). It consisted of stacked iron balls enclosed with "iron top and bottom plates over which were bent the ends of a cylinder formed from sheet tin" (Ripley 1970, 267). Canister for twelve-pound mountain howitzers differed by consisting of spherical lead balls with calibers in the mid-.60s. When fired, the cannon blast broke the canister apart, sending the iron or lead balls flying out in an expanding pattern from the muzzle, much like a massive shotgun.

Fragments of explosive projectiles—common shell and spherical case—and fuses that ignited these are the most common artillery-related artifacts that we found on the battlefield. Shell and case are similar in appearance: both are hollow cast-iron spheres (case has thinner walls than shell) with a threaded hole for a fuse, and both were filled with black powder. Case was also filled with lead balls of the same size used for .69 caliber muskets (around .64 or .65). Some are known to have been filled

FIGURE 15. Nested six- and twelve-pound shell fragments. Photo by William B. Lees.

with conical Minié balls. Due to shortages of lead, some Confederate case was filled with small iron balls (Ripley 1970, 270; Johnston 2018, 82). The fuse for both was a timed device ignited by the muzzle flash when the gun was fired.

Case was intended to explode in the air over massed troops, in effect to extend canister's range by showering soldiers with tightly clustered shrapnel. On the other hand, shell has a thicker wall and was intended to explode near the ground. It was typically used to engage enemy artillery—to dismount guns or kill crews and teams. Solid cast-iron spherical shot, not found at Honey Springs, would have been used against structures, fortifications, or artillery. An unknown number of the larger-caliber lead balls, discussed later, certainly had their origins in the explosive spherical case or may have been lead-ball canister fired from twelve-pound mountain howitzers (Ripley 1970, 268).

One complete unexploded six-pound projectile was found during the survey, but it is unknown whether it is case or shell. It was not available for reanalysis, but photos show the Bormann time fuse was intact and was punched for about two and one-half seconds. It was either lost be-

FIGURE 16. Unexploded six-pound cannonball found south of Elk Creek. Photo by William B. Lees.

fore it was fired or was fired but did not explode. The latter was relatively common. During the 1995 field season, Gary Moore showed me an unexploded six-pound explosive shell or spherical case set for about two seconds that he found in the Wooded Forty. He also had an unexploded Tennessee Pattern solid shot (bolt) for the Confederates' small rifled gun.

Fuses include one unthreaded iron specimen from the Moore donation, which may be of Confederate manufacture. We found one brass Bormann fuse support and four fragmentary fuses. The lead and tin alloy Bormann fuse screwed into a threaded hole in the cannonball on top of a support plug. This plug covered an opening used to add powder during manufacture. The support plug prevented damage to the soft alloy fuse when the gun was fired (Biemeck 2013, 247; Ripley 1970, 276). After determining the distance to the target, the gunner estimated the number of seconds required for the projectile to reach its target and "punched" the fuse at a corresponding tick, exposing an embedded black-powder trail that led to the main charge.

Parts of firearms found during our work are a percussion lock mechanism, side plate, ramrod ferrule, barrel band, musket sling hook, and

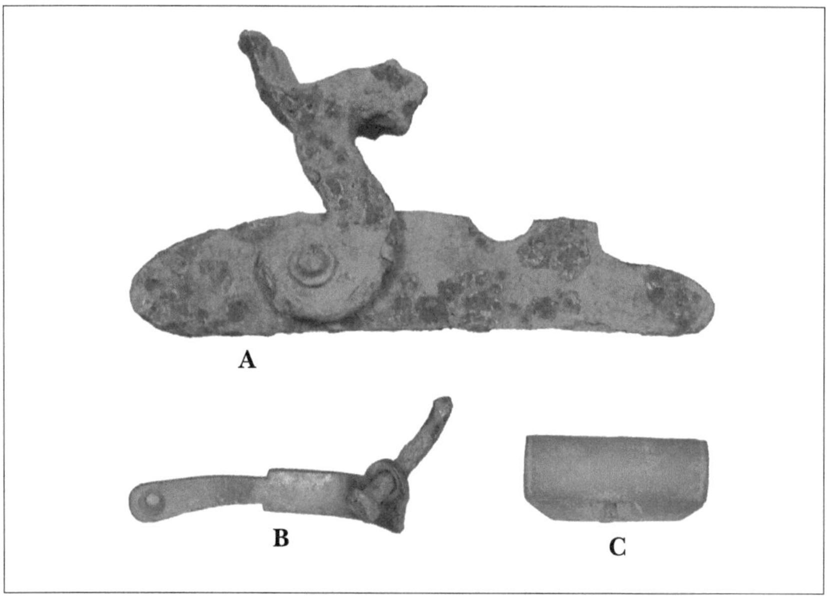

FIGURE 17. Lock (A), side plate (B), and ramrod ferrule (C) for a common rifle. Photo by William B. Lees).

revolver cylinder. Although few, these items add to our understanding of the arms present at the battle. The percussion lock mechanism, side plate, and ramrod ferrule were found close to one another and are probably from the same weapon. The shape of the lock plate, hammer, side plate, and ferrule compare favorably to examples from civilian gunsmith-made American "plains rifles" and "trade rifles" of the early nineteenth century. Similar non-martial gunsmith-made weapons in everyday civilian use for hunting and defense during the nineteenth century were referred to as sporting or common rifles in documents of the Civil War era.

The iron barrel band from Honey Springs is immediately recognizable as a mid-barrel band from a martial weapon because it has a swivel loop for a shoulder sling. Designed to hold the barrel fast to the stock, this is consistent in size to those used on .69–.71 caliber US or foreign martial muskets made up to the 1850s. The sling hook allowed adjustment of the length of a leather or cloth shoulder sling.

The revolver cylinder is highly corroded but is for a .36 caliber weapon such as the Colt or Remington. Cylinders were easily removed for cleaning

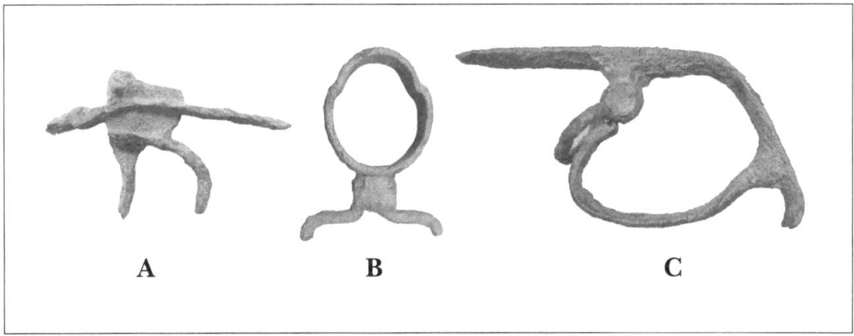

FIGURE 18. Shotgun double trigger (A), musket barrel band (B), and musket trigger guard (C). Photo by William B. Lees.

and loading, and extra loaded cylinders were sometimes carried. Revolvers were readily available and heavily used by US and Confederate officers and cavalry throughout the war.

In the Moore donation are a double trigger mechanism and a trigger guard. The double trigger mechanism (see figure 18) is from a civilian double-barrel shotgun. The heavy iron trigger guard (see figure 18) is bent and broken but is clearly from a martial weapon because it is fitted with a loop for a shoulder sling. It is highly corroded but is consistent with a guard for US rifle-muskets of the Civil War and is distinctly different from those used on imports such as the Enfield and the Austrian Lorenz.

Bullets for muzzle-loading rifles (rifles, rifle-muskets, and rifled muskets); breech-loading and magazine carbines and rifles; and pistols and revolvers were common finds at Honey Springs. Included are conical compression ammunition for rifle-muskets (eighty-five specimens), a few conical bullets for the common rifle (three), conical bullets and cartridges for breech-loading carbines and rifles (twenty-five), and conical bullets for pistols and revolvers (twenty). Round (spherical) ball ammunition was also used in some of these weapons but are discussed later in this chapter for reasons that will become apparent.

Rifle-muskets were designed to fire the compression bullet invented by Captain Minié in 1849 (D. Thomas 1997, 3). The US Army adopted the rifle-musket using the Minié ball as the Model 1855. Many were in the hands of regulars and at arsenals when the war broke out. It was used in the Civil War alongside its descendants (the M1861 and M1863) and

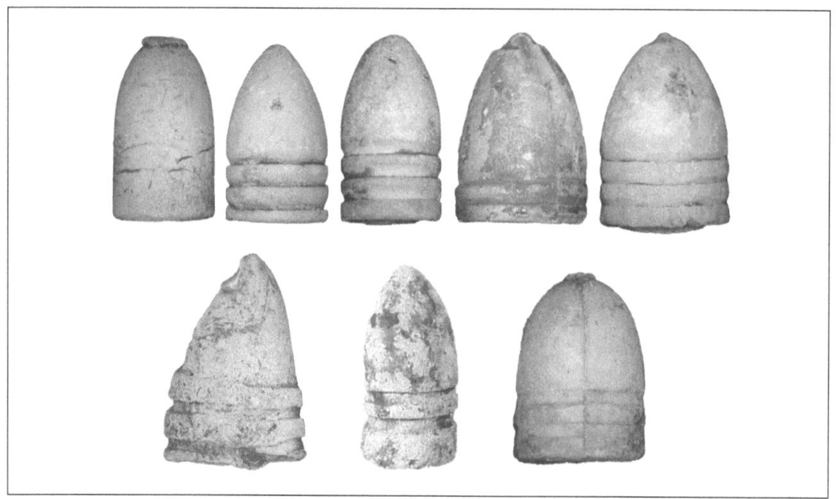

FIGURE 19. Minié ball varieties. Top row (left to right): Enfield, .58 standard, .58 standard (two specimens), .69 two-cannelure, .69 three-cannelure; bottom row (left to right): .69 "Italian," .58 Gardner, .69 similar to Gardner. Photo by William B. Lees.

Confederate manufactured versions, with similar effect (W. B. Edwards 1962). Likewise, virtually the same weapon was in use throughout Europe, and many countries sold these as well as older, obsolete smoothbore weapons to both sides during the war. Some older smoothbore muskets, such as the US Model 1842 and European equivalents, were used throughout the war, but some of these had been rifled to increase accuracy. The latter are referred to as "rifled muskets." The well-regarded US Model 1841 rifle in .54 caliber was originally designed to use a spherical ball. In the late 1850s, the Minié bullet was adopted for use in this weapon. Serving this wide range of weapons and manufactured widely in both the north and south, the Minié bullet varies in form but could be used interchangeably in any rifle of the proper caliber. We found several general varieties of the Minié bullet at Honey Springs: the standard Minié as designed by Captain Minié (with multiple cannelures or grooves around the base) and Enfield, "Italian," and Gardner varieties.

The standard Minié ball has two or three cannelures or grooves around the skirt. Many of these from Honey Springs have been fired, and some are heavily disfigured by impact. Most were intended for use in .54 or

.577/.58 caliber weapons, but a few were used in larger, obsolete .69–.71 caliber rifled muskets. The size difference between .54 and .577/.58 caliber Miniés is small, making it difficult to distinguish between the two for bullets damaged by impact. Due to differences in length, shape of nose, and depth of cavity, weight does not convincingly distinguish one from the other. The fifty fired and unfired specimens in this caliber range all have three grooves. They vary by characteristics just mentioned and by deformation by firing and impact.

The eleven unfired specimens have deep grooves with sharp leading and rounded following edges as per Captain Minié's original design. Based on measured diameter, five were for use in .54 caliber and six in .577/.58 caliber firearms. Unfired specimens are of particular use to archaeologists because their placement on the field marks a specific location during the battle of a soldier who lost or discarded this bullet (collectors call these bullets "drops").

The thirty-nine fired Miniés include many that are disfigured, making caliber and rifling measurement difficult if not impossible. These were roughly evenly divided between those with minimal, moderate, and low impact. The number of these rifle-fired bullets in "yaw" (tumbling), especially those that struck with a high velocity, is remarkable (bullets that experienced yaw are identified by damage to the side or base related to striking or grounding while actively tumbling). Bullets will eventually tumble as their velocity decreases. Tumbling can also happen immediately on leaving the barrel if insufficient or poor-quality powder is used (D. Scott et al. 2019). For a bullet to strike with high velocity while tumbling is probably an indication of issues with powder quantity or quality coupled with a nearby target or obstruction.

Of these fired bullets, only eight had rifling impressions that were sufficiently clear to allow comparison to that from known weapons. Three had four lands and groove impressions comparing favorably with the Pattern 1853 Austrian Lorenz in .58 caliber. The other five had seven lands and groove impressions and are probably for .54 caliber weapons. Observed rifling on these bullets is consistent to breech-loading carbines such as the Merrill and Confederate Maynard but also a variety of nonmartial rifles. One disfigured bullet has a land impression consistent with the three-land and three-groove pattern of the .577 caliber Enfield rifle-musket.

Fourteen Miniés are of a size used in .69–.71 caliber rifled muskets. Three of the five unfired specimens have three cannelures, one has two, and another has two broad, flat grooves. The two-cannelure bullet was pulled using a worm, which has left a distinctive mark on its nose. Bullets were pulled for a variety of reasons, but in battle this was probably because of jamming midway in the barrel from fouling or due to failure of the powder charge to ignite.

The nine fired specimens include two with double cannelures and six with triple cannelures. Three of these bullets suffered high-velocity impacts while actively tumbling and another two with moderate velocity. Others show little evidence of impact but were clearly fired. Largely due to the lack of documented examples for comparison, the consistent rifling marks observed on these bullets suggest only that they were fired in similar weapons.

Sixteen bullets are identified as Enfield-variety. These differ from Captain Minié's bullet because they have no cannelures around the skirt, and typically they are a bit longer and have rounded noses. Six of the seven unfired specimens range in caliber from about .559 to .569, which is appropriate for the .577 caliber bore of the British Enfield rifle-musket for which they were intended. Confederate rules for bullet manufacture published in August 1862 specified that the diameter of bullets for the Enfield was to be .562 caliber (D. Thomas 2010, 45). The seventh unfired Enfield bullet was seated and has a measured diameter of .571 caliber, but a worm impression shows it was pulled and never fired.

The nine fired specimens include four with very clear patterns of rifling consistent with that of the Pattern 1853 Enfield imported in quantity by both the United States and the Confederacy during the Civil War (D. Scott et al. 2019). Two struck with high velocity, one with medium velocity, and six with low velocity. While not seemingly earth-shattering, the fact that these Enfield-pattern bullets do appear to have been fired in the Enfield is useful since they could have been used in any weapon of a similar caliber. For example, standard three-groove Minié balls are known to have been packaged by arsenals for use in "U.S. or Enfield Rifles" (D. Thomas 1997, 162). A three-groove Minié discussed above has a rifling pattern consistent with that of the Pattern 1853 Enfield.

Three Confederate arsenal-made Gardner Minié balls were found at Honey Springs. One is unfired and the other two show low-impact damage to their sides. The Gardner has two broad, flat grooves midway up the bullet and a distinctive base. Frederick J. Gardner's Confederate patent for this bullet hinged on directly attaching the paper cartridge into a prepared base that was crimped to hold the paper. Confederate arsenals produced Gardner bullets in .54, .58, and .69 caliber. The specimens from Honey Springs are likely for a .58 caliber bore. An unfired .69 caliber bullet, discussed earlier, with rounded nose and two broad, flat grooves is similar to the Gardner, but does not have the patent Gardner base (D. Thomas 2010, 210–13).

The final Minié variety is referred to as "Italian" by collectors (S. Phillips 1971, 22). Thomas and Thomas (1996, 48) say, "[These bullets] have become known as 'Italian Carcanos,' but there is no proof of their foreign manufacture. Most likely they were cast in the South." This distinctive variety is represented by two fired specimens, both of which appear to be about .69 caliber. They are distinct because rather than grooves they have two wide raised bands wrapping the skirt. Confederate use, especially at mid-war, is suspected. Neither of these bullets, although fired, shows any impressions of rifling, although their raised bands do show barrel abrasion. One of these struck on its side with a high velocity and is virtually flattened. The other struck a jagged object, possibly a splintered tree, at medium to high velocity while tumbling.

Another somewhat peculiar bullet found at Honey Springs is the so-called Pickett. These are cone-shaped projectiles that may have a solid base or a basal cavity, with calibers commonly in the mid-.40s but ranging from .35 to .56 (D. Thomas 2003, 280–81). The Pickett was widely used for civilian common rifles. Often found on Civil War battlefields, these may have been used by sharpshooters. Thomas is, however, hesitant to necessarily ascribe them to Civil War use (D. Thomas 2003, 279). The three Pickett-style bullets from Honey Springs are all fired and have estimated calibers from .41 to .49. The .49 caliber specimen has clear barrel abrasion but no clear rifling impressions. It also appears to have been carved to accentuate the cone shape, or it may have originated as a different type of bullet and then been purposefully carved into the characteristic cone shape of the Pickett.

Although breech-loading weapons such as the Hall rifle had long been in use by the US military, the widespread adoption of breech-loading and magazine weapons, and the widespread use of metallic cartridges, was

FIGURE 20. Breechloading bullets and metallic cartridges. Left to right: Merrill, Sharps, pin-fire (Lefaucheux). Photo by William B. Lees.

a sea change accelerated by the Civil War (W. B. Edwards 1962, 136). These weapons had relatively distinctive bullets, and some had unique metallic cartridge cases that allow us to identify the presence of the Merrill, Sharps, Spencer, and Henry at Honey Springs. Bullets for these weapons are easily distinguished from conical bullets designed for muzzleloading weapons because the bases are solid and the circumference is slightly larger than the bore. Because the bullet was loaded at the breech, its larger size forced the lead into the grooves of the smaller barrel rather than having a skirt that expanded to engage the rifled bore.

The Merrill carbine was a single-shot .54 caliber breechloader with 1858 and 1861 patents (Coates and Thomas 1990, 33; W. B. Edwards 1962, 119–21). Large numbers of Merrill carbines and lesser numbers of rifles were purchased early in the war by the US government, and many fell into Confederate hands through capture. Four bullets characteristic of those designed for the Merrill were found during our surveys. These have solid bases, draw to relatively acute points, and have a single broad, flat groove near the base and two forward grooves with sloping leading edges and sharp trailing edges. One is unfired. Rifling impressions confirm that the others were fired in a Merrill (D. Scott 2019). All show low-velocity impact.

Like the Merrill, the Sharps was a single-shot breech-loading weapon that saw significant use by cavalry (carbine) and, to a much lesser extent, infantry (rifle) during the Civil War. Although based on an 1848 patent, the New Model 1859 was adopted by the United States, with the purchase of 80,512 carbines and 9,141 rifles (Coates and Thomas 1990, 34; W. B. Edwards 1962, 293–95). Although the form of bullets varies, the twelve specimens from Honey Springs were all the "tie-base" variety, with an expanded stud on its otherwise solid base used to tie on its linen cartridge. Like the Merrill, the Sharps was sized slightly larger than the bore to facilitate the bullet engaging the rifling in the barrel. Ten of these are fired and struck with low to high impact.

Three other bullets have solid bases suggesting that they were also fired in breech-loading weapons. One of these measures .491 caliber and has a relatively distinctive three- land and three-groove rifling pattern that compares favorably with several popular breechloaders of the Civil War: the Smith, Maynard, and Morse. The bullet itself has a single narrow groove midway up the base, possibly over a narrow constriction. This does not match the style of bullets made for any of these weapons, but this does not necessarily mean it was not fired in one. The Morse was of Confederate manufacture, and the Smith and Maynard, although in use by US troops, were used by Confederate cavalry through capture. The second of these solid-base bullets suffered a high-velocity impact but it is similar in weight to Merrill cartridges from Honey Springs and may have been fired in one. The last of these unidentified solid-base bullets was fired and has a relatively intact base with a measured caliber of .498. I could not match this to any specific weapon.

The .52 caliber Spencer rifle and carbine used a metallic rim-fire cartridge and had a seven-round magazine (Coates and Thomas 1990, 35; W. B. Edwards 1962, 144–50). US Ordnance Department tested this weapon, patented in early 1860, but did not initially adopt it due to concerns over the availability of its specialized rim-fire metallic cartridge ammunition. By 1863, however, due to its reliability and availability of a sufficient supply of ammunition, it saw rapid adoption by US cavalry and, to a lesser degree, infantry. Two fired Spencer cases were found during the Honey Springs survey, attesting to the spread of this weapon to the Far West by this time.

The Henry, predecessor of the famous Winchester, was also an 1860 patent and received similar skepticism from the US Ordnance Department over its specialized rim-fire metallic case ammunition. Even with an impressive sixteen-round magazine, this weapon was never officially adopted by the US military. Many Henry rifles, in .44 caliber, were purchased privately, mainly by officers. A gold-plated Henry presented to Major General Blunt by his staff officers was donated in 1936 to the Kansas Historical Society (Kansas Historical Society n.d.). Three fired Henry cartridges and a single fired solid-base Henry bullet were found at Honey Springs. The cases each had signature double firing pin marks, and one has an "H" head stamp. Their presence at Honey Springs attests to the widespread if not profuse adoption of this arm.

When most people think of Civil War sidearms, army (.44) and navy (.36) caliber revolvers made famous by Colt come to mind. As with shoulder arms, sidearms including revolvers underwent a significant evolution by the outbreak of hostilities in 1861 from flintlock to percussion, smoothbore to rifled, and single-shot to revolver, some using metallic cartridges. The army and navy caliber revolvers were indeed staples of Civil War armies, North and South. Still, other manufactures in the United States and Europe (for example, Adams, Kerr, Lefaucheux, Remington, and Savage) and several southern contractors supplying the Confederacy (for example, Spiller & Burr and Griswold & Gunnison), operated during the conflict and produced very serviceable weapons. Brigadier General Cooper carried a .36 caliber Spiller & Burr during the Civil War, now in the collections of the Oklahoma Historical Society. In addition to popular army and navy caliber weapons were revolvers such as the imported LeMat in .40 caliber. The LeMat also had a .60 caliber smoothbore barrel below the smaller rifled barrel. The former was designed to fire buckshot and was the issue sidearm for several Confederate cavalry regiments (Coates and Thomas 1990, 60). The Richmond arsenal produced cartridges, including prepared buckshot cartridges, for the LeMat (D. Thomas, 2010).

In the decade before the war, the United States worked on updating single-shot muzzle-loading pistols in .58 caliber by changing out flint for percussion locks and rifling the barrel, and by adopting as their preferred ammunition the Minié ball. These improvements were also captured in the Model 1855 pistol produced in US armories. Commonly called "horse pistols" because of their use by dragoons and other mounted troops, these weapons were essentially obsolete but were in arsenals throughout the country in 1860. Some similar weapons were probably also purchased in Europe by US and Confederate agents in a frenzy to equip large volunteer armies in 1861 (W. B. Edwards 1962, 292).

In addition to martial weapons manufactured in the United States or purchased in Europe, an extensive range of other pistols and revolvers were available before and during the Civil War. They were carried as personally purchased weapons by individuals in all branches of service north and south. However, infantry soon found that the weight and bulk of their kit was a fundamental adversary. The Colt Pocket Model 1849 in .31 caliber was popular. Still, a wide range of other revolvers such as the .31 and .41 caliber Volcanic along with numerous single-shot pistols ("boot pistols") and derringers were readily available and heavily marketed to soldiers for private purchase. Use of privately owned sidearms, as well as quartermaster acquisition of sidearms of any description in the far western theater and Indian Territory, was likely even as late as 1863.

Twenty conical bullets associated with use in sidearms were found during our survey. A conical bullet measuring .44 caliber has a single groove above a slightly constricted base like those made for Colt revolvers. It has a distinct seven-land, seven-groove pattern that matches well with Colt Dragoon and Model 1860 revolvers recorded by Douglas Scott (D. Scott 2019). Three other bullets, probably in navy caliber, also appear to be Colt pattern bullets. One fired and one unfired bullet of about .44 caliber are the Remington pattern, two seem to be Adams pattern (one probably .36 and one .44), and another, probably .44 caliber, might be a Kerr pattern bullet. Also found was an ordinary revolver bullet with a slightly constricted base that I could not associate with any weapon. The other ten bullets I believe were used in sidearms were extremely distorted by high-velocity impact, making specific identification impossible. All appear to be in the upper .30s and mid-.40s calibers. Gary Moore found a single metallic pin-fire cartridge in the Wooded Forty. This cartridge has been fired and is likely for a .44 caliber Lefaucheux revolver. While conical bullets were available for most revolvers, spherical ball (round ball) ammunition was commonly used, especially by the Confederacy.

Spherical ball ammunition is by far the most common artifact found during our work at Honey Springs, with a total of 480 specimens. These are also the most difficult to differentiate by use: were they used or intended for use in a smoothbore small arm as ball or buckshot (or "buck and ball," a combination of both), as a single ball in a rifle, or in a revolver or single-shot smoothbore or rifled pistol? Alternately, some may have been used in artillery as lead-ball canister (used primarily in mountain howitzers) or as shrapnel contained in spherical case. Size (caliber) and marks and damage from firing and impact provide the best clues for determining use. It is unfortunate that while many can be conclusively assigned a specific use, others cannot, and we remain uncertain whether they were dropped or discarded or simply do not bear the telltale scars of having been fired.

A key feature of spherical ball ammunition is caliber. Unlike other types of ammunition, caliber for round balls can be accurately estimated, even for the most damaged specimens, using a formula developed by Daniel M. Sivilich (1996; 2016, 23–27). His work is based on comparison of archaeological specimens with known calibers and predicts the circumference (caliber) of a sphere based on the weight of the lead.

Numerous balls from Honey Springs have without doubt been fired in small arms. This conclusion is firmly based on the presence of land and groove impressions ("rifling") on the ball, "banding" (a result of firing in a smoothbore, where the ball develops a flattened band from contact with the inside of the bore), buckshot impressions on large balls (buck and ball), and partial banding and impressions of other balls on buckshot. Partial banding and damage from contact with other small-caliber balls also results from buckshot loads in shotguns or large-caliber muskets (DeMuth, Nicholas, and Munger 1978).

Ninety-three balls were fired in relatively small-caliber rifled small arms. This was determined by different types of damage seen on the bullets, including clear land and groove impressions or by patterns of fabric "patch" that show or strongly indicate firing in rifled weapons. These patch impressions are distinct from a few others that resulted from impact with uniform or clothing of an enemy combatant.

Calibers for these balls were estimated using the Sivilich formula (Sivilich 2016) and broadly distributed from .321 to .615 caliber. Most rifle-fired balls are less than .50 caliber, but seven are between .52 and .61 caliber. Details on these larger balls are indistinct or non-conclusive as to specific weapons used. They likely were fired in larger-caliber civilian weapons, and their low number is striking. The remainder and vast majority cluster broadly around two calibers popular for Civil War revolvers, the navy .36 caliber and army .44 caliber. While conical bullets available

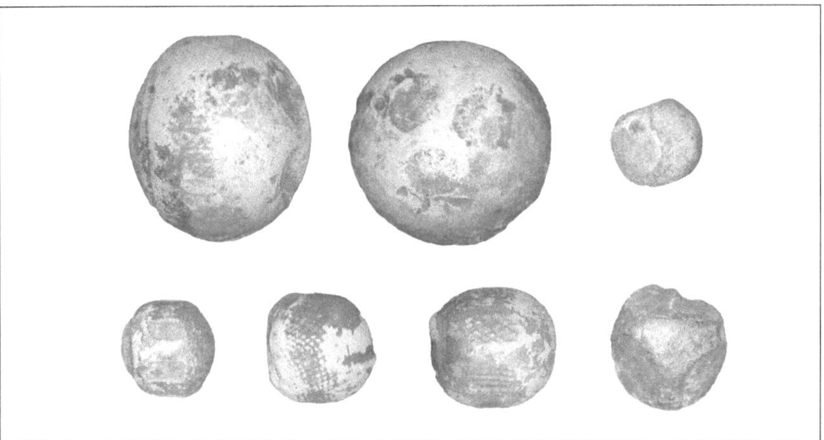

FIGURE 21. Fired spherical ball ammunition. Top row, left to right: .68 caliber ball showing banding and indentations of buckshot, same ball turned to show buckshot indentations, buckshot showing partial banding; bottom row, left to right: ball showing rifle lands and grooves, ball showing patch impression, ball showing partial patch and lands and grooves, buckshot. Photo by William B. Lees.

for these weapons have already been discussed, round balls were also commonly used in revolvers. It is probable that some were fired in these army and navy revolvers and in revolvers and pistols of other calibers. However, the range of balls between .30 and .49 caliber, most with a seven-land and seven-groove pattern, means they could have been fired in a dizzying array of martial and non-martial revolvers and pistols and an equally dizzying array of common rifles (D. Scott et al. 2019). While this lack of certainty may seem disappointing, these rifle-fired balls, as part of the overall collection, allow an important general characterization. In the following chapters, where I discuss how these balls are represented in the different fields of conflict at Honey Springs, I will bring some further light to this diversity.

Some of these balls show additional interesting individual characteristics. On the front of two balls, which struck with medium and high velocity respectively, is a clear fabric impression of what was probably clothing worn by an enemy soldier. Two others show similar but faint fabric impressions. About one-fourth of the bullets struck with high velocity, one-fourth at medium velocity, and the remainder at low or no velocity. It is important that half of these bullets either lost velocity and fell to the ground or were fired with such low velocity (insufficient or poor gunpowder) that impact caused little or no damage.

Overall, calibers are highly variable, which is both a reflection of the diversity of weapons and corresponding calibers in use during the Civil War as well as variation in actual finished bore sizes and in mass-produced and hand-cast lead ammunition. This observed diversity of calibers probably most directly reflects the wide range of different weapons in use in the Indian Territory. In 1863, this diversity was almost certainly higher than anywhere else under arms during the Civil War and included many common rifles of variable calibers.

Another fifty-two round balls are strongly banded, showing that they were fired in small arms. The distribution of these banded balls by caliber falls into three general clusters: .30 –.46, .52–.57, and .65–.69. It is notable that balls ranging from .65 to .69 caliber account for nineteen or around a third of the specimens, compared to zero among the rifle-fired balls. Nine of these balls impacted with a medium velocity, while the remainder struck at little or low velocity, meaning they were essentially spent and would have done little harm. Confederate commissioner of Indian affairs Sutton S. Scott derided the quality of the gunpowder in use by the rebels at Honey Springs, saying it was barely sufficient to "drive the ball out of the piece" (S. Scott 1888, 1097). Four of these large-caliber banded balls also have distinctive impressions of buckshot that show these were the large ball in a buck-and-ball round. Large-caliber smoothbores were notoriously inaccurate, but buck and ball increased the likelihood of inflicting some sort of wound on an enemy. The seven balls measuring between .52 and .57 caliber were probably fired in shotguns or fowlers but show no buckshot impressions as do some of the larger balls. One of these was pulled and discarded, and two hit with a high impact, one with medium, and three with low.

Most banded balls are smaller than .46 caliber and cluster around the mid-.30s to the upper .40s. Fourteen buckshot-size balls ranging from .32 to .45 caliber were fired in a large-caliber smoothbore weapon, either as part of a buck-and-ball round or shotgun-fired buckshot. The buckshot shows impressions of other similar-size balls but also have partial banding on that part of the ball that engaged with the inside of a larger-caliber bore. Analysis of the partial banding on one confirms that it was fired in a bore in the mid-.60 caliber range, while another was in the upper-.50 caliber range. Still, twelve of these small-caliber spherical balls are banded around their entire circumference showing they were not buckshot but rather were fired as an individual round in a small-caliber smoothbore. Except for one with medium-impact damage, all showed little evidence of impact.

Although not banded, another thirty-five balls were fired with other balls, possibly from small arms. Five, ranging from .67 to .69 caliber, have at least one ball impression. Two have three impressions of smaller balls characteristic of the large ball in a buck-and-ball round. The other three have only one ball impression each, one of which is notably larger than buckshot; these may be lead balls contained in artillery case.

Smaller balls include thirteen that have one or typically two impressions of similar-sized balls and are probably the buckshot from a buck-and-ball round. The remaining seventeen all have multiple ball impressions but in character differ from other balls similar in size by being more angular or battered. I believe these were buckshot stacked tightly and fired in a larger-caliber weapon, probably a shotgun. Confederate use of shotguns is well documented. D. Thomas (2010, 184) illustrates prepared cartridges of buckshot of .69 caliber that could be fired in either muskets, rifle-muskets, or shotguns of that caliber. These were manufactured at the Augusta and Columbus, Georgia, arsenals. He also illustrates two charges of buckshot removed from cartridges that show considerable variability in size and finished shape, reflecting lower standards of manufacture for this type of round.

I will add a caveat here regarding numbers. The relatively small size of buckshot, and more so as caliber decreases, probably results in underrepresentation in our finds. As the smallest of our finds, these were the least likely to be indicated by the metal detectors in use in the mid-1990s and, to a lesser degree, today. Although I cannot put a number to this, keep in mind that the buckshot recovered, and especially the smaller varieties, may underestimate the importance of shotguns at the Battle of Honey Springs.

Finally, two balls with no banding or rifling have distinctive marks that show they were pulled with a worm and are thus certainly small-arms ammunition. One of these is about .44 caliber and was probably not reloaded and fired after being pulled. The other, of about .66 caliber, was pulled and then apparently reloaded and fired as it shows a medium-velocity impact.

The 180 spherical balls from Honey Springs that were fired in rifled or smoothbore small arms (or, perhaps in a few cases, artillery) represent only 37.5 percent of all the spherical ball ammunition found during our survey of Honey Springs. The remaining 300 balls are, unfortunately, more difficult to assign to either small arms or artillery. These are thus the largest single category of artifacts found during our survey. The reason these are lumped into a category of "unknown use" is that there is simply no physical evidence that will allow me to establish whether these balls were fired in rifle, smoothbore, or artillery (as canister or case shrapnel), or whether they represent ammunition that was simply not used. Still, over half show damage from very high–, high-, or medium-velocity impact that tell us they are ammunition that was fired during the battle.

The impact-damaged balls occur across the caliber spectrum along with those with little or no impact damage. Balls fired in smoothbores may not have banded if undersized or fired with insufficient or poor-quality powder, and they may not have impact damage if they hit the ground after their initial velocity was expended. This would include buckshot fired as part of a round of buck and ball or fired as a buckshot load in a shotgun. Some may represent ammunition intended for rifled or smoothbore small arms that was lost or discarded during the battle, although it is unlikely this would account for more than the 20 percent documented for Minié balls at Honey Springs.

Of note, though: the distribution of these spherical balls across calibers is similar with that for rifle- and smoothbore-fired specimens with a few exceptions. The primary divergence is with rifle-fired balls, which have very few specimens above .55 caliber. The balls fired in smoothbores and the unattributed balls discussed here both have peaks in the upper-.60 caliber range. Unfortunately, these peaks could relate to use in shotguns and large-caliber martial smoothbores, and in mountain howitzer canister and case for six- or twelve-pound cannon.

Still, there are significant spikes in balls with no evidence of impact in the mid-.40 and upper-.60 caliber ranges. These are probably best explained as undamaged balls from buck and ball and buckshot for shotguns in the .40s, and by spherical case shot in the .60s. Spherical case

FIGURE 22. Lead ball resting on a reproduction US Model 1861 rifle-musket. Photo by William B. Lees.

explode in the air, throwing some shrapnel balls backward or upward, countering their forward thrust; these likely would have had little damage from a subsequent impact.

Finally, two balls provide individual stories of interest if not importance. The first is a spherical ball of about .54 caliber that struck with a high to very high velocity but otherwise shows no evidence of how it was fired; it is not marked by banding, rifling, or fabric patch. This ball struck firmly against a smooth, cylindrical object forever molded into the soft lead (see figure 22). On July 17, 1863, at Honey Springs, the only perfect explanation is that this ball struck a musket barrel. Since there is no evidence for this ball being fired in a rifle or musket, I believe it most likely was mountain howitzer canister or artillery case shrapnel.

The other unusual ball appears to have been modified in an attempt to increase its lethality by cutting six slices and pushing the lead slightly outward around its circumference (Sivilich 2016, 73–76). This ball has no evidence of rifling, banding, or fabric patch, but it does show

FIGURE 23. Lead ball carved to increase lethality. Photo by William B. Lees.

medium-velocity impact, probably a ricochet or glancing blow. It is .635 caliber by weight, making it right for use in a .69 or .70 caliber musket or as shrapnel in artillery case or canister. Because the modification would have made it impossible to load into a musket, its use in artillery is suspected. If so, this modified ball would have likely been inserted during manufacture of the projectile rather than in the field. While these last two items may individually not tell us much about the battle itself, they very poignantly illustrate and connect to the human reality of that conflict.

While these conclusions about spherical ball ammunition address a large percentage of battlefield finds at Honey Springs, they are admittedly general and somewhat less than satisfying. Nonetheless, the findings speak to the importance of artillery, though with less clarity than iron fragments of exploded cannonballs. They also comment on the realities of loss and discard during the battle, but with less certainty than conical bullets.

An additional twenty-five disfigured items were probably once lead ammunition. Thirteen of these are melted and twelve severely chewed by animals. None can be identified as round or conical in original form, and thus they are not included in the above discussions. Evidence from campsites suggests soldiers used black-powder cartridges to start cooking fires while in camp (bullets were melted in the process) or that wet or damaged cartridges or pulled bullets were thrown in fires for discard (Balicki 2010, 71–72). Some of the melted lead found at Honey Springs might reflect this since the Confederate troops camped along Elk Creek before the battle, and Union troops camped on the battlefield afterward. Also likely is that some of the melted lead represented bullets, shrapnel balls, or canister balls embedded in trees that later burned in natural fires or during clearing of land for agriculture.

The popular convention has it that chewed bullets are signs of soldiers "biting the bullet" when in pain in the field or hospital. Soldiers did indeed chew bullets, but perhaps for reasons other than to deal with pain. A range of animals from deer and swine to rodents also are known to have chewed bullets. I have not analyzed the tooth marks on the Honey Springs bullets; most, due to size, were probably made by rodents. Swine (whose tooth impressions are easily mistaken for human) and deer are likely responsible for a few others (Sivilich 2016, 102–15).

Sixteen additional round balls from the final survey in 1999 were not available for reanalysis. There was no existing recorded information on which to describe caliber and any damage related to use. These are included in the totals and shown on some maps but are not otherwise discussed.

Although the preponderance of ammunition in the Honey Springs collection is no surprise, I believe the importance of spherical ball ammunition stands out as exceptional on a Civil War battlefield, especially one at mid-war. Almost 70 percent of all ammunition, including iron artillery shrapnel, iron canister balls, and copper alloy arrow points, is spherical ball ammunition. This substantial percentage serves, I think, to identify two critical themes in the overall conflict. First, a considerable portion of these balls are from artillery. These balls were shrapnel released with the explosion of spherical case ammunition fired from six- and twelve-pound guns or were lead-ball canister fired in twelve-pound mountain howitzers. This conclusion flows easily from accounts of the battle in official records and other sources.

A second theme is the importance of civilian weapons used at Honey Springs. I have shown that much of the spherical ball ammunition was fired in small arms. The variability of calibers in balls smaller than .52 speaks clearly to the range of weapons such as civilian common or "country rifles," shotguns, and privately purchased single-shot pistols and revolvers.

FIGURE 24. Arrow points. Photo by William B. Lees.

The use of these non-martial weapons is not missing from the documentary record, but evidence of their presence in the artifacts provides proportion and importance beyond what comes from a reading of vague or general characterizations of the arms in use. Although rare finds, parts of firearms found at Honey Springs reflect this as well; evidence of civilian common rifles and shotguns is as frequent as that for martial weapons.

Although matches with specific civilian weapons were not possible, civilian rifles and smoothbore weapons of various calibers were used extensively during the conflict. The use of shotguns (or other large-caliber smoothbore weapons loaded with shot) is supported by buckshot damaged by firing; this is distinct from buckshot fired as part of a buck-and-ball cartridge. Although revealing the importance of civilian weapons, the spherical ball ammunition also speaks to the battle's martial weapons. The collection contains clear examples of fired buck-and-ball rounds that were standard for US and foreign import muskets in the .69–.71 caliber range. There is specific and inferred evidence in spherical ball ammunition for the use of army and navy caliber revolvers (also revealed by the finding of a revolver cylinder on the field).

Potentially the most interesting artifacts found at Honey Springs were eight rolled-metal arrowheads. These are made from a thin copper alloy sheet to form a cone that is closed at the tip, which is quite sharp. Native American artisans probably crafted these from pieces of copper alloy cooking pots or kettles. The tightly closed tips set these apart from similar cone-shaped "tinklers" that were suspended from clothing on cordage or leather. Tinklers differ from the Honey Springs artifacts in that their points are open to facilitate fastening. Gregory Perino named the closed tip devices "Kaskaskia points" and noted their presence from the Great Lakes to Oklahoma (Perino and Good 1970). According to Perino (1977, 58): "This is a conical metal arrow point usually made of kettle brass or copper. The thin metal was rolled or hammered onto a tapered mandril to form a cone with a point on one end and a socket for hafting on the other."

Perino also notes that these points "may be a substitute for the conical antler tip arrow point used earlier" (Perino 1977, 58). He illustrates points from MacIntosh County (Choctaw), along the Red River and Lake Texoma (Chickasaw), and Hughes County (Creek/Choctaw), Oklahoma (Perino 1977, 58, plate 29). Richard Drass (1980) notes a similar point from a historic Muscogee site in Okmulgee County. Three similar rolled-metal points were found during the excavation of a Choctaw house from the 1830s to 1850s in southeastern Oklahoma (Larry Haikey, personal communication, 2001). A rolled-copper Kaskaskia point found in the Apalachicola River in Florida is possibly associated with Seminole use of this area in the early nineteenth century (Horrell et al. 2009). The Seminoles are known to have used the bow in the Second Seminole War (1835–42) (Mahon 1967, 123). I have seen a similar point in a private collection from Cabin Creek where battles were fought in 1863 and 1864. The 1863 Battle of Cabin Creek was two weeks before the Battle of Honey Springs. Indian troops, on both sides, fought at both places.

The eight points found during our work at Honey Springs range from 1.37 to 2.7 inches in length. All have a tightly closed tip, but one is slightly blunted and another slightly rolled over by impact. The specimen with the blunted tip also opened along its seam, probably also the result of impact. An additional three "rolled copper cones" were found during the 1972 University of Tulsa excavation near Honey Springs, which Cheek (1976, 70) suggests may have been used as clothing decoration ("tinkling cones" or tinklers). Illustrations of two of these show they are about 1.5 inches long and like the smaller specimens found during our survey (Cheek 1976, 47, figure 23 k–l). These also seem to have tightly rolled tips identical to those found during our work. I believe these are also points rather than tinklers.

A cane arrow (*oski naki*) with a similar rolled-metal point, said to be of Choctaw origin, is in the collections of the Museum of the Red River (Choctaw Nation of Oklahoma n.d.). The School of Choctaw Language website (2011, 3) notes, "Rolled metal points, like the one on this arrow, are known on Choctaw sites dating back to the 1730s. Arrows of this general description were being used by some Mississippi Choctaws until at least 1900, and some Oklahoma Choctaw hunters into the mid-1900s."

Buttons are another item that connects the archaeologist with an individual's location in the past—where threads failed and it fell to the ground. Most of the buttons from Honey Springs were manufactured for US military use. Four are three-piece (stamped front and back, wire eye) copper alloy construction, bearing an eagle with a shield on the front. One of these has "Scovill * Extra" and three "Scovill Mfg * Waterbury [Connecticut]" stamped into their backs. Another is the back and eye only, marked "Scovill Mfg C * Waterbury," and is undoubtedly a US button as well. These buttons include two suitable for officer and enlisted frocks and fatigue blouses (sack coats), and one is suitable for cuffs.

Scovill was established in 1802 and began contracting with the US Army and Navy to produce uniform buttons in 1812 as the nation went to war with Great Britain for the second time. This company was incorporated in 1850 as Scovill Manufacturing Company and broadened its product line with additional military items, including fuses and munitions. They were a major US contractor during the Civil War, once again broadening their line to help supply the nation's rapidly expanding armed forces. The buttons marked Scovill Manufacturing date after 1850 (Scovill Fasteners n.d.).

Three additional three-piece buttons have an eagle and shield device on the front. Two have an "I" for infantry within the shield, and another has a "D" for dragoon. None are marked on the back. The infantry buttons are of a size suitable for officer's frocks and enlisted men's fatigue blouses, and the smaller dragoon button is suitable for cuffs. The "I" and "D," along with companion branch buttons for artillery and cavalry were phased out in 1855. Still, use of these buttons continued into the Civil War as supplies were exhausted. Service designations were adopted by the Confederacy, and a rebel button with a large "I" for infantry was found in the Wooded Forty by Gary Moore.

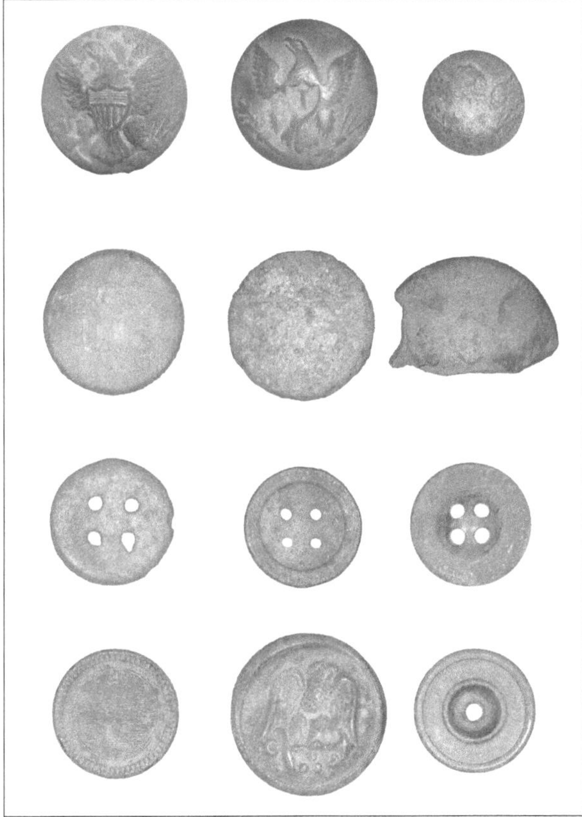

FIGURE 25. Military and civilian buttons.
Top row, left to right: US Army general service, infantry, dragoon; second row, left to right: early US Army general service brass, US general service pewter, three-piece brass rifleman; third row, left to right: pewter, two-piece iron, civilian brass trouser button; bottom row, left to right: civilian, US Navy, and civilian one-hole.
Photo by William B. Lees.

Three other US buttons found during our survey were long obsolete by the Civil War. A one-piece cast pewter button bearing a large "US" is of a size suitable for use on uniform coats. This button is highly corroded but appears to be a style that featured the letters US separated by a tiny star and issued in 1808 through the 1830s. Another one-piece cast copper alloy button has a spread eagle over "US," which is in turn over a horizontal oval wreath. The back has a cast eye surrounded by two concentric lines separated by eleven randomly placed five- and six-pointed stars. This is a greatcoat (overcoat) button in use in the 1820s (D. F. Johnson 1948, 65). The other is a three-piece button stamped with an eagle and shield, with an "R" for rifleman in the shield. This button is in very poor condition and is folded over onto itself. The US Regiment of Riflemen was authorized in 1808 and discontinued in 1821 (Fredriksen 2000).

Troops who established Forts Smith, Gibson, and Towson would likely have worn buttons such as the "US" and rifleman buttons, and they may have been lost along the Texas Road well before the Civil War by US troops moving within or through the Indian Territory. That said, either button may have been on an obsolete uniform stored in a southern state arsenal and seized and issued to Confederate troops early in the war. It was also common practice to issue obsolete uniform items as treaty annuities for the Indian nations in the Indian Territory and elsewhere.

Seemingly out of place is a navy button of a style introduced slightly before the Civil War. It has a left-facing eagle perched on a horizontal anchor circled by stars over a stack of three cannonballs. Unfortunately, only the front of this button was found, so there is no information from the manufacturer's mark on the back. This general style of button was used well into the twentieth century. While it might seem unusual at a Civil War battlefield in Oklahoma, it also may have been on clothing worn by a Native American combatant.

Important to any uniform were trouser buttons used to close the fly and attach suspenders to trousers. These were simple four-hole buttons, which early on were one-piece cast pewter but began to be replaced by two-piece tin buttons shortly before the Civil War. We found two one-piece pewter buttons and a single two-piece tin button at Honey Springs. A civilian one-piece four-hole copper alloy button of the same size may also have served as a trouser button.

Other civilian buttons were also found that I believe may have been on clothing of combatants at Honey Springs. These are a three-piece button with a stamped, abstract decorative front and a single-hole copper alloy button with a scalloped rim. Civilian buttons may, once again, have found their way to the ground before or after the Civil War by civilian traffic on the Texas Road. Still, I believe it likely that they were from

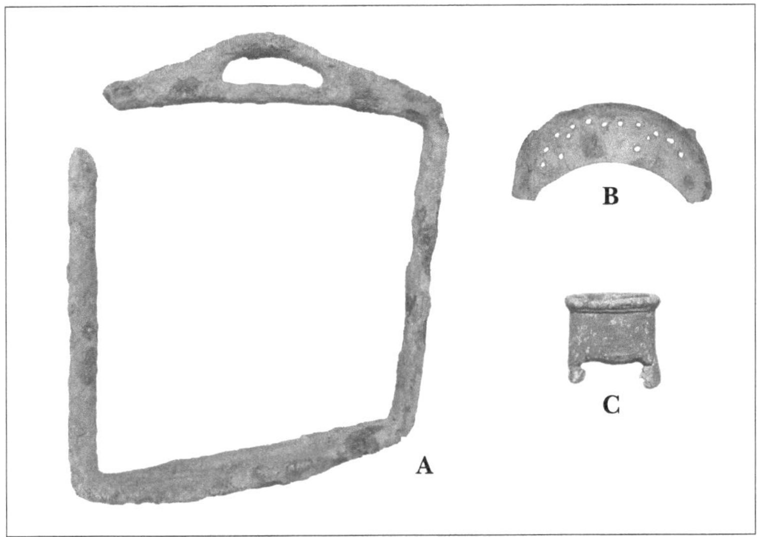

FIGURE 26. Stirrup, heel protector, and canteen spout.
Photo by William B. Lees.

privately purchased clothing that may have been used to some degree by Union troops and probably to a great degree by those aligned with the Confederacy.

Military equipment was an uncommon find at Honey Springs. Equipment included a few US issue items. Equally rare are civilian items that may have equipped Confederate-allied troops and, less likely, US soldiers. Although it is uncertain how widespread this practice was, Thomas White of the US Sixth Cavalry, wounded at Honey Springs, furnished his own horse and horse equipment from at least May 1862 up to and beyond the Battle of Honey Springs (National Archives 1891).

US pattern mass-produced canteens are represented by a single canteen spout, made of pewter, and a finger loop for a canteen stopper. US canteens were made by soldering together two stamped tinned sheet metal halves and soldering a pewter spout on top. The finger loop is made of heavy iron wire and has a stem that passed through the cork and was held in place by a small nut. A chain or light cordage attached the loop and cork to the canteen.

A single copper alloy hook is from a US Model 1855 double bag knapsack. It is probably from a knapsack carried by one of the well-supplied federal soldiers who brought it from Fort Gibson on the grueling march to Honey Springs. This hook was used to fasten the strap.

One copper alloy toe protector provides rare evidence of footwear. It is curved, semicircular in shape, with the outside edge turned up to form a lip. The tap would have fit onto the underside of the shoe's toe and been held in place with a row of small nails. Two rows of nail holes are visible on the tap; one broken nail remains in one of these holes. This artifact resembles two found in Civil War camps that are illustrated in Stanley Phillips's *Excavated Artifacts from Battlefields and Campsites of the Civil War* (S. Phillips 1974, 157). McBride and Sharp (1991, 160) describe similar examples from Civil War contexts.

Other items include one civilian stirrup, one fragment of a civilian spur, two spur/stirrup buckles, two iron bits, and two copper alloy harness buckles. The lightweight stirrup is of iron construction, and the spur is a copper alloy. The spur/stirrup buckles are D-shaped and made of a copper alloy. It is difficult to be sure that these civilian items equipped soldiers at the Battle of Honey Springs. Their location among residue of combat, shown in later chapters, adds to the probability of use in this conflict.

We found two heavy padlocks during our survey. The padlocks are both heart-shaped; their bodies are a similar three inches wide by three inches tall. They have an iron hasp and a body made of sheets of iron riveted together. Each had a copper alloy drop (swinging key-hole cover) and brass escutcheons around the keyhole itself. One of these locks is intact and the other is represented by four parts found in proximity. The intact lock has an elaborately shaped drop stamped with " . . . NT" (a poorly executed "Patent" stamp). The drop from the other lock is stamped with "Patent" below "W. R." topped with a crown. W. R. probably refers to King William (William Rex), who served as England's monarch between 1830 and 1837 (B. Johnson n.d.).

Moore found three similar padlocks in the Wooded Forty. Five nearly identical padlocks from a battlefield are unusual. I believe they are likely residue of the battle rather than items in prior or later use by civilians living or traveling along the road. While other explanations are possible, I think these may have been artillery ammunition chest locks lost during the confusion of battle. Roswell W. Lee's Confederate battery was under

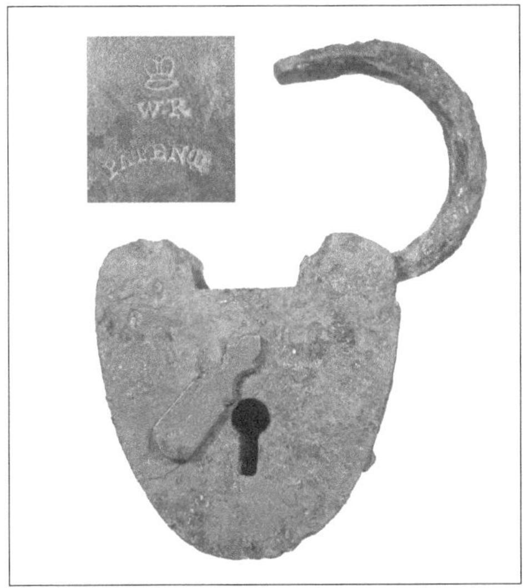

FIGURE 27. Complete padlock and detail of "WR" marked drop from another. Photo by William B. Lees.

pressure to retire from the field, possibly leading to loss of locks that gun crews would have removed in preparation for the fight.

The most personal of personal items found on the battlefield is a wedding band. This narrow band (.162 inches) fit a person with a size ten finger. This disfigured band was once probably gold-plated; all that remains is the copper or copper alloy base.

Three parts of pocket watches found at Honey Springs would likely have been in the hands of an officer. They were found in different locations and thus represent parts of three separate watches. These three parts include the back dust cap or cover and two parts of the movement. The dust cap is made of gold plate on a copper alloy base and is marked "John Beesley Liverpool." The dust cap style shows this as a key-wind, key-set watch probably made in the 1840s or 1850s (Scott Stuart, email message to author, December 31, 2001).

The top of a traveling inkwell is one of the more interesting items in the collection. This artifact is made of what appears to be a silver-plated copper alloy. It fit over a larger vessel that held ink, or an ink bottle, and

FIGURE 28. Detail of pocket watch dust cap marked "John Beesley LIVERPOOL." Photo by William B. Lees.

has a hinged lid. Hand-engraved on this lid is a five-pointed star and other decoration. Fremantle (1864, 6) noted the use of stars adorning the hats of Texas troops in 1863. Inkwells would have been common possessions of officers, and the star may suggest a Confederate association.

Speaking to the portability and popularity of pocket musical instruments, they are found anywhere that soldiers congregated including forts, camps, hospitals, and battlefields (S. Phillips 1974, 131). We found one iron mouth harp or jaw harp at Honey Springs and several remnants of harmonicas. The harp was heavily corroded, and the reed was missing. Two identical harmonica reed plates were found together and certainly represent a single instrument. One side of each copper alloy plate, almost four inches long and one inch wide, has remnants of what is probably nickel plating. Separate finds include another complete reed plate and four fragments of others.

The only coin that possibly relates to the battle is a Liberty Seated half-dime minted in 1854. In 1863 this coin would have been in circulation for almost ten years, which would account for its worn condition. US mints produced Liberty Seated half-dimes between 1837 and 1873 (Yeoman 1984, 100–101).

FIGURE 29. Top of inkwell with hand-engraved star motif. Photo by William B. Lees.

Four carved or modified lead items, presumably once bullets, may have been the handiwork of soldiers with time on their hands. One is a hollow cylinder that weighs 10.9 grams and is three-quarters of an inch long; the weight is consistent with a .50 caliber ball. Another item is a circular disc, pounded flat, with a small hole punched in its center. It is less than an inch in diameter and weighs 7.87 grams, about the weight of a .44 caliber ball. Another is a shaped rectangular block almost one inch long and weighing 35.89 grams. The weight is more than even a .69 caliber spherical ball; this may have been made from a .69 caliber Minié ball. The final item is a squared, solid cylinder that weighs 27.6 grams, about the weight of a .68 caliber ball. Each is eccentric and reflects soldiers' attempts to pass time. Their function, if any, is now lost to the ages.

Prior to our archaeological survey, these artifacts lay buried in fields to the north and south of Elk Creek. It is my conclusion after examining each that they had lain there since they fell to the ground during the Battle of Honey Springs. By adding the critical characteristic of location to the discussion, it is now possible to begin a consideration of the relationship of this residue of conflict with the landscape on which the battle transpired and to consider the questions posed in the first paragraph of this chapter.

The Fields of Conflict

Our survey stretched for a winding three miles from just south of Oktaha to just north of the rebel headquarters at Honey Springs near modern-day Rentiesville. Surveyed areas included state-owned land managed by the Oklahoma Historical Society and a variety of adjacent private landholdings, some of which the state has since purchased. We included private land because findings on state land showed us that adjoining areas were also involved or because historical narrative pointed to these as likely to have been engaged. In all cases where we found archaeological evidence of Civil War conflict, we bounded these by sufficient negative evidence (lack of finds) to tell us that we had identified the edges of each concentration of artifacts. Thus, while I acknowledge other concentrations of battle-related items may exist beyond the area we searched, I am confident they would be separate from, rather than a continuation of, anything we defined.

Well-bounded concentrations of artifacts defined during our survey are the first place we can see the fields of conflict of the Battle of Honey Springs. A battlefield is not always, or even usually, seen archaeologically as a continuous spread of artifacts across the landscape. As the historical narrative in chapter 1 suggests, the Battle of Honey Springs included several instances of intense fighting that were separated by less severe or even no action. Archaeologically, this might look like denser concentrations of artifacts separated by areas with fewer or even no artifacts. The battle includes the initial 10:00 a.m. engagement north of Elk Creek and fighting during the rebel retreat. Because Brigadier General Cooper seems to have attempted to direct the rebel fighting during this retreat, it would in today's parlance be called a retrograde action (a planned strategic withdrawal or retreat). Backing up a bit, the skirmish that happened in the early morning hours that day, July 17, five miles to the north near Chimney Mountain, is logically a part of the Battle of Honey Springs. We did not extend our investigations that far north.

The maps showing the distribution of all battle-related artifacts found during our surveys clearly show two well-bounded concentrations. The largest straddles Elk Creek, extends less than one mile north of the creek, and below turns southwest for another one-third mile. Although battle-related artifacts are found continuously through this area, the battle told

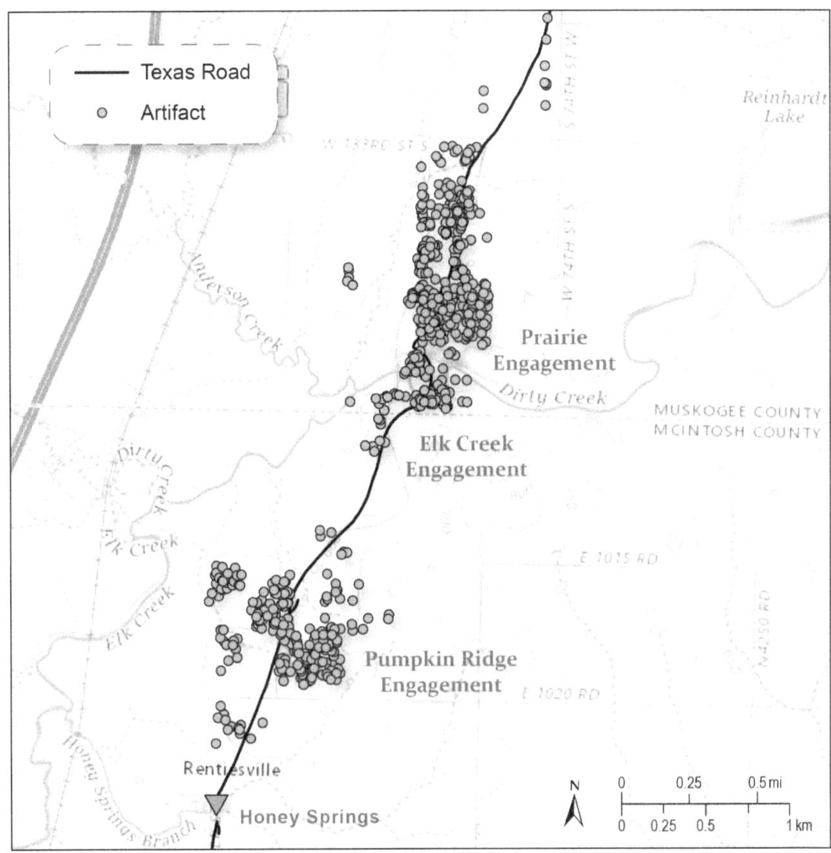

FIGURE 30. Distribution of all battle-related artifacts along route of Texas Road. Map by Katherine Sims.

from recorded memory shows logic in dividing what happened north of the Elk Creek valley from what happened to the south. Adopting this logic, I break the concentration straddling Elk Creek into what I will call the Prairie Engagement (north of Elk Creek) and the Elk Creek Engagement (along and south of Elk Creek), realizing that this is a somewhat arbitrary naming. I draw the line separating these areas at the pronounced bluff at the southern edge of the Prairie Engagement, placing all the valley in the Elk Creek Engagement. As this analysis unfolds, one question I will evaluate is whether archaeology will uphold my separating the Elk Creek Engagement from what happened on the prairie above.

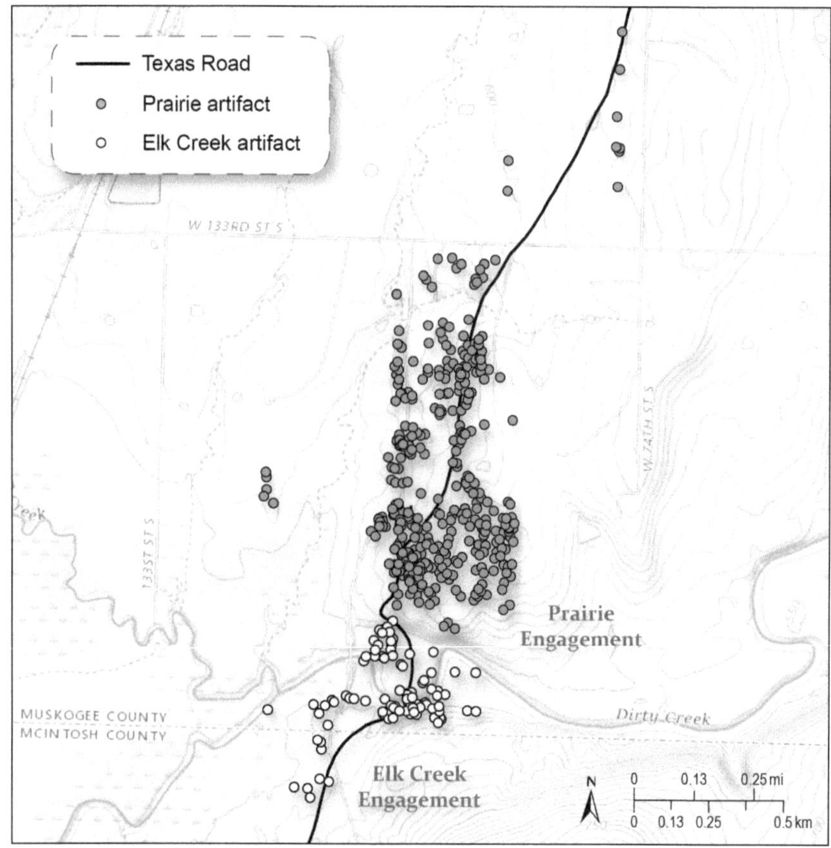

FIGURE 31. All battle-related artifacts in Prairie Engagement and Elk Creek Engagement. Map by Katherine Sims.

While this does seem to make sense given the memory of the battle from after-action reports and other accounts, the breadth of what I have here defined as the Prairie Engagement seems narrow and its length along the Texas Road extreme. From the edge of the prairie overlooking the Elk Creek valley, what I have termed the Prairie Engagement runs some 1,300 yards or about three-quarters of a mile to the north. Blunt says his troops went into bivouac one-half mile north of the rebel line and that his initial troop deployment as the battle opened was halfway between (a quarter-mile or about 440 yards north of the rebel lines). Accounts talk of the US troops closing on the rebel line before engaging, which makes sense given that some regiments carried smoothbores with a short effective range. Although I expect there was overshot, the US and rebel lines were probably no more than 100 yards distant when battalion and regimental fire began. Although artillery had a greater effective range and was in action earlier and at greater distance, small-arms overshot from foes separated by only 100 or even 200 yards may not account for the 1,300-yard spread of artifacts on the Prairie Engagement. Why the artifacts are spread so far along the Texas Road emerges as a question of some importance.

Placing the US or rebel line on the modern landscape thus becomes essential to address my concerns about the stretch of battle along the Texas Road. The implications of this for understanding the extent of artifacts along this road is significant. If fighting was in the middle, bullets to the north and south could more easily be ones that were overshot, but if the fight was backed up to the prairie's edge to the south, those far to the north become problematic. The question becomes whether what I have defined as the Prairie Engagement continues to make sense on closer examination of the physical evidence. There may be more to the story of fighting in this area than memory alone seems to present.

Although I do not see a meaningful break in the distribution north of Elk Creek to suggest a subdivision, that is not the same as saying this area is internally homogenous. The densest concentration of artifacts is in fact at the very southern edge of the prairie; logic would have this as the core of the 10:00 a.m. engagement. To the north, artifacts decrease in density before picking up roughly midway between the bluff edge and the stream that crosses the Texas Road to the north, likely where Blunt rested his troops before battle. Artifacts continue up to and beyond the stream. Is the dense concentration of artifacts at the south end of the prairie the core of the 10:00 a.m. fight? If so, are the artifacts in the northern end of the Prairie Engagement overshot ammunition from fighting to the south, or is a different explanation wanting?

The breadth of the Prairie Engagement is also intriguing since it seems at odds with accounts that say it stretched for one mile (Wiley Britton) or one and one-half miles (Major General Blunt). The reality on the ground is that the area engaged is only about one-third of a mile wide, although a small cluster of conflict artifacts was found to the west (Anderson Creek Area). Once again, identifying the breadth of the fighting along and in front of the rebel line requires its identification on the modern landscape. This will be addressed in chapter 4 when I look at patterns in the location of artifacts in each defined engagement. The question that will follow is this: how does a much shorter breadth of fighting correlate with memory of the troops engaged on both sides and with the reality of the landscape on which this conflict occurred?

A second sizeable, bounded concentration, which I will call the Pumpkin Ridge Engagement, is south-southwest from the first. Separated from the Prairie and Elk Creek Engagements by about one-third of a mile, a stretch where no battle-related artifacts were found, this concentration is the broadest. The breadth of this engagement is a maximum of about two-thirds of a mile, and its extreme reach along the Texas Road is well over three-quarters of a mile. But, like the other engagements, the distribution of battle finds in this area is uneven. Most of the artifacts are along a ridge roughly perpendicular to the Texas Road, but even these are broken by an area where few were found. North along this road, artifacts trail off in lesser numbers, and to the south there are two small clusters defining the furthest-south evidence of conflict found during our survey. Although internally quite varied, based on memory and landscape I think calling this a distinct engagement does make sense.

The general distribution of the artifacts in the Pumpkin Ridge Engagement does differ markedly from that observed in the other conflict areas at Honey Springs. While I believe these belong together, the separation of clusters of artifacts by areas where few or none are found is interesting and will require an explanation as to why this is so and why it differs from what is seen elsewhere. Differences in length of combat, numbers of troops involved, and type of fighting will need to be considered in searching for an interpretation. Insights from an imperfect historical memory of this part of the fight lead me to wonder if the observed overall pattern in the distribution of artifacts is related to combat by mounted adversaries.

These three engagements represent the main concentrations of conflict-related artifacts and are the basis for all subsequent analysis. Each straddles the Texas Road as reconstructed from visible remnants of this once essential route. Still, there are two other very small scatters of battle-related artifacts north of Elk Creek. Already mentioned is one located to the west of the Prairie Engagement but separated from it by

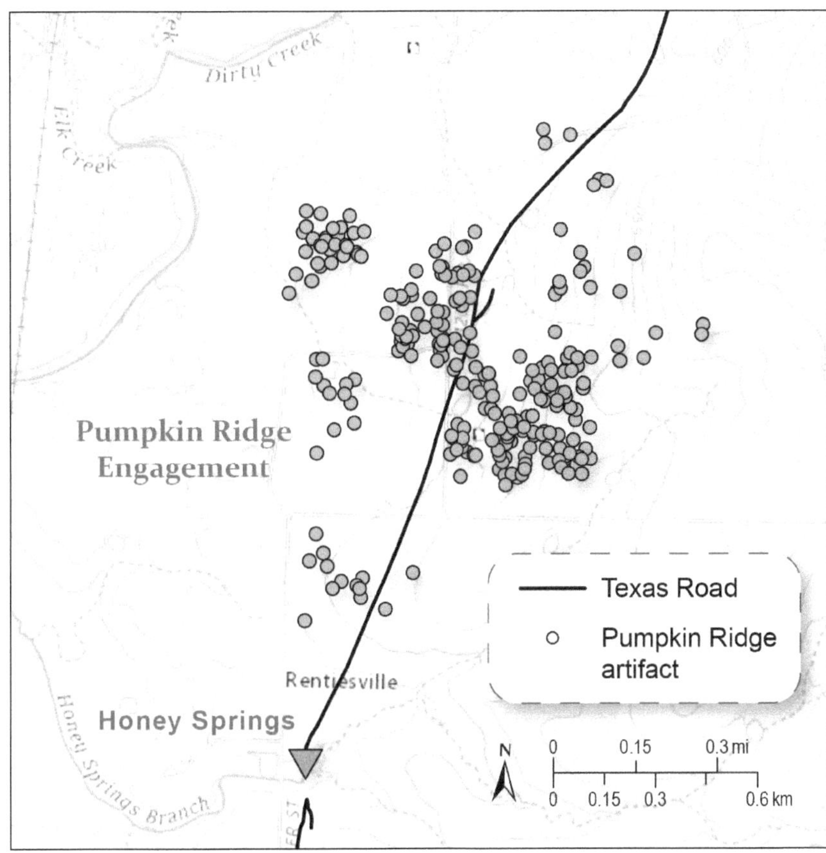

FIGURE 32. All battle-related artifacts in the Pumpkin Ridge Engagement. Map by Katherine Sims.

about one-quarter mile (Anderson Creek Area). It is across a small unnamed branch of Anderson Creek (which flows intermittently across the prairie and ultimately into Elk Creek). The other scatter may simply be the northern periphery of the Prairie Engagement, and I give it only passing discussion. This area lies just beyond the north end of property owned by the Oklahoma Historical Society in an area only surveyed at the reconnaissance level. With the caveat that the survey covered a small percentage of this area, the results show a significant drop-off in the evidence of conflict to the north. This was the basis for our decision to curtail surveys in this area. What we did find aligns roughly along the Texas Road, although the road is difficult to see here with the naked eye. Our survey maps show artifacts in two north-to-south alignments, which reflect the location of our reconnaissance survey transects. Neither of these small artifact scatters warrant, on their own, the label "engagement."

Defining the three engagements is the first significant finding of our archaeological project, although breaking the larger Battle of Honey Springs down in this manner is, at this point, provisional. Still, though analysis may argue for a more nuanced understanding of these bounded concentrations of artifacts, they do define in a very concrete way where fighting took place during the Battle of Honey Springs. Before this, scholars based their theories of where the actual fighting occurred on anecdotal reports of battlefield finds and different interpretations by historians, both lay and professional, of where the events described in recorded memory occurred. Looking back, we can say that the Oklahoma Historical Society got it right in terms of the land they initially acquired, which the National Park Service listed on the National Register of Historic Places in 1970 (upgraded to a National Historic Landmark in 2013). In making decisions, OHS scholars were guided by the most visible part of the battlefield landscape: the preserved swales of the Texas Road and the remains of Honey Springs itself. And while generally understanding that the engagement started with fighting centered on the Texas Road north of Elk Creek and continued with fighting around the bridge across Elk Creek, the existence of a significant concentration of battlefield artifacts, which I am calling the Pumpkin Ridge Engagement, was unknown until our study. The OHS developed the existing park road and interpretive park trails in the years following our field research. I was still at the OHS at that time, and we took full advantage of our new archaeological insights in designing these park improvements.

The terrain is a critical factor for understanding the Battle of Honey Springs. Understanding the landscape of the fields of conflict initially defined as the Prairie, Elk Creek, and Pumpkin Ridge Engagements and the Anderson Creek Area, and for the larger battlespace, is essential for understanding what the antagonists in this fight confronted and strategically used to their advantage. Between the location of the early morning skirmish of July 17 and the northern edge of the Prairie Engagement, late nineteenth-century land surveys suggest soldiers would have seen open prairie with tree cover along streams. I will not speculate on the precise location of the initial skirmish near Chimney Mountain, described by Lieutenant Colonel Campbell of the Sixth Kansas Cavalry as being on a "rise of ground" (Campbell 1888, 452).

More certain is the location of Prairie Mountain, where Cooper says his aide-de-camp Lieutenant T. B. Heiston remained to assess Blunt's strength. Three miles north of Elk Creek is a prominent ridge that rises a good 150 feet and would have provided rebels with an excellent view of the approaching federal force. From Prairie Mountain, the Texas Road probably followed the top or west side of a ridge that leads to the primary Texas Road crossing of Elk Creek (a toll bridge). Lyman A. Darling remembered the old Texas Road that ran "along the top of the ridge east of town (Oktaha)" (Darling 1976, 136). This route is unbroken by stream tributaries until within the Prairie Engagement, to which I now turn my attention.

Somewhere on this field is where the primary engagement began, along the road that was key in how both the US and rebel commanders organized their troop deployment. From the south, this road climbed onto the prairie from the entrenched Elk Creek valley, bordered on the north by steep, rock-strewn bluffs. As the road emerged on the prairie it sloped gradually upward before reaching a high point where it began a gradual downward slope to the north. This high point is almost five hundred yards from the current channel of Elk Creek. Standing today on the north bank of Elk Creek, this point is a full sixty-six feet higher (elevation 607 ft.); there are about one hundred or so yards of gradually downward-sloping ground behind this point (to the south) before the ground drops precipitously down the bluffs to the creek bottoms below. This point of high ground on the Texas Road, or slightly behind it to give cover, is a logical place for rebel troops to have formed their line, depending on how far the timber north of Elk Creek then extended. Guided in part by field observations from our surveys in the 1990s, I have always believed this is where, or is very close to where, Cooper's lines crossed the Texas Road on the morning of July 17. Using elevation tools of the US Geological Survey's National Map (USGS National Geospatial Program), it is possible to model the extent of a rebel line based on the identified high point on the Texas Road with corresponding high points to the east and west. The result, shown in figure 33, is a curving line that may match Major General Blunt's description of the rebel line being a

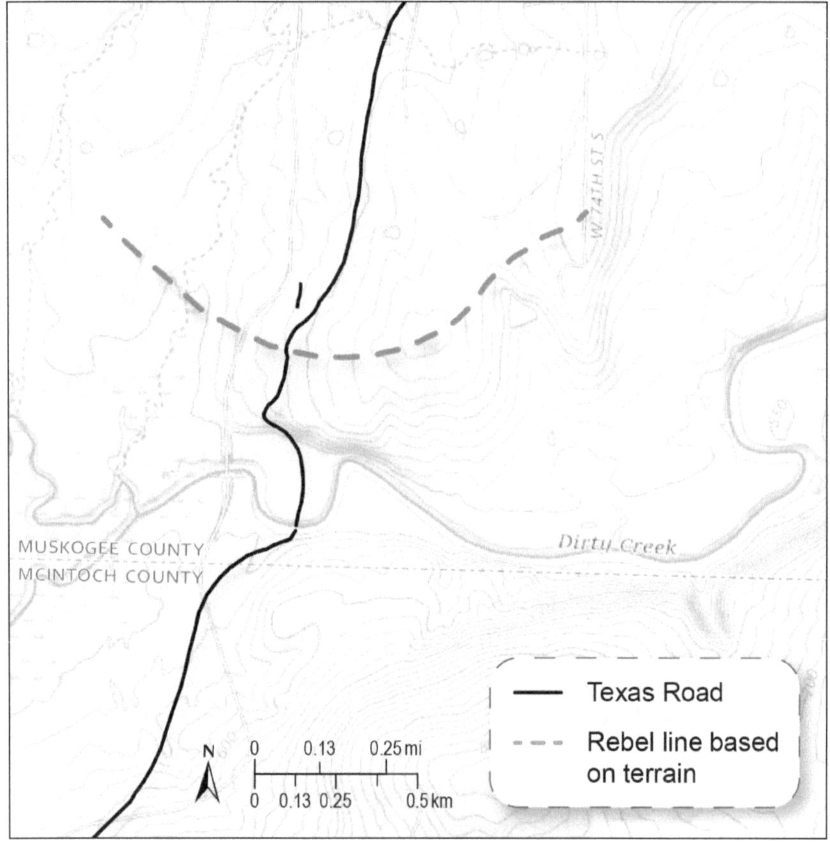

FIGURE 33. Possible location of rebel line (dashed line) based on terrain. Solid line is the Texas Road. Map by Katherine Sims.

"partial semi circle, the road running through the center" (Blunt 1863). The validity of this model of the placement of the rebel line on the landscape is a question that I will address with the archaeological findings, in part by comparing it with an alternate placement to the north, suggested by the 1896 General Land Office survey plat map.

Neither Cooper's orders before the battle nor any of the US or Confederate reports made after the battle are precise about the timber or its extent; Cooper talks of the importance of denying federals "the cover of the timber." Lieutenant Colonel Welch of the Twenty-Ninth Texas talks about small bushes, and an anonymous account mentions sassafras bushes (Welch 1863; *Standard* 1863a). Blunt refers to the Confederates being "concealed under cover of the brush." His subordinate officers talk about brush, timber, timber and brush, woods, a cornfield with a rail fence, and a hill, all viewed from positions, presumably, before the rebels forfeited their initial line and withdrew south of Elk Creek.

During subdivision of land by the General Land Office (GLO) in 1896, the northern edge of "timber" was mapped to extend a half-mile north of Elk Creek at the Texas Road, well beyond where I am tentatively placing the rebel line but still conceivably matching the after-action reports from 1863. The portrayal of cultural features and vegetation was secondary to the goals of the GLO contract surveyors. Surveyor notes thus provide no help in characterizing the specific nature of vegetation in this location. Symbolically, their maps do little more than to distinguish between prairie and areas with some woody growth. There may have been a transition of immature brushy growth, which might explain Union officers' differing descriptions. The elevation model supports what I think is the best estimation of the rebel line's location, but this would become illogical if mature timber or woods extended as much as one-quarter mile farther north, which the GLO maps may show for 1896. The line between prairie and timber showed in 1896 is, then, an alternate theory on the location of the rebel line.

If you go north from the bluffs along the ridge where the Texas Road runs, two terrain features could have provided some cover during the battle. The first is an indistinct saddle (a dip along a ridge crest) some 450 yards (one-quarter mile) north of the rebel line (but near the location of the rebel line alternate). It is more pronounced west of the Texas Road. At its greatest, this saddle might provide US soldiers as much as ten to twelve feet of cover from the rebel line, although the height of standing soldiers, artillery, and horses would diminish this greatly. However, if the tree line extended to this location in 1863 as it may have in 1896, and hence the location of the rebel line, this saddle may have provided additional cover from advancing US troops.

About one thousand yards north of the rebel line, an intermittent tributary stream, Anderson Creek, that ultimately flows into Elk Creek, crosses the battlefield. Swales of the Texas Road are today clearly visible where it crossed this stream. Along its course, this could have provided between twelve and twenty feet of cover from the location I propose for the rebel line. In his report of the battle, Blunt noted, "As my men came up wearied and exhausted, I directed them halted behind a little ridge, about one-half mile from the enemy's line, to rest and eat a lunch from their haversacks" (Blunt 1888g, 447–48).

This stream is slightly more than one-half mile from where I think the rebel line stretched. What Blunt refers to as a ridge is what I believe to be the southern slope rising out of the valley. Years ago, I noted that when you walk south along the route of the Texas Road toward the rebel line, the ascent out of this valley is very gradual, but it is a considerable distance, say about one-eighth of a mile or more, before you can look south and see the ground where I believe the rebels were posted.

Leaving his bivouac, Blunt says he formed his forces into two columns, marched them down on the left and right sides of the Texas Road, and deployed them into line of battle about one-quarter mile from the rebel line. This would place his deployment at the saddle previously mentioned. These landscape features running along the Texas Road north of Elk Creek—the point of high ground which I favor as the placement of the rebel line and two terrain features providing cover—may thus correlate with Blunt's descriptions of his steps taken in the initial deployment of federal troops at Honey Springs. For this to work, however, the edge of the timber in 1863 had to be farther south than shown on the GLO map.

If the edge of the timber, and therefore also the rebel line, was farther north than I propose, there is no credible alternate for a sheltered area along the Texas Road where Blunt's troops took bivouac before the battle. I therefore stand by my conclusion based on topography; once again, this is a question that archaeology is well suited to resolve. I will take this up in chapter 4 when I look at each of the individual engagements for clues to answer this and other questions.

I am therefore presuming the identified topographic high point along the Texas Road as it emerges onto the prairie north of Elk Creek is in fact the approximate point the rebel line crossed the Texas Road. The curved line shown in figure 33 extends a total of about one mile, which is less than Blunt's description of Cooper's line "extending 1 ½ miles, the main road running through their center" but matches Britton's later memory (Blunt 1888g, 447–48; Britton 1922, 275). To the east along this line the ground slopes upward to one of the highest points on the prairie, where it then drops off precipitously into a steep ravine cutting north into the uplands from the Elk Creek bottoms. But Cooper's line may have crossed the head of this ravine as it curved northward, where an even higher elevation is reached. There, however, the land drops off sharply, and it is unlikely, I think, that Cooper would have extended beyond this point. To the west of the Texas Road, the land becomes low-lying and intersects with intermittent tributaries of Elk Creek and areas that are today at least periodically wet or marshy. As shown on figure 33, however, the line may have curved to the north onto rising ground between tributary streams.

Beyond the approximately half-mile wide unbroken prairie through which the Texas Road courses, Cooper's troops may have been dispersed with the intention of preventing flanking actions by enemy cavalry. In fact, Cooper says his troops on the flanks were positioned at the upper and lower fords rather than being deployed into line of battle north of Elk Creek. Cooper's advice in his general orders before the battle is instructive here: "These smaller creeks will be used in case of attack by the enemy to penetrate to Elk Creek, and thus flank the different positions near the fords. These can be used by our troops to advantage in gaining a position in advance of the general line of the prairie to flank the column of the enemy" (Heiston 1888, 462).

In his report, Brigadier General Cooper mentioned escorting part of the Second Cherokee Regiment to the right before the battle and "reconnoitering the enemy from the high prairie, where [he] had a full view of [the enemy]" (D. Cooper 1888, 459). The far right of the prairie east of the Texas Road, before it drops into the ravine as mentioned earlier, is one candidate for this vantage as it reaches an elevation of around 645 feet. This vantage would have provided a probably unrestricted view for a considerable distance across the open prairie north along the Texas Road. About one-third of a mile across the ravine to the northeast is a higher vantage of over 660 feet, which is another candidate for Cooper's point of observation. This is on the far right of the line I show in figure 33.

The archaeological footprint of the Prairie Engagement shows evidence of fighting across the southern end of the prairie between the intermittent stream and marshes to the west and the ravine to the east. The footprint of fighting between these points covers only about one-third of a mile. Of note, although the Texas Road at this point is on high ground, this ground increases in elevation to the east, culminating in the highest elevation just before the ravine. It is possible this point of high ground is what Captain Edward Smith was referring to when he said his Second Kansas Battery fired on the "rebel position on the hill" (E. Smith 1888, 454).

Could Cooper and Blunt have deployed most of their troops into line of battle within this prairie? In terms of numbers, Cooper's forces engaged at Honey Springs are poorly recorded. Although reports place this number at around 6,000, this is difficult to support. Cooper posted his left and right on Elk Creek guarding the upper and lower fords. His center was on the Texas Road and was anchored with Roswell Lee's four-gun battery. Arrayed to either side were the Twentieth and Twenty-Ninth Texas and the Fifth Texas Partisan Rangers. We do not know the total strength represented by these units. Blunt says the Twentieth Texas was 300 strong in the battle, although a report printed shortly after the battle says they were "only 262 men" (*Standard* 1863a, 1). This same source says one-quarter of DeMorse's Twenty-Ninth Texas "were in the rear as horse holders" and that two or three companies were "detached as skirmishers and posted in a Branch at a right angle to the line of battle" and did not see action (*Standard* 1863a, 1). Even at half strength, these factors would have meant that DeMorse only had about 375 men available to fight, including the skirmishers that may not have been engaged. Presuming a similar relative strength for the Texas Partisan Rangers, the rebels would have had to deploy in a single rank with no reserves to cover the half-mile prairie north of Elk Creek. If Indian allies were deployed into line on either side of the Texans, the rebel line would, of course, have been extended. This question of rebel deployment will be revisited in later chapters.

Blunt's US forces would have matched Cooper's center well. With the Texas Road as center, the right wing (Judson's Brigade) was the First Kansas Colored Infantry (mustering 500 total), the Second Indian Home Guard (368 total), and the Third Wisconsin Cavalry (five companies). On the left (Phillip's Brigade) was the Second Colorado Infantry (six companies, 274 total), First Indian Home Guard (745 total), and the Sixth Kansas Cavalry (four companies, 238 total). As mounted troops, as many as one-quarter of the Indian Home Guard would have been to the rear, holding horses. Blunt would have been able to deploy easily in front of Cooper's center in double ranks. Rebel lieutenant colonel Welch remembered that the federals advanced in four ranks, suggesting a lack of sufficient space to deploy in the optimal two (Welch 1863). An anonymous account suggests the federals may have advanced in eight ranks (*Standard* 1863a). From position a quarter mile north of the rebel center, Blunt could have easily extended his cavalry (probably less than 500 men total, with some to the rear holding horses) in skirmish order to counter Cooper's shifting some troops up from the fords on Elk Creek to reinforce the main rebel line.

The Anderson Creek Area is minimal in size and in the number of artifacts. It is on a point between two intermittent tributaries of Anderson Creek, itself a branch of Elk Creek. It sits at about 563 feet and overlooks the marshy bottoms of Anderson Creek, which are fifteen to twenty feet lower in elevation. While isolated from the Prairie Engagement, this area is located about one-half mile west of the Texas Road, roughly along the position earlier suggested as the rebel line. The setting of this concentration would have been a good location for troops guarding or pressing the rebel left—for example, the flanking action of the Wisconsin Cavalry.

Leaving the prairie above Elk Creek, the Texas Road snaked south and west and found its way down the bluffs to the creek terrace or bottoms. There it crossed Elk Creek near the remains of a bridge built after the war, which may be in the approximate location of the private toll bridge used during the battle (most say the Civil War–era bridge was slightly downstream). The terrace along the creek was where those troops assigned to the center probably camped before the battle: Twentieth and Twenty-Ninth Texas and Fifth Texas Partisan Rangers. Lee's Light Battery was reportedly in position on the Texas Road the night before the battle. The importance of Cooper's admonition to prevent the federals from gaining the cover of the timber on the north side of the creek is evident when you look at the topography here; the timber was on the bluffs over Elk Creek. If the federals gained possession of these bluffs, they would have had a commanding position over rebels in the valley below. Further, the steep slopes of a towering hill (Pumpkin Ridge) to the south would have effectively constrained the movements of fleeing rebels or those attempting to defend the bridge and fords of Elk Creek.

South of the main crossing of Elk Creek, the Texas Road veered to the southwest as topography necessitated; as noted earlier, the Elk Creek Engagement artifacts do likewise. Here the route of the Texas Road is affected by the presence of "Pumpkin Ridge," whose 820-foot peak is about one-half mile southeast of the middle crossing (toll bridge) of Elk Creek and trends east to west and, with a much-diminished height, crosses the Texas Road between Elk Creek and Honey Springs. From the south bank of Elk Creek, the steep, boulder-strewn slopes of this ridge ascend more than 250 feet from the creek terraces before leveling off on the climb to its highest point. This pronounced ridge is part of a region along Elk Creek of higher ground with steep bluffs along its edge, known as the Rattlesnake Mountains.

The slopes of this ridge were likely wooded then as they are now; this is how they are depicted on the 1897 GLO survey. Regardless, the Texas Road skirted this hill toward the southwest as the Elk Creek bottomlands and terraces widened. After traveling through a gradually rising, rolling plain for about three-quarters of a mile, the road turned south-southwest to Honey Springs. Before it reached Honey Springs, the road crossed the western toe of Pumpkin Ridge. It is on this toe and surrounding slopes that the Pumpkin Ridge Engagement is situated.

The Pumpkin Ridge Engagement represents a large concentration of artifacts in probably only a slightly smaller area than the Prairie and Elk Creek Engagements combined. It appears a bit amorphous and spreads wider on either side of the Texas Road than do the Prairie and Elk Creek Engagements. An elevation profile (cross-section) along the Texas Road's approximate alignment through this area shows the elevation attains a height of about 612 feet, compared to about 540 at Elk Creek and 584 at Honey Springs. The edges of the Pumpkin Ridge Engagement range from a low of 565 feet in the northwest corner—bordering the Elk Creek bottoms—to 687 feet on the ascent to Pumpkin Ridge overlooking the main ford. While this may not appear like much of a rise, one thing is certain: when you are standing on the south edge of the Pumpkin Ridge Engagement you are looking down on Honey Springs and, in 1863, the rebel headquarters. In fact, this is the only high ground on the Texas Road between Elk Creek and Honey Springs.

Major J. Nelson Smith of the Second Regiment Colorado Volunteers described action that may refer to this ground, in support of Captain Henry Hopkins's battery south of Elk Creek. Smith remembered, "After rallying my companies, we crossed the stream, and discovered the enemy on a hill, or rise of ground in the advance" (J. N. Smith 1888, 455). Hopkins noted of this same action that his battery, "opened upon the enemy's cavalry, upon a hill beyond, causing them to fall back quite precipitately, the shell bursting in their immediate vicinity. Again, moving forward one-quarter of a mile, a line of the enemy's cavalry was discovered and driven back after the firing of a few rounds of shell" (Hopkins 1888, 456–57). The rebel cavalrymen initially engaged here were probably Gillette's Texans who Cooper implies were the first to attempt to slow the federal pursuit south of Elk Creek. Brigadier General Cooper reported that Colonel Walker's Choctaws and Chickasaws, who had just returned from a misguided scouting expedition to Prairie Springs, then "charged the enemy, who had now planted a battery upon the timbered ridge about 1,000 yards north of Honey Springs" (D. Cooper 1888, 457–461). One thousand yards from Honey Springs is the middle of the concentration of artifacts of the Pumpkin Ridge Engagement. Cooper's is the only account that mentions timber being on this ridge.

There can be little question that the landscape in the Honey Springs battlespace helped define the outcome of the day's action. Approached from the north, the land along the Texas Road was a gently rolling prairie. At Elk Creek, this prairie was about one-half mile wide and well suited for establishing a defensive line with a clear field of fire to the north. To the west, the land was (and still is) substantially lower and intersected by small tributaries, which are today marshy and in 1863 probably lined with various trees. To the east, a significant ravine with relatively steep slopes projects into the uplands that trend north, as does the creek. The lower ford is probably below this ravine, and there was ample ground along the creek for camps of Cooper's right wing. This challenging topography on Cooper's wings may explain why he initially placed his right and left flanks guarding the upper and lower fords of Elk Creek rather than deploying them into line to the north.

From the prairie above, which backed on the steep bluffs of Elk Creek, the Texas Road meandered down to the main ford and toll bridge on Elk Creek, which was at this point constricted by the rocky bluffs to the north and the steep, rock-strewn slope of Pumpkin Ridge to the south. The Texas road skirted this hill toward the southwest before turning roughly south to Honey Springs. As the route progressed southwest, the land along Elk Creek flattened and broadened. As the road turned south to

Honey Springs, it ascended gently rolling ground across an upland toe, and then descended toward Honey Springs. Although pursuit continued for over a mile from this high ground, it is here where I believe the last major fighting of July 17 ended. Overall, it is not surprising that Brigadier General Cooper reported, "The nature of the ground precluded the possibility of personally observing all the movements of our troops and the conduct of the men and officers" (D. Cooper 1888, 461).

CHAPTER THREE

From History to Artifacts

IN WRITING A REPORT, account, or reminiscence of the Civil War, the witness-narrator sometimes mentions observed material culture, the "tools, weapons, utensils, machines, ornaments, art, buildings, monuments, written records, religious images, clothing, and any other ponderable objects produced or used by humans" (Encyclopaedia Britannica 2018). These mentions can be a vital link between the memory of conflict and its physical, archaeological footprint by connecting with the people who were there. How were the different regiments and partisan units present at the Battle of Honey Springs uniformed, armed, and equipped? For example, was the Sixth Kansas Cavalry the only unit that carried the Sharps carbine? If so, distinctive bullets used in this weapon mark the location of this unit on the battlefield; dropped specimens show where a particular trooper stood during the fight, and fired examples show the location of this unit's enemy targets.

Eyewitness records of battles, whether they be officer after-action reports or a soldier's journal, memoir, or letter, sometimes mention specific equipment and weapons. More often, inference on material culture comes from documents or recorded memory dating before or even after the battle. These include the same officer and personal accounts, but also vital are quartermaster and regimental records. Both are essential references for the Battle of Honey Springs. All must be used with caution, of course, because descriptions often oversimplify a more complex condition or may not reflect last-minute changes in arms or uniform. It is also an unfortunate truth that it is not easy to piece together how soldiers were dressed and equipped on any particular day. Rarely, it seems, was this of sufficient interest to warrant recording in reports, letters, or memoirs. Further, as I mentioned in chapter 1, written accounts are not as common in the Indian Territory as in the states. Similarly, the preservation of military records is uneven between the US and Confederacy and rare for the Confederate-allied Indian regiments.

This chapter reviews inferences from the historical record on how the different armies, and regiments and battalions within armies, may have been equipped.[1] While I will look at this broadly, remember from the preceding chapter that the archaeological finds related to the Battle of Honey Springs are overwhelmingly associated with artillery and small-arms ammunition—primarily bullets and exploded artillery shells. Over 93 percent of artifacts thought to be from the battle are so associated. These are the most important because they were expended, lost, or discarded due to the fighting. Other artifacts, such as buttons from uniforms or metal parts from equipment, are also essential but were never intended to be expendable and thus occur at much lower frequencies in the archaeological assemblage. The reason I take the deepest dive into accounts from reports and memory of the arms and ammunition is, therefore, because of their pivotal importance for the archaeological study of the battle. Still, in looking beyond the arms and ammunition to how the participants were clothed, uniformed, and equipped, I not only address the relatively few artifacts so associated but also present a tapestry useful for imagining the culturally diverse participants and the realities facing the opposing armies in 1863 in the Indian Territory and surrounding states.

The units that fought at Honey Springs present a human and organizational diversity uncommon in the American Civil War. "*Indians and Negroes,* with a slight sprinkling of white troops, comprise this command" is how Blunt's army was described in a July 12, 1863, letter from Fort Gibson (*Daily Conservative* 1863a, emphasis in source). Fighting for the United States were White, Indian, and Black regiments. The Indian and Black units formed in reaction to the flood of Indian refugees and free and self-emancipated Blacks to Kansas following the outbreak of hostilities. These troops provided much-needed numbers in a military department lacking in troops. Still, the enrollment of African American and Indians as regiments of regular soldiers in the US army was altogether new.

Confederate troops included White regiments and partisans from Texas. Given Texas's long Spanish heritage and Mexican governance before US statehood, these units certainly also included Hispanic or "Tejano" soldiers. Indian regiments from the Five Civilized Tribes joined

TABLE 5. Units present, strength, and arms at Battle of Honey Springs

US units at Honey Springs: Maj. Gen. James G. Blunt		
Service	**Unit**	**Strength and arms**
Artillery	Hopkins's (Third) Kansas Battery (independent) (Capt. Henry Hopkins)[1]	Three six-pound guns, Model 1840/1841 One twelve-pound field howitzer Army and navy caliber revolvers
	Smith's (Blair's) Second Kansas Battery (independent) (Capt. Edward A. Smith)[2]	Two six-pound guns Two twelve-pound guns, Model 1857 Navy caliber revolvers, cavalry sabers
	Battery attached to Sixth Kansas Cavalry[3]	Two twelve-pound mountain howitzers
	Battery attached to Third Wisconsin Cavalry	Two twelve-pound mountain howitzers
Infantry	First Kansas Colored Infantry (Lt. Col. John Bowles)	500 officers and men (full regiment) .69 Model 1842 muskets
	First Indian Home Guard (mounted) (Col. Stephen H. Wattles)	745 officers and men (full regiment) Common rifles (various calibers), US Model 1840 (.54), US Model 1842 rifled musket (.69), foreign rifled muskets (.69–.71)
	Second Indian Home Guard (mounted) (Lt. Col. Frederick W. Schaurte)	368 officers and men (full regiment) US Model 1841 rifle (.54), US Model 1841/1845 rifle (.58), foreign rifled muskets (.69–.71), US Model 1842 musket (.69); Sharps breech-loading rifle (.52); Enfield rifle (.58)
	Third Indian Home Guard (mounted) (Col. William A. Phillips)[4]	623 officers and men (full regiment) US Model 1840 rifles (.54), US Model 1840/1845 rifles (.58), US Model 1842 rifled muskets (.69); foreign rifled muskets (.69–.71)
	Second Colorado Volunteer Infantry (Maj. J. Nelson Smith)	276 officers and men. Six companies (A, B, E, G, H, I) .58 Springfield rifle-muskets (A, G, H) .54 Austrian rifle-muskets (E, I), .69 Model 1842 rifled muskets (B)

1 This battery originated with the Second Kansas Cavalry, who were issued Merrill carbines and the Lefaucheux Revolvers.

2 The left section (six-pound guns, commanded by Second Lieutenant Aristarchus Wilson) of Smith's battery counted forty-three officers and enlisted men at Fort Blunt on July 12, the last day they were attached to the Second Colorado Infantry.

3 This battery of mountain howitzers was retained by Judson's Brigade when the Sixth Kansas Cavalry was moved to Phillips's Brigade on the US left just before the battle began.

4 There is little evidence that the Third Indian Home Guard was deployed in the fighting that began at 10:00 a.m. on July 17.

(*continued*)

TABLE 5. (*continued*)

Service	Unit	Strength
Cavalry	Sixth Kansas Cavalry (Lt. Col. William T. Campbell)	211 officers and men in four companies (A, C, F, H) Sharps, Merrill, and Hall carbines, Colt revolvers (.36 and .44), Remington and Lefaucheux revolvers (.44), cavalry sabers and light sabers
	Third Wisconsin Cavalry (Capt. Edward R. Stevens)	Five companies (B, G, H, I, and M) Merrill carbines (.54), Lefaucheux and Colt revolvers (.44), cavalry sabers
Confederate (CSA) and Confederate-allied units (CSA-A) at Honey Springs: Brig. Gen. Douglas H. Cooper		
Artillery	Lee's Light Battery (CSA) (Capt. Roswell W. Lee)	Three twelve-pound mountain howitzers One 2 ¼-inch mountain rifle
Infantry (mounted)	First Cherokee Regiment (CSA-A) (Maj. Joseph F. Thompson)	Variously armed, probably with common rifles, Texas rifles, and various foreign rifled muskets and muskets
	Second Cherokee Regiment (CSA-A) (Lt. Col. James M. Bell)	
	First Choctaw and Chickasaw Regiment (CSA-A) (Col. Tandy Walker)	
	First Regiment Creek Mounted Volunteers (CSA-A) (Colonel Daniel N. McIntosh)	
	Second Regiment Creek Mounted Volunteers (CSA-A) (Lt. Col. Chilly McIntosh)	
Cavalry	Twentieth Texas Cavalry (dismounted) (CSA) (Col. Thomas C. Bass)	262 men Enfield rifle-muskets (.58?)
	Twenty-Ninth Texas Cavalry (CSA) (Col. Charles DeMorse)	One-quarter of enlisted holding horses Shotguns
	Fifth Texas Partisan Rangers (CSA) (Col. Leonidas M. Martin)	Probably shotguns
	Scanland's squadron (CSA) (Capt. John C. Scanland)	
	Gillette's squadron (CSA) (Capt. Levi Elliott Gillette)[5]	

[5] Also called Gillette's Company

these Confederate troops as allies. Warde's description of these Indian troops as Confederate allies draws a significant distinction between them and others more unambiguously under Confederate government control (Warde 2013). Because of this, I refer to the army commanded by Brigadier General Cooper at Honey Springs as "rebel" rather than "Confederate" (a term also commonly used in US reports of the Indian Territory). When speaking of the individual rebel units, I refer to them as either Confederate or "Confederate-allied," following Warde's terminology.

US Cavalry, Mounted Troops, and Infantry

Determining the small arms carried by the troops engaged at Honey Springs in July 1863 is a significant challenge. The Union infantry and cavalry engaged were the First Kansas Colored Infantry, regiments of Indian Home Guard (mounted), a battalion of the Second Colorado Volunteer Infantry, and battalions of the Sixth Kansas and Third Wisconsin Cavalry. Although supplying US troops in the Trans-Mississippi West was a significant challenge at the outset of the conflict, by 1863 this situation improved, and troops were receiving uniforms and equipment on a regular basis, although not necessarily on par with troops to the east. That said, western troops also are known to have adopted slight variations in uniform often related to their "western individualism," but these variations, like wide-brimmed hats, may as likely have reflected practicality in the open, harsh environments in which they operated.

The recruitment of the First Kansas Colored Infantry began in Leavenworth, Kansas, in August 1862 and resulted in the mustering of a battalion of six companies into federal service on January 13, 1863. Earlier, while operating as state militia, the First Kansas participated in the October 29, 1862, Battle of Island Mound, Missouri. There it became the first African American unit to engage in combat in the Civil War (Spurgeon 2014, 97). On November 10, 1862, the *Daily National Republican*, published in Washington, DC, proclaimed, "Thus the first black blood has been spilled in fighting with the enemies of the Union." Descriptive rolls of the First Kansas show that many of the enlisted men were born in neighboring Missouri, but also included were substantial numbers from Kentucky and states throughout the South and its other borders.

Between January and May 2, 1863, recruitment of the remaining four companies was completed. The regiment moved afterward to Baxter Springs, Kansas. On June 27, the unit joined a supply train bound for Fort Gibson and participated in the Battle of Cabin Creek on July 1 and 2. Following the US defeat of the rebel forces at Cabin Creek, the First Kansas and the rest of the train proceeded to Fort Gibson, arriving there on July 5. The First Kansas was heavily engaged at the Battle of Honey Springs.

As to uniforms and general appearance, Spurgeon (2014, 75) says their initial issue derived from surplus available at Fort Leavenworth and included a mixture of obsolete (gray) and new blue uniforms and forage caps. It is likely their arms were also issued from surplus. Captain Ethan Earle of Company F noted, "Prior to the battle at Island Mound, our rifles had been exchanged for tolerable good muskets, though of an old pattern and very heavy" (Earle 1873, 98). These may have been unconverted Austrian Consol-Augustin tube lock muskets.

In May 1861, Major General John C. Frémont was appointed commander of the Department of the West, headquartered in St. Louis. One of his first duties was the procurement of arms for his department, as none were available. In his short tenure in the West, which lasted less than a year, he made several purchases, but significant were twenty-five thousand Austrian Consol-Augustin pattern 1841 muskets. These were .70 caliber tube lock smoothbore muskets; the tube lock required a specialized primer. Frémont had fifteen thousand of these rifled and converted to standard percussion locks but apparently issued the other ten thousand as smoothbore tube locks (W. B. Edwards 1962, 133–34). Spurgeon (2014, 76–77) speculates that, because of bias against Black troops, the First Kansas was recipient of some of these substandard weapons.

The unit received new uniforms and equipment well before the Battle of Honey Springs. Based on records for Company F, in the first three months of 1863 at Fort Scott the regiment commonly was issued replacement jackets, pants, shirts, drawers, socks, shoes, caps, blankets, overcoats, knapsacks, haversacks, canteens, and tents (Earle 1863b). Clothing issued to Company F on July 10 at Fort Gibson were one cap, thirty jackets, twenty pairs of pants, sixty-one shirts, twenty-four pairs of drawers, forty-four pairs of shoes, no socks, two blankets, and six shelter tents (Earle 1863c). Although the descriptions are vague, they certainly refer to standard issue uniform items for the time and probably the familiar dark-blue wool sack coats, white shirts, sky-blue pants, ankle-high brogans, and dark-blue forage caps.

Britton says the First Kansas used one of the most recently improved patterns of Springfield muskets during the Battle of Honey Springs (1882, 279, 334). In the "Summary Statements of Quarterly Returns of Ordnance and Ordnance Stores on Hand in Regular and Volunteer Army Organization" (hereafter "summary statements") for the second quarter of 1863, the First is shown to be consistently armed with the smoothbore US Model 1842 musket. They had on hand spherical ball and buck-and-ball ammunition in roughly equal numbers for these weapons (National Archives 1983c, 65). Regimental history of the First Kansas mentions their firing buck and ball into rebel lines during the battle of Honey Springs (Adjutant General of the State of Kansas 1896, 246–50).

Confirmation of the rearming of the First Kansas just before the Battle of Honey Springs comes from the account book of Captain Earle of Company F. Receipt at Fort Scott of sixty "US Muskets" and accoutrements is listed for March 10, 1863, as is the return of "all the brass mounted guns and bayonets" (Earl 1863a) The brass-mounted guns are certainly the Austrian Consol-Augustin muskets they had apparently used with great effect until that time. An entry for May 4, 1863, provides additional confirmation of rearming through inventory of Springfield percussion muskets, .69 caliber cartridge boxes, and .69 caliber round ball and buck-and-ball cartridges (Earle 1863d, 68). The summary statement of ordnance on hand for the second quarter of 1863 confirms that the entire regiment was armed with these weapons and ammunition (National Archives 1983c, 65). While rearmed with better weapons, these were certainly not the most recently improved pattern of musket alluded to by Britton. In 1863, these smoothbore muskets were considered by the United States to be Third-Class weapons.

Wiley Britton recorded an account from a private in the federal Indian command who had seen the First Kansas in the spring of 1863 at Baxter Springs and said,

> that they wore military caps, dark blue coats and light blue trousers, and every man had his shoes polished black, and as he thought, made a fine appearance; that the barrels of their muskets and bayonets were polished as bright as silver; that they were well drilled;

> that he saw them drilling, and that when the order was given, "order arms," the butts of their muskets struck the ground with a thud, all at the same instant, and that on the drill ground they went through beautiful movements with their arms on their shoulders and with glistening bayonets in the sunlight. (Britton 1922, 243)

These soldiers were equipped with the standard US infantry uniforms and .69 caliber smoothbore muskets that they would carry to Honey Springs.

The three regiments of Indian Home Guard had been organized from Indian refugees in Kansas and other Indians disenchanted with the Confederate cause and treatment. Some African Americans found their way into these regiments as well, including self-emancipated refugees from the Indian Territory (Warde 2013, 132). The formation of these regiments had begun in the spring of 1862 at LeRoy on the Neosho River in southeastern Kansas (also site of a federal camp) (W. A. Phillips 1888b, 58). Several mass desertions diminished the large Osage membership in the Second Regiment. Phillips replaced them with Cherokees formerly aligned with the Confederacy who also filled the new Third Regiment's ranks.

The US military has a long relationship with Native Americans as allies and scouts. Recruiting them into regular Indian regiments was new, and this had challenges due to the recruit's time-honed traditions of warfare and concepts of being a warrior. The results, according to Rein (2013, 4) was that "[Indian troops] modified almost every aspect of federal military life, including uniforms, drill, the personal use of government-issued weapons, and desertion, in ways that would have resulted in severe punishment for other troops." Desertion was more akin to liberal use of unauthorized furlough to tend to personal and family responsibilities (Confer 2007, 97). Similarly, Confederate brigadier general Cooper, facing severe shortages of supplies, took advantage of a system of liberal furloughs to let his Confederate-allied Indian troops subsist at home rather than at Fort Smith, formalizing a process that was probably already commonplace (Confer 2007, 100–101; Steele 1888a, 30).

Before departing their camp in Kansas for the 1862 Indian Expedition, the First and Second Indian Home Guard (the Third was not yet formed) wore new uniforms. Witnesses noted that this included "small military caps," probably the regulation fatigue or forage cap commonly worn by federal units (Abel 1919, 122–23). A June 25, 1862, letter quoted in Abel (1919, 123) describes the Indian regiments as they headed south into Indian Territory: "The first and second Indian Regements left for the Indian Territory in good stile and in fine spirits the Indians with their new uniforms and small Military caps on their Huge Heads of Hair made rather a Comecal Ludecrous appearance they marched off in Columns of 4 a breast singing the war song all joining in the choruse and a more animated seen is not often witnessed."

In an apparent attempt to pay homage to the Native traditions, Colonel William Weer, commanding the Indian brigade, arranged for "a grand 'ball play' in the day time, & a 'war dance' at night" on the day before departure of the expedition (Weer 1862).

The Third Regiment was the last to be formed. Clothing receipts for Company E for December 1862 show that individuals were drawing regulation items including hats (trimmed), fatigue blouses, trousers, drawers, flannel shirts, greatcoats, cavalry boots (the Indian Home Guard was mounted), blankets, and gum blankets. These hats were not the caps described above but were some form of wide-brim, high-crown hat. This may have been the US Model 1858 wide-brimmed dress hat (the "Hardee" or "Hancock") but may also have been a more practical hat with a lower crown such as the "Burnside," common in Civil War–era photos of Kansas soldiers (Howell 1982, 9–11). Whatever the hat form, Third Regiment soldiers drew trimmings including feathers, badges (designating branch of service), eagles (an eagle ornament used to pin up the brim on one side), and cords with tassels such as specified for the M1858 hat (Military History Collections 1862a).

Britton recalls that shortly after US troops under Phillips occupied Fort Gibson in the spring of 1863, the Indian command received new clothing, arms, and ammunition. He observed, however,

> There was a marked difference in the appearance between the Indian and white soldiers when dressed in the new uniform. What was known at that time as the "Hancock Hat" was issued to the Indian soldiers, while the white soldiers generally wore the regulation cap. The Indian mounts were nearly all ponies. Care was not taken to see to it that the clothing issued to the Indian soldiers fitted them properly. The pants legs were frequently too short or too long, and

> the coat rarely ever fitted as a white soldier would have insisted that it should, giving the Indian soldiers a comical appearance, mounted on their ponies with badly fitting clothing, and wearing "Hancock Hats," with their long black hair falling over their shoulders, and legs astride their mounts coming down near the ground. (Britton 1922, 226)

Britton's reminiscence suggests that the First, Second, and Third Regiments were at least nominally wearing regulation US uniforms in the months before the Battle of Honey Springs. While Britton notes their "Hancock Hat" (Model 1858) as being unusual, other units such as the famed "Iron Brigade" or "Black Hats" wore this headwear with distinction throughout the war, as did many officers, including US General Winfield Scott Hancock. Following Rein's observation stated above, what is certain is that the members of the Indian regiments would have taken their issue uniforms and made it their own following the cultural norms and traditions of warriors. Rein (2013, 8) suggests that the issue of the Hardee hat to the Indian regiments was, in fact, due to a cultural preference for wide-brimmed hats by the Indian troops. Clothing was, of course, not the only way Indian warriors expressed culture and traditions. War dances, war songs, tactics, and preferred means of fighting are commonly noted in accounts of Union- and Confederate-allied Indian troops operating in the Indian Territory and vicinity during the Civil War.

An unidentified image of a Native American soldier is reproduced by Rein (2013) to illustrate the possible appearance of a member of the First Indian Home Guard (see figure 34). He wears what are likely a dark-blue cavalry shell jacket and sky-blue pants and a Burnside-pattern hat adorned with a feather. He holds a Model 1858 Remington revolver, a cavalry saber, and a belt with a rectangular sword belt plate (Wilson's Creek National Battlefield n.d. b). A photograph in the collections of the Oklahoma Historical Society shows Ezekiel Proctor, a Cherokee who served in the Third Indian Home Guard. He is wearing a loose-fitting unbuttoned coat over what at first appears to be a vest but that seems to have the collar of a mounted services jacket. He also wears a rectangular sword belt plate and a low wide-brimmed Burnside-pattern hat festooned with a feather. An image identified as Seminole John Chupco in 1865 (see figure 35) may portray standard issue sky-blue trousers, white flannel shirt,

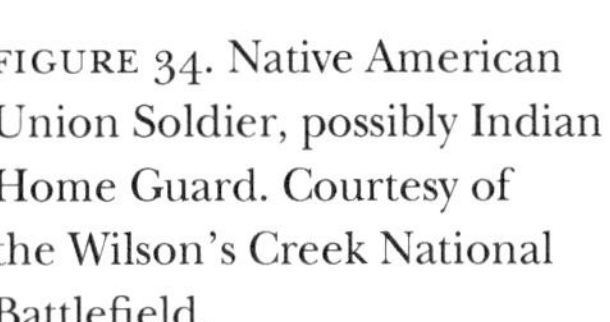

FIGURE 34. Native American Union Soldier, possibly Indian Home Guard. Courtesy of the Wilson's Creek National Battlefield.

FIGURE 35. Private John Chupco, Seminole, First Indian Home Guard, 1865. Courtesy of the Oklahoma Historical Society.

and an unbuttoned sack coat. Around his neck is what appears to be a multicolored neck cloth or tie, and he is wearing a dark, broad-brimmed Burnside-pattern hat with a feather and the crossed-saber device of cavalry. Unlike the first two images, which probably date prior to the Battle of Honey Springs, the photo of Chupco is substantially later. The hats shown in each of these figures are similar: each with a low crown and a rim that turns up.

In January 1863, Colonel Phillips reported of his Indian Home Guard regiments that the first was armed with hunting rifles of various calibers, the second with Prussian rifles and muskets, and the third with Mississippi and Prussian rifles (W. A. Phillips 1888b, 58). Abel (1919, 101) notes that the first four hundred rifles used to arm the Indian Home Guard (the First Regiment) were "Indian Rifles" from the federal arsenal at Fort Leavenworth. These are not inconsistent with the First Regiment's "hunting rifles" described by Phillips. The summary statements of ordnance for the second quarter of 1863 list no arms for most companies of the First Regiment but show that Company C had US Model 1841 rifles in .54 caliber and Belgian or French rifled muskets in .69 caliber, and that Company G had Model 1842 rifled muskets in .69 caliber and Austrian or Prussian rifled muskets in .69 caliber (National Archives 1983c, 40).[2] Since there was no place to list non-martial common rifles on the summary statements, it is possible this is what the other companies carried. Still, Johansson (2016, 21) says the First Indian carried the .54 caliber US Model 1817 "Common Rifle," and some had older weapons.

Although Phillips said the Second Indian Home Guard was armed with Prussian rifles and muskets, Coates and Thomas (1990, 92) list them as having the Model 1841 (Mississippi) rifle in .54 caliber. The summary statements for the second quarter of 1863 list no arms for most companies of the Second Regiment but show that Company C had US Model 1841 rifle in .54 caliber; US Model 1841/1845 rifle in .58 (Model 1841 rebored to .58 caliber); US Model 1842 .69 caliber smoothbore; Austrian and Prussian rifled muskets in .69/.70 caliber; Austrian, Prussian, or Saxony rifled muskets in .71/.72 caliber; .52 caliber Sharps breechloading rifles; and an Enfield rifle-musket in .58 caliber. For this one company, rifles and rifled muskets predominated, with a fair number of .69 caliber smoothbores and only thirteen Sharps rifles. I again speculate that companies with no arms listed may have been carrying common rifles (National Archives 1983c, 40).

The Third Regiment may not have been engaged in fighting in the study area. Still, Phillips has the Third Regiment with Model 1841 (Mississippi) and Prussian rifles, while Coates and Thomas (1990, 92) list them with Model 1840/1845 rifles in .58 caliber. Ordnance reports for Company E of the Third Regiment dated December 31, 1862, show issue of elongated ball ammunition (Minié ball) in .58 and .69 caliber; these are consistent with the Model 1840/1845 (rebored Model 1841) and the Prussian Rifle (Military History Collection 1862b). An April 1863 inventory of ordnance and ordnance stores for Company L of the Third Regiment combined with information from summary statements of ordnance on hand for the second quarter of 1863 shows the Third Regiment was armed with US Model 1841 rifles in .54 caliber; US Model 1841/1845 rifles in .58 caliber; US Model 1842 smoothbore and rifled muskets in .69 caliber; Austrian and Prussian rifles in .69/.70 caliber; Austrian, Prussian, or Saxony rifled muskets in .71/.72 caliber; and two worn Merrill carbines in .54 caliber (Military History Collection 1863; National Archives 1983c, 40).

These records suggest that companies of the Indian Home Guard, as was relatively common, may not all have been carrying the same weapons. This discussion calls into question Britton's statement that the Indian Home Guard received new arms on arrival in July 1863 at Fort Gibson. Also made clear is the general diversity of types and calibers of weapons in each of these regiments.

By any account, by 1863 the small arms described above in use by the US Indian and Black troops at Honey Springs would have been classified as Second- or Third-Class arms by the US Ordnance Department. Common rifles would have defied classification in this system, which probably accounts for their absence in ordnance returns. The exception to this is the so-called Mississippi rifle in .54 and .58 calibers (Models 1841 and 1841/1845) that was still designated as First Class. While some White regiments in federal service still used weapons such as the Austrian Lorenz and US Model 1842 smoothbores, these were the exception. The heavy use of these Second- and Third-Class weapons by Black and Indian troops, especially in the West, is not surprising given prevailing racial prejudices (Confer 2007, 99).

The Second Colorado Volunteer Infantry was organized by Colonel Jesse H. Leavenworth in February 1862, incorporating four existing independent companies, all of which had seen service against Confederates and Indians in New Mexico. General David Hunter commanding the

Department of Kansas furnished Leavenworth with "1,000 stand of arms, 200,000 ball cartridges, and a battery of field artillery complete," which arrived in Denver in May 1862 (Leavenworth 1888, 172). The battery was the Ninth Wisconsin Battery, which did not accompany Colorado troops when deployed eastward in Kansas. The arms issued by Hunter may be those described by regimental quartermaster James Burrell: "There was in that arsenal when placed in charge of the R. Q. M., every conceivable fire-arm and weapon that might equip or adorn a hunter or mountebank [a charlatan] in all the variety of styles of every state in the union, all the way back to the days of the old revolution" (Burrell 1877a, 2). These substandard weapons apparently stayed in Colorado.

In March 1862, Leavenworth noted that the Second Colorado had "marched for the States" from their headquarters at Fort Lyon, Colorado Territory, and informed Major General E. V. Sumner, "Should you require good mounted troops, I can assure you you will find the mountain men of the Second Regiment Colorado Volunteers as good material as any to make them from" (Leavenworth 1888, 173). Lieutenant Colonel Theodore H. Dodd moved his battalion of six companies (A, B, E, G, H, I) to Camp Leroy in eastern Kansas at the end of June 1862 (Schofield 1888d, 347). They accompanied a supply train from Fort Scott to Fort Gibson, arriving there on July 8, 1863 (Colorado State Archives 1863). Quarterly summary statements dated May 1, 1863, show Company A, G, and H with the .58 caliber Springfield rifle-musket, Company B with .69 caliber rifled muskets, and Company E and I with .54 caliber Austrians, probably the Lorenz rifle-musket (National Archives 1983c, 9; Rein 2020, 86). It is likely that this regiment in late 1862 and 1863 would have been issued the then-standard dark-blue sack coat and sky-blue trousers, along with forage caps and standard equipment. With the soldiers having been recruited in Colorado, wide-brimmed hats may have been favored.

Formation of the Third Wisconsin Cavalry was completed in January 1862, and it moved to St. Louis in March and to Fort Leavenworth, Kansas, in May. The Second Battalion was at Fort Scott, Kansas, in June. The following year, after constant and active campaigning, companies B, G, H, I, and M left Fort Scott with a supply train for Fort Gibson on June 20, and were attacked by rebels under Cooper and Watie at Cabin Creek on July 1 and 2. When they arrived at Fort Gibson, the Third Wisconsin was assigned to the Third Brigade, Army of the Frontier. On July 17, they

FIGURE 36. (*Above*) Corporal George Henry McCoon (right), saddler in the Third Wisconsin Cavalry, and unidentified man, Fort Scott, Kansas. Courtesy of the Kansas State Historical Society.

FIGURE 37. (*Left*) Benjamin Fullager, Company A, Third Wisconsin Cavalry. Courtesy of the Wilson's Creek National Battlefield.

participated in the Battle of Honey Springs as a battalion commanded by Captain Edward R. Stevens (of Company I) (Quiner 1866, 909–14).

Two images of Third Wisconsin soldiers give insight into their appearance before the Battle of Honey Springs. The first (figure 36) is an image taken at Fort Scott and shows two mounted members of the regiment.

They are both wearing what appear to be dark-blue fatigue blouses (sack coats) and sky-blue trousers, with indeterminate footwear. The soldier in the foreground is Corporal George Henry McCoon, the company saddler. He is wearing what is probably a forage cap. McCoon is equipped to travel, with a revolver in hand, a cavalry saber in the scabbard, two blanket rolls, and a haversack. Behind McCoon is a trooper with a wide-brimmed hat and without weapons or other equipment. Another image (figure 37) shows Benjamin Fullager of Company A, probably after his enlistment in 1861. He is holding a cavalry saber and is wearing a mounted services or shell jacket, what are likely sky-blue trousers, and a forage cap. These images are not necessarily inconsistent. As a saddler, McCoon may have routinely worn the fatigue sack coat, whereas Fullager wore the regulation cavalry shell. A photograph published by Warren (2012, 42) shows the Haney brothers of Company M, which was at Honey Springs. This image shows veteran soldiers, one wearing a shell jacket and the other what appears to be an unbuttoned sack coat over a vest, with a generous neck cloth (tie).

Coates and Thomas (1990, 94) list the Third Wisconsin Cavalry as equipped with the Merrill carbine. The summary statements for the second quarter of 1863 show Company B equipped with the Merrill carbine, the .44 caliber Lefaucheux revolver, and cavalry sabers. No arms are listed for the other four companies present at Honey Springs. The .54 caliber Merrill was a single-shot breech-loading rifle that used a paper cartridge. It was first used by the US military before the Civil War and was purchased in quantity for use primarily by cavalry once the conflict began (McAulay 1981, 62–68).

The Sixth Kansas Volunteers were formed beginning in July 1861 and initially operated as a battalion. In October, a mix of cavalry and infantry companies were combined to obtain a full complement of soldiers. In March 1862, the regiment was reorganized as the Sixth Kansas Volunteer Cavalry and moved to Fort Scott. Various battalions operated in eastern Kansas and through the summer in the Indian Territory. In the fall they served in Southwest Missouri, the Indian Territory, and Northwest Arkansas. In December, a detachment of the Sixth assisted in the capture of Fort Gibson. On July 4, 1863, the regiment accompanied Major General Blunt in his relocation to Fort Gibson. On July 17, Companies A, C, F,

FIGURE 38. Earls King, Sixth Kansas Cavalry. Courtesy of the Butler Center for Arkansas Studies, Central Arkansas Library System.

and H were engaged at the Battle of Honey Springs (Adjutant General of the State of Kansas 1896, 73–92).

Wiley Britton, who was with this unit before and at Honey Springs, describes pickets from the Sixth using their Sharps carbines to exchange fire with rebels across the Arkansas River near Fort Gibson in the spring of 1863 (Britton 1922, 228). Second quarter 1863 summary statements show that the Sixth carried .52 caliber Sharps, .54 caliber Merrill, and .52 caliber Hall breech-loading rifled carbines, although Sharps outnumbered the others two to one. Sidearms were Colt revolvers in .36 and .44 calibers, smaller numbers of .44 caliber Lefaucheux revolvers, a single .36 caliber Remington revolver, and a mix of standard and light cavalry sabers (National Archives 1983b, 31–32).

FIGURE 39. Henry Gable (right) and unidentified man, Sixth Kansas Cavalry. Courtesy of the Butler Center for Arkansas Studies, Central Arkansas Library System.

Photographs of members of the Sixth Kansas Cavalry show a uniform not inconsistent with that depicted for the Third Wisconsin Cavalry (as in figure 37). In figure 38, Earls King of Company I (not present at Honey Springs) is wearing a cavalry shell jacket and a belt with a rectangular sword belt plate (Butler Center for Arkansas Studies n.d. a). He has a Colt revolver in hand and what is probably a carbine sling over his shoulder. He is not wearing a hat. King enlisted soon after the Battle of Honey Springs. In figure 39, an image featuring Henry Gable of Company K (also not present at Honey Springs) shows a veteran soldier wearing what appears to be a shell jacket and holding a sword in one hand and a Colt revolver in the other (Butler Center for Arkansas Studies n.d. b). An image tentatively identified as Jacob H. Bartles shows a soldier with a shell jacket, Sharps carbine attached to sling, and revolver in holster on a belt with an oval plate (Warde 2013). He has a wide-brimmed hat (possibly the Model 1858 Hardee hat) and no sword. Bartles served with Company A, which was at Honey Springs. These three images show a fairly consistent kit and provide confirmation of weapons as well.

The uniforms of the US troops engaged at Honey Springs appear to have been consistently drawn from quartermaster storehouses supplied with regulation issue items that were then in mass production. Dark-blue sack coats were probably the norm for the enlisted infantry (First Kansas and Second Colorado). Shell jackets possibly mixed with some sack coats are suggested for cavalry (Kansas and Wisconsin) and mounted infantry (Indian Home Guard). Photographs show forage caps and wide-brim hats, possibly in the same regiment. Photos of the Indian Home Guard and Third Wisconsin may show that the low-crown, Burnside-pattern wide-brimmed hat was a standard issue item. Small arms were a mixture of First-Class weapons within a majority of Second- and Third-Class weapons. Although the weapons varied in quality, the US troops were certainly fully armed with serviceable weapons.

Confederate and Confederate-Allied Cavalry and Mounted Troops

Identifying small arms carried by Confederates and Confederate-allied Indians at Honey Springs is more difficult than for the US troops. Rebel cavalry and mounted troops at Honey Springs were the First and Second Cherokee Regiments, First and Second Creek Regiments, First Choctaw and Chickasaw Regiment, Twentieth Texas Cavalry (dismounted), Twenty-Ninth Texas Cavalry, Fifth Texas Partisan Rangers, Scanland's squadron, and Gillette's squadron (company).

Harbinger of things to come, at least concerning arming the Confederate-allied Indians, is found in Colonel Douglas H. Cooper's Order No. 23, Headquarters of the Indian Department, dated October 22, 1861 (D. Cooper 1861). This order instructed Colonel Drew to arm his Cherokee regiment by local purchase from private citizens. Warriors in his regiments with serviceable arms were asked to turn them in to the regiment in exchange for their appraised value; they would then be issued back to this same person but as property of the Confederate States. Whether or not this process of formal purchase and issuing back took place, the widespread use of civilian firearms continued in the Indian Territory up to and beyond the Battle of Honey Springs.

Regarding clothing and uniforms, Whit Edwards has summarized the Confederate reality in the West:

> The Trans-Mississippi Confederates were a hardy group of warriors who from the outset of war found themselves required to provide their own arms and supplies. That is not to say that the Confederate quartermasters failed to supply them with goods. The men in the field did receive shipments of food, harness, tentage, ammunition, some arms, and even infrequent shipments of clothes. However, those shipments were far from adequate, leaving some companies going into battle with full knowledge that their arms would come from fallen comrades in their front. When faced with situations like that, it is understandable that uniforms were low priority. (Whit Edwards 1995, 435)

This generalization fits well the situation in the Indian Territory, although specifics are hard to tease out of a historical record seemingly unconcerned with these details.

Confederate Indian Territory had its closest connections, especially at the war's beginning, with Texas. The Lone Star State garrisoned forts along the Red River such as Washita and McCulloch and sent troops to aid in Colonel Cooper's attempts to drive the federals out of the territory's northern reaches in 1861. The fall of New Orleans—the Indian Territory's long-standing source of imported material—to the United States in November 1861 made Texas even more important. Confederate priorities on the East Coast and in Tennessee and a tightening US blockade of the Gulf Coast (Galveston, Texas, was first blockaded on July 2, 1861) made it increasingly difficult to supply war material to Texas and the Indian Territory. Increased federal control of the Mississippi River leading up to the surrender of Vicksburg in July 1863 compounded problems of Confederate supply of the Trans-Mississippi West.

Many fabled Texas regiments, such as John Bell Hood's Texas Brigade, left the state early on, taking most of the state's arsenal with them and leaving little for new regiments being formed to take their place (Madaus 1997, 17). In a letter to Major General James B. Magruder in

December 1862, Texas governor Francis R. Lubbock summarized the state of the remaining Confederate troops, "The Confederate States troops at this time within the state and the State troops are probably sufficient for its defense, but they are all of them to some extent, and some of them wholly, destitute of arms" (Lubbock 1886, 896). Magruder relayed these concerns to the Confederate secretary of war on December 13, noting, "All the rifles and shot-guns at one time in the hands of her citizens have been sent with her troops to the army elsewhere, and she is absolutely now without any whatever, except the few with which the troops in the field here are badly armed" (Magruder 1886a, 898). However, on December 9, 1862, Major General Magruder asked that the "well-armed troops" of DeMorse's Twenty-Ninth Texas Cavalry be retained in Texas for its defense (Magruder 1886b, 896).

In early April 1863, British lieutenant colonel Arthur James Lyon Fremantle landed in Mexico to begin a three-month fact-finding tour of the South. After crossing the Rio Grande into Texas, he entered the camp of officers of James Duff's cavalry, whose "dress consisted simply of flannel shirts, very ancient trousers, jack-boots with enormous spurs, and black felt hats, ornamented with the 'lone star of Texas'" (Fremantle 1864, 6). Later Fremantle's journal recorded that members of Duff's regiment "were dressed in every variety of costume, many of them without coats." He added, "All wore the high black felt hat. Notwithstanding the peculiarity of their attire, there was nothing ridiculous or contemptible in the appearance of these men, who all looked thoroughly like 'business'" (Fremantle 1864, 7)." In May 1863, Fremantle observed a regiment of Pyron's (Second) Texas Cavalry in Galveston, as they marched out of town. He noted, "[Pyron's regiment was] dressed in every variety of costume, and armed with every variety of weapon; about sixty had Enfield rifles; the remainder carried shotguns (fowling pieces), carbines, or long rifles of a peculiar and antiquated manufacture. None had swords or bayonets—all had six shooters and bowie-knives. The men were a fine, determined looking lot" (Fremantle 1864, 39). These descriptions of Texas troops, dating to mid-1863, are apt for the Texas troops' appearance at Honey Springs. Portraits of Texas troops that Madaus (1995) used to illustrate the use of shotguns also confirm Fremantle's description of a wide variety of dress, including civilian attire, "battle shirts," and in some cases broad-brimmed hats.

Although little is available to describe the equipment carried by the Twentieth Texas Cavalry (dismounted), important insight is provided by a letter to the *Rocky Mountain News* from Captain George West, Company H, Second Colorado Volunteers. West reported, "About eighty prisoners were captured by us, most of them belonging to the Twentieth Texas Infantry. The prisoners captured were armed with new Enfield rifle-muskets, marked 'Tower 1862,' showing that this early in the fight Mother England was patting the southern branch of her descendants upon the back to some purpose" (West 1877, 2). Although not attributing them to any particular regiment, Blunt noted of weapons collected after the battle that they included "two hundred stand of arms, mostly English Enfield rifles" (Blunt 1863, 3).

When first assembled in Clarksville in July 1862, recruits of the Twenty-Ninth Texas Cavalry came variously clothed and equipped. "Aside from a few well worn butternut-colored uniforms belonging to some of the veterans . . . all of the men looked strangely alike—mud-colored or gray homespun hunting jeans; red-and-white checked or brown wool shirts; heavy, muddy brogans; wide, low porkpie hats, or an occasional Stetson. Most men carried squirrel guns or double barrel shot guns, and a few had muskets" (Felmly and Grady 1975, 9). To better equip his troops, Colonel DeMorse traveled to Richmond to attempt to procure suitable equipment and arms but lamented that there were none of the desired tents, revolvers, or shotguns available. In Columbus, Mississippi, DeMorse obtained his needed tents, clothing, and shotguns, which he shipped to Clarksville (Felmly and Grady 1975, 13–17). In May 1863 a soldier in the Twenty-Ninth wrote, describing skirmishing with the enemy across the Arkansas River, "Our guns are mostly ineffective at long range, but two or three rifles, and some of the largest bore shot guns, loaded with balls, carry over" (*Standard* 1863b).

Little is known about the clothing or armament of the other Texans at Honey Springs—the Fifth Texas Partisan Rangers and Gillette's and Scanland's squadrons. It is likely their clothing was consistent with that observed by Fremantle. Their weapons were probably shotguns.

At Honey Springs, the Texas regiments were opposed on the field by the First Kansas Colored Infantry. Several descriptions of the shots coming into the ranks of the First Kansas exist and are informative. A correspondent of the *Missouri Democrat* identified only by the initials

W. H. S. wrote that the First Kansas "advanced to within about forty paces of the enemy, who then opened upon them a terrible fire of buckshot" (W. H. S. 1863, 1). An article by an unnamed correspondent of the *New York Tribune*, reprinted in the *Cincinnati Daily Commercial* (1863, 4), reported, "Colonel Williams fell at the first fire, shot through the upper part of the right lung by a musket-ball, and three other slight wounds from buckshot." These accounts probably describe fire from shotguns or large-caliber smoothbore muskets loaded with buckshot, spherical ball ammunition, or buck-and-ball rounds.

The Indian troops fighting as allies with Confederate troops at Honey Springs probably fit Fremantle's description of Texas troops more closely than their Union opponents with their more standardized uniforms and weapons. The Indians were likely carrying various civilian common rifles of varying calibers similar to those noted for the US First Indian Home Guard. In 1861, Albert Pike suggested that Indian troops be armed with plain muzzle-loading rifles of large bore and that "an Indian would not pick up a musket [smoothbore] if it lay in the road" (Pike 1900, 360). The same probably held true for shotguns. Clothing was probably consistently inconsistent and civilian in nature but distinct from the Texans in the reimagining of dress along traditional lines, including accessories and adornments. It was not uncommon as well for Indians to wear surplus military coats, which might explain some early nineteenth-century buttons found on the battlefield. Confederate-allied Indians would have equally embraced warriors' traditions—including war paint, dances, and songs—described earlier for the US Indian Home Guard.

Although recalling a time before the Battle of Honey Springs, Allison Sparks's description of the appearance of Cooper's Indian troops (First Choctaw and Chickasaw Mounted Rifles, First Creek Regiment, Creek and Seminole Battalion) during the 1861 Opothle Yahola campaign is informative:

> The Indian warriors, as I noticed were well supplied with rations, and rode small ponies and were dressed in a garb ranging from a common gent's suit to a breech clout and blanket, most of the full bloods wore only the latter, their faces were painted in such a manner that many of them were frightful to even look upon. [The] most common way of painting appeared to be about three lines of deep

FIGURE 40. This image is thought to depict a Confederate-allied Cherokee soldier later killed at the Battle of Honey Springs. Courtesy of Hindman Auctions.

red from the edge of the hair down the forehead and met between the eyes. Then a large red spot on either cheek that would resemble the outline picture of the sun with spangles, all of red, sometimes black spots, too, were painted and sometimes the eyes were made red, and the mouth outlined to each ear and some were painted black down to the eyes, then the balance of the face red. Some had head coverings that were the skins from the heads of buffalo, bear, panthers, cougars, calves, etc., and quite a number wore the horns taken off with the hide of buffalo, and others wore no head covering, only a single feather. (Sparks 2014)

Sparks also remembered war dances and songs prior to battle.

Images of Confederate-allied Indians are exceedingly rare, but the one in figure 40 is particularly useful. This image is thought to depict a Confederate-allied Cherokee who was killed at the Battle of Honey Springs. This waist-up image shows what appears to be a Colt revolver in his right hand and a civilian broad-brimmed hat turned up at the front. The rest of his dress is civilian. If the attribution is correct, this individual would probably have been with either the First or Second Cherokee Regiments. An image printed by Warren (2012, 49) purporting to be Lieutenant Pleasant Porter of the First Creek Regiment may depict him during the Civil War. He has what may be a Colt revolver in hand, civilian attire including a tie and greatcoat, and a wide-brimmed hat with a plume.

Colonel James Madison Bell of the First Cherokee Regiment provides a compelling description of the state of Indian troops then in camp in the southern Indian Territory less than two months after the Battle of Honey Springs: "One thousand are without arms and many have not Clothing to change, without shoes and what any one in their right sense would say was in a deplorable condition looking more like *Siberian exiles* than Soldiers" (Dale and Litton 1995, 137, emphasis in source). In February 1864, Brigadier General William Steele filed a report on "operations in the Indian Territory in 1863" that provides general insights about the conditions in the Indian Territory (Steele 1888a, 28–36). Steele had just been relieved of command for cause. His report must be viewed as an attempt to defend his reputation as an officer; some of his claims may thus be exaggerated in his favor. Referring to the winter of 1862–63, Steele reported that Cooper's brigade was poorly clothed and equipped and poorly armed (many were without arms) (Steele 1888a, 30).

Shortly after the Battle of Honey Springs, extracts from ordnance reports of Cooper's brigade listed 2,854 long arms, of which over 84 percent were shotguns (1,078), common rifles (460), Texas contract rifles (450), muskets (416), and Enfield rifles (265). The shotguns, common rifles, and muskets were listed as old and worn. Texas rifles were made under contract with the State of Texas and were poorly regarded. The Enfield was the only First-Class weapon of this bunch and was probably largely in the hands of the Twentieth Texas. Smaller numbers of Mississippi rifles, "Minié muskets," Minié rifles, Belgian rifles, breechloading Sharps rifles, Hall carbines, Colt rifles, and Maynard carbines rounded out the list (Madaus 1995, 164, 166). Cooper's Indian troops were noted as being armed mainly with common sporting rifles, some of which were flintlocks, although the 460 enumerated were not enough to arm the 2,743 Indians present for duty in early August (Schaumburg 1888, 1052; S. S.

Scott 1888, 1098). Except for the Twentieth Texas, apparently armed with late-model Enfield rifle-muskets, the Texans were probably armed in a similar fashion with shotguns. The shotguns and Enfields specified would have armed almost all of the 1,416 Texans present, suggesting that the disparate other weapons were in the hands of Indian troops.

With exception of the Twentieth Texas, the only US or rebel unit apparently consistently armed with the Enfield, and the fact that the remainder of Texans probably carried shotguns, distinguishing other rebel units from each other and from the variously armed federal units, especially the Indian Home Guard, is extremely difficult based on found ammunition. That said, the insights gained from this review shows well the reality of arming both US and rebel troops who fought in the Indian Territory midway through the Civil War.

US and Confederate Artillery

Artillery present at Honey Springs comprised sixteen guns. The twelve US guns were four with Hopkins's Kansas Battery, four with the Second Kansas Battery, and four mountain howitzers attached to the cavalry (two each with Sixth Kansas and Third Wisconsin). The Confederates had only four guns, all with Captain Roswell W. Lee's Light Battery. Although Blunt had superior artillery at this engagement, he nevertheless reported on July 30, "My artillery is . . . very poor; have not a rifled gun in the command." This comment reflected the inadequate supply of the army in the Far West (Blunt 1888c, 411).

The Second Kansas Battery was formed at Fort Scott beginning in August 1862 by Major Charles W. Blair, commanding the Second Kansas Cavalry, under orders from Brigadier General James G. Blunt, then commanding the Department of Kansas. The Second Kansas was a six-gun battery with two sections of six-pound iron guns and one section of twelve-pound iron field howitzers, all said to be captured Confederate guns. These were replaced with brass guns of the same size before the Battle of Honey Springs (Swain 2017). Only two sections of this battery were present at Honey Springs, commanded by Captain Edward Smith. A six-pound section under Second Lieutenant Aristarchus Wilson (Left Section) was attached to the Second Colorado Infantry and accompanied a supply train from Fort Scott to Fort Gibson, departing on June

16 and arriving at Gibson on July 4. With Wilson's section of artillery, a Confederate attack at Cabin Creek on July 1 and 2 was repulsed. The twelve-pound section (Center Section) under Smith accompanied Major General Blunt when he moved his headquarters from Fort Scott to Fort Gibson on July 5, arriving there without incident on July 11 (Kansas National Guard n.d.; E. Smith 1888, 454).

The second quarter 1863 summary statements show the Second Kansas Battery equipped with four bronze six-pounder guns (Model 1840/1841) and two bronze twelve-pounder light Model 1857 guns (commonly known as Napoleons), of which one six-pound and one twelve-pound section were at Honey Springs. The summary statements list ammunition on hand for the entire battery: for the six-pounders (only two were in the Indian Territory), there were 444 shot, 564 case, and 478 canister, and for the twelve-pounders there were 17 shot, 100 shell, 57 case, 43 canister, and 152 canister for mountain howitzer. Members of this battery were armed with 128 navy caliber revolvers and 23 sabers (National Archives 1983a, 17–20; Swain 2017).

On October 27, 1862, Company B of the Second Kansas Cavalry was reorganized as Hopkins's Kansas Battery, commanded by Captain Henry Hopkins. It is referred to as the Third Kansas Battery in the quarterly summary of ordnance immediately prior to the Battle of Honey Springs (National Archives 1983a, 17–20). Guns captured by the Second Kansas Infantry "at Old Fort Wayne" equipped this battery. Blunt reported, "The battery captured consists of three 6-pounder brass guns and one 12-pounder brass field howitzer, with horses, harness, and caissons complete" (Blunt 1885, 328). Hopkins's battery was moved to Fort Gibson, arriving on March 1, 1863 (Civil War Archive n.d.; Swain 2018). According to the summary statements for the second quarter 1863, immediately before the Battle of Honey Springs this battery was equipped with three bronze six-pound Model 1840/1841 guns and one bronze twelve-pound mountain howitzer and had 196 shot, 406 case, and 196 canister for the six-pounders, and 166 case and 150 canister for the twelve-pounder. The battery was further said to have thirty-five navy and eleven army caliber revolvers and no sabers (National Archives 1983a, 17–20; Swain 2018).

The Sixth Kansas Cavalry, commanded by Lieutenant John P. Grassberger, had a section of two bronze twelve-pound mountain howitzers when stationed near Fort Gibson before the Battle of Honey Springs

(Campbell 1888, 452). Ordnance summaries for the second quarter of 1863 show they had 12 shell, 120 case, and 48 canister for these guns (National Archives 1983a, 17–20; Swain 2017). The Third Wisconsin Cavalry had another section of twelve-pound mountain howitzers (Stevens 1888, 453). No information on sidearms carried by these batteries is recorded.

The single Confederate battery—Roswell Lee's Light Artillery—had "three 12-pounder mountain howitzers and an experimental 2 ¼-inch bronze mountain rifle, one of only 18 produced at the Tredegar Iron Works in Richmond" (Guttman n.d.; Steele 1888a, 32). Lee's Light Battery was formed in Texas in 1863 (Barr 2011). Brigadier General Cooper does not comment on problems with artillery ammunition in his report on the Battle of Honey Springs. Still, several reports before the battle from Brigadier General William Steele suggest that it may have been in short supply. On July 1, Steele, from his headquarters at Fort Smith, reported, "All the artillery with General Cooper is a mountain battery, and that is almost without ammunition, a requisition made in May not having been filled, as far as I have heard" (Steele 1888c, 902). On July 5, he advised Cooper that he was expecting the ammunition to arrive at Fort Smith and would ship it along up the Arkansas River when it did (Steele 1888b, 906). On July 10, he reported that Cooper's battery had "little, if any, ammunition" (Steele 1888d, 917). On June 26, Major General Blunt reported, "The rebel force [Cooper] in front of Colonel Phillips has lately received a large train of supplies from Texas" (Blunt 1888e, 337), but the nature of these supplies is unknown. They obviously had enough ammunition to fire "shot, shell, and cannister" at Hopkins's battery to devastating effect as the battle opened on the prairie north of Elk Creek (Hopkins 1888, 456).

From the above historical information, insight into the origins of different ordnance found on the battlefield is possible. Easiest is the artillery: both US and Confederate troops had twelve-pound smoothbore cannon; either side could have fired ammunition for twelve-pounder guns. Although the twelve-pounders were a mix of light field howitzers and mountain howitzers, the bores were all 4.62 inches, and fractured cannonballs would be indistinguishable, one from the other. The only explosive ammunition for twelve-pound guns found during our survey was shell. Lead ball and iron ball canister could have been fired by any of the six- or twelve-pound smoothbores present at Honey Springs (US or Confederate). Only the United States had six-pound artillery (smoothbore); ammunition of this size found on the battlefield is, therefore, US ammunition and was fired by either the Second Kansas Battery or Hopkins's Kansas Battery. Case was the only six-pound explosive ammunition found during our work on the battlefield. Finally, the Confederates had a 2 ¼-inch rifled cannon, and ammunition of this size would be so associated although none was found during our survey (one solid bolt for this gun was found by Gary Moore).

As far as small arms—rifles, muskets, and sidearms—there are only a few items that can easily be associated with specific units. The rebel Indian regiments allied with the Confederacy were probably armed with common rifles of variable caliber, Texas rifles, and a variety of Second- and Third-Class military muskets and rifles, most of which were old and worn. These units certainly account for some of the spherical ball ammunition along with some conical bullets (Minié varieties and Pickett) found during our work. For the Confederate cavalry—all Texans—we know that the Twentieth Texas stands out as having been consistently armed with the Enfield rifle-musket, probably firing a .58 caliber Minié bullet. Several Minié and Enfield variety bullets fired in these weapons were found, and the probability of their association with the Twentieth Texas is higher than for other units that may have had a few Enfields among their various arms. The Twenty-Ninth Texas was armed with shotguns as their weapon of choice, from which they were probably firing buck-and-ball ammunition. The remaining Texas troops—Fifth Texas Partisan Rangers and Scanland's and Gillette's squadrons—were probably armed with some assortment of non-martial weapons, but I suspect the shotgun predominated. Ball, buck and ball, and shot were probably fired from these weapons and were common finds on the battlefield.

The Federal Indian Home Guard soldiers were, I believe, armed with a variety of weapons as described by Colonel Phillips in January 1863. There is no good evidence I have seen that these regiments were re-armed prior to the Battle of Honey Springs based on summary statements of ordnance on hand. The First Indian Home Guard carried common rifles of various calibers, but two companies had martial rifle-muskets or rifled muskets in a variety of calibers. The common rifles would have used spherical ball ammunition, but the martial rifles may have used spherical ammunition or the conical Minié ball. The Second Indian troops were armed with many common rifles but also a variety of martial rifles and smoothbores in a range of calibers. Similar to the First Regiment, these would have used spherical ball ammunition, with the martial rifles possibly using Minié ball varieties in the stated calibers. Although probably not engaged at Honey Springs, the Third Regiment appears to have been armed with a mix, probably including common rifles and martial rifles in a variety of calibers.

The First Kansas Colored Infantry carried .69 caliber smoothbore muskets that fired spherical ball or buck-and-ball ammunition. A ledger of equipment issued to Company F annotated with "July 17 at Honey Springs" shows that spherical ball cartridges and buck-and-ball cartridges were issued in roughly equal numbers on the day of the battle (Earle 1863d). The Second Colorado Infantry were armed with .58 caliber Springfield rifle-muskets, .69 caliber rifled muskets, and .54 caliber Austrian rifle-muskets. Conical Minié bullets varieties in .54, .58, and .69 caliber would have been issued for these rifles.

As Wiley Britton had remembered, the Sixth Kansas Cavalry carried the Sharps carbine but they also were armed with .54 caliber Merrill and a few .52 caliber Hall carbines. Sidearms included army and navy caliber Colt and army caliber Lefaucheux revolvers and regular and light cavalry sabers. Company B of the Third Wisconsin Cavalry carried .54 caliber Merrill carbines, navy caliber Colt revolvers, and cavalry sabers; it is uncertain if the rest of the regiment was so armed. Although the ammunition used in the Merrill and Sharps carbines is relatively distinctive, it is obvious that it would be difficult to distinguish between these battalions of cavalry based on ammunition found on the battlefield, given the uncertainty about the arms of the Third Wisconsin. Although in small numbers, the Sharps and Merrill were also probably used by some rebel soldiers.

Information on the clothing and equipment may seem less than satisfying due to the lack of specific detail in most cases. Still, a general picture emerges that contrasts the two armies in the field at Honey Springs. On the one hand, Blunt's federal troops were all to some degree wearing and equipped with some version of the US uniform common throughout the Trans-Mississippi West. On the other hand, soldiers under Cooper's command differed in that the dress, and, to perhaps to a large degree, the equipment favored a civilian origin with a mixture of Confederate-issued and captured US items. In very general terms, then, this translates to the probability that items of standard US Civil War issue, such as buttons, can be more confidently associated with Blunt's army, while civilian and obsolete federal items (for example, early US buttons) can more confidently be associated with Cooper's rebels. Interpretation, then, is a probability problem, where location and context become as important as an item's form.

The picture that emerges of the armies engaged at Honey Springs in July 1863 is thus one of contrast and sameness. Contrast comes most clearly in terms of clothing, with the federal army more closely resembling US standards than not, and the rebels differing markedly with what memory suggests is predominately civilian clothing intermixed with some Confederate uniforms, especially among the Texans, and probably uniform elements such as coats among the rebel Indians. Although better documented for the federal Indians, the attire of Indian soldiers in both armies certainly reflected their cultural belonging. While the opposing Indian warriors certainly shared similar cultural traditions of warfare, I wonder what effect the organization of regiments would have on the expression of their "own ways of fighting" on the battlefield. How would this be expressed in white-officered regular US regiments versus those tribally organized and officered regiments serving as Confederate allies?

Sameness comes from a consideration of the arms used in this battle, especially contrasted with the mid-war status quo in the eastern armies. The White US troops were armed on par with the times. It can be argued that the Texans were likewise, with one regiment equipped with First-Class Enfield rifle-muskets and the others probably consistently with shotguns, which remained widely in use by Confederate cavalrymen throughout the war. Even the Black soldiers of the First Kansas had been recently rearmed, although with Third-Class smoothbore muskets. The real sameness comes from the Indian regiments on both sides, who were armed with a wide-ranging assortment of firearms, almost exclusively Third Class or worse, heavily favoring common rifles. Sameness also comes from the fact that many if not most of the weapons in the hands of Indian regiments used spherical ball ammunition, as did the shotguns of the Texans. This and the use of spherical balls in artillery case and canister is why lead balls make up most of the finds at Honey Springs. Sameness also is seen in the artillery. Although the United States had the only six-pound guns, and the Texans a single small-bore rifled gun, all had twelve-pound guns firing generally identical ammunition. This sameness, with notable exceptions, was discussed in chapter 2.

I have yet to consider another essential bit of information about each artifact: its location in the landscape and its spatial relationship to other finds. So far I have only used location to show where fighting occurred and where it did not. I will move next to adding location to the artifact information presented in chapter 2 to look at the internal structure of the Prairie, Elk Creek, and Pumpkin Ridge Engagements and seek patterns that will help us understand, and sometimes raise new questions, about what happened in each.

CHAPTER FOUR

Understanding the Fields of Conflict

WHEN CONSIDERED TOGETHER, several distinct areas of fighting constitute the Battle of Honey Springs. The initial skirmish near Chimney Mountain lies outside the scope of this study. The others, on land that is now the Honey Springs Battlefield public heritage site, were delimited above as the Prairie, Elk Creek, and Pumpkin Ridge Engagements. Even a cursory comparison of the artifacts found in these three areas shows that they differ in obvious ways (see table 6). First, most of the artifacts (52.9 percent) were found in the Prairie Engagement, followed by the Pumpkin Ridge Engagement (35.6 percent) and the Elk Creek Engagement (12.3 percent). Length of combat, number of combatants engaged, or nature or intensity of the fighting in these areas might explain the observed differences. The initial conflict north of Elk Creek is described in many officer reports as lasting for hours, starting with an artillery exchange of over one hour and followed by at least an hour of engagement by infantry and cavalry. I have questioned whether this fighting alone explains the spread of artifacts for over three-quarters of a mile up the Texas Road. A more complex story north of Elk Creek could comment on this and the preponderance of artifacts in this area. This is a new question born out of archaeology that I will begin to look at in this chapter.

The fighting at Elk Creek and generally to the south did not, according to officer reports, involve all the federal troops that were initially engaged or rebel troops that were potentially available. It also appears that many Confederate or Confederate-allied regiments withdrew quickly if engaged north of the creek, with those engaged in the center described as withdrawing in rout. This may explain low numbers of artifacts along Elk Creek. Accounts vary on the length and intensity of fighting in this

TABLE 6. Overall artifact profile of three engagement areas

Description	Prairie	Elk Creek	Pumpkin Ridge
Artillery shell fragments and fuses	46 (76.6%)	5	9
Firearm parts	5	0	1
Conical bullets for rifle-musket	65 (76.4%)	5	15
Conical Bullets: Pickett	0	0	3
Breech-loading and magazine bullets and cartridge cases	12	2	11
Conical sidearm ammunition	6	5	9
Spherical (round) ball ammunition	235 (48.9%)	54	191 (39.7%)
Arrowheads	1	2	5
Civilian and military buttons	7	5	5
Other military equipment	6	3	3
Padlocks	1	1	0
Personal Items	6	7	5
TOTALS	390 (52.9%)	89 (12.3%)	257 (35.6%)

area, but most do not say it was hard-fought or a long-lasting affair, offering another explanation for lower artifact numbers. The higher numbers in the Pumpkin Ridge Engagement certainly relate to the formation of new rebel resistance by the arrival of reserves, and in particular the First Choctaw and Chickasaw Regiment, which had not been engaged since very early in the morning near Chimney Mountain. At the same time, no accounts suggest this was a long-lived affair, and I was surprised that the total number of artifacts found here was so high. As this is a newly defined field of conflict that is imperfectly mentioned in memory, understanding what happened here and how it relates to the larger battle narrative is another new question as I move into detailed analysis of the archaeological findings.

A few brief observations about the relative occurrence of several different types of artifacts help in thinking about how the engagements are similar or different. Numbers for artillery ammunition, for example, show that a preponderance (76.6 percent) was found in the Prairie Engagement, with the remainder roughly split between the other areas of fighting. This exceeds the observation that roughly half of all artifacts were found on the prairie. Still, this does underscore an importance of artillery in the Prairie Engagement that does not differ from expectations drawn from memory. Minié balls fired from martial weapons, possessed by both armies, show a distribution similar to artillery ammunition with a preponderance (likewise 76.6 percent) found on the prairie and the rest elsewhere. Two types of Minié balls, with presumed rebel use, are found only on the prairie. Did units using this ammunition not participate after the initial fight?

A final artifact type will complete this brief inter-engagement comparison: spherical ball ammunition, the most common artifact type at Honey Springs. The comparison across the battlefields of spherical balls fired in small arms (rifles and smoothbore) is interesting. In general, there are roughly the same percentage in the Prairie Engagement (43.3 percent) and on Pumpkin Ridge (46.6 percent), with a significantly smaller number along Elk Creek (10 percent). It follows that—unlike martial small arms and artillery—common rifles, muskets, shotguns, and sidearms seem equally important in the Prairie and Pumpkin Ridge Engagements.

Still, these numbers are different for the 259 balls of uncertain use: a slightly greater percentage are found in the Prairie Engagement (50.9 percent compared to 37.9 percent on Pumpkin Ridge). This difference is explained, I believe, because the subset of unattributed balls in the .64–.68 caliber size are overwhelmingly more common north of Elk Creek (80.6 percent) than in either the Elk Creek or Pumpkin Ridge Engagements. The preponderance of these large-caliber balls north of Elk Creek is almost certainly linked to the use of many of these in artillery rounds such as canister or case. Percentages for spherical balls less than .64 caliber are similar for those with and without evidence of having been fired in small arms. Because of this, and in contrast with the evidence for balls in the .64 to .68 caliber range, I believe these unattributed specimens are most likely related to a similar use in small arms.

Although contrasting mainly the Prairie and Pumpkin Ridge Engagements, these brief observations reveal some contrasts in the importance of artifacts between different areas of fighting. These are with little doubt related to some of the factors that are preserved in memory that record differences between engagements in who participated, the intensity and duration of fighting, and perhaps also the type of the fighting itself. Although these observations will be useful as I proceed, one can only go so far with this sort of general comparison of percentages. Fundamentally more useful is to consider each engagement in turn by looking at the spatial distribution of found artifacts (using maps) in search of patterns that more specifically and accurately anchor events to landscape, provide the opportunity for explanation, and invariably raise new questions in need of answers.

In the process of developing a general narrative of the conflict in the Prairie, Elk Creek, and Pumpkin Ridge Engagements, I believe an overarching question is whether my breakdown of the fighting into three clearly bounded engagements will hold against an intra-engagement analysis based on the distribution of found artifacts. From the outset I said that my splitting what appeared on the maps as a continuous concentration of artifacts on both sides of Elk Creek into the Prairie and Elk Creek Engagements would need to be borne out by this analysis. Also, questions have earlier been raised about the difficulty in using memory alone to explain the way artifacts are distributed along the Texas Road north of Elk Creek.

In chapter 2 I presented a fundamental question about the Prairie Engagement: where was the rebel line at 10:00 a.m. on July 17, 1863? I offered two theories on this placement, one based on my reading of the landscape and the other on the late nineteenth-century land surveys. Following on this, was Blunt's description of the spacing of his bivouac and initial deployment north of Elk Creek accurate? I believe it was, but if I am wrong about where the federal line was, then I am wrong about the accuracy of his claim. The resulting implications for the on-site interpretation are large. Also, Cooper and Blunt both indicated that the severe fighting north of Elk Creek was at the center of the rebel line. Are their descriptions confirmed by archaeology, and was the fighting so concentrated that this is what explains the surprisingly narrow breadth of the archaeological residue of fighting on the prairie?

Likewise, the Pumpkin Ridge Engagement shows an unexpectedly large number of artifacts and an interesting array of lesser concentrations, some slightly separate from the others, that may require more nuanced definition. Can these observations be used to clarify an unfortunately vague accounting from memory? How intense was fighting on Pumpkin Ridge? What units were involved? How did the nature and character of the conflict compare with that on the prairie and along Elk Creek?

Loitering around the edges of these relatively specific questions are a few puzzlements that are at the heart of my goals in writing this book. Of importance is the question of Indian agency as participants in the Indian Territory's Civil War catastrophe. Agency can be interpreted using the few available photographs and in memory mainly derived from White observers. It is, however, difficult to see archaeologically. I believe the rolled-metal arrowheads found at Honey Springs may provide an unusually clear window into the question of agency. Is their use by Indian combatants on July 17, 1863, supported archaeologically, and, if so, does their presence speak to expression of culture or of expediency to address a shortage of arms or poor gunpowder?

Other questions that drive me toward a broad conclusion relate to Cooper's choice of the landscape for battle and the effect of that choice on the chances of success defending his position or conducting a retrograde withdrawal (retreat). Put differently, to what degree did Cooper's stated reliance on poor-quality gunpowder or Steele's blame of him for poor defensive preparation contribute to rebel loss? How does the triangulation of history, landscape, and archaeology contribute to the explanation of Cooper's ultimate defeat at Honey Springs? Returning to Indian agency, how might Confederate-allied Indians have viewed the outcome of the day's fighting?

After introducing the battle-related artifacts and using their distribution on the landscape to bound the areas of fighting in chapter 2, I now turn to the vital work of searching for patterns in maps of artifacts in each of the three engagements. During battle, items are used, lost, or discarded by those involved; their locations are thus a physical link to the day's tragic activities. Artifacts found on battlefields all relate to participants in distinct yet complementary ways. Those lost or discarded may include bullets, for example, dropped when retrieving ammunition from a cartridge box or bullet pouch; buttons that popped off clothing; and coins that fell from pockets. Such items mark, if but for a moment, the precise location of a soldier on the battlefield. When these sorts of things are found, the connection between place and person is immediate and often profound for the archaeologist or project volunteer. Less-direct evidence of the location of soldiers is the expended ammunition for small arms and artillery. These mark soldiers, or more typically groups of soldiers, as they moved across the battlefield or stood in place in a fighting line or serving a battery of artillery. These items provide less precise information on location, since bullets or artillery shells did not necessarily reach their human targets or may have traveled beyond.

Artifact locations and maps showing their distribution on the landscape are thus crucial for interpreting—using archaeology—how commanders deployed and moved forces on the field and how individuals reacted to events as they unfolded. These not only speak to the internal structure of each engagement, by triangulation with memory and landscape, they also allow construction of interpretations of the day's events. Still, looking at a map of all artifacts in a conflict area can be overwhelming, so I have prepared this chapter through a thorough look at distributions of different types of artifacts, each being a separate lens into the battle. Breaking the findings down in this way allows nuanced understandings of how the locations of artifacts differed across the battlefield (different types and calibers of Minié balls, for example). These differences relate to troop placement, movement, and engagement over the course of the fighting. Deconstructing the overall pattern in this way and then rebuilding a narrative based on layered interpretations of troop position and movement is what enables archaeology to become a driving force in a new description of the Battle of Honey Springs. By linking memory to artifacts that we have found, memory is in turn linked in increasingly specific ways to the landscape. The result is a narrative of the battle where memory is anchored to the landscape through the intermediary of artifacts left on the field on July 17, 1863. This place-specific analysis is the basis for what I will do in the next chapter: analyze the resulting narrative using KOCOA military terrain analysis. There I will consider how the landscape may have affected decisions made by the commanders and combatants and how it may have itself influenced the outcome of the day's events.

The Prairie Engagement

As argued in chapter 2, no clear visual distinction between the Prairie and Elk Creek Engagements was discernable simply by looking at the distribution of finds along and to the north of Elk Creek. Instead, I have

FIGURE 41. Metal detectors on the edge of the prairie overlooking the Elk Creek valley during the 1994 survey. Pumpkin Ridge is in the distance. Photo by William B. Lees.

separated these engagements based on topography and memory. Topography supports treating these as two adjoining but distinct conflict areas; the steep, rocky bluff overlooking Elk Creek sheltered the valley from view of those engaged on the prairie to the north. This bluff almost required disengagement before combatants could move south. The memory of what happened at the creek is unfortunately vague but suggests that this area differed in terms of officers' intent and tactics, and in terms of who participated.

The artifacts found north of Elk Creek are the most numerous and diverse of the conflict areas—this is, after all, where Blunt's and Cooper's troops collided and by all accounts had their most desperate fighting. Looking at the overall map, the pattern of artifacts seems to defy the descriptions of the battle by the narrow confinement to a width of only about one-third of a mile, with the Texas Road slightly west of center (see figure 30). This width is much less than Blunt's proclamation describing a rebel line stretching a mile and a half wide. Had we not explored areas to the east and west of this concentration to verify its limits, I might think this pattern reflected an arbitrary edge to our survey rather than the actual boundary of an area of intense fighting. All that we found in either direction was a concentration of artifacts discovered about one-quarter mile further west (Anderson Creek Area). To the east, we found no evidence of fighting.[1] The outlying concentration may provide testament to Blunt's claim by showing that, perhaps, rebel troops were deployed beyond the area most heavily engaged on July 17.

Details of what occurred on the peripheries may be worked out with additional survey, but the breadth of the core fight is, I believe, accurately defined. However, as worked out in chapter 2, the extent of the artifacts north of the bluff edge overlooking Elk Creek exceeds 1,300 yards (about three-quarters of a mile). Blunt's description of his sheltered bivouac being one-half mile north of the rebel lines and his deployment into line of battle midway between these two points (440 yards) easily fits within this north to south extent of artifacts. Still, given that memory says the federal line advanced to within 100 yards or so before fully engaging, I question whether the evidence of battle stretching north along the Texas Road can be reconciled with memory of what happened on the morning of July 17. Identifying the location of either Blunt's line of initial deployment or the rebel line, or ideally both, is critical in addressing this question.

To explore this and other questions, the next task is to examine patterns of different types of artifacts within that defined area that I am calling the Prairie Engagement. I accomplished this through a tedious process of producing and reviewing maps (layers) using geographic information systems (GIS), searching for insight about what they show. GIS allows the generation of different maps of single or multiple artifact layers, limited only by choice and design; for Honey Springs, I used fifty-one base layers of different types of battle-related artifacts. These were projected over various base maps (topographic, photographic, and LIDAR [USGS 3D Elevation program or 3DEP]) relating the finds to the modern landscape. Maps showing single or multiple layers are readily generated, and specific artifacts or groups of artifacts in any layer can be brought in or left out to further refine a map. Of course, it is impossible to publish all the generated maps that I consulted. I include here only those that best illustrate my discussions.

In presenting the results of my analysis of the Prairie Engagement, I draw first on some significant insights about the use of artillery. This is my favorite starting place because the armament of the batteries is well

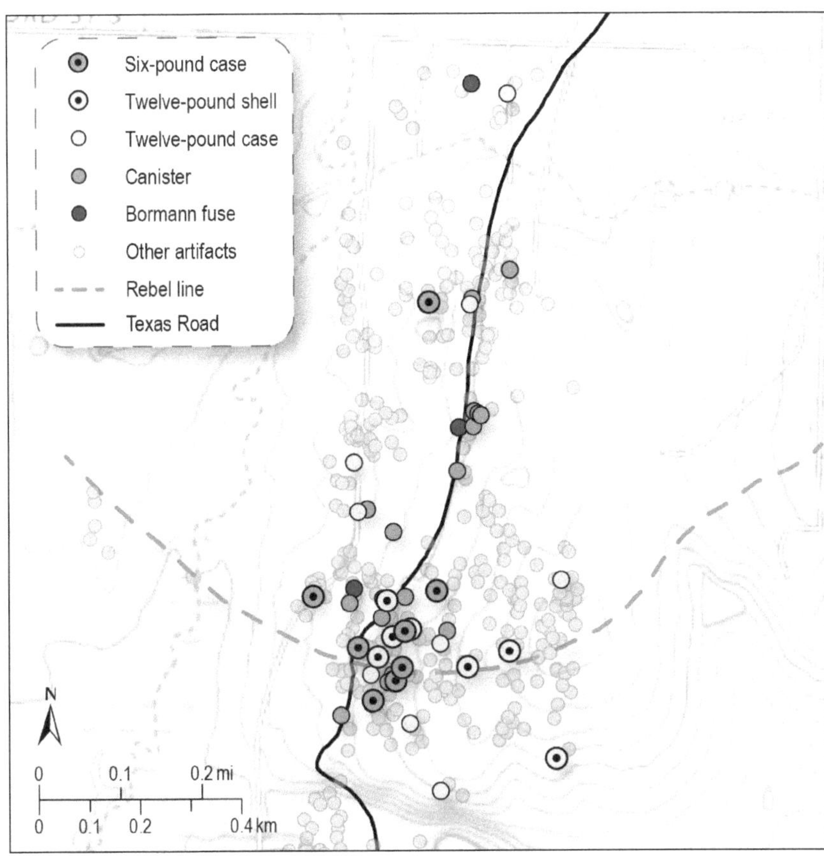

FIGURE 42. Artillery artifacts on the Prairie Engagement. Map by Katherine Sims.

documented. The exploded cannonballs and iron canister balls found on the battlefield are also a clear and direct residue of the Honey Springs battle since there is no other way to explain their presence in this landscape. I believe artillery also presents an excellent example of the process of breaking apart similar artifacts into meaningful groups and then rebuilding them into a generalized overall interpretation. While I accept many other artifacts as battle residue, artillery shell fragments and iron canister are the gold standards.

I see a revealing pattern when I examine a map of the prairie north of Elk Creek (see figure 42) showing the exploded cannonball fragments, fuses, and iron-ball canister. These occur on both sides of the Texas Road, with a noted concentration perpendicular to the road immediately north of the bluffs overlooking Elk Creek. This concentration extends disproportionately to the east of the road on what would have been the rebel right (federal left). When plotted, the unattributed spherical lead with a caliber above .60 mirrors this concentration with a few exceptions; as reviewed at the start of this chapter, these are most likely lead ball shrapnel or canister. The same is true for many unattributed balls in the .50 to .59 caliber range, many of which may therefore also be shrapnel or canister.

To better understand artillery, it is necessary to look at different sizes and types of ammunition. I start by looking at those fired from six-pound guns. These are important because only the US Second Kansas Battery and Hopkins's Kansas Battery were so armed; the other US batteries and the Confederate battery had twelve-pound guns with one exception. That exception was a Confederate small-caliber rifle firing a Tennessee Pattern shell, none of which were found during our study.[2] Most of the six-pound cannonball fragments—all case—were located closely along the Texas Road just north of the Elk Creek bluffs. A lone piece is farther north along the Texas Road, which is problematic; I may have miscategorized this small fragment as six- rather than twelve-pound.

Because these fragments are from cannonballs from US six-pound guns, their location supports a highly compelling argument for where the rebel line crossed the Texas Road. In chapter 2, I suggest an optimal location for the rebel line based on terrain, and this is exactly where these six-pounder fragments were found. I had proposed an alternate theory on the location of the rebel line based on the 1898 GLO land survey map showing the woods' edge north of Elk Creek. Archaeology shows clearly that the edge in 1898 was as much as one-quarter mile north of where it was in 1863. The concentration of six-pound cannonball fragments is not the only evidence that my terrain-based placement of the rebel line is correct, but it is the most compelling. Supporting this is the observation that many lead balls of .60 or more caliber cluster around these six-pound case fragments; again, case contained lead ball shrapnel of this size. Within this cluster was one .65 caliber lead ball that had been intentionally cut to increase its ostensible lethality. I suggested in chapter 3 that this modified ball (see figure 23) may have been inserted into case or canister during manufacture; its place of discovery makes this interpretation more likely and suggests that it had been inserted into an artillery projectile that was ultimately directed at Cooper's line.

Of possible related importance is a heavy iron padlock found close to the Texas Road in the same area as the concentration of six-pound cannonball fragments. This padlock complements in style and size three others Gary Moore found in the Wooded Forty (although I do not use that terminology to discuss our finds, our padlock find was also in this same area). I mention the Moore finds because heavy padlocks are not a common archaeological find, and four in proximity are, I would say, exceptional. In terms of the battle narrative, these are near the Texas Road and Confederate battery location. I believe these are related to Lee's battery and possibly served as locks on ammunition chests. Loss of these locks during a hasty retreat after enduring suppressing enemy fire is easy to imagine.

The plot of twelve-pound shell fragments complements that of the six-pound case. This finding further underscores my conclusion about the location of the rebel line. These twelve-pounder fragments are found within the dispersion of six-pound specimens and extend to the east into the rebel right. No exploded cannonball fragments—either six- or twelve-pound—extend west of the Texas Road. Fragmentary twelve-pound shells occur only with US six-pound case fragments north of Elk Creek and are not found along Elk Creek or in the Pumpkin Ridge Engagement. Because of this, although both the US and Confederate batteries had twelve-pound guns, I believe these fragments came from the muzzles of US cannon. This finding argues that Lee's Confederate battery did not have, or did not fire, explosive shell ammunition.

However, either US or Confederate cannoneers could have used twelve-pound case, fragments of which we found on the prairie north of Elk Creek. These also would have contained lead ball shrapnel or, possibly in Confederate arsenal-made rounds, iron ball shrapnel. Most twelve-pound case fragments occur along the rebel line at the Texas Road and east and were probably fired by US guns. Still, several others are north of this line along and on either side of the Texas Road. I believe these represent fragments of rounds fired by the Confederate battery, although fragments found at one thousand yards north are at extreme range for their mountain howitzers. One fragment found relatively close to the rebel line is near two Confederate iron shrapnel balls. Although seemingly close to their own line, these are as much as two hundred yards or more northeast of the probable location of the rebel battery. The other pieces thought to originate from Confederate guns are associated with clusters of large-caliber lead balls that are probably shrapnel from case ammunition. Bormann time-fuse fragments found at and north of the rebel line also indicate that these were on explosive case or shell used by both US and Confederate batteries.

The iron ball canister pattern mirrors that for case. Thus, many are concentrated at the rebel center on the Texas Road and others north along the road. This pattern shows federal cannoneers fired canister as well as twelve-pound case at the rebel center. The rebels appear to have fired canister rounds up the Texas Road as far as about 750 yards, which is well beyond effective range of their mountain howitzers, but most did not travel this far. These were possibly fired along the Texas Road as Blunt was bringing up his troops after their bivouac. No accounts from memory, however, mention the Confederate battery firing before US deployment into line was complete.

Like artillery, conical, solid-base bullets and cartridge cases for breech-loading and magazine carbines are easily associated with Civil War combat. While relatively few, the location of these bullets and cartridge cases on the Prairie Engagement is instantly intriguing when compared to the unfolding internal structure of this area as so far presented. Along the rebel line are a dropped Merrill carbine bullet and a cluster of fired breechloader bullets. This dropped Merrill is just one hundred yards up the Texas Road from the rebel center and may relate to the advance of the Wisconsin Cavalry, armed with Merrill carbines, into the rebel flank during its withdrawal, which "forced the enemy to fall back upon their center" (Stevens 1888, 453). An unidentified fired bullet for a breech-loader is four hundred yards southeast and is near two .54 caliber Minié balls that, based on examination, appear to have been fired in a Merrill carbine. Three hundred yards in advance of the rebel right and four hundred yards from their left are single fired Henry cartridge cases. The Henry case four hundred yards out is close to Blunt's probable point of deployment, and that at three hundred yards is slightly in advance. It is possible, perhaps, that these are good indications of that line and even conceivable one or both may be associated with the Second Kansas or Hopkins's batteries.

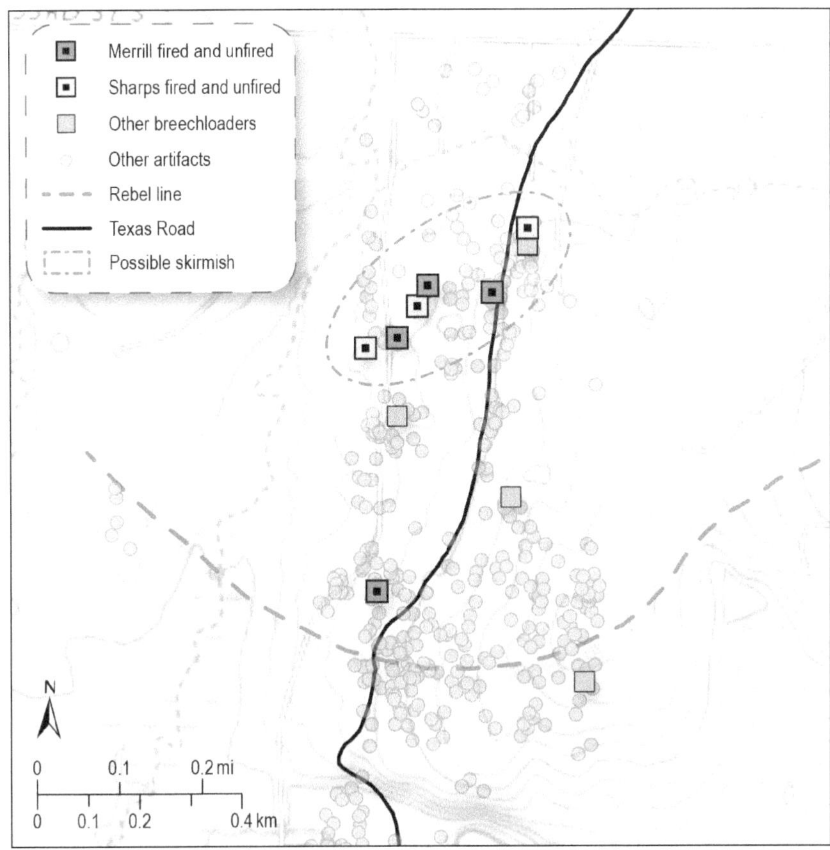

FIGURE 43. Breechloading bullets on the Prairie Engagement. Possible skirmish evidence encircled. Map by Katherine Sims.

Still farther north of the rebel lines and Blunt's probable initial line of deployment are two fired Spencer cartridge cases, three fired Merrill bullets, and one dropped and two fired Sharps bullets. No units are known to have been equipped with Spencer carbines, but given their specialized cartridges these may have been in US hands. The locations of the fired Sharps and Merrill bullets complicate the story of the Prairie Engagement. These are spread out in a line about one-quarter mile long that trends southwest from the Texas Road, at a location that I believe would be between the bivouac site and the initial US line to the south (see figure 43). Based on what we know of armaments, these fired bullets

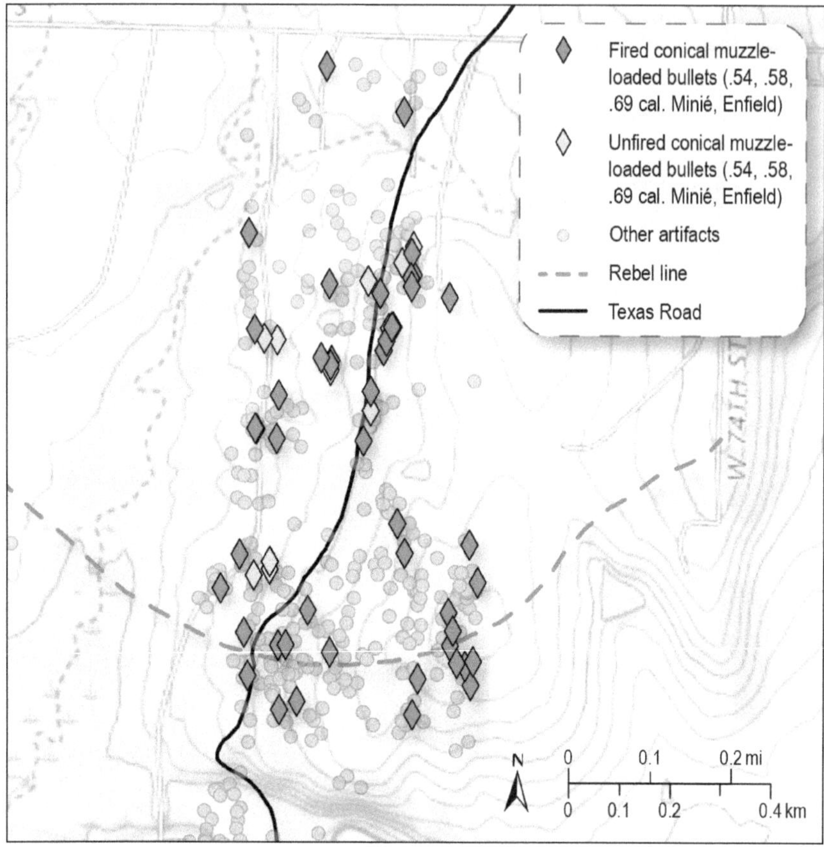

FIGURE 44. Conical muzzle-loading bullets on Prairie Engagement. Map by Katherine Sims.

indicate that the Third Wisconsin (Merrill) and/or the Sixth Kansas Cavalry (Sharps and Merrill) were engaging enemy in this general vicinity. The dropped Sharps bullet along the Texas Road is nearby and may thus be related. The question arises, where were the US cavalry troopers located when they fired these rounds, and who were their targets? These bullets are convincing clues for active combat in the northern part of the Prairie Engagement sometime on July 17.

Moving on from these breech-loading and magazine bullets and cases, I next consider the Minié balls. As far as martial weapons, these conical compression bullets designed for the rifle-musket had an effective range of several hundred yards and could be lethal at substantially longer distances. For a variety of reasons, including that not all battalions or regiments were so armed, fighting generally and at Honey Springs happened in a space well within that effective range. The US Indian Home Guard carried some rifles, rifle-muskets, or rifled muskets that used these bullets, as did all of the Second Colorado Infantry. The Twentieth Texas carried the Enfield rifle-musket, probably in .577 caliber. Other rebel units, Texan or Indian, may have counted some sort of martial rifle among their various arms. The presence of shotguns, fowlers, various common rifles, and smoothbore muskets on both sides, as well as the clouds of black-powder smoke produced by all, inspired if not required the close-in fighting characteristic of the period.

The pattern of all conical Minié balls on the Prairie Engagement does, in general, mirror that noted for other artifacts already, with a concentration south along the rebel line separated by a decrease in finds up to the location that I favor as the federal line of deployment. At that point and to the north the number of finds pick up, but they begin to drop off again close to the intermittent stream along which I believe the US troops bivouacked. Looking at the distribution of Minié balls by type in the battlefield provides only partial clarity because of overlap of weapons used by the US and rebel units; we are left with considering what is most probable.

The dropped bullets, of course, show the location of individual soldiers sometime during the battle. Three Minié balls found about 150 yards in front of the rebel line, near its center, may show the location of the US line at some point. Since these were not fired, their actual caliber is known: two are .54 caliber and the other is .58 caliber. As these were found right along the Texas Road, I would hazard that these are best associated with the Second Colorado, whose soldiers carried .54 caliber Austrians (Lorenz) and .58 caliber Springfields. The other dropped Minié balls are, however, located some 400 to 700 yards north of the rebel line. These are one .54 caliber, four .58 caliber, three .69 caliber, and two Enfield variety .577 caliber bullets. US regiments were armed with weapons that could have fired all of these, but the Enfield variety bullet is best associated with the Twentieth Texas. Again, given the variability of arms in use by Indian regiments and Texans, caution argues against taking speculation on regimental association too far. What is clear, however, is that the dropped Minié balls concentrate generally along and west of the Texas Road between the possible line of Blunt's deployment and the site of the bivouac. Alone, it is possible to suggest these were dropped by US troops as they moved into position from bivouac. On the other hand, is it possible these are somehow correlated with the just discussed dropped and fired bullets for breechloaders?

Fired Minié balls in the southern concentration of bullets are exactly what I would expect. Most of these are distributed along the rebel line on both sides of the Texas Road, but most are to the east, on the rebel right. Although I say these are along the line, the rebel line was by design not dressed (straight) but rather conformed to the edge of the brush, which Blunt described as forming a "partial semi circle, the road running through the center" (Blunt 1863). It is significant that the line I propose based on topography mirrors Blunt's description of a partial semicircle (see figure 33) and that the found bullets provide additional support for the line's location. Bullets found in this area include twenty of .54/.58 caliber broadly distributed along the line. Three fired .69 caliber Miniés and a single .58 caliber Enfield variety are also along the rebel right. The .54/.58 caliber bullets are best associated with the troops of the Second Colorado Infantry who were formed in line immediately east of the Texas Road in front of where these bullets were found. An association with Indian Home Guard is also possible. While I cannot accurately gauge the caliber of these bullets due to impact damage, two have rifling impressions showing four lands and grooves. These were probably fired from a .54 caliber Austrian rifle-musket such as those carried by the Second Colorado and are, in fact, directly south of the three dropped Minié balls in front of the rebel lines, two of which are .54 caliber.

The rest of the fired Minié balls are more difficult to explain. These are distributed north of a line that corresponds to Blunt's possible line of deployment and reach up to, with a few beyond, the intermittent stream along which I believe Blunt bivouacked his troops. Roughly half of these are clustered along and immediately east of the Texas Road, while the remainder are more broadly distributed to the west. These include one .69 caliber Minié ball, two "Italian" variety Minié balls, three Gardner Minié balls, eight Enfield variety Minié balls, and twelve .54/.58 caliber Minié balls. While the Italian, Gardner, and Enfield bullets are easy to associate with the rebels, the .54/.58 caliber bullets are, based on what

I know, most easily associated with Indian Home Guard or more likely Second Colorado Infantry.

These dropped and fired Minié balls located in the northern half of the prairie field are in the area where we found dropped and fired breech-loading bullets probably associated with US cavalry. These carbine bullets were unexpected given the deployment elsewhere of the US cavalry during the battle as it commenced at 10:00 a.m. Their presence suggests units so armed were engaged in this area at some point. The fired Minié balls in this area, which overlap the distribution of carbine bullets, are another matter. Given the range of the rifle-musket and trajectory of ammunition fired from it, it is possible these are overshot balls from rebel rifles fired at the advancing US troops, either when first deployed or more likely upon closing and engaging with the rebel line. Most rebel troops were, however, armed with various caliber common rifles and fowlers and shotguns, the exception being the Twentieth Texas, armed with Enfield rifle-muskets. One way to examine whether these bullets represent overshot is to look at evidence of impact velocity with the presumption that bullets fired from a distance ranging from three hundred to one thousand yards would have lost velocity before hitting the ground, decreasing impact damage.

The Minié balls most likely to have been fired by rebels toward advancing US troops are for the Enfield in the hands of the Twentieth Texas. For the eight that were found in the north half of the prairie, those farthest south, about three hundred to four hundred yards north of the rebel line, show low to moderate impact, while those farther than six hundred yards show low impact. This is consistent with expectations of bullets fired from the rebel lines as identified by terrain and archaeology. In contrast, the only Enfield bullet near the rebel lines, fired from as close as fifty yards, shows a high-velocity impact. Other Minié balls confidently thought to have been used by rebels are the Gardner and "Italian" varieties. These are only found in the northern half of the Prairie Engagement. I could not reexamine the Gardners for this study, which had all been fired, but the two "Italian" bullets showed medium- and high-velocity impacts in an area where Enfields showed low impact. This suggests to me that the Enfields may very well be bullets fired from the rebel lines that finally came to rest on the northern reaches of the Prairie Engagement but that the "Italian" and perhaps the Gardner (they were found very close to one another) may have been fired relatively close to where they were found.

In considering this, it is extremely useful to look at impact damage on the fired .54/.58 caliber Minié balls. These have the closest association with US troops, which is supported by the large number that are found within, and apparently fired into, the rebel line. Of those found along the rebel line, I have already mentioned two that appear to have been fired from Austrian rifle-muskets and impacted with a medium velocity. These are accompanied by four other Minié balls that show a high-velocity impact, including one that is smashed flat, and another nine that hit with a medium velocity. This is what I would expect of bullets that were fired into the rebel line by troops that were relatively close.

This pattern of impact velocity is not measurably different from that found for .54/.58 caliber Minié balls found in the northern half of the Prairie Engagement. Four of these had a high-velocity impact, and another three hit with a medium velocity (for several others, impact velocity estimates were not available). The difference between the impact velocity of these bullets from the northern half of the prairie were markedly different than for the Enfield bullets, which showed consistently low-velocity impact in the same area. This comparison leads me to conclude that while the Enfields may be overshot from fighting in the south of the Prairie Engagement, the .54/.58 Minié balls probably were not. It follows that most of these bullets relate to some sort of fighting that occurred in this northern area and that this might be related to evidence already presented from the carbine ammunition and the Confederate "Italian" variety Minié balls. Although there was only one .69 caliber Minié ball in this northern area, it too had a high-velocity impact, while three along the right of the rebel line had low-, medium-, and high-velocity impacts. The Minié balls thus provide additional evidence for conflict, rather than overshot, in the northern half of the Prairie Engagement. This cannot easily be explained as being part of the general engagement that began between Blunt's and Cooper's forces at roughly 10:00 a.m. on July 17.

With only four specimens, small, solid-base conical bullets probably fired in revolvers are rare in the Prairie Engagement. Two of these are along the Texas Road on either side of the intermittent stream and Blunt's pre-battle bivouac. Both are fired; one is .40 caliber and the other .44 caliber, the latter possibly fired in a Colt Dragoon or Model

1860 revolver. Although the smaller-caliber bullet was not definitively identified as fired in a revolver, it seems likely. Given the short range of revolvers, their presence in the bivouac area is surprising but may relate to other evidence of fighting in this vicinity.

Another two fired conical revolver bullets were found along the right of the rebel line. One is heavily damaged by impact but is probably about .36 caliber. The other is also about .36 caliber and is a Colt pattern bullet. The evidence on this bullet—seven lands and grooves roughly equal in width—is consistent with several varieties of Colt revolver. Navy caliber Colts were carried by the Sixth Kansas Cavalry, who were active against the rebel right, but were also probably in the hands of many others, including rebels. Either way, these probably speak to the close fighting spoken of in numerous accounts.

Spherical ball is the largest category of ammunition but has been the most difficult to interpret. Nonetheless, maps provide some clear patterns (and some less than clear) that help measure the fighting north of the Elk Creek valley. As discussed earlier, included are balls that evidence proves were fired in small arms, and others that show no evidence of their intended use, whether in small arms or artillery. As has already been confirmed, a considerable number of the latter, certainly those above .60 caliber but possibly also including some in the .50s, were probably artillery lead ball canister or shrapnel.

Round balls that were fired from rifled small arms are identified by the presence of land and groove impressions and by impressions of cloth patch in the soft lead bullet. The thirty-five found in the Prairie Engagement were variable calibers between .30 and .50 with four above .50 caliber. Some of the smaller balls may have been fired by single-shot pistols or revolvers of variable calibers, but most were likely, and for larger balls certainly, fired in common rifles in wide use by Indian troops on both sides.

Of note, however, the rifle-fired balls found in the northern part of the Prairie Engagement cluster along the Texas Road and to the west along the US right. Although representing only thirteen specimens, these with one exception have clear land and groove impressions. The single exception has no rifling marks but does have impression of fabric patch. Except for one .61 caliber ball, these are of variable sizes between .38 and .46 caliber, popular for pistols and revolvers but also for many common civilian rifles. Six struck with low velocity, six with medium velocity, and only one with high velocity (the .61 caliber ball). Velocity of impact seems, therefore, to mimic that for the Enfield variety Minié balls found in this area that I speculated had been fired from a considerable distance. That said, while most may be overshot, it is possible some with medium- and high-velocity impact may relate to fighting in this area suggested by the carbine bullets and some Minié balls.

On the other hand, the nineteen rifle-fired spherical balls located along the rebel line concentrate from the Texas Road east for about one-quarter mile, consistent with most other ammunition. Most of the rifle-fired balls have clear land and groove impressions, although five have fabric patch showing they were fired in rifles. Calibers range from .36 to .47, with three above .50 caliber. Seven of these struck with low velocity, six with medium velocity, and six with high velocity. These skew more to the medium- and high-velocity impact than those found farther north, comparing favorably with what was observed for conical bullets. Thus, impact damage on rifle-fired balls suggests that, in general, those found on the northern half of this engagement may have traveled farther—and may represent overshot—than those that were found along the rebel lines. If those to the north are indeed overshot, possibly fired from the rebel line, they would have most likely come from rifles of rebel Indian combatants. Likewise, those found along the rebel line would have been fired by Indian combatants on either side. Because of the widespread use of weapons of variable calibers by the Indian regiments, attribution to any particular unit is impossible.

Twenty-one round balls show full or partial banding and/or have impressions of other balls, showing that they were fired in smoothbores, including shotguns. Two of the larger banded balls have impressions of smaller buckshot characteristic of buck and ball. These could have been fired from .69 or .70 caliber martial weapons or shotguns of large but variable caliber. Other large, banded balls without impressions of buckshot were probably fired alone in either martial weapons or shotguns. Also, several smaller partially banded balls with impressions of other balls could have been part of buck-and-ball rounds but could also simply represent buckshot fired from shotguns.

Only five banded balls are found in the northern part of the Prairie Engagement. Two large balls, .64 and .68 caliber are some four hundred yards north of the projected rebel line, about at the initial US line of deployment. One of these is clearly the large ball in a buck-and-ball round. Farther north are three buckshot. All these struck with little or low velocity. Unlike rifled weapons, either martial or common, smoothbore weapons including shotguns are not effective at this range, and it is even questionable if these could be overshot from the fighting farther south. The possibility does exist that these, despite their low-velocity impact, were fired during whatever altercation occurred in the northern part of this area of engagement.

Closer in along the center and right of the rebel line are sixteen banded balls and one ball that has been pulled. The .66 caliber pulled bullet has scars from the worm used to remove it and was found just east of center on the rebel line. The banded balls cluster in an area very similar to that seen for the exploded cannonballs and Minié balls. Like those found farther north, most of these struck with low velocity, with only two of medium- and two of high-velocity impact. This once again probably speaks to the nature of smoothbore weapons and shotguns rather than the distance from which they were fired.

Eight of the balls along the rebel line are .64 to .67 caliber, probably intended for martial muskets such as the .69 caliber smoothbores carried by the First Kansas but which could also have been fired in shotguns such as those of the Twenty-Ninth Texas. Another five are .52–.54 caliber balls probably fired from shotguns, and the other three balls are buckshot fired either as part of a buck-and-ball round or simply as a buckshot load in a shotgun. The distribution is such that they range on either side of the line I have drawn as the most likely location of the rebel line. I think it fair to say that some of the large-caliber balls found at the southern edge of this area were fired toward rebels by the First Kansas, and that those to the north were fired by the shotgun-wielding Twenty-Ninth Texas.

To some degree, the distribution of these balls on the Prairie Engagement mirrors that for conical bullets. First, there is a dense scatter along the southern part of this area roughly following the rebel line as identified by terrain and by the location of exploded US artillery ammunition. This scatter is convincingly associated with the fighting along the rebel line during the general engagement that began mid-morning. To the north there is a marked drop-off before the pattern of balls fired from small arms again picks up, roughly halfway between the rebel line and the suspected location of the US bivouac. While this is generally similar to the distribution of conical Minié balls, the pattern of small-arms-fired balls is of markedly lower density.

This general pattern holds as well for spherical balls without evidence of use in small arms; there is a substantial concentration at the center and east along the rebel line, in an area consistent with other artifacts discussed above but a little larger. Density decreases until about the location of the US line and extends well north of that line. Balls in the .60 caliber range, however, are most heavily concentrated along the rebel line and do not extend nearly as far north as smaller-caliber balls. These larger balls are likely artillery canister or shrapnel, and the fact that they do not reach any farther north is significant. To the north of the rebel line, these larger balls do correlate with exploded cannonball fragments and are interpreted to have resulted from fire from the rebel battery during the engagement on the prairie that began at roughly 10:00 a.m.

Overall, the distribution of small-arms ammunition, dropped and fired, on the Prairie Engagement is very useful in defining action along the rebel line during the 10:00 a.m. engagement. It also provides important and I think undeniable clues that this is not the whole story of the Prairie Engagement. Although evidence of fighting in the northern part of this area seems at odds with memory about the Battle of Honey Springs, passing accounts provide clues to a possible explanation. This question will be further explored in the final chapter.

Directly related to munitions are two firearm parts found in the Prairie Engagement.[3] One is a barrel band to a martial musket. Its location is on the US right about one-tenth of a mile to the west of the Texas Road. Being about halfway between the suspected US bivouac area and the rebel lines, this is probably from a US weapon. Although a single item, it may be evidence that Major General Blunt's federal line was fully deployed at this location. A musket sling hook, also from a martial weapon, was found along the Texas Road, also at the approximate location where I believe Blunt deployed his troops into line. Although only a few items, their locations are consistent with what I would expect if my interpretation of the US and rebel lines is correct.

A final armament found on the Prairie Engagement is a single rolled-copper arrowhead with no impact damage. This arrowhead was within the cluster of exploded six-pound artillery shells that identifies the rebel center. Still, this is not proof this arrowhead relates to the battle because it is also along the Texas Road and could have resulted from hunting or travel along this route before or after the Civil War. Also, no Confederate-allied Indians are reported to have deployed at this location. I will return to this question again.

Other artifacts found at Honey Springs provide an intimate view of the individual soldier as these come from personal possessions, clothing, or equipment. Buttons, pieces of equipment, and personal items mark, like dropped bullets, precise locations of a soldier at some time during the battle. These can be used to evaluate some of the conclusions I have offered, or questions implied, based on the just-completed consideration of certain munitions found on the battlefield.

Because some of the soldier-carried items are not government-issued, it is important to evaluate whether they are battle-related. In so doing, where we found them is critical. Using location, I assessed the strength of their correlation with known martial artifacts or with areas used by the combatants before or after the battle (camps). In a similar fashion, I earlier showed how bullets fired from civilian rifles and shotguns complement those fired from martial weapons to create a compelling map of the fighting. A single bullet fired from a civilian weapon may be suspect, but the collective is not. While we are now dealing with smaller numbers of items, how well they correlate with the fighting pattern remains critical.

We found seven military buttons in the Prairie Engagement. Four were north of and three in the vicinity of the rebel lines. Those to the north are one US general service button found along the Texas Road between where I think the bivouac was and where Blunt extended his troops into line of battle. This button may relate to the movement of US troops down this road. This general service button was a standard issue to US troops during the Civil War. The other three US buttons cluster near the barrel band discussed above, thought to mark the US line's location at some point. These include two US general service buttons similar to that just mentioned, and one infantry button with the letter "I" on the US eagle's shield. This cluster of buttons near the barrel band is intriguing because it is within a swale that crosses part of the Prairie Engagement. I recall pondering during fieldwork whether this cluster of artifacts in this slightly

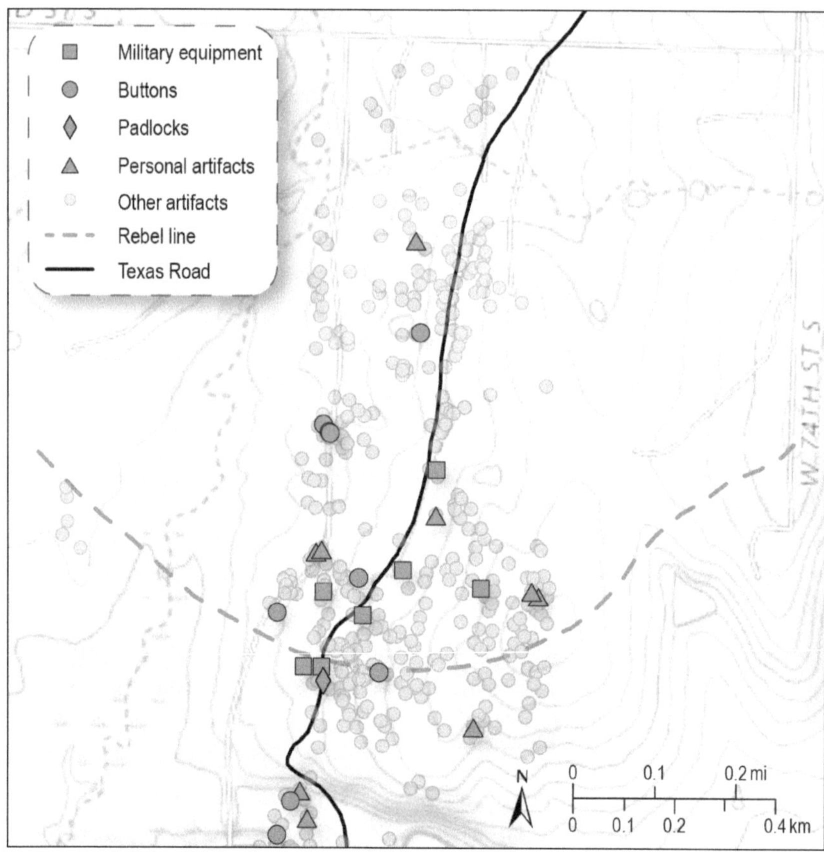

FIGURE 45. Buttons, equipment, padlocks, and personal items on the Prairie Engagement. Map by Katherine Sims.

sheltered location might represent a place of refuge for wounded soldiers. Either way, memory combined with archaeology tells us that this location would have been on or near Major General Blunt's initial line of battle.

The three buttons near the rebel line include another US infantry button like those just described. It was found just west of the Texas Road, some 150 yards in front of where I place the rebel line. It is near three dropped .54/.58 caliber Minié balls discussed earlier that I think may mark the US line at one point during the battle. Also present is a small cast-pewter four-hole trouser button located along the rebel right. This type of button was standard issue on US military uniforms at the outbreak of the Civil War. The third button is of interest because it was obsolete at the war's outbreak. It is a one-piece cast-copper-alloy greatcoat button with a flying eagle over "US" on the front. This button dates from the 1820s and was within the rebel left.

The US infantry button was, I believe, probably lost by a US soldier during the close-in fighting in front of the rebel line. Either US or rebel soldiers could have lost the pewter trouser button found along the rebel line. Standard issue for US soldiers, federal uniforms and buttons fell into rebel use through capture at the outbreak and during the Civil War. On the other hand, the 1820s greatcoat button was likely on the uniform of a Confederate or allied Indian soldier. Obsolete uniforms, especially coats, were widespread trade and annuity items valued by various tribes throughout the nineteenth century. Of interest, this button was on the rebel left, which is where the Confederate-allied Muscogee regiments were to be deployed.

We found six artifacts that I identify as military equipment in the Prairie Engagement, including military-issue and civilian items. First was a canteen spout found along the Texas Road between the initial US line and the rebel line. Slightly west of the Texas Road and near or within the rebel line was a hook from a US model 1855 knapsack. These military items could conceivably have found their way into Confederate service through capture. Still, based on my understanding of the equipping of the rebel troops present at Honey Springs, I believe they mark a US soldier's location. Two bits, one stirrup, and a stirrup/spur buckle are close to or within the rebel line. While these are civilian items, their placement on the battlefield correlates with the military-issue equipment items and an area of intense fighting. This association suggests to me that they are artifacts related to the battle.

Except for a single button on the Texas Road north of the US lines, the buttons and equipment items occur almost entirely where I place the initial US and rebel lines and the area in between. These artifacts each mark the location of an individual soldier during the battle and add support for this interpretation of the initial lines of battle. Increasingly, clarification of where Blunt deployed his troops makes me believe that some of the fired small-arms ammunition found farther north represents overshot in what would have then been an open prairie, and, increasingly more likely, some may be evidence of fighting focused in this area.

Six personal possessions found in the Prairie Engagement are once again windows into a location where an individual once stood. These items are an 1854 half-dime, parts of musical instruments, and two carved bullets. The half-dime showed moderate wear consistent with being in circulation for a decade. It was found not far from the intermittent tributary where I believe Blunt's troops bivouacked before the battle and may have been lost during the morning of July 17 by a US soldier.

We found most of the other items just north of the rebel lines. The harmonica parts and mouth harp could have easily fallen out of a soldier's pocket while advancing or engaged in fighting, especially if lying on the ground for protection or suffering from a wound, or worse. Alternatively, these items may relate to the camps US soldiers made on the battlefield on the evening of the battle; this area would have been on the open prairie north of the contested woods (but possibly too close to the grim remains of battle). The two carved lead items—probably once bullets—located close by the rebel line may represent the idle passing of time by soldiers before the fighting or by a federal soldier afterward. Based on correlation with the undisputable residue of battle, my interpretation is that these all represent soldier-owned personal items. Although cracked only slightly open, they are a window to the personal side of the soldier's life.

Prairie Overview

What I am calling the Prairie Engagement is thus, at first blush, a confusing concentration of artifacts that seemingly only show the boundaries of fighting and nothing more. On closer examination, this confetti becomes an archaeological layer cake made up of dozens of slices of different artifacts stacked one on the other. By looking at individual layers (maps) and seeing how one differs or complements the others, a story of the fighting emerges. This story confirms Major General Blunt's telling of his deployment from bivouac into line of battle facing his rebel antagonist aligned along the edge of the woods north of Elk Creek. It shows that Brigadier General Cooper established his line of battle in the most advantageous topographic setting a short distance north of the bluffs overlooking Elk Creek—far south of where the GLO mapped the edge of timber thirty-five years later.

The distances reported by Blunt appear correct based on the archaeology; Blunt bivouacked in a sheltered area about one-half mile north of the rebel line. US six-pound case concentrated on the Texas Road proves the rebel center's location. US twelve-pound shell focused there and to the east provide further confirmation and show that US batteries targeted the rebel right along with the center. Although the bivouac area—a valley one-half mile north of the rebel line—revealed few telling artifacts of the Union's brief repose, it emerges as the only viable option based on the physical evidence of the battle and the area's terrain.

Fragments from Confederate twelve-pound case suggest a minimal response to the US attack by the rebel battery but clearly illustrate the disparity of firepower available to US and rebel forces, and probably also the US batteries' effective suppression of Confederate artillery. Large-caliber spherical balls, most certainly lead ball shrapnel from six- and twelve-pound case, further illustrate the targets of US and rebel cannoneers. Looking at the maps of the lead ball shrapnel's dispersion, the distance between the rebel and US lines begins to be visible, consistent with Blunt's description of being one-quarter mile apart. The maps also show US troop movement closer to the rebels where the heaviest evidence of fighting is clearly shown by the archaeology-revealed residue of the fight.

Small-arms ammunition, dropped and fired, builds on the artillery layers in several essential ways. Maps of dropped conical bullets show that most are north of the rebel line. While I at one time thought this might hint at the deployment of the US troops, first advancing along the Texas Road in columns of companies and then deploying into line on both sides of the road, undeniable evidence of localized fighting in the northern half of the Prairie Engagement calls this into question. Careful consideration of the location of conical bullets and spherical balls fired in small arms leads to several important conclusions. First, this ammunition shows close-in fighting along the rebel line at the center and east. Conical bullets show the work, I think, of the Second Colorado Infantry as it attacked the rebel right, and certain spherical balls speak to an exchange between the shotgun-wielding Twenty-Ninth Texas and the First Kansas Colored Infantry, which was armed with smoothbore muskets.

The few firearm parts, military buttons, military equipment, and personal items provide important insight into not only where the rebel lines were located, which is clearly shown by munitions, but also where the

United States initially deployed into line of battle. While a few of these items are found north along the Texas Road and could relate to movement of US troops down that road, the majority are in a broad band that I think corresponds to the initial US and rebel lines and the area between them. These as much as anything else help to confirm Blunt's description of his initial deployment being one-quarter mile north of the rebel line. Most of these types of artifacts are found at Blunt's initial line of deployment and in front of the rebel line, where intense, close-in fighting occurred at the center and along the right. The pattern behind the rebel line, which certainly includes bullets fired south toward the rebels, falls off sharply before reaching the bluff edge, about one-tenth of a mile. This argues that the bluff at the south edge of the Prairie is the edge of fighting that occurred before the rebel withdrawal. Still, it is possible some of the munitions in the Elk Creek valley represent overshot from the prairie above. I will address this further when I discuss the Elk Creek Engagement.

The initial US and rebel lines as I have reconstructed them are thus roughly 440 yards apart, closing to 100 yards or less. Still, the artifacts of the Prairie Engagement stretch from the edge of the bluff over Elk Creek to beyond the saddle where I think Major General Blunt bivouacked his troops, about three-quarter miles farther north. There are thus substantial numbers of artifacts well north of the mid-morning engagement. I have shown that some, in particular the Enfield bullets, are likely rebel overshot. In contrast, Sharps and Merrill carbine bullets, along with Confederate Gardner and "Italian" varieties and .54/.58 caliber Minié balls, seem to relate to localized fighting well north of where I think Blunt established his first line of battle.

Finally, the maps of artifacts from the Prairie Engagement show consistently that the core, intense fighting was only about one-third of a mile (less than six hundred yards) wide. The items in the Anderson Creek Area to the west of the main concentration show there was minimal engagement beyond this core area and that Blunt's observation of a rebel line a mile and a half wide might be close to correct. But if the rebel line did stretch this far, it was certainly not as a continuous line of soldiers. It is nonetheless easy to account for most US and rebel troops being deployed into line of battle within this third of a mile. It is also easily conceivable that troops may have been posted substantially farther west and east to protect flanks and access to other fords across Elk Creek. Further, Blunt never said he deployed his troops across a similar mile-and-a-half front. What is clear from archaeology is that the Battle of Honey Springs started with intense fighting on a front only one-third of a mile wide.

It is revealing that the width of fighting shown by the archaeology matches my analysis of the topography of the Prairie Engagement presented in chapter 2. The prairie along what is now confirmed as the rebel line stretches only so far before being interrupted by intermittent streams and marshy ground to the west (Anderson Creek Area is across one such stream) and a steeply sloped ravine to the east. It is likely that terrain, as much as anything else, defined the conflict's core as Cooper and Blunt observed it on July 17, 1863.

While the overall confetti pattern of residue in the Prairie Engagement does clearly speak to an evenness of engagement between US and rebel, analysis of different layers has shown interesting imbalances within. One is the general unevenness of artillery and a striking focus of US artillery on the rebel center and right. Conical bullets and spherical balls fired in muzzle-loading rifles, spherical balls fired in smoothbores, buckshot fired in shotguns, and personal items, buttons, and equipment all showed unevenness. It is, in fact, this unevenness that underlies the interpretive power of archaeological research; for the archaeologist, the battlefield is more than the sum of its parts.

Although the implications are far from crystal clear, overall patterns of artillery ammunition and bullets—and the buttons, equipment, firearm parts, and personal items—show several things. First, the center of the rebel line is clear from the artillery artifacts and supported by the distribution of other types of artifacts. Based on that, it seems the most contested part of the Prairie Engagement was along and to the front of this line for probably no more than one hundred yards. To the north well beyond that is evidence that I think relates to Blunt's initial deployment into line, from which he advanced his troops after the artillery barrage had ended. It is significant in arguing for the line of deployment of US troops that virtually all the items that would have been with individual soldiers, such as buttons, equipment parts, and personal items, were within five hundred yards, ranging from slightly behind where I place the rebel line to the location where I think Blunt initially deployed US troops. Although the location of this US line is described by Blunt, its archaeological footprint is less than obvious. The location of these artifacts provides what is probably the strongest support for the accuracy of Blunt's description of it being halfway between the rebel line (here established based on terrain and archaeology) and the US bivouac (established largely based on terrain). The most surprising result of this analysis is that beyond this to the north is a newly identified localized area of conflict. This and the limited breadth of fighting north of Elk Creek require further consideration and explanation. I will return to both in the final chapter.

The Elk Creek Engagement

The Elk Creek Engagement is separated from the fight on the prairie above by terrain (located out of sight in the entrenched Elk Creek valley) and from the Pumpkin Ridge Engagement by distance. The question of overshot from the Prairie Engagement landing in the valley below is important and could be a confounding factor for interpretation of this area. It is also, perhaps, important to remember stories in the introduction about the camps along Elk Creek being "cleaned out" by relic collectors, which might also make the archaeological footprint of this part of the story foggy.

Still, we know from memory that fighting did happen along Elk Creek at the bridge, whose Civil War location is uncertain, and probably also at the lower ford as Phillips's brigade (US left) pushed the rebels into the valley. In the valley, rebels sought to protect their retreat by stopping or slowing the US advance. But US Major General Blunt sent only part of his force in pursuit. This may have been because of his confidence in progression of the battle and possibly also to guard his hard-fought ground against rebel counterattack.

Looking at the Elk Creek valley's archaeological footprint, I begin as I did for the Prairie Engagement with artillery. We recovered only one iron canister ball, one fragment of twelve-pound case, and three fragments of six-pound case. There are also what I think to be five spherical lead-case shrapnel. The three fragments of six-pound case cluster in a line crossing Elk Creek, slightly below the remains of the post–Civil War bridge. This tight placement is not a likely result of overshot. Four probable lead ball shrapnel are nearby. Because Major General Blunt held Captain Edward

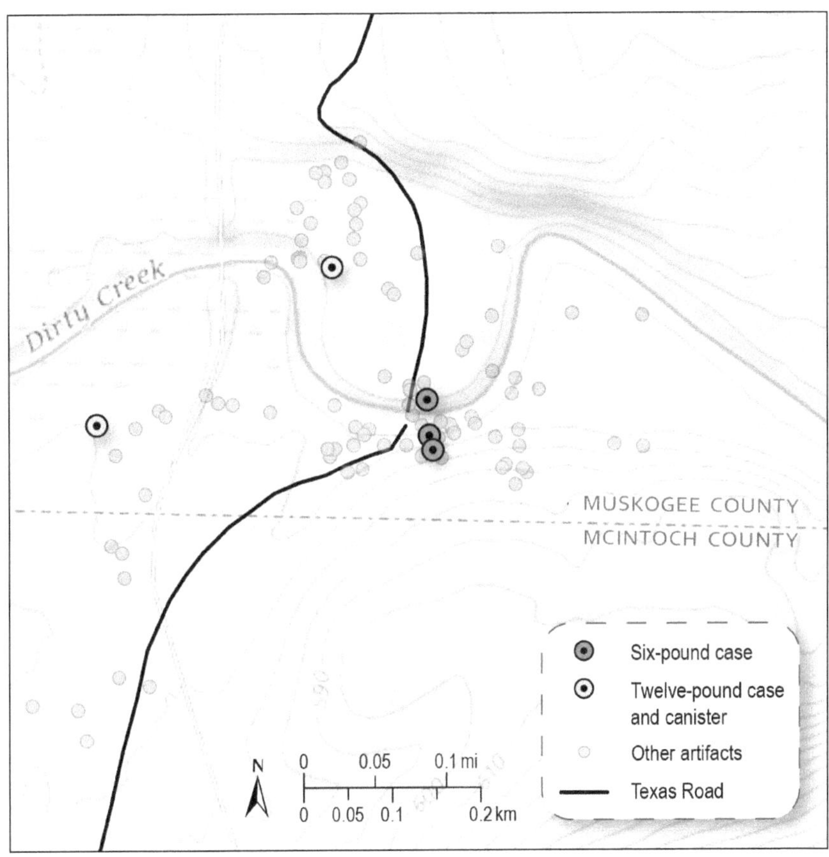

FIGURE 46. All artillery artifacts on the Elk Creek Engagement. Map by Katherine Sims.

Smith's battery on the Prairie Engagement, I can confidently say that Hopkins's Kansas Battery fired this six-pound case, possibly toward the bridge. While Hopkins does not say, I think he ordered his battery to follow the retreating rebels along the Texas Road and engaged the defenders of the bridge below. Britton appears to confirm this by saying that Hopkins's battery moved up to the former position of the rebel guns as they retreated. From that position, they shelled the rebels holding the bridge (Britton 1899, 122). Given the topography, I think the six-pound case was probably fired from a position a bit closer to the bluff edge or on the road as it sloped toward the creek bottom.

FIGURE 47. Post-battle stone bridge abutments as they appeared in 2001. Photo by William B. Lees.

These three fragments of six-pound case (and possible shrapnel) anchor the densest cluster of finds in the Elk Creek valley. This pattern is characterized by a prominent cluster of discoveries along and mainly south of Elk Creek at the bottom of a U-shaped bend.[4] Most believe the post–Civil War bridge was west of or upstream from the bridge that was present during the battle. LIDAR images of this area clearly show the scars of the post–Civil War bridge just west (upstream) from the cluster of six-pound case fragments. LIDAR also shows ravines on the south side of Elk Creek, both east and west of the probable location of the Civil War bridge.

William Rex Howland remembered his father's story of Confederate-allied Indians taking cover in a ravine west of the bridge during an attempt to hold back the US advance (Foreman 1937e). We found four dropped or discarded Minié bullets along the ravine to the east of where I think the bridge was located. These were three Enfield and one standard three-ring variety. The Enfields I most easily attribute to the Twentieth

Texas, but these could also have been carried by other regiments in either army.

Other artifacts in the vicinity of the exploded six-pound case are a complete padlock and parts of another, both found on the south side of Elk Creek. These padlocks are like those found in the Prairie Engagement during our survey and in the 1980s by Gary Moore. As I have previously speculated, they may relate to the Confederate cannon of Lee's Light Battery that memory says may have briefly halted at or deployed near the bridge. These finds support the conclusion that the bridge was in this location. Also in this vicinity are metal parts of a stopper from a military-issue canteen, a civilian button, a civilian iron spur, harmonica reed plates, and part of an inkwell. The inkwell has a cover engraved with a five-point star, which I speculate may signal an association with Texas and Texas troops. Farther afield but still in this same general area on the south side of Elk Creek is an unfired Adams revolver bullet that a soldier cut in half.

A fired Henry cartridge case was found in the cluster of artifacts near the bridge. We found two similar cases in the Prairie Engagement in locations suggesting they were carried by an officer with one of the US regiments. The cartridge case by Elk Creek supports an argument that one of the associated weapons may have also been engaged in fighting at the bridge. In addition, we found two rolled-copper arrowheads, one on each side of Elk Creek, near the bridge's probable location. One of these, located on the south side of the creek, has impact damage, while the other does not. Considering that one had impact damage, a possible explanation for these items at this location is that Confederate-allied Indians used the bow in defense of the bridge.

Fired small-arms ammunition is rare in this area. The only fired Minié ball from the Elk Creek valley is a standard three-ring variety found along the ravine east of the suspected Civil War–era bridge. In addition, there are two conical solid-base bullets, probably fired in army caliber revolvers near the bridge, and some spherical ammunition. Notable are three large-caliber smoothbore-fired balls (.65–.67 caliber) possibly fired from martial arms but also possibly from shotguns. One of these was at the suspected bridge and two along the ravine to the east. The large-caliber balls may have been fired toward rebel defenders at the bridge, although this is highly speculative. If so, these may have come from the large-caliber smoothbore muskets of the First Kansas soldiers who Lieutenant Colonel Bowles noted skirmished “with the enemy from the high bluffs” during their retreat (Bowles 1888, 450). Finally, a smattering of smaller balls, most having no evidence of having been fired, are in this area; perhaps some are from buck and ball fired by the First Kansas.

The preponderance of the artifacts in this concentration associated with the six-pound case and presumably also with the bridge were discarded or lost at the spot where they were found. They are clearly not overshot. Likewise, the fact that the fired small-arms ammunition fits nicely within the distribution of these discarded or lost items is compelling evidence that they are not overshot from the Prairie Engagement.

Another defined artifact cluster is on the north side of the creek surrounding the place where the Texas Road descends to the bottom from the bluff. Of note, four US military buttons are part of this cluster. A US general service button was just off the Texas Road as it entered the bottoms from the prairie above, and two obsolete buttons were relatively close by along the north bank of Elk Creek. One dates before 1821 and was made for the US Regiment of Riflemen. The other dates prior to the 1830s and is a greatcoat button marked with “US” and an eagle. I have suggested that these outdated buttons—manufactured decades before the Civil War—may have been worn by Confederate-allied Indians. Finally, a four-hole trouser button commonly used during the Civil War was on the south bank of Elk Creek. Also in this vicinity is part of a pocket watch.

In this cluster are also the single iron-ball canister and most of the spherical ball ammunition found along Elk Creek. Given the proximity of this lone canister ball to the bluff edge, and the fact that no other iron canister was found south of the Prairie Engagement, I believe that it may be overshot. The spherical ammunition includes a roughly equal number fired in rifles and smoothbores, and an equal number that showed no clear evidence of having been fired. Together these are in a diffuse band north and northwest of the probable bridge location. Most of these vary in size from .30 to .54 caliber and are most easily associated with common rifles and fowlers. If I were to hazard a guess, I would say this pattern reflects firing to the north from the south side of Elk Creek by rebel soldiers armed with civilian rifles and smoothbores. This may reflect William Rex

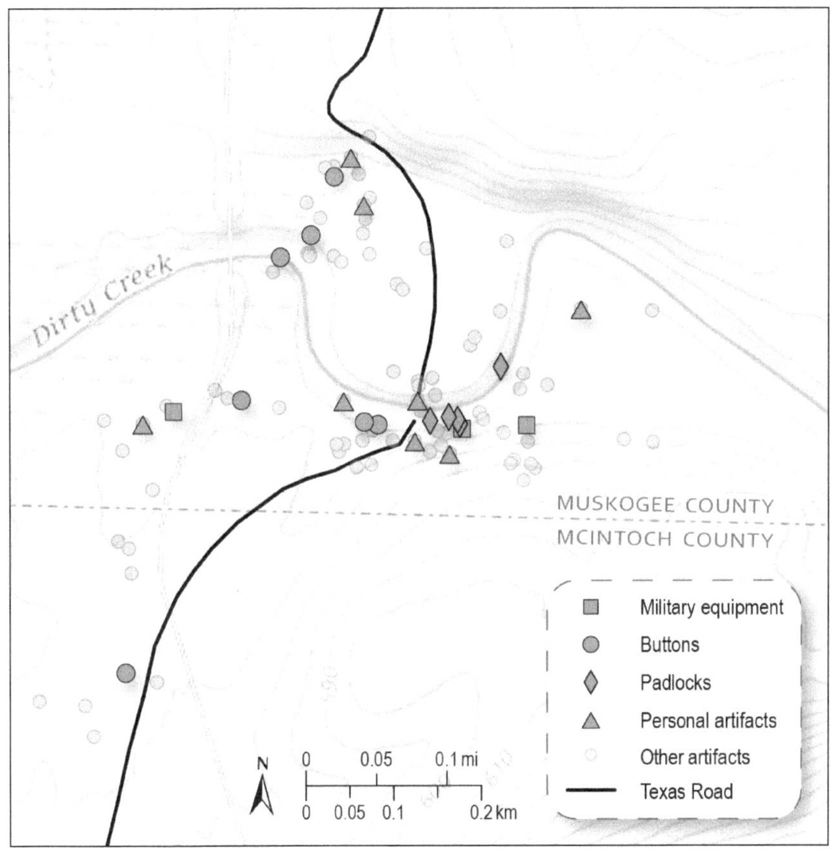

FIGURE 48. Buttons, equipment, personal items, and padlocks on the Elk Creek Engagement. Map by Katherine Sims.

Howland's account about his father's experience: "The Federals made several attempts to take the bridge, each time meeting the deadly fire of Major Howland's Indian riflemen" (Foreman 1937e).

Finally, there is a relatively thin scattering of artifacts that trends southwest along where the Texas Road must have traversed as it headed to Honey Springs; evidence for this road's exact route is elusive along this stretch. A heel plate like others often found in Civil War camps, a civilian button, and part of a pocket watch were found along an alignment that may reveal the route of the Texas Road as it snaked south to Honey

Springs. A single twelve-pound case fragment is on the western side of this scattering. A conical bullet probably fired in a navy caliber revolver, a solid-base conical bullet from an unknown breechloader, and a few spherical ball ammunition round out the finds. These finds are not dense or numerous, and they mainly show, I think, not only the route of rebel retreat but also that it was at this point lightly contested.

Given the distance of many of these finds from the prairie north of Elk Creek, the seeming association with a likely path of the Texas Road, and correlation with lost or discarded items, I think it unlikely that any of the finds are overshot. The exception may be the single twelve-pound case fragment found west (upstream) from the Texas Road's possible route and below the upper ford. Conversely, this case may have been fired by Hopkins's battery, which participated in the pursuit of the retreating rebels. If so, the target may have been rebels taking position or simply in retreat along the Texas Road as it curved southwestward from the bridge.

While the few civilian items (personal items, buttons, equipment) in the valley may relate to pre- or post-battle use of this area or rebel camps along the creek, their distribution on the landscape mirrors that of military-issue items easily associated with the battle. Further, these are consistent with things that would have been in use by Indian troops and probably Texans. Likewise, there can be no doubt that military buttons, equipment, and personal items found on both sides of Elk Creek below the prairie and roughly along the Texas Road may relate to rebel camps. It is equally likely that these items, especially those clustered around the exploded case and items along the Texas Road, are the residue of the fighting at the bridge and the retreat along the road; similar items were found along the rebel lines to the north.

The general correlation of these lost items with fired munitions further supports the conclusion that overshot is not an issue of serious concern for the interpretation of fired ammunition found in the valley. Ruling out overshot and considering the interpretation I have offered that show US attack on the bridge, rebel defense of Elk Creek, and the route of a poorly contested withdrawal along the Texas Road, I conclude also that the archaeological remains in the Elk Creek valley do provide useful information on the Battle of Honey Springs despite years of artifact mining by collectors.

Elk Creek Overview

Only about 13 percent of the artifacts found during our study were in the Elk Creek valley. I see no evidence that bullets or artillery shell fragments fired on the Prairie Engagement above fell in significant numbers along Elk Creek, probably due to the blocking nature of woods along the bluff. Some artifacts may relate to the camps in this area before the battle; artifacts other than ammunition are in fact over four times more common in the valley than in the engagements to the north and south. Due to the attraction of things found in campsites, metal detector hobbyists may have frequented this area more than others. Still, some clear patterns emerge from our finds that contribute to an understanding of what happened after the rebel withdrawal from the prairie and the final engagement a mile to the south. Despite years of collecting, the fight along Elk Creek is still visible archaeologically.

The numbers of artifacts that we found match my expectations from my reading of relevant memory. Union officer after-action reports tell us that not all units engaged on the prairie followed the retreating rebel army across Elk Creek and farther south, and most sent only several companies. Although William Howland's secondhand account talks of this being the most intense fight, Lieutenant Colonel Welch reports that by the time the left of the Twenty-Ninth Texas got to the creek no other rebel units remained, and he barely escaped US troops in hot pursuit. Other reports barely mention this action or say it was short and passing. The number of artifacts that we found probably relate more to the numbers of combatants engaged and the fighting's fleeting nature, no matter how intense it might have briefly been.

The artifacts from the Elk Creek valley thus present convincing evidence for the location of the bridge in use during the Battle of Honey Springs, its defense by rebel Indians positioned south of the creek, and its attack by US artillery from the bluffs above. Also revealed are artifacts that I believe are distributed along the route of the rebel retreat, along the Texas Road toward Honey Springs. Between the last artifact along this route and the first seen on Pumpkin Ridge is a stretch along the Texas Road of about one-third mile. The footprint of the battle shows that there is about one-half to three-quarters of a mile between fighting along Elk Creek and the resumption of intense fighting on Pumpkin Ridge overlooking the Confederate headquarters at Honey Springs. I now turn to that.

The Pumpkin Ridge Engagement

The memory-based narrative of the Battle of Honey Springs following the rebel retreat from their initial position north of Elk Creek seems to describe a running fight possibly as far as Honey Springs itself. The only contemporary illustration of the battle was published in *Frank Leslie's Illustrated Newspaper* (1863) and shows US cavalry charging Cooper's burning headquarters at Honey Springs.[5] When we embarked on our fieldwork, we fully expected to find evidence of fighting for the two miles between the Prairie Engagement and Honey Springs. As was made clear in the preceding chapter, what we found was entirely different: limited action along Elk Creek and an impressively large (at least in area) fight on high ground between Elk Creek and Honey Springs: the Pumpkin Ridge Engagement.

The map of battle-related artifacts found on the Pumpkin Ridge Engagement portrays an area of conflict stretching slightly over three-quarters of a mile along and two-thirds of a mile perpendicular to the Texas Road. A close study of the map shows a more complicated distribution; a light scatter of artifacts on the northern edge leads into a dense, somewhat oval band of artifacts perpendicular to and crossing the Texas Road. An isolated cell is a bit farther down the ridge toe to the east, and two other less dense cells are to the southwest. One of these is across a small intermittent tributary of Elk Creek from the main band of artifacts. The other is farther south along the Texas Road as it slopes downward toward Honey Springs. The southernmost is one-quarter mile from the springs at Honey Springs.

The oblong core of the Pumpkin Ridge Engagement is oriented almost perfectly northwest by southeast. While roughly perpendicular to the Texas Road, which is angling south-southwest at this point, the artifacts can be seen to better align with an expanse, or ridge, of unbroken high ground. The intermittent stream mentioned earlier defines the southern edge of the ridge on which most of the residue of fighting was found. Therefore, within the Pumpkin Ridge Engagement, while a core of intense conflict stretches along the Texas Road for one-third of a mile,

FIGURE 49. The Battle of Honey Springs (*Frank Leslie's Illustrated Newspaper* 1863). From the Lincoln Financial Foundation Collection, courtesy of the Indiana State Museum and Allen County (IN) Public Library.

the pattern of artifacts betrays broad clusters that may represent cells of close-in fighting or a cluster of troops who were the target of soldiers elsewhere on the field.

Memory suggests that the fighting in this area probably involved mounted troops on both sides, which may explain the various concentrations of artifacts. If these concentrations do originate from mounted combat, the fact that they are so well separated from each other may argue that the fight was brief. Movement of mounted troops over any prolonged length of time would, I expect, result in a more even distribution of conflict-related artifacts than what we found.

Turning to the artifacts, there is one unexploded six-pound cannonball (case or shell), two fragments of six-pound case, three fragments of twelve-pound case, and three Bormann time-fuse fragments. The unexploded cannonball is at the leading edge of the cluster defining the Pumpkin Ridge Engagement, some eight hundred yards north of the fragments. It is certainly associated with Hopkins's Kansas Battery. Its Bormann time fuse is punched for 2.5 seconds, indicating it was either

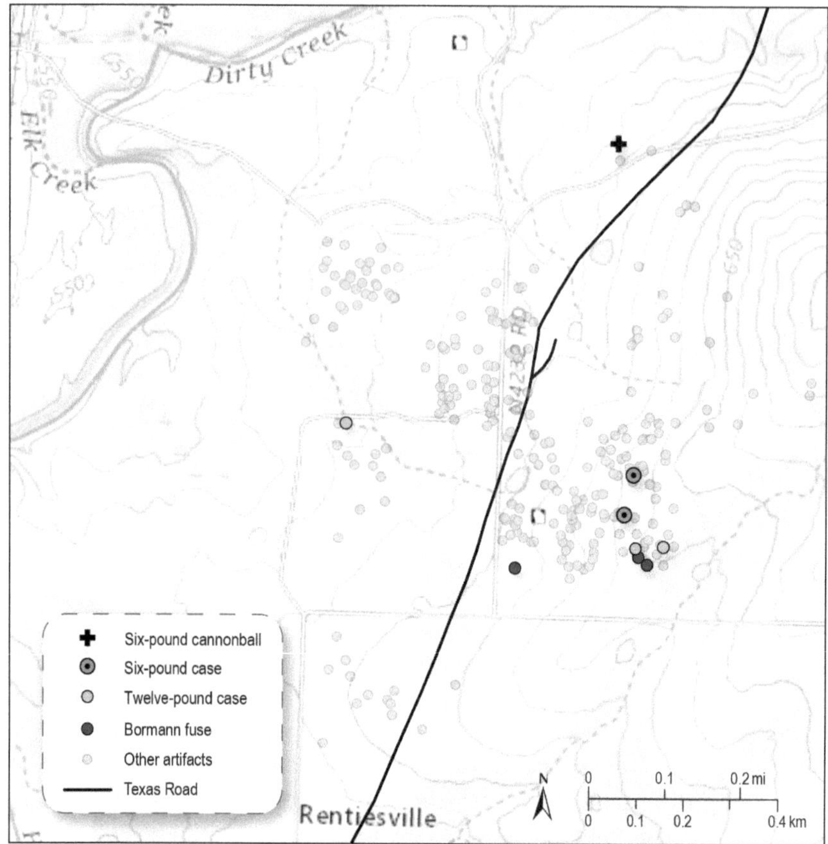

FIGURE 50. Artillery artifacts on the Pumpkin Ridge Engagement. Map by Katherine Sims.

fired and did not explode or was lost or discarded prior to being fired (possibly when the battery was moved forward). A cannonball punched for 2.5 seconds would probably travel about eight hundred yards before exploding, so it seems plausible that this marks the location of the battery that fired the exploded fragments. Conversely, if this US round was fired and did not explode, the battery firing it would have been deployed very close to Elk Creek and well out of range of Pumpkin Ridge. I believe the former explanation is the most plausible.

Except for one piece of twelve-pound case, the exploded fragments are all on the east side of the Texas Road at the crest of Pumpkin Ridge. Hopkins's US battery fired the six-pound and probably also the twelve-pound

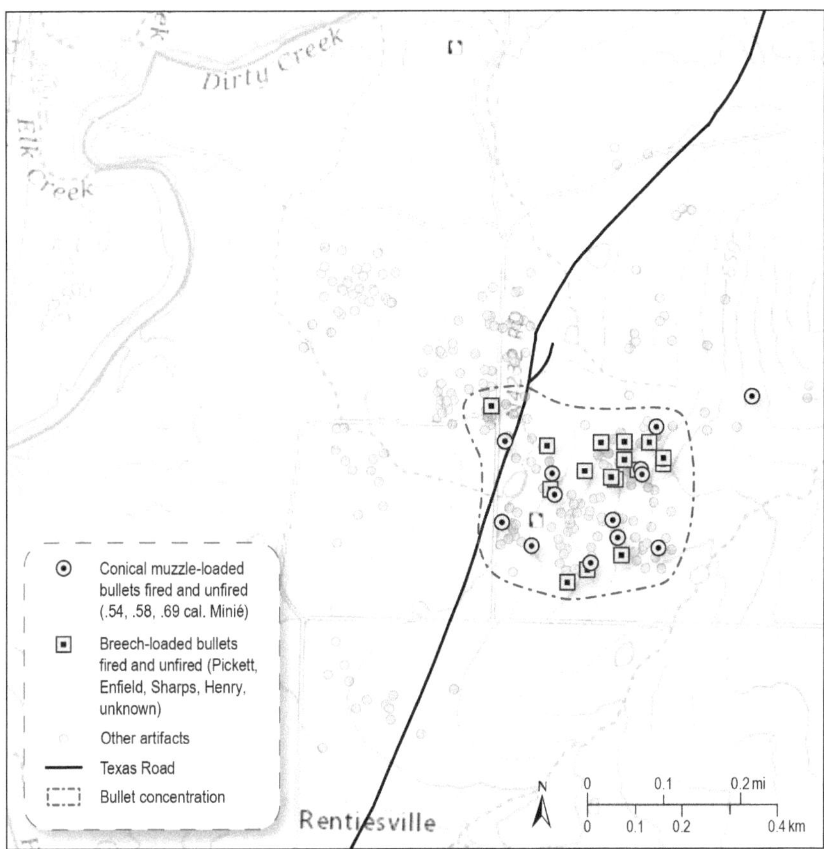

FIGURE 51. Breech-loaded bullets and Minié balls on the Pumpkin Ridge Engagement. Map by Katherine Sims.

case. Several large lead balls found on Pumpkin Ridge cluster around these case fragments and probably represent shrapnel. First described in chapter 2, one of those close to an exploded six-pound case appears to have struck a musket barrel (see figure 22). The cannonball fragments may relate to Hopkins's description (1888, 457), "Lieutenant Aduddell moving to the left of the road with one section, opened upon the enemy's cavalry, upon a hill beyond, causing them to fall back quite precipitately, the shell bursting in their immediate vicinity." The artillery artifacts once again clearly show the location of rebel positions (targets) at midday, on the last high ground before reaching Honey Springs. The evidence shows that a US battery directed fire at both sides of the road, but most was found to the east.

When I look at the hundreds of other artifacts found in the Pumpkin Ridge Engagement, the location of conical bullets (mainly Minié balls) fired in martial rifles and bullets fired in breech-loading or magazine small arms is striking. These twenty-nine bullets concentrate tightly along and east of the Texas Road in roughly the same location as the exploded cannonballs. They do not occur along the road in advance or to the south. One of these is a dropped Sharps bullet found on the Texas Road; the Sixth Kansas Cavalry carried Sharps carbines. Nine fired Sharps bullets are to the southeast of the lone unfired bullet at a distance of at least 242 yards; it is easy to speculate that Kansas troopers fired toward rebel targets from a direction suggested by the dropped specimen. That the fired specimens struck primarily with medium velocity (five) and high velocity (2) suggests that if the Kansas Cavalry had been on the road where indicated by the lone dropped round, they had moved southeast before firing. This thought of directional movement is, of course, highly speculative. Also, a single Henry bullet and an unknown breechloader bullet, both fired, are in the same area as those fired from Sharps rifles.

In precisely the same area east of the Texas Road are nineteen conical muzzleloader-fired bullets. Included here are Minié balls of standard (.54/.58) and .69 caliber, Enfield variety Minié balls (.58 caliber), and Picket bullets in variable caliber. Seven of these are .54/.58 caliber Minié balls that I have before attributed to the Second Colorado Infantry. One is dropped (.58 caliber), and the others hit with low to relatively high velocities (three low, one medium, two high). Another six are .69 caliber Minié balls, one of which is unfired and the others with impact velocity similar to the .54/.58 caliber variety. The only units I know were armed with rifled muskets in this caliber are the Second and Third Indian Home Guard and one company of the Second Colorado Infantry, although rebel units may have carried any number of similar weapons. Only two Enfield variety Minié balls were found here, including a dropped .58 caliber and a fired bullet that hit on its rear with medium to high velocity. While I have associated these with the Twentieth Texas on the Prairie Engagement, I will not do that here because of the low numbers involved and the fact that Enfield rifle-muskets were certainly in the hands of any of the units armed with various weapons, including Indian regiments on both sides. Finally, there are three fired Pickett-style bullets in variable calibers. I would associate these with Indian regiments on either side, although, of note, they are not found elsewhere on this or the Prairie or Elk Creek Engagements. As mentioned in chapter 2, Dean Thomas (D. Thomas 2003, 279) is hesitant to associate these with Civil War combat, but their presence in the Pumpkin Ridge Engagement is strong evidence of their use during this battle.

Nine conical revolver-fired bullets overlap the pattern of the other conical bullets along the Texas Road and to the east. Despite the small number, they are found on Pumpkin Ridge in greater frequency than anywhere else north or south of Elk Creek. One is unfired and is a .44 caliber Remington-style bullet. Others are intended for .40 caliber as well as army and navy caliber revolvers, some with styles like those made for Adams, Colt, Kerr, and Remington models. Two struck with high velocity, two with medium velocity, and the rest with low velocity. Speaking clearly to the use of revolvers in this area is a navy caliber revolver cylinder. This was found almost four hundred yards southwest of these bullets, across the intermittent stream from the heavily engaged ridge. A large number of Confederate and allied Indian troops may have carried revolvers. Fewer US troops, certainly including cavalry and officers and probably also some members of the Indian Home Guard, would have been so equipped. The use of revolvers probably indicates close fighting due to the limited range of these weapons.

The tight clustering of both the breechloading and conical muzzle-loading bullets within an area five hundred yards in diameter, and these not being found at all in the wider battlefield, shows a correlation that bespeaks a common purpose of those who fired them. To this can be added the revolver bullets and the artillery, both of which overlap significantly with the breechloading and conical muzzle-loading bullets. The question arises as to whether these conical bullets represent the concentrated fire of troops so armed as part of the larger fight on Pumpkin Ridge or instead should be considered separately from a larger dispersion of spherical ball ammunition. Is this one synchronous fight or perhaps two or more slightly separated in time?

As seen elsewhere, the spherical ball ammunition includes some with evidence of being fired in rifles and smoothbores (forty-five fired in rifles and thirty-six in smoothbores), and others having no evidence of being fired (ninety-six). The former were, I believe, fired in military muskets, trade or civilian common rifles, shotguns, and fowlers. The latter are probably also from these same weapons and were either dropped or more likely simply do not show the evidence of having been fired.

The rifle-fired balls are of variable caliber from .36 to as high as .57, but those above .49 caliber are rare. The balls fired in smoothbores, excepting buckshot, range from .32 to .67, with those above .49 being the exception. Buckshot ranges from .30 to .35 caliber; the majority show distinctive damage resulting from being tightly packed in a shotgun (as opposed to a buckshot in a buck-and-ball round). When the distribution of *only* spherical ball ammunition is examined for the Pumpkin Ridge Engagement, what looked like an oblong distribution spanning the Texas Road now appears as two distinct concentrations. Thus, along the ridge where most of the conflict artifacts are found, there are three equidistant clusters of spherical balls, with the same two across the intermittent tributary to the south and the same scatter of specimens along the northern, leading edge of this engagement. Density is not the same, however, with the clusters straddling the Texas Road containing more specimens than are found elsewhere.

This is most striking for the balls fired in smoothbores, with most of these being to the east of the Texas Road and overlaying the aforementioned concentration of artillery and conical bullets. The larger numbers of smoothbore-fired balls here are the result of five in the .65 to .67 caliber range, which were probably fired in martial smoothbores such as those carried by the First Kansas Colored Infantry or from shotguns such as were probably carried by Gillette's Texans. Regardless, these large-caliber balls are found nowhere else on Pumpkin Ridge; the correlation with the conical bullets is both striking and significant.

Balls identified as buckshot fired in shotguns are found only in the clusters crossing the ridge and not in those to the south across the tributary stream. Other balls of this size with no clear evidence of use mimic and amplify (because of their larger numbers) the pattern of the shotgun-fired balls. The frequency of these shotgun-fired balls in the fighting along Pumpkin Ridge confirms the importance of these weapons at Honey Springs. While not surprising, this is an important outcome of this research and sets this battle apart from those fought in the eastern theaters at this same time. These shotguns were most likely in the hands of Gillette's Confederate cavalry.

When the other balls without evidence of firing are plotted, most are seen to occur in the concentrations that span the Texas Road although with more connectedness in between. While these concentrations contain the most specimens, that at the ridge toe to the west shows significant numbers. What is striking is that all the balls above .60 caliber, which are possibly artillery shrapnel, are found to either side of the Texas Road, with most in the concentration to the east. While this seems compelling evidence that these may be shrapnel, they also correlate with the distribution of balls of this size clearly fired from smoothbores. Either way, these larger balls, both with and without evidence of firing, correlate very strongly with the artillery and conical bullets and not with the larger spread of spherical balls across the Pumpkin Ridge Engagement.

It is important to note five rolled-copper arrowheads found along the Texas Road near but a bit west of the concentration of artillery, conical bullets, and large-caliber smoothbore-fired spherical ammunition. Two of these arrowheads show distinctive evidence of impact. I do not believe it to be a random coincidence that these occur at this location, given they join others found at the center of action on the rebel line in the Prairie Engagement and at the probable bridge location at Elk Creek.

Artifacts other than fired and dropped ammunition help to flesh out the Pumpkin Ridge Engagement. On the northern edge of this area are two buttons, a US Navy button and a US dragoon button. I remain skeptical that the navy button is related to the battle, partly because its possible date of manufacture extends well beyond the Civil War (only the front is present). Still, as I have said earlier, it is as plausible as other types of civilian and obsolete military buttons that we have found. The dragoon button was obsolete before the war but could have been in use on either a US or rebel uniform.

Along the ridge, in the dense concentration to the east of the Texas Road, are a civilian button and a US general service button. Within the southernmost cluster, across the intermittent tributary, is a military issue tin trouser button and a civilian trouser button. The civilian button and the navy button (if of Civil War use) are most likely associated with Indian troops or Texans, and the US buttons are probably best explained by the presence of federal troops.

Also on the ridge are two harness buckles and one stirrup/spur buckle, which are the only items falling into the equipment category. In terms of personal possessions, we found a fragment of a harmonica reed plate and part of a pocket watch in advance of the ridge. A carved lead item, another harmonica reed plate, and a wedding band were found relatively close together near the Texas Road.

While some of these artifacts are more closely associated with Civil War combat than others, their discovery in direct correlation with concentrations of battle-related artifacts is compelling evidence that they are also so associated. As items that identify locations of individuals at some point they complement dropped ammunition to anchor actions to the locations of people. All are relatively close to the Texas Road, and most are along the road as it crosses the most intense area of fighting across Pumpkin Ridge. Prior to fighting on Pumpkin Ridge, of course, retreating rebel soldiers used the Texas Road as they headed to Honey Springs and beyond.

Whether or not the fighting on Pumpkin Ridge seems more intense because it represents the superposition of two or more clashes during the rebel retreat or was just the focal point of a single action remains subject to speculation. I will revisit this later, but the question is whether it is appropriate to put some time—if only a moment—between the US attack on Gillette's Texans and the fight between US troops and Tandy Walker's Choctaws and Chickasaws as they returned from their reconnaissance-in-force to the east.

Pumpkin Ridge Overview

More than anything else, our finds at the Pumpkin Ridge Engagement help to clarify the nature of the larger Battle of Honey Springs. This finding is reflected in the on-site interpretation there today. After a clear break from the fighting at Elk Creek, this location stands out as a major and final engagement on July 17, 1863. Although this action is certainly mentioned in accounts of the day written from memory, the archaeology has made clear that Honey Springs was not a continuous running fight and that the battle was over when the US troops reached Cooper's burning headquarters at Honey Springs. While the accuracy of the illustration published in *Frank Leslie's Illustrated Newspaper* has been questioned, I think it is probable that the Sixth Kansas Cavalry, whose presence in the Pumpkin Ridge fight is almost certain, were the first US troops to reach the headquarters. This lithograph is a fair depiction of their appearance at Honey Springs, regardless of whether they charged the burning Confederate depot.

In defining this last fight, the evidence from artillery, although based on only a few finds, provides striking evidence for a rebel position straddling the Texas Road. To the east of the Texas Road fired and a few dropped bullets from martial rifle-muskets and breech-loading carbines correlate with exploded cannonballs and further set this area apart. Large-caliber spherical balls possibly fired in martial smoothbores are also found here almost exclusively. Coupled with the artillery, this small-arms ammunition is most easily associated with the US Sixth Kansas Cavalry and the Second Colorado Infantry of Phillips's brigade. The First Indian Home Guard was also part of Phillips's brigade, but their arms were predominately common rifles firing spherical ball ammunition.

This evidence is, of course, within a broader distribution of other artifacts in the Pumpkin Ridge Engagement. Beyond this concentration most ammunition are spherical balls fired in small arms or having no evidence of use. Most of these balls were probably fired in or intended for use in rifles and smoothbores of variable caliber that are best associated with use by US or rebel Indian regiments. Shotguns firing buckshot and possibly large-caliber balls are indicated in the main concentration along the ridge, possibly associated with Texans, which, based on memory, would be Gillette's troops.

Overall, analysis of the Pumpkin Ridge Engagement shows a pattern of fighting distinctly different from that seen in the Prairie Engagement. Although conflict artifacts are spread over a large area, they are also concentrated in multiple clusters of spherical balls with an overlay of artillery and conical bullets. The nonlinear pattern of fighting is distinct from that observed in the Prairie Engagement and to me seems best explained by an engagement of mounted adversaries that probably was of limited duration. This is entirely consistent with memory. The main question that has emerged from this analysis concerns the relationship between the pattern of spherical balls and the smaller pattern of artillery, conical bullets, and large-caliber rounds fired in smoothbores. Do these distinct but overlapping patterns reflect a synchronous if complex single action, or might they possibly represent different, asynchronous actions, even if separated by only a moment?

Summary of the Findings

The archaeological work that we conducted in the 1990s and the analysis presented so far in this book have resulted in the identification of distinct locales of conflict in the OHS's Honey Springs Battlefield. In chapter 2 I broke the conflicts into areas that I named the Prairie, Elk Creek, and Pumpkin Ridge Engagements. On reflection of the data, these monikers have validity, but the reality is at least the Prairie and Pumpkin Ridge Engagements may be more complicated. In the Prairie Engagement is evidence of conflict that must have occurred before the general fighting began at 10:00 a.m. but is poorly recorded or not recorded in memory. On Pumpkin Ridge the patterns of artifacts suggest that there may have been overlapping engagements here as well, but here these are consistent with memory.

By analyzing the placement and pattern of artifacts on the Prairie Engagement, I have confidently located the line formed by Confederates and Confederate-allied Indians on the morning of July 17, 1863. Based on this and the patterns of a variety of artifacts, the valley of a small intermittent stream at the north end of the state battlefield park is presented as the only viable candidate for the location of the US bivouac. Virtually all the battlefield residue is between this point and the confirmed location of the rebel line, and the archaeological evidence points to the deployment of Union forces into a line of battle roughly halfway between. The distances between these points are as described by Major General Blunt in his after-action report.

Archaeology revealed a few surprises. There is tantalizing evidence from fired bullets from breech-loading and magazine carbines and some conical rifle-musket bullets of fighting in the northern half of the Prairie Engagement that may have occurred separate from, and prior to the general engagement that began about 10:00 a.m. The evidence suggests that the US cavalry and possibly the Second Colorado Infantry (and possibly also the First Indian) may have been involved against unknown rebel soldiers. Also, the extent of fighting in the Prairie Engagement was much less than implied by Blunt's proclamation that rebel troops were lined up for a mile and a half. While there may be some truth to this, the core fighting in the area we surveyed was limited to a front of about one-third of a mile. Lesser engagement may have characterized the rebel right and left flanks; we found possible evidence of this in a small scatter of artifacts to the west. Within the core area of fighting, which stretches for a half-mile along the Texas Road, I see an unsurprising imbalance in the use of artillery. While it is also unsurprising that the Union batteries focused their attention on the rebel center at the Texas Road, the location of the single rebel battery, it was surprising that they also focused on the rebel right to the exclusion of the left.

Evidence from small arms complements that from artillery. Along the rebel line, from the center and down the line to the east is evidence of fighting after the US closed to within one hundred yards or less following the cessation of the artillery bombardment. Evidence of US fire into the rebel lines by rifle-muskets, probably of the First Colorado, and muskets of the First Kansas Colored Infantry is compelling. Bullets fired by the Twentieth Texas from their Enfield rifle-muskets are found far north of their intended targets where they fell to the ground after losing velocity, supporting accounts that the rebels fired high. Spherical ball and buck-shot probably fired by the Twenty-Ninth Texas from their shotguns is found closer to their intended targets but probably only due to the lesser range of these weapons.

Although memory and scholars give much attention to the fighting of the First Kansas at Honey Springs, accounts from the Second Colorado and First Indian Home Guard testify to the intensity of the fight to the east of the Texas Road. A brief note in the Leavenworth *Daily Conservative* (1863c) reported, “We learn from a reliable source that the First Indian and Second Colorado did the heaviest part of the fighting at Honey Springs. The First Colored did all that was required of them, but their position was such that less fighting devolved upon them than upon the two regiments named above.” I think the litter of bullets along the rebel center and right and to the front reflects this memory, although this does not diminish the work of the First Kansas.

The artifacts found in the Elk Creek valley relate directly to the fighting in this area; I believe only a few may be overshot from the battle on the prairie above. While some of the personal and other non-martial items may relate to rebel camps, bullets and artillery ammunition reflect the fighting of July 17. The location of fragments of six-pound case reveal, I believe, the location of the Civil War–era bridge across the creek. Overall, I believe the evidence shows a lopsided contest between artillery and

Confederate-allied Indians. The artillery was certainly Hopkins's Kansas Battery firing south from the bluffs toward the bridge. There is evidence that ravines on either side of the bridge were involved, as described in memory, and that rebels fired toward the bluffs probably from positions south of Elk Creek. However, the evidence shows that the fighting in this area was brief and that it involved small numbers, probably from only a few of the units engaged earlier on the prairie.

Perhaps the most unexpected finding during our field survey was between Elk Creek and Honey Springs. We expected to see a continuous running fight but knew that the rebels made at least one concerted attempt to slow the advance of the pursuing US troops. We found a single, large area of conflict, ideally situated on the only high ground between Elk Creek and Honey Springs. Detailed analysis suggested a possibly more complex story. While memory of this fight exists, primarily in after-action reports, it is vague and provides few clues of the Union participants, the nature of the fight, and location. As described in memory, US artillery fired on this high ground, perhaps when Gillette's squadron stood in front of the advancing US troops. The patterns of found artifacts show the greatest concentration along a low ridge crossing the Texas Road, but these are discontinuous and comprise multiple cells in the general area of engagement. Exploded cannonballs, bullets from Sixth Kansas Cavalry carbines, and Minié balls fired by weapons known to have been common in the Second Colorado Infantry were found clustered in a small area adjacent to and east of the Texas Road on the point of highest ground between Elk Creek and Honey Springs. This seems to attest to the importance of Phillips's brigade (the US left) in pursuing the rebels. Taken separately, the spherical ball ammunition, including rifle and smoothbore-fired balls and balls that have no evidence of use, show a pattern of five cells in the area of engagement. Three of these are along the ridge, and two are farther south across an intermittent tributary. The densest cells are two that bridge the Texas Road and are more connected than not; the one to the east of the road is overlapped by the concentration of cannonball fragments and conical bullets for carbines and rifle-muskets. For those with evidence of having been fired, the balls were from common rifles and smoothbores (shotguns and fowlers) of variable calibers, probably also including some pistols and revolvers. Of note, buckshot fired in shotguns, almost certainly in the hands of Texans, was only found along the ridge.

Beyond identifying the last of the areas of general conflict that comprise the Battle of Honey Springs, research on the Pumpkin Ridge Engagement raises some important questions. Although occupying the same space, the distribution of artillery and conical bullets overlies only a small part of the larger concentration of artifacts. This larger concentration is really five cells of spherical ball ammunition, probably from weapons commonly used by rebel Indian regiments and Indian Home Guard. Even though they overlap, do these two patterns result from a singular action, or were there two actions slightly separated in time and differing by troops engaged? Memory, although vague, is entirely consistent with the latter.

Analysis of the artifact patterns between and within the Prairie, Elk Creek, and Pumpkin Ridge Engagements has provided insight into questions outlined at the beginning of this chapter. Still, unexpected findings have posed new questions that require additional consideration. First, however, I will use the specific footprint of the Battle of Honey Springs as revealed by archaeology to evaluate the engaged landscape using KOCOA terrain analysis. Ultimately this will all lead to consideration of the final question: why was Brigadier General Cooper defeated?

CHAPTER FIVE

Understanding the Terrain of Conflict

I USED THE CONCEPT of "battlespace" in chapter 2 to frame the competing interests of US major general Blunt and Confederate brigadier general Steele in late June and early July 1863. Blunt's central focus was protecting the US interests at Fort Gibson and the Indian Territory north of the Arkansas River. Steele's was, conversely, driving the US garrison out of Fort Gibson and the Indian Territory, and possibly invading Kansas. Thus, the mutual antagonists were simultaneously projecting force into the area by, in Blunt's case, supplying, fortifying, and reinforcing Fort Gibson and, in Steele's case, concentrating troops at Honey Springs and Fayetteville, Arkansas, able to attack the US supply route and the fort itself. Eventually Steele attempted to focus all his forces at Honey Springs to facilitate an all-out attack on Fort Gibson. This posturing was, of course, conflict involving numerous smaller armed clashes, but we also know that it led to a focused, brutal armed confrontation known as the Battle of Honey Springs.

This battlespace that I described was defined by a landscape, on the edge of the Great Plains, with a long history of cultural use. The Five Civilized Tribes' use of this area after resettlement in the early nineteenth century is especially pertinent to our story. Seen in a larger narrative of the Civil War, the Battle of Honey Springs appears as part of a contest between warring sections of the United States. Still, it occurred on the sovereign lands of another nation and included opposing Indian combatants who were neither US residents nor citizens. The motives of the Indian Nations for engaging in battle at Honey Springs had origins that included decades-long tensions from a forced and internally contested removal. Those Kansas refugees who enrolled in the US Indian Home Guard also wanted to be able to return their families to homes in the

Indian Territory. At the same time, those fighting as allies of the Confederacy fought to uphold the complicated reasons behind these alliances. Motives of African American participants included freedom from enslavement and the end to the institution of slavery itself. For some of the formerly enslaved, their homes were in the Indian Territory. Those who wished to return probably wanted to do so with citizenship rights in the Indian Nations where they had been enslaved.

Motives for the Confederacy included protecting Texas and Arkansas without using White troops in demand elsewhere; preservation of southern institutions, particularly slavery; and access to resources such as salt, beef, and produce. Motives of the United States were self-serving in seeking a solution to a refugee crisis in Kansas and protecting the free state's southern border. Although Kansas had rejected slavery from its formation at the end of the first iteration of the Civil War (Bleeding Kansas), by spring of 1863 the US national narrative had also shifted to include emancipation along with preservation of the Union as overarching goals. In the rearview mirror of history, the US interest was part of a contest for expansion into, and federal control of, the American West that was ultimately concluded during the "Greater Reconstruction" that followed the war.

As we consider the terrain of the Battle of Honey Springs, we must concurrently consider the complex cultural mosaic of the Indian Territory and the Indian, Black, White, and Hispanic participants and where, how, and why they fought. Since the terrain is the common denominator for both sides in the Battle of Honey Springs, the use of the KOCOA approach to terrain analysis will tie together several important threads implied or developed throughout this book. While I used battlespace on a reasonably broad scale to balance the competing US and rebel interests in controlling the same territory, KOCOA terrain analysis is the most valuable and appropriate tool for bringing together memory, landscape, and archaeology when looking at our much smaller study area.

KOCOA was not developed for use in historical or archaeological study but rather as a military training tool "to inform commanders and junior leaders about their area of concern for them to make informed decisions on their courses of action in battle" (D. Scott et al. 2019, 35). Used in reverse, it is a tool that can help identify battlefields and their critical components by using clues preserved in memory to identify critical locations on the modern landscape. In some cases, memory is sufficiently robust to place events on the contemporary landscape accurately. In many cases, however, memory is insufficient to establish events on the landscape with confidence and can lead to widely contradictory and possibly inaccurate interpretations of where and how things transpired. In cases where memory is lacking or vague, and even where it appears sufficiently detailed, archaeology provides a new line of evidence whose link to the landscape is undeniable.

> The importance of the archaeological or physical record is not its richness but that it is an independent line of evidence that tells a different story or enhances the documentary record and oral tradition. The value of archaeological research and the recovery and documentation of physical evidence of past conflict lies not in the artifacts alone but in the context in which they are found. Historical documents and oral testimony are accounts derived from human memory and can contain intentional and unintentional bias. The archaeological record has its own bias, one of preservation, not one of intent. The archaeological record of a conflict is not dependent on human memory; rather it is the debris and evidence left behind by violent events. It is there and recoverable. The archaeological record cannot speak for itself, but it is interpretable. This independent line of evidence can be recovered, recorded, and interpreted. Its real power is that it can be used to correlate, corroborate, or contrast documentary sources or oral testimony to determine the best fit or the accuracies of various information sources. (D. Scott and McFeaters 2011, 121)

Archaeologists use the five attributes of KOCOA terrain analysis to organize a backward-facing discussion of a battlefield landscape. "Key Terrain" refers to "ground that must be controlled to accomplish the mission" or provide a significant advantage. "Observations and Fields of Fire" are the "ability to see friendly and enemy forces." Fields of fire are "areas that weapons cover/can fire on efficiently." Although both rely on observation, certain fields of fire could include some areas concealed from direct observation (consider use of mortars during the Civil War). "Cover and Concealment" are "protection from enemy fire, observation, and surveillance" and, of course, correlate with "Observations and Fields of Fire." Concealment prevents or makes observation difficult, but cover may also protect from fire. Of course, cover generally provides concealment as well. "Obstacles" are "natural or human-made landscape features that prevent, impede, or divert movement." An obstacle may give an advantage or a disadvantage depending on objective. An "Avenue of Approach and Withdrawal" is, ideally, a "relatively unobstructed ground route that leads to and/or away from an objective or key terrain and does not come under enemy fire." Although "Avenues of Approach" are sometimes constructed or improved during a campaign, they often take advantage of existing roads and waterways (Department of the Navy 1990; McKinnon, Roth, and Carrell 2020, 9).

In chapter 1, I reviewed memory of the Battle of Honey Springs that included accounts written near the date of the battle and others set down many years later. Some are secondhand accounts committed to paper after the storyteller-witness had passed. Unfortunately, references to what could be considered key landscape and cultural features are exceedingly rare and often without the specificity necessary to relocate them on the modern landscape or even, in some cases, to understand what was being observed. In other cases, memory recalls a cultural feature that was once part of the visible landscape but that has since vanished.

In general, descriptions of Honey Springs terrain based on participant memory can rarely be used to identify its location today. Regarding the Prairie Engagement, landscape features mentioned in US reports are the Texas Road, site of the US bivouac, edge of timber north of Elk Creek, hill on which rebels were visible, erosional ditch, and cornfield. The Texas Road is key terrain, and its route is sporadically visible throughout our study area. The edge of timber is another critical terrain feature for this fight because this is the position of the rebel line and because Major General Blunt relates this feature to the location of his bivouac and his initial line of battle. Unfortunately, the only record of where the woods gave way to prairie postdates the battle by almost thirty-five years. Still, the archaeological evidence discussed in the preceding chapter establishes where the rebel line crossed the Texas Road, which at the same time places the edge of the timber in 1863. This is as much as one-quarter mile south of where it was mapped in 1898.

Insight on key terrain from Confederate brigadier general Cooper's after-action report is disappointing by what is not said. Of significance, he states, "The nature of the ground precluded the possibility of personally observing all the movements of our troops and the conduct of the men and officers" (D. Cooper 1888, 461). It simply seems that he was not an intimate witness to the fighting or, rather, that he was not inclined to spell out the details of his defeat. Unfortunately, with one exception, officer reports that he used to compile his summary are not preserved if they ever existed; his report mentions only waiting to receive an accurate record of dead and wounded. More informative is Cooper's General Orders No. 25, which gives insight into what he saw as important in terms of landscape. Still, even this is less than specific. He clearly identified the timber north of Elk Creek as essential to control (key terrain). He was also aware of the importance of quickly deploying troops camped along Elk Creek to guard against enemy attacks along the branches of the Texas Road leading to multiple fords. He was concerned about enemy use of "creeks, bayous, and wooded ways" as routes to infiltrate the creek bottoms and saw their value for the movement of his troops northward into battle. He ordered work be done to clear pathways for the movement of his troops along Elk Creek and between the various rebel camps along the creek and the timber on the north side (Heiston 1888, 461–62).

Welch's report on the action of the Twenty-Ninth Texas talks about dismounting "under cover of the timber" and proceeding "across the skirt of timber into the prairie." Here he said, "The whole space in front of us was covered with small bushes, which concealed our positions, and almost masked the approach of the enemy" (Welch 1863). Another account of the Twenty-Ninth talks of them being pushed back into a clearing. "[Here] the enemy had the advantage of the cover of Sassafras bushes before our line, and our men then had *no* cover" (*Standard* 1863a, 1, italics in source).

Regarding the site of the US bivouac, Blunt (1888g, 447) says this was "behind a little ridge, about one-half mile from the enemy's line" and Schaurte (1888, 451) of the Second Indian Home Guard only that it was "to the north of and near Elk Creek timber." The small stream valley about a half-mile north of the archaeologically verified rebel center on the Texas Road matches Blunt's estimate. The residue of the battle stretches up to and slightly beyond this valley and indicates that Blunt's initial deployment of troops into line was halfway between this stream and the rebel line. Since there are no other options farther north along the Texas Road, this valley emerges as the only viable option for where US troops sheltered before the battle.

Captain Smith of the Second Kansas Battery, from a vantage just west of the Texas Road, mentions firing on "the rebel position on the hill" and that the rebels then retreated "in the direction of a small cornfield" in his "immediate front" (E. A. Smith 1888, 454). The prairie does rise east of where Smith's Second Kansas Battery was then posted, and this may be what he referred to as a hill, though it does not otherwise seem to be one. Brigadier General Cooper's after-action report mentions viewing the approaching federals from "the high prairie," which may also refer to the high ground along the right wing of his troop line (D. Cooper 1888, 459).

The cornfield Smith mentioned is probably the same referenced by Lieutenant Colonel Bowles of the First Kansas when he says that his right pressed the enemy back to a cornfield where they " broke and fled in confusion" (Bowles 1888, 450). A report in the *Delphi (IN) Journal* says, "[Shortly after sunrise,] our advance proceeded to feel the enemy, whom they found very strongly posted in the brush and cornfields, behind rocks and fences" (W. H. S. 1863, 1). Finally, Captain Stevens of the Third Wisconsin Cavalry on the right flank of the Union line reported that his mountain howitzers "opened upon the enemy, posted behind a rail fence, in the edge of a corn field" (Stevens 1888, 453). Several different witnesses thus report a cornfield in their reports of the fighting north of Elk Creek. Whether these reports are of one or more fields, all seem to point to their location being at or west of the Texas Road. Although the map of the battlefield published by Wiley Britton (1899, 113) is not to scale and is not without issue, he does show a field behind the Twentieth Texas and immediately west of the Texas Road (see figure 12). Britton also mentions "an impassable ditch or washout" (121) encountered by the right of the Second Colorado Infantry as they advanced toward the rebel line. However, no other mention is made of this seemingly important feature, and no evidence of one was noted during fieldwork or, more recently, by examining LIDAR (3DEP) images of this area.

Reports of fighting at Elk Creek and along the Texas Road to the south are also limited and highly vague. Both Blunt and Cooper mention fighting at the Texas Road bridge over Elk Creek (Blunt 1888g, 448; D. Cooper 1888, 459). Lieutenant Colonel Welch of the Twenty-Ninth Texas only remembered that his regiment fell back and made a stand on

Elk Creek or a branch, where they found they were alone and facing the enemy "passing rapidly to [their] rear, on the right" (Welch 1863, 2). Lieutenant Colonel Bowles of the First Kansas Colored Infantry noted that they "advanced in line for a distance of 3 miles, skirmishing occasionally with the enemy from the high bluffs in front and to the left." It is unclear exactly what the "high bluffs" refer to, but south of Elk Creek this would refer to some part of Pumpkin Ridge (Bowles 1888, 450). Major Smith of the Second Colorado noted only, "We crossed the stream [Elk Creek], and discovered the enemy on a hill, or rise of ground in the advance" (J. N. Smith 1888, 455). Captain Hopkins of Hopkins's Kansas Battery described pursuing the retreating rebels along the Texas Road and how, from a position on the prairie beyond Elk Creek, they "opened upon the enemy's cavalry, upon a hill beyond" (Hopkins 1888, 456). Hopkins then described moving forward one-quarter mile and firing on advancing cavalry. Brigadier General Cooper may have also described this when he wrote that Walker's Choctaws and Chickasaws charged "the enemy, who had . . . planted a battery upon a timbered ridge about 1,000 yards north of Honey Springs" (D. Cooper 1888, 460).

Hopkins's reference to the "enemy's cavalry, upon a hill beyond" seems to describe a rebel line in the Prairie Engagement (possibly established by Gillette's squadron). Hopkins moved forward a quarter-mile, possibly occupying Gillette's position, from where he fired on approaching rebel cavalry, possibly Walker's First Choctaw and Chickasaw Regiment. Hopkins's second position was perhaps what Cooper referred to as being one thousand yards north of Honey Springs.

Finally, Blunt mentioned that the Confederate commissary buildings "were 2 miles south of where the battle commenced" (Blunt 1888g, 448). Brigadier General Cooper, of course, also mentioned his headquarters and especially its abandonment and destruction. He further underscored the importance of using the Briartown Road rather than the Texas Road as his retreat route to deceive his enemy (D. Cooper 1888, 460). From Honey Springs, the Texas Road headed southwest toward North Fork Town, while the road to Briartown headed to the southeast in the direction of expected Confederate reinforcements. Cooper wrote his report from his new headquarters on Imochiah Creek, near its confluence with the Canadian River, in the vicinity of Briartown.

FIGURE 52. Prairie along the Texas Road at north end of the battlefield in 2019. This probably resembles conditions in 1863. Photo by William B. Lees.

KOCOA and Honey Springs

Although KOCOA as an acronym starts with "Key Terrain," its ending, "Avenues of Approach," is central to understanding terrain because of the importance of the Texas Road. Swales of the Texas Road also are visible on the modern landscape, and they comprise one of the few terrain features noted in memory that is clearly evident today. As I reviewed in the introduction, this road was established in a corridor of open prairie bordering the western edge of the Ozark and Ouachita uplifts. The prairie represented a clear and relatively uninterrupted route between Honey Springs and the Arkansas River near Fort Gibson. As was once typical, a road's name described where it was headed, which, of course, is relative. Cooper thus referred to what I am calling the Texas Road as the Gibson Road. He recognized its strategic importance and had placed pickets at fords on the Arkansas River to protect against federal passage to the south. Concerning Cooper's defense of Honey Springs, the Texas Road was first crucial for allowing his troops to move freely to the north and, significantly, where he had to stop any federal advance toward his headquarters.

TABLE 7. Discussion of KOCOA elements for the Prairie Engagement

Key Terrain	High ground on bluffs on north side of Elk Creek and on either side of the Texas Road
Observations and Fields of Fire	From their position north of Elk Creek, the rebels probably had relatively unobstructed observation north along the Texas Road at least to the small valley used by the US troops for bivouac and possibly for a considerable distance beyond. Their field of fire from this position would have been similarly open and would have included the valley (bivouac) by use of explosive artillery ammunition such as case and shell. From their position of bivouac a half-mile north of the rebel lines, the federals would have had limited observations and fields of fire until they moved south out of the valley onto the prairie. When they were able to observe the rebel position, they found them concealed in brush that probably provided only minimal cover.
Cover and Concealment	Wooded area north of Elk Creek was used by rebels to conceal their defensive line from observation. This provided minimal cover, and there is no indication that any effort was made to construct works for cover. Intermittent tributary valley a half-mile north of rebel lines was used by US troops for bivouac, providing both concealment from observation and cover from small arms.
Obstacles	The woods in which the rebels were posted, along with some rocks and rail fences along their line, were an obstacle for the US force, not only in terms of dislodging and engaging the rebels but also in their pursuit if they were successful.
Avenues of Approach and Withdrawal	The Texas Road as it crossed the prairie toward the Elk Creek crossings was the avenue of approach for the US army and avenue for withdrawal if they were unsuccessful in defeating the rebels.

Brigadier General Cooper's General Orders No. 25 identified the "timber on the north side" of Elk Creek as key terrain, although he did not use this term (Heiston 1888, 462). Cooper talked in his after-action report about terrain being a challenge for his observation and management of the battle. However, he did not discuss it in any detail and instead used vegetation as his primary descriptor. Therefore, it is not apparent from these documents where his battle line was meant to be or where it was ultimately established. Still, the terrain provides many clues as to where a threat from the north should be defended. For some of the same reasons that the Texas Road crosses Elk Creek where it does, the landscape presents an obstacle to an advancing army.

Elk Creek is itself a formidable obstacle, with steep bluffs in some areas. It is approached along the main road and via roads to several fords above and below. On the south side of the creek and to the east are Pumpkin Ridge and the Rattlesnake Mountains, which are formidable. To the west of the road, as Elk Creek curves to the south, numerous tributaries and marshy areas also pose obstacles to a mid-nineteenth-century army in a hurry to advance. To approach Honey Springs along the Texas Road is the best option as bypassing to the east or west would be both difficult and time-consuming. If passage is attained along this road, the path to Cooper's headquarters two miles to the south is relatively unimpeded. None of the obstacles I just described would prevent an army that had crossed Elk Creek from advancing on Honey Springs directly along the road or from multiple directions after Pumpkin Ridge flattens out and is no longer an obstacle. Terrain analysis thus shows that Cooper needed to prepare to defend the Texas Road on the prairie above its main crossing on Elk Creek.

Although Blunt says the rebel line stretched for a mile and a half, with the Texas Road at its center, and that it was a partial semicircle at the edge of the timber, Cooper's General Orders No. 25 and after-action report provide no helpful insight into its placement or extent (Blunt 1863; Heiston 1888). US reports and accounts frequently mention that the rebels took advantage of vegetation for concealment from observation, while Blunt noted, "We were compelled to advance over the open prairie" (Blunt 1932, 244). Blunt took advantage of a shallow intermittent stream valley for cover from enemy fire and concealment from observation during a short bivouac. From there he advanced in columns of companies to conceal his numbers and plans for deployment. The archaeological footprint of the Prairie Engagement identifies the location of the rebel line where it crossed the Texas Road and provides beneficial information on how it extended, or at least where it was engaged, to either side. Of interest, this shows that the line was engaged only for a total length of about one-third of a mile but that the evidence of conflict (mainly small arms and artillery projectiles) was primarily at and to the east of the road. Of importance, the rebel position was on the highest

FIGURE 53. The Texas Road near the center of the rebel line in 2001. Photo by William B. Lees.

ground north of Elk Creek before the ground sloped gradually to the north. The heavily engaged right wing of the rebel line was, in fact, on a high point that may have been the "hill" noted by Captain Edward Smith and the "high prairie" where Cooper viewed his adversaries to the north. The road was thus not at the center of the archaeologically documented fighting, although it may at first have seemed so to General Blunt and other US observers. Unknown to them, the crest of the high ground where rebels were aligned gave way to a backward slope where the road swung to the west to take advantage of a more manageable approach to the valley below, the bridge across Elk Creek, and the road to the upper ford.

In addition to the fighting at the Texas Road and east of it, archaeology shows a point of minor conflict to the west. This isolated evidence of fighting is across a tributary of Elk Creek. This suggests that the rebel line was indeed longer than the footprint of conflict at the center suggests but also that it was, at least to the west, dispersed or intermittent based on terrain and cover. Lieutenant Colonel Welch of the Twenty-Ninth Texas wrote about sending a company up "a small brushy ravine, that extended into the prairie" on their left that might correlate with these artifacts (Welch 1863, 2). Many accounts say the rebels were under cover of timber, woods, or brush that provided concealment from observation of the US troops. In his General Orders No. 25, written several days before the battle, Cooper allowed that "in timbered places the line may be extended" (Heiston 1888, 462). Although Cooper never mentioned terrain, I suspect features such as streams and marshes were factors in decisions on deployment made by different rebel units and individual soldiers before or during the fighting north of Elk Creek.

I believe the archaeological footprint of the Prairie Engagement clearly shows what the opposing commanders saw as the key terrain on the morning of July 17, and it is undoubtedly the key contested terrain of the battle. This was an area of concealment under cover of brush and woods with an unobstructed view across open prairie north along the Texas Road. To the west were several tributaries of Elk Creek with accompanying marshes. Behind this key terrain was a steep rocky bluff descending to Elk Creek, which complicated options for any rebel withdrawal. Cooper in his General Orders said, "The enemy must, if possible, be prevented from gaining the cover of the timber on the north side" (Heiston 1888, 462). This is important because this timber was on high ground overlooking the Elk Creek valley through which any rebel withdrawal had to pass. Archaeology and memory show that Hopkins's battery availed itself of this high ground to shell the retreating rebels in the valley, probably at the bridge, causing them to withdraw.

The terrain was also tricky to the east and included bluffs and steep descents to the Elk Creek bottoms. These steep but passable slopes along with the Texas Road itself are shown from memory to have been avenues for the withdrawal of rebel troops from the prairie above and for advance of US troops of Phillips's brigade into the valley. The lack of a significant archaeological footprint in this area suggests that the withdrawal was rapid. Here options available to combatants narrowed as the valley was confined by prairie edge to the north and Pumpkin Ridge's steep and rocky slopes to the south. In thinking about Bowles's account of his First Kansas soldiers skirmishing with rebels from the high bluffs, it

FIGURE 54. Rock-strewn bluffs at the south edge of the Prairie Engagement above descent to the Elk Creek bottoms, 2019. Photo by William B. Lees.

is uncertain if he was saying that his soldiers were firing on rebels from bluffs or whether the rebels were in fact the ones on bluffs. The only topography that I would refer to as bluffs that would have been encountered by the First Kansas would have been on the south edge of the Prairie Engagement or across the valley on the heights of Pumpkin Ridge. There is probably only about a quarter-mile where this description makes any sense; as you go south, the slope of Pumpkin Ridge becomes gradual. At that point, well before the ridge overlooking Cooper's Honey Springs headquarters is crossed, this description of high bluffs no longer describes the landscape along the Texas Road. I believe Bowles may have been describing his soldiers firing into the Elk Creek valley from the overlooking bluff before they then joined the pursuit of the rebels through the valley and south. As discussed in the preceding chapter, there is some archaeological evidence along Elk Creek that supports this conclusion.

In the Elk Creek valley, memory tells of a rebel holding action at the bridge, variously called brief or sustained. This action may have involved rebel troops then taking advantage of both concealment from observation and cover from fire in one or both ravines flanking the south approach to the bridge. Archaeological evidence does support fire from small arms of variable calibers toward the north side of the valley, where the Texas Road descended to the bridge. These bullets were probably fired from common rifles, probably in the hands of Confederate-allied Indians such as described by Howland in 1937 based on the memory of his father (Foreman 1937e). The attack on the rebels at the bridge is indicated by fragments of artillery ammunition probably fired by Hopkins's battery from a location overlooking the bridge, probably near the route of the Texas Road. It seems from the relatively small footprint of fighting in this area that rebels quickly withdrew, likely given the apparent fact that the US had gained the high ground overlooking the Elk Creek bottoms; with this, these bottoms provided little tactical advantage for the rebels. Although the Elk Creek valley's terrain complicated this initial part of the rebel withdrawal, the avenue of retreat along the Texas Road became advantageous as the valley broadened and flattened to the south-southwest. Rapid movement of the rebels along the Texas Road is shown by the decline in artifacts beyond the southern edge of the Elk Creek Engagement. It does not pick up again for a quarter to a third of a mile farther south.

Key terrain for the Elk Creek Engagement does appear, based on archaeological evidence, to be associated with the creek itself, particularly the bridge but also the ravines on either side of the bridge. At the time of the Civil War, the bridge location was, I think, where the exploded six-pound artillery shell fragments were found, although no direct evidence of the bridge itself is known to exist. Cooper also obviously saw the bluffs above Elk Creek as key terrain because of his admonition that they must not fall into US hands. Given his knowledge of the terrain between that point and Honey Springs, he probably saw no way to recover from such a loss. He certainly also knew that US troops occupying these bluffs would command the valley below and could easily counter rebel troops even if they had been posted in number on Pumpkin Ridge across the valley. This reality is probably why, in his General Orders No. 25, Cooper proposed holding Walker's, Gillette's, and Scanland's troops in reserve as much as two miles away at Honey Springs rather than closer to his lines north of Elk Creek.

TABLE 8. Discussion of KOCOA elements for the Elk Creek Engagement

Key Terrain	Elk Creek bridge and fords above and below the bridge
Observations and Fields of Fire	Depending on vegetation in the valley, which is uncertain, US troops probably had commanding observation and field of fire into the bottoms along Elk Creek from the captured bluffs to the north. Rebel troops' field of fire was certainly most effective in the bottoms toward the Texas Road as it descended into the valley on the way to the bridge. Once again, the nature of vegetation in the valley at the time of this fight is not well understood.
Cover and Concealment	For the advancing US troops, the bluff and woods overlooking Elk Creek provided both cover and concealment. For rebel troops, ravines to the east and west of the bridge would have provided cover and concealment. The wooded slopes of Pumpkin Ridge might also have provided the same.
Obstacles	The bluffs and steep slopes of the Elk Creek valley, tributaries and marshes upstream, and Pumpkin Ridge to the east on the south side of the valley were major obstacles for both sides to overcome during this fight. While these made defense of the bridge and fords difficult for the rebels, they also certainly slowed the federal troops as they pressed their retreating foes.
Avenues of Approach and Withdrawal	The Texas Road, including the bridge on the main road at Elk Creek and alternate crossings by ford above and below the bridge, was the avenue of approach for US army and the avenue of withdrawal for Confederate troops and allied Indians.

Brigadier General Steele was highly critical of Cooper's preparation for a battle that seemed inevitable and had caused Cooper to issue his General Orders No. 25. Noting that Cooper occupied his position before the battle and had plenty of time to prepare, Steele criticized him for "having taken no steps to strengthen his position" (Steele 1888a, 32). Although one account talks about the rebels being "behind rocks and fences," there is neither suggestion by Cooper that formal defensive cover was to be constructed nor any other accounts suggesting that any such preparation was done (W. H. S. 1863, 1). Defensive works consisting of dug entrenchments and piled rocks and timber could have been completed and certainly would have helped Cooper defend his line, although the outcome may not have been different. Also, positions established on the steep slopes of Pumpkin Ridge overlooking the main crossing of the

Texas Road might have been more effective in slowing the US pursuit than making a stand in the bottoms. This would probably have been less effective without artillery on these heights, which Cooper simply did not have available to deploy in that manner. Certainly, the utility of defensive works had been established by the summer of 1863 at places such as Lexington, Missouri; Fredericksburg, Virginia; and Vicksburg, Mississippi; and they had been used the first week of July at Gettysburg, Pennsylvania. Cooper also had knowledge of construction of defensive earthworks at Fort Gibson and had himself ordered rifle pits (trenches) constructed to defend crossings of the Texas Road at the Arkansas River. Still, the construction of defensive works in advance of an anticipated battle was and would remain the exception in the Far West.

Whether Brigadier General Cooper thought of anything as key terrain south of his initial planned deployment is unknown. Holding Walker's well-regarded First Choctaw and Chickasaw Regiment in reserve was both an expression of military confidence in his ability to prevail at Elk Creek and, perhaps, the wisdom of a sound military mind preparing for the worst. But whether he envisioned a second or a third line of defense between his initial position and his headquarters at Honey Springs is unknown. He did note in his report of the battle that he took an active part in actions south of Elk Creek intended to slow if not stop the federal advance (D. Cooper 1888, 460). Nevertheless, whether by prior discussion among the rebel commanders or not, what was key terrain south of the Elk Creek Engagement is clearly shown by the archaeological footprint of the Pumpkin Ridge Engagement.

Running through this most southern part of the Honey Springs Battlefield is the intermittent scar of the Texas Road, a cultural feature imprinted on the land and thus a visible element of key terrain. As it was on the prairie to the north, the Texas Road was key because it represented the route to Honey Springs. Midday on July 17 it ceased to be Brigadier General Cooper's road to Fort Gibson and became the avenue for the invading Union army to attack his headquarters. Between Elk Creek and Honey Springs, the key terrain chosen for the final fight of the Battle of Honey Springs was determined possibly in advance but likely as the retreat unfolded. The key terrain, probably chosen by Confederate captain Levi Gillette, is also the last best defensible high ground south of Elk Creek along the Texas Road. Before the archaeological survey, this final

TABLE 9. Discussion of KOCOA elements for the Pumpkin Ridge Engagement

Key Terrain	High ground of Pumpkin Ridge as it crosses the Texas Road between Elk Creek and Honey Springs Honey Springs and the headquarters buildings and camps
Observations and Fields of Fire	Memory suggests that both US and rebel troops had relatively clear fields of observation along the Texas Road after it emerged from the constricted valley of Elk Creek. However, the ability of the US troops to observe rebel troops regrouping at, or coming forward from, their Honey Springs headquarters was restricted. Once the US occupied the former rebel position (Gillette's) on top of Pumpkin Ridge, they could then see Walker's counterattack as it unfolded. US observers at this point would also have a clear line of observation to Honey Springs and south along the Texas Road.
Cover and Concealment	Similar to what is noted for observations and fields of fire, the combatants on the Prairie Field probably had no cover and little or no concealment. Cover and concealment was available, however, for any regrouping or reserve troops, such as Walker's Choctaws and Chickasaws, who were behind the engaged rebels (Gillette's?) on the top of the ridge.
Obstacles	Other than some possible wooded area as mentioned by Cooper in his after-action report, there are no known obstacles.
Avenues of Approach and Withdrawal	The Texas Road as it proceeded on the prairies south of Elk Creek was the avenue of approach for the pursuing US army and the avenue of withdrawal for Confederate troops and allied Indians. The Briartown Road was, according to Cooper, used to deceive the federals as the retreating rebels headed east rather than southwest along the Texas Road, and it was Cooper's final avenue of withdrawal from the battle. The Briartown Road was the anticipated route for Cabell's reinforcements.

battle's location and its nature were not known. The discovered archaeological footprint establishes the location of fighting as a broad sweep of land on either side of the Texas Road overlooking both the road north to Elk Creek and the Confederate headquarters to the south. This is the best place to mount a defense of Honey Springs, and that is certainly why it was selected, perhaps by Gillette. The rebel defender probably had a clear field of observation and a clear field of fire to the north toward the approaching enemy. There was, however, little hope of cover or concealment for either US or rebel combatants (although Cooper mentioned a timbered ridge in his report, which may refer to this area). The only certain obstacles were soldiers set to challenge each other for control of this piece of land. Still, Gillette's squadron and Walker's regiment certainly understood that any challenge to the advancing US troops would be successful only if it facilitated a retreat of the defeated rebel army.

Overall, the original position selected by Cooper to defend his headquarters at Honey Springs against attack by US troops from Fort Gibson was probably the best option available given the most probable avenue of approach: the Texas Road. Rugged terrain to the east and west of the Texas Road at Elk Creek almost required an army desiring rapid advance to follow this route. North of Elk Creek, Cooper identified key terrain to be a location with concealment in woods but on high ground with a commanding view of the prairie to the north along the Texas Road. Obstacles for Blunt were these woods, tributary streams and marshes to the west, a bluff behind the rebel lines, steep slopes to the east, and Pumpkin Ridge to the south. Blunt took advantage of a valley about a half-mile north of Cooper's troop line to gain concealment and cover from fire for a brief rest of his troops, weary from a rainy night's march. In between was an open and deadly field of fire. Although it is unclear, there is no archaeological evidence in memory that suggests Cooper's troops constructed any significant defensive works to provide cover beyond what little the woods afforded.

Although the terrain selected by Cooper, as shown clearly by the archaeology, receives high marks from KOCOA analysis, his avenue of withdrawal from this position is flawed, but he had few alternate choices with the resources he controlled. He backed his troops up against the Elk Creek valley with its adjacent bluffs and steep slopes. The valley is constricted on the other side by the prominent Pumpkin Ridge rising steeply from the creek bottom. Although the valley broadens out along the Texas Road as it heads south-southwest, until reaching there any rebel troops would have been dominated by small arms and artillery fire from US troops occupying their former positions. Archaeology and memory agree that this is indeed what happened. Any fighting in this area, no matter how intense, certainly did not last long. This conclusion is supported by the commanding positions afforded the US troops once they pushed the rebels off the bluffs overlooking Elk Creek and by clear accounts from memory of the disorganization of the rebel withdrawal.

Some rebels may have taken refuge on the steep slopes of Pumpkin Ridge and engaged Union troops from that position as they followed the main body of retreating rebels down the Texas Road, although we found no evidence for that. Still, the next and final pronounced conflict occurred on the ridge overlooking Honey Springs. It is likely that Gillette's squadron first attempted to hold back the advancing US troops and artillery and were attacked, and possibly forced to withdraw, by Hopkins's battery and troopers of Phillips's brigade. Whether the federals first occupied Gillette's former position on the ridge or not, it appears that Walker's Choctaws and Chickasaws advanced to this same ground, either in support of Gillette or alone. Certainly understanding that their role was to slow rather than stop the US advance, Walker and his allied Indians subsequently withdrew. Blunt's troops took possession of Honey Springs and pursued the retreating rebels for another mile and a half or so, and the Battle of Honey Springs was over.

As seen throughout this book, and re-centered in this chapter, terrain and its vegetation and cultural features played a major role in establishing the parameters within which the Battle of Honey Springs unfolded and helped measurably define how it transpired. With an ever-increasing focus on the study area, the landscape has proven critical. Once the battle was joined, terrain did not decide the outcome but certainly limited the possibilities.

Terrain analysis puts the Battle of Honey Spring into perspective that would, I think, be clearly understood by the combatants engaged on July 17, 1863. Still, some questions linger on the edges of information provided by archaeology, memory, and landscape. I will consider these in my next and final chapter, where I will offer speculations on why, for example, the rebel line was engaged primarily at the Texas Road and east. These speculations will focus on thinking about how to properly contextualize the warfare that happened at Honey Springs not as a quotidian event of the American Civil War but as one of a unique subset that occurred on lands of another sovereign nation and by combatants with different motives and histories of—and approaches to—warfare.

CHAPTER SIX

Reading Between the Lines

THE GOAL OF THIS BOOK is to present a solid new line of archaeological evidence on the Battle of Honey Springs as the basis for a re-envisioned story of this tragic event. I have employed a landscape approach, using concepts of battlespace and KOCOA terrain analysis, to reconcile converging lines of evidence from memory and archaeology with the land itself. In my pursuit of answers to old questions, this process has led me to new ones that by their very utterance have been enlightening. Throughout, I have kept my eye on the complex historical and cultural context of this event, both original and more recently imposed, and the need to strive for balance in a story whose participants did not equally contribute to its memory.

The first question I asked, which inspired my journey into the field in 1994, was simply whether a sufficient residue of battle existed to support the investigation of the fighting using battlefield-scale archaeology. The answer is demonstrated throughout this book and is a resounding yes! But, at the same time, it is obvious that this physical, archaeological evidence of the battle began diminishing as the smoke cleared on July 17, 1863. Artifacts have been lost from the ravages of time, through souvenir and relic collecting by the curious, picked up by farmers as they tilled fields, and removed by the systematic mining of the battlefield landscape by hobbyists armed with metal detectors of ever-increasing sophistication. And, yes, between 1994 and 1999, we also removed artifacts from the battlefield. Still, we preserved them and their all-important location in a study and museum collection housed at the Oklahoma Historical Society. Further, artifacts that may remain on battlefield lands owned by the State of Oklahoma are protected by law from unauthorized excavation or removal.

It is hard to tell what effect artifact collecting has had on our ability to see the battlefield patterns at Honey Springs. In the 1980s, Gary Moore collected from the Wooded Forty, which we now know contains the intersection of the rebel lines and the Texas Road (referred to in memory as the rebel center). Despite this, this place still held battle-related artifacts during our archaeological survey that evidenced some of the core fighting on the prairie above Elk Creek. The rebel camps along Elk Creek were also reported to have been heavily collected in the 1980s, if not before and after. The fact that we found fewer artifacts in this area than elsewhere may be partly the result of the work of earlier collectors. Still, the distribution of what we did find along Elk Creek shows patterns that we can interpret today. It is also likely that the lower numbers in the valley reflect the brevity of fighting in this area, where there were only a small number of combatants compared to the fight on the prairie and perhaps also the fight to the south on Pumpkin Ridge.

I also answered a related question in this book: where was the Battle of Honey Springs fought? Of course, in a general way, everyone knew the location of the battle, also known as the Battle of Elk Creek. Honey Springs and Elk Creek are well-known place names, and the route of the Texas Road connecting them is still visible in the modern landscape. But the rest is shrouded by a fog and not immediately evident when you read the official after-action reports of the officers in charge. Things are less clear when you walk the ground with those accounts in hand. Where exactly was Cooper's initial line of battle? What exactly was the nature of the fighting during the rebel retreat?

When we finished our last day of fieldwork in 1999, we knew the answer to these questions in a general sense. We had held in our hands the bullets and exploded cannonballs fired on July 17, 1863, and knew precisely where they had been found. We had opened a new "archive" of the Battle of Honey Springs, used here to describe the location of the Prairie, Elk Creek, and Pumpkin Ridge Engagements. Relying more on recorded memory but still anchored by archaeology and terrain analysis, I have verified the site of Blunt's bivouac and where he deployed his troops into a line of battle on the morning of July 17. Relying first on archaeology and terrain and drawing from memory, I have shown where the rebel line crossed the Texas Road and what part of it was engaged in fighting with Blunt's army. This conclusion matched my predicted location based on elevation and, along with KOCOA analysis, showed that it was optimally situated. Next, I have identified a likely location for the bridge across Elk Creek and shown how what I think was brief fighting transpired in its vicinity. Finally, I have shown precisely where the rebels mounted their final attempt to hold the advancing federal army on the last high ground before Honey Springs itself. These fundamental findings contribute significantly to our evolving understanding of the Battle of Honey Springs.

As is always the case with any research into the past, be it historical or archaeological, new questions arise. These are often more important than the questions that initially drove the research. Sometimes questions arise when research does not support the scholar's expectations (theory, hypothesis), which results in a substantial but straightforward question: why not? In other cases, new findings require explanation because they also defy expectations. Perhaps because they come to us in this fashion, these questions sometimes become the most powerful way to see a new interpretation of past events. These cause the scholar to rethink the premise of their underlying assumptions, which, as we recognize more and more these days, are often culture-bound or at least bound by a long-standing cultural-historical narrative that may have flawed origins. Scott and Fox's work at the Little Big Horn showed how this process works using archaeology to allow Native American memory into the official history by proving its factual basis (D. Scott and Fox 1987).

A number of discoveries stand out to me in terms of having been unexpected: 1) the stretch and breadth of the fighting north of Elk Creek, 2) evidence of localized fighting in the northern reaches of the Prairie Engagement, 3) fighting on Pumpkin Ridge that covered an area at least equal to that on the Prairie,[1] 4) seemingly overlapping patterns of conflict on Pumpkin Ridge, and 5) confirmed use of the bow and arrow in the conflict. These findings concern the materiality of the battle and its very footprint on the modern landscape. In addition, this material evidence supports and leads to a consideration of broader questions:

- How does material evidence of conflict localized in the northern half of the Prairie Engagement relate to fighting along the rebel line that began at about 10 a.m. on July 17, 1863? Does memory recall this fighting?

- Compared to memory suggesting that Blunt's army engaged a much longer front, how can the limited breadth of material evidence of fighting along the rebel line of the Prairie Engagement be explained?[2]
- Are seemingly overlapping material patterns of conflict on Pumpkin Ridge evidence of a complicated synchronic battle, or are they the result of different events separated in time?
- There is no memory of the use of the bow and arrow at Honey Springs, but arrow points were found and correlate with other evidence of battle. Is the conclusion that bow and arrow were used in this fight reasonable? If so, do they reflect cultural expression or military expediency?
- The question that must follow all the others is how to explain Cooper's defeat at Honey Springs. I couched this earlier as a choice between Cooper's blaming loss on poor-quality gunpowder and Steele's criticism of his lack of defensive preparation. However, the answer may be more complicated and may invoke other factors entirely.

I will take these questions in turn. I introduced this chapter in the last by discussing "questions [that] linger on the edges of information provided by archaeology, memory, and landscape." These questions seem just out of reach of the evidence presented, but an answer might come by extrapolation from all three. Whether you call the result speculation, opinion, or interpretation, it is common practice because it is essential. The study of the past often requires boundaries to be stretched to investigate what is not necessarily entirely knowable (at least not with the data at hand). Still, in so doing, it is essential that the stretch is firmly tethered to fact and that the result is consistent with possibility. That is, I will stop short of invoking aliens to explain the human experience at Honey Springs.

The Other Conflict on the Prairie?

The archaeological analysis presented in chapter 4, supported by examination of terrain in chapter 5, affirms the location of the initial rebel line as it crossed the Texas Road in the southern part of the Prairie Engagement. Identifying the location of the rebel line and other admittedly less-conclusive archaeological data supports Blunt's characterization of the initial US deployment being one-quarter mile to the north. However, we found a significant distribution of battle-related artifacts far north of this location. Using bullet type and impact velocity, I explain some of the fired bullets in this area as rebel overshot. Still, others appear to be residue from localized fighting. How does this unexpected evidence of combat relate to the 10:00 a.m. US attack on the rebel line at the southern edge of the prairie?

The first clues to fighting in the northern half of the Prairie Engagement came from dropped and fired bullets for breechloaders and magazine rifles (Sharps, Merrill, Spencer). These were found west of the Texas Road and between where I believe the US bivouacked and where they initially deployed into line of battle. The Sharps and Merrill bullets are best associated with US cavalry deployed on the right and left flank and are seemingly out of place where found. The Sixth Kansas Cavalry had both Sharps and Merrill carbines, while the Third Wisconsin may have been armed only with the Merrill carbine. Nearby were various Minié balls whose impact velocity adds them to evidence for localized fighting; these include several associated with rebel use and others possibly related to the Second Colorado Infantry or Indian Home Guard. Since the archaeological footprint of the Prairie Engagement shows clearly that the most intense fighting was close-in along a rebel line at the southern end of the prairie, this evidence to the north was not expected based on recorded memory of the general conflict that began at 10:00 a.m. I believe the only explanation of the evidence is an engagement of some sort that occurred earlier that morning, possibly well before most US troops had gone into bivouac.

Some brief accounts from memory may refer to fighting in this area early in the morning of July 17. After skirmishing with the enemy near Chimney Mountain, Lieutenant Colonel Campbell of the Sixth Kansas Cavalry moved toward Honey Springs. He later reported, "I then advanced and came up with the enemy, posted in force under cover of timber at Elk Creek. Here I came to a halt and sent a company forward to reconnoiter; found the enemy strongly posted in the woods, their line extending on the right and left of the road. I kept up a brisk fire on them; *they, however, kept under cover*" (Campbell 1888, 452; emphasis added). The brief report of the Third Wisconsin Cavalry, which also probably arrived on the scene earlier than other US troops, does not mention any skirmishing before the primary battle (Stevens 1888, 453).

Lieutenant Colonel Otis G. Welch described the deployment of the Twenty-Ninth Texas Cavalry to the left of the Twentieth Texas. One company deployed in a ravine to the west (probably that which eventually crosses the northern part of the battlefield) and a squadron of two companies under Captain John Harmon as skirmishers in advance of the main body. Of the action before the advance of the US Infantry, Welch noted, "A constant fire was kept up by the skirmishers of both sides" (Welch 1863). Welch also noted, "The whole space in front of us was covered with small bushes, which concealed our position, and almost masked the approach of the enemy." There is no mention of how far advanced these skirmishers were posted or if they were also concealed by this cover. Still, the Twenty-Ninth was west of the Texas Road, which aligns with the evidence of conflict in question. Thus, Welch's memory fits well with Campbell's account but does not easily seem to explain the evidence of engagement of US cavalry and others so far to the north of the rebel lines.

A reminiscence by Blunt's chief of staff, Colonel Thomas Moonlight, may shed light on these carbine and other bullets. Waiting for the infantry and "heavy artillery" (Second Kansas and Hopkins's Kansas Battery) to come up, he remembered, "I made use of the time by climbing on the top of a farm house. With the aid of a spy glass and hidden by the chimney I discovered the rebel line of battle, and by throwing out a company of Cavalry as skirmishers drew a portion of their force, partly to satisfy myself and partly to keep others engaged until the arrival of the command" (Lindberg, Matthews, and Moonlight 2003, 31). Moonlight implies that Blunt and his staff along with the cavalry (both Sixth Kansas and Third Wisconsin as Blunt's bodyguard?) arrived, as would be expected, before the infantry and Smith's and Hopkins's batteries. Bullets found in the area in question, which I believe is behind Blunt's initial deployment, include those for the Sharps rifles and Merrill carbines carried by the Wisconsin and Kansas cavalries. Few bullets for breechloaders were found on the Prairie Engagement outside of this concentration. The possibility that the pattern of carbine bullets may reveal the location of an early morning skirmish before Blunt's deployment of his army at 10:00 a.m. is significant.

Accounts such as that by Colonel Moonlight suggest the engagement of US cavalry with rebels early in the morning in advance of Cooper's line. Still, the evidence I have so far presented indicates that the Second Colorado Infantry and perhaps Indian Home Guard, both of which were mounted, may have been involved as well as, of course, rebel fighters. Whether the evidence in question relates directly to Campbell's, Welch's, or Moonlight's account may never be known, but, significantly, the archaeology identifies a distinct area of conflict that must have occurred before the general engagement began. This is best explained by the action of skirmishing well in front of rebel lines, probably well before the bulk of Blunt's army arrived on the scene.

The Breadth of Cooper's Line

Conventional wisdom on the breadth of Cooper's initial line of deployment comes from Blunt's description that it stretched for a mile and a half. However, another witness, Wiley Britton, said it was only a half-mile on either side of the Texas Road (Blunt 1888g, 447; Britton 1922, 275). Considering what to expect of an archaeological footprint, it would follow that evidence of fighting would extend along Cooper's entire line, presuming Blunt deployed his troops to match Cooper's and that the antagonists engaged evenly. Unfortunately, there is no memory that provides clear insight on this.

Presuming that the center of the rebel line was the Texas Road as multiple sources attest, we can see that archaeology demonstrates that US firepower was focused there and to the east with little evidence on the rebel left. Despite conventional wisdom drawn from either Blunt's or Britton's remembrance, archaeology shows the US attack on Brigadier General Cooper's line was focused along a front of only about one-third of a mile, with little evidence farther afield. Identifying the unexpectedly limited breadth of this engagement is a significant finding. Although not self-explanatory, this archaeological fact is not inconsistent with terrain analysis results. KOCOA analysis has shown that the archaeological footprint of fighting along the rebel line is precisely what both Cooper and Blunt must have recognized as key terrain. In open prairie on either side of the Texas road, the rebel right occupied the highest ground with the best available observation points and fields of fire toward an enemy approaching along the Texas Road. Yet I suspect that Blunt also knew this was the easiest path to Honey Springs.

Cooper's General Orders No. 25 described his thinking about deployment but is not very specific. In his after-action report, he attempted to explain his implementation and modifications of this plan as the battle unfolded on July 17. On examination, much remains in doubt. Roswell Lee's battery was said to have been in position at the Texas Road since the evening before the battle. Cooper deployed Scanland and Gillette from reserve at Honey Springs to "support the Creeks at the upper crossing of Elk Creek" (D. Cooper 1888, 458). Walker's Choctaws and Chickasaws were to remain in reserve at Honey Springs with pickets sent out toward Prairie Springs. However, Walker seems to have mistaken the command and taken the entire regiment on a reconnaissance-in-force in that direction and was unavailable until the Pumpkin Ridge fight had begun. Not mentioned by Cooper was that Colonel Stand Watie, in command of the Cherokee regiments, had taken a brigade of unknown size to Webbers Falls and was not present on July 17.

Regarding the Muscogees, Lieutenant Grayson complained that the Second Creek Regiment received no orders to deploy into action from their position, presumably at one of the upper fords (Grayson and Baird 1988, 61–62). It is unclear if any soldiers from the First or Second Creek (or Gillette's or Scanland's squadrons that Cooper sent to support the Muscogees) deployed into action on the rebel left. Cooper does say that he ordered the Muscogees to move toward the main road and support DeMorse and Martin, who were supporting Bass and then deployed on both sides of the Texas Road. Still, an unsigned article published on September 12, 1863, in the *Standard* of Clarksville, Texas, states, "[The rebel troops] were so posted with reference to anticipated points of attack by the enemy, that Martin's regiment and the two Creek regiments were never under fire. General Cooper issued an order for them to come to the support of DeMorse's regiment, which though called a part of the centre, really occupied the extreme left of the line actually engaged; but the order got to them too late to be effectual" (*Standard* 1863a).

Captain Stevens of the Third Wisconsin later mentioned moving to the right to flank the enemy, forcing the rebels toward their center (Stevens 1888). He may have engaged some Muscogees or, perhaps more likely, skirmishers DeMorse had posted along a stream to the west of their main position (*Standard* 1863a). Still, the regimental history of the Third Wisconsin contains only one sentence on the Battle of Honey Springs (Quiner 1866, 913–14). While memory leaves some doubt, it seems probable that the Muscogees and Gillette's and Scanland's Texans on the left remained mainly behind the lines. The archaeological footprint of the fighting supports this conclusion by showing little US engagement by the artillery or small arms west of the Texas Road, which implies that the federals in command perceived no threat from that part of the field. Perhaps confirming this is a statement by Lieutenant Colonel Schaurte of the Second Indian Home Guard who claimed that his regiment was the first to establish a position across Elk Creek (Schaurte 1888, 452). The Second was on the US right, to the right of the First Kansas Colored, who were heavily engaged with Texans to their front. It seems likely that the Second Indian's race across Elk Creek was facilitated by the fact that there were few or no rebels opposing their advance.

Initially Bass's soldiers of the Twentieth Texas were at the center supporting Lee's battery.[3] DeMorse and his Twenty-Ninth Texas (and possibly Martin's Fifth Texas Partisans) were to Bass's left. Cooper ordered one-half of Bass' regiment to the far right to support First Cherokee skirmishers under Captain Tinnin as the battle began. Therefore, Cooper deployed at least half and possibly more of Bass's unit to the right of Lee's battery. Lieutenant Colonel Bowles of the First Kansas Colored Infantry was on the US right adjacent to (west of) the Texas Road. He reports that his men engaged directly with DeMorse's regiment. Lieutenant Colonel Schaurte, with 368 soldiers of the Second Indian Home Guard, was to the right of the First Kansas and reported only that they were deployed as skirmishers and entered the timber. He did not indicate that they received any serious opposition as they fought. As noted earlier, soldiers of the Second Indian Home Guard were the first US troops across Elk Creek. US casualty reports from their right wing echo these observations: the First Kansas suffered thirty-two total casualties. In contrast, the Second Indian Home Guard reported only three, and the Third Wisconsin Cavalry reported none (Return of Casualties 1888). Some of these casualties may have come later, but most were probably from the fighting in the Prairie Engagement.

Rebel casualties on their left are also telling. Significantly, there are none reported for the First and Second Creek Regiments. On the other hand, over 80 percent of casualties reported in the Clarksville *Standard* were from the Twentieth and Twenty-Ninth Texas and Lee's battery (*Standard* 1863c). The logical conclusion from these numbers is that the Muscogee regiments were not engaged in the day's fighting. All the evidence, therefore, shows that the rebel left was initially composed of Texans who may have numbered only around five hundred men but possibly less and certainly not many more. These numbers would put them relatively equal in opposition to the five hundred men of the First Kansas.

In considering why the rebel left was not fully deployed, Grayson's criticism that orders were never received cannot be discounted. At the same time, it would be wrong to ignore the possible role Native American traditions of warfare, as evidenced in the 1861 exodus of Opothle Yahola and the Battle of Pea Ridge, may have had in how Muscogees and other Native Americans at Honey Springs engaged in the initial fighting on the Prairie. What caused Blunt to say that the rebel line stretched for a mile and a half is uncertain. Although memory suggests that the Muscogees were never deployed, is it conceivable that some Muscogee soldiers made themselves visible as Blunt brought his troops up but then moved back into the valley as the US artillery deployed? Or was Blunt simply misled by the deployment of the Twenty-Ninth Texas troops as they moved along the brush toward their position at center and deployed skirmishers up a brushy tributary to the west? Regardless of the reason, there seems no question that there was little for Blunt's artillery, infantry, mounted troops, and cavalry to engage to the west of the Texans.

Although archaeology clearly shows that the rebel right wing was heavily engaged, like the left, it does not extend as far as memory might suggest. To the right of Lee's battery and Bass's Twentieth Texas, who were in support, memory shows that some soldiers from the Second Cherokee were present. To their right, some First Cherokee soldiers deployed as skirmishers and were reinforced by half of Bass's Texans. Opposite the rebels, the Second Colorado with 276 men in six companies was on the federal left adjacent to and east of the Texas Road, and to their left was the First Indian Home Guard (745 men) and the Sixth Kansas Cavalry (238 men) (Colorado State Archives, 1863; Kansas Adjutant General's Office 1863a and 1863c). The Second Colorado engaged directly with Bass's Twentieth Texas and perhaps the Second Cherokee. Lieutenant Colonel Campbell reported that his Sixth Kansas troopers, deployed as skirmishers, and the First Indian Home Guard heavily engaged unidentified rebels on their right (Campbell 1888, 453).

The rebel right (First and Second Cherokee Regiments) was handicapped by the absence of the First Regiment's Colonel Watie, who was in overall command, and Colonel Adair of the Second Regiment. Again, Watie was at Webbers Falls during the battle with an unknown number of his regiment, leaving Lieutenant Colonel James M. Bell in command. Adair was ill, and Major Joseph F. Thompson commanded in his absence. In a letter to Bell, Brigadier General Cooper lamented, "It was regretted exceedingly that it so happened that Col Watie was not present on that occasion, as his service & well known gallantry would have given great encouragement to the Officers and men of his command" (Dale and Litton 1995, 140–41). That Watie went to Webbers Falls probably indicates that Cooper was unaware of Blunt's immediate plans to attack Honey Springs by bringing his army directly down the Texas Road.

The archaeological footprint of conflict on the rebel right definitively shows that rebel antagonists, which would undoubtedly have included Texans and some Native American troops, were deployed along the rebel line when the US artillery opened up. It is probable that not all of the Cherokees had moved up from their camps along Elk Creek to join those initially on this line, or at least waited until the Union artillery paused and fighting with small arms began. Some who were available, including Cherokees, may have sought refuge behind or in the valley during the bombardment. Still, the Second Colorado, First Indian Home Guard, and Sixth Kansas reported significant resistance to their advance toward the rebels and into the woods. Cooper reported that the right wing collapsed when the center broke, and a general retreat began (D. Cooper 1888, 459).

Casualties show the intensity of fighting on the rebel right: the Second Colorado suffered nineteen, and the First Indian Home Guard and the Sixth Kansas suffered eight and five respectively. One of the Sixth Kansas casualties was Private Thomas White who was wounded on the prairie but before the general fighting commenced. Once again, some of these casualties may have occurred later in the day, although Major J. Nelson Smith, covering action of the Second Colorado at Elk Creek and to the south, reported no casualties. Casualties among the Twentieth Texas were the heaviest of any rebel regiment, over 48 percent (sixty-nine) of total rebel casualties. In comparison, the First and Second Cherokee Regiments account for less than 13 percent (eighteen) for the day (*Standard* 1863c).

While it seems certain that most of Blunt's troops were deployed into line (including mounted troops assigned to hold horses) north of Elk Creek, it is also certain that many of Cooper's were not. Cooper's report of the battle shows that the majority of one of his best and probably largest regiments, Colonel Walker's First Choctaw and Chickasaw Regiment, was not only held in reserve but also had mistakenly undertaken a scout to the east. Walker was only able to join the fight after the final action had begun on the ridge above Honey Springs. Further, Cooper described the Muscogee regiments and two Texas regiments (Scanland's and Gillette's) being at the upper ford immediately before the battle. He says only that he directed the Muscogees to support DeMorse's Texans. Grayson says he never deployed his Muscogees into the fight due to a lack of orders to do so. Finally, Cooper talks of finding many of the Cherokees in camp along Elk Creek as the battle was beginning and states that he ordered them up to the line; it is uncertain how they responded. In addition, one of Cooper's most able officers, Colonel Stand Watie, was on detached duty on a raid to Webbers Falls with an unknown number of Cherokee troops. While the raw numbers, as reported by Blunt and Cooper, suggest the rebels had as much as a two-to-one numerical advantage, the evidence suggests their effective numbers were not that divergent. It is even possible that the rebels had fewer deployed soldiers than the US troops they opposed in the Prairie Engagement (D. Cooper 1888).

There is no other way to reconcile the archaeological footprint of fighting in the Prairie Engagement than through a conclusion that Blunt's artillery engaged the rebel center and right because that was where they observed the threat. The lack of evidence of heavy small-arms engagement on the rebel left suggests that a threat there never materialized, which is implied by memory from Cooper and Grayson and, indirectly, from US officers of the Second Indian Home Guard and the Third Wisconsin Cavalry. US and rebel casualty reports also support this conclusion. Archaeology shows that the rebel right was more heavily engaged by US artillery and small-arms fire. Memory, including US and rebel casualty reports, also shows more resistance to Phillips's brigade (Second Colorado, First Indian Home Guard, and Sixth Kansas Cavalry) as they engaged the rebel right.

Interpreting Pumpkin Ridge

The discovery of broadly distributed evidence of fighting along the Texas Road as it crosses Pumpkin Ridge is a significant outcome of our project. Chapter 5 used memory recorded in after-action reports to identify this as the probable location where Gillette and Walker contested US troops advancing toward Honey Springs after the opening battle and the subsequent fight at Elk Creek. Based on the archaeological footprint of fighting first presented in chapter 2, there is no other place where this could have occurred. Cooper's after-action report all but says it was Gillette who fell back along the Texas Road from Elk Creek to hold, if only briefly, the advancing US troops. Although challenging to tie to the modern landscape, the memory from the US after-action reports leads me to believe that Hopkins's battery and advancing members of Phillips's brigade attacked Gillette's position. I think that exploded US cannonball fragments fired from Hopkins's position eight hundred yards north along the Texas Road mark Gillette's initial position.

Hopkins noted that after crossing Elk Creek, one of his sections moved to the left of the road and "opened upon the enemy's cavalry, upon a hill beyond, causing them to fall back quite precipitately, the shell bursting in their immediate vicinity" (Hopkins 1888, 457–58). Smith likewise reported that his two companies of Colorado Infantry, which had moved across Elk Creek, "discovered the enemy on a hill, or rise of ground in the advance." His report continued, "Here Hopkins' battery, supported by my infantry, opened upon the enemy, who fled in confusion after the second fire" (J. Smith 1888, 455). He then noted, "[I moved my] two companies forward in support of the battery until we occupied the enemy's former position" (J. Smith 1888, 455).

Importantly, Hopkins described moving his battery forward until "a line of the enemy's cavalry was discovered and driven back after the firing of a few rounds of shell" (Hopkins 1888, 457). I believe the location described by both Smith and Hopkins, where they moved forward and occupied the former rebel position, is one and the same as the contested ridge crest identified by US artillery shell fragments and small-arms ammunition from Phillips's brigade, which fought Texans and rebel Indians armed with shotguns and common rifles. The significant small-arms ammunition along this ridge crest suggests that it was contested by US and rebel adversaries, while the smaller clusters of small-arms ammunition, largely from common rifles, probably related to the eventual withdrawal of rebels toward Honey Springs. Due to the physical evidence of the use of shotguns, it seems probable that the US move to occupy this former rebel position was actively contested by Gillette's Texans who apparently remained nearby.

What happened next is unclear. Did Gillette's troops withdraw, or were they reinforced by Walker prior to close-in fighting along this ridge? The ammunition fired from common rifles there, as in the two clusters found to the south, could have emanated from the First Choctaw and Chickasaw Regiment and may also be associated with the similarly armed First Indian Home Guard who were part of Phillips's brigade, although memory is unclear as to whether they were present in this part of the fight. Here Cooper's after-action report may help. He remembered, "The Choctaws, under Colonel Walker, opportunely arrived at this time, and under my personal direction charged the enemy, who had now planted a battery upon the timbered ridge about 1,000 yards north of Honey Springs" (D. Cooper 1888, 460). Cooper's description of the US battery location places it precisely within the concentration of artifacts that I associate with Phillips's Brigade. That he says Walker arrived after the US battery had been moved forward to this position suggests that he was not present when Gillette was driven from the ridge crest by US artillery.

Although the precise sequencing of events on Pumpkin Ridge may forever be uncertain, the record best supports the following sequence: 1) Captain L. E. Gillette's Texas squadron first occupied and was then driven off this ridge by fire from six- and twelve-pound cannon of Hopkins's Battery from a position some eight hundred yards north along the Texas Road, 2) a battalion of Phillips's Brigade, including companies of Second Colorado Infantry, Sixth Kansas Cavalry, and possibly First Indian Home Guard, advanced to hold the former rebel position on the ridge crest while the battery was moved forward, 3) Phillips's advance was briefly contested by Gillette before he withdrew toward Honey Springs, and 4) with US troops and artillery now posted on the ridge some one thousand yards north of Honey Springs, Walker's late-arriving regiment perhaps combined with Gillette demonstrated briefly against his adversaries before strategically withdrawing to follow the rest of the retreating rebel army. I believe it unlikely that the rebel rear guard, composed largely if not entirely of Indian troops, would have spent much time within range of artillery on high ground knowing full well that their adversaries were well equipped with canister and shell. By reading the accounts from memory, this progression would have happened quickly.

The distribution of artifacts in the Pumpkin Ridge Engagement, in five clusters of spherical ball ammunition and one overlapping concentration of artillery ammunition and conical bullets, probably also speaks to the fleeting nature of the fighting. In additional thinking about this fight, Gillette's Texans and Walker's regiment were mounted and probably remained so. Likewise, Gillette may have engaged mounted US troops who then engaged Walker's mounted regiment. The clusters may relate to nonlinear, mounted, and rapidly changing positions. The fact that artifacts were found clustered rather than evenly scattered probably also speaks to the ephemeral nature of the fighting. That many of the combatants were Native American may be a factor as well, with the arrangement of cells possibly reflecting different concepts of mounted warfare such as was observed at the Battle of Pea Ridge, Arkansas (Pike 1883, 288). My work at Mine Creek, Kansas, which was a battle of mounted cavalry, all White troops, shows by example more formal alignments of soldiers than seems to be the case on Pumpkin Ridge (Lees 1998). Conversely, the cells may reflect the engagement of combatants who were rapidly arriving on the scene and may also relate to the possible presence of areas of trees or brush on this ridge.

A Case for Agency

As the reader knows, eight rolled-metal arrow points were found during our survey in each area of engagement, in all cases close to the Texas Road. Although seemingly not the most critical question, whether these artifacts relate to the Battle of Honey Springs addresses a broader question of agency for Native American participants in this fight. There are, of course, many ways that you might explain arrowheads along the Texas Road. But it is impossible to explain away the association of these projectile points with evidence of fighting on July 17, 1863. As is shown in chapter 4, they correlate with the rebel line in the Prairie Engagement, the bridge across Elk Creek, and the center of fighting on Pumpkin Ridge. It follows that they do result from the fighting in each of these areas. To argue otherwise would be to reject the data at hand.

There are no accounts of the use of the bow at Honey Springs. However, the use of this traditional weapon in Great Plains warfare at this time and later is well documented, although the form of the metal points used on the plains (cut or manufactured from flat sheet metal rather than rolled to a point) is different from those found at Honey Springs. The archaeology conducted at the 1864 Sand Creek Massacre site provides a perfect case study of the diverse weaponry, including the bow, carried by Cheyennes in 1864 (Greene and Scott 2004). In 1863, Captain Asaph Allen of the Ninth Kansas Cavalry Volunteers at Fort Halleck, Idaho, described an encounter with 250 Utes he later described as "better mounted and armed than the troops, having Hawkins' rifles, revolvers, bows and arrows, and spears" (Allen 1888, 444). Less understood is the use of this weapon in conflict situations by the Indian nations in eastern Indian Territory during this same time.

The bow and arrow was a standard weapon in the Choctaw and Chickasaw nations during the antebellum period and until well after the Civil War. Born in 1857, Choctaw Thomas H. Graham remembered, "I never saw any kind of weapon except bow and arrow and the old muzzleloading rifle until I was grown" (Foreman 1937d, 255). Choctaw Arthur J. Cline had similar recollections, "There were a few old Choctaw Warriors near Stringtown, who still used the bow and arrow, but most of the Indians in the early seventies [1870s] adopted the Winchesters, carrying them in scabbards attached to their saddle" (Foreman 1937b, 122). Muscogee John Chupko, born in 1866, remembered, "There weren't many rifle guns. Some had #44 Winchesters and some old Musket or breech loading guns. Old Indians didn't care about guns. They used bow and arrow" (Foreman 1937c, 91–92). Use of the bow was an essential skill to master for Choctaws seeking to become warriors (Yarbrough 2021, 154).

A carte-de-visite in the collections of the Wilson's Creek National Battlefield shows a seated "Osage warrior" in traditional clothing holding a bow and arrow (Wilson's Creek National Battlefield n.d. a). A description of this image suggests that he may have been a member of the Second Regiment of Indian Home Guard, which initially included many Osages. Other Osages, however, served with Confederate-allied units. Regardless, this Civil War–era photograph well illustrates the contemporary importance of the bow in Indian Territory and vicinity.

At the Battle of Round Mountain on November 19, 1861, Muscogee and other Indian refugees following Opothle Yahola to Kansas engaged with Texas cavalrymen and Confederate-allied Indians (Muscogees, Seminoles, Choctaws, and Chickasaws) under Colonel Cooper using both bullets and arrows. With the Texas Cavalry, Allison Sparks remembered in published reminiscences, "When within 40 or 50 yards we received a volley of balls and arrows that were discharged by a hidden enemy who had concealed themselves behind the bank" (Sparks 2014). In remembering Confederate-allied Indians, Sparks also noted, "Their arms were as varied as their apparel and were old rifle, guns and bows and arrows mostly" (Sparks 2014).

An interview in 1937 with full-blood Cherokee Elizabeth Watts, born in 1859, provided an account of the use of the bow and arrow by Confederate-allied Indians at the March 1862 Battle of Pea Ridge, Arkansas. According to the biographical sketch compiled from this interview, "General Pike also had a fight in Arkansas and they called it Pea Ridge. His Indian troops fought Indian style with bow and arrow, and the North whipped them there" (Foreman 1937a, 288). Brigadier General Curtis's report of March 13, the week after the battle, confirms, "General Pike commanded the Indian forces. They shot arrows as well as rifles, and tomahawked and scalped prisoners" (S. Curtis 1888a, 195). Elsewhere in her interview, Watts noted, "The early weapon was the bow and arrow. The bow was usually made out of Bois-De-Arc or Black Locust, the arrows out of Swamp Dog Wood, and the bow string out of squirrel skin. Later muzzleloading guns and cap and ball pistols. But many would rather have the bow and arrow" (Foreman 1937a, 287).

That the bow and arrow was a familiar weapon is only one factor. I have already reviewed Confederate complaints of substandard powder and noted that Walker's Choctaws and Chickasaws felt their firearms were useless as a result. Thus, if present among the arms carried by Confederate-allied Indians at Honey Springs, the bow and arrow would be an alternative to poorly performing firearms. It is much less likely that the US Indian Home Guard soldiers carried the bow and arrow, due to better supply and more focus on "standard" military training in Kansas. Speculation may remain on who had these weapons. Still, despite the lack of memory, archaeology does confirm their use at the Battle of Honey Springs.

Do the arrowheads support Cooper's criticism of the quality of gunpowder used during the battle, particularly referencing the complaint from Colonel Walker (D. Cooper 1888, 460)? Perhaps. Evidence of the use of the bow remains limited in the face of battle residue that is overwhelmingly from firearms. Still, after taking command in January 1863, Steele reported on the lack of weapons among his troops at Fort Smith, including those who would later fight at Honey Springs (Steele 1888a, 30). Steele also reported that Cooper's troops engaged in September 1863 at Perryville, Choctaw Nation, included many unarmed and almost all with "indifferent" weapons (Steele 1888a, 33). While no mention of this shortage is made immediately before the Battle of Honey Springs, I suspect that at least some rebel combatants carried no firearms. Thus, the lack of firearms may as easily explain the use of the bow as would substandard gunpowder.

Archaeological evidence of the bow at Honey Springs joins only a few references to them in conflicts between regular US and rebel troops. Mentioned above is the use of the bow by Opothle Yahola's followers during their contested departure from the Indian Territory in 1861 and by Confederate-allied Indians during the Battle of Pea Ridge in 1862. The Native Americans at Pea Ridge included Confederate-allied regiments present at Honey Springs the following year. In addition, regular federal army troops in the West became all too familiar with the use of the bow by Native American antagonists during the Indian war that followed the Dakota War of 1862. In 1862, Joseph Howland Bill in his "Notes on Arrow Wounds" declared, "The arrow is a weapon of the greatest antiquity. It is one with which, in this country, at least, we are all familiar" (Bill 1862, 365). While many scholars believe this US participation in the Indian Wars falls outside of regular Civil War conflict, Greater Reconstruction theory presents a compelling argument that this should be rethought. This theory holds in part that the Indian Wars of the 1860s and later were part of a larger struggle for control by the federal government, of which war with the southern states in rebellion was but a part.

Many Native Americans fought during the Civil War, including in predominantly Native American companies or regiments (Hauptman 1995). Still, I know of no other accounts of the use of the bow in Civil

War conflict involving regular US and Confederate troops. Because of lack of a record of use of the bow it may be easy to discount archaeological finds as D. Thomas (2003, 279) does for the Pickett bullet: "Unfortunately, there is no way to distinguish bullets with a military association from those which may have been dropped or fired by nineteenth-century hunters." His argument may work for collector-found specimens but not necessarily for those found through battlefield archaeology. The Pickett bullets and arrow points found at Honey Springs correlate well with other artifacts that I am confident were used in the battle.

However, these distinctive arrow points from Honey Springs speak to a topic broader than their use in this battle. Hinted at by White observers is the persistence of traditions or practices of dress and combat. These traditions were "curious," "comical," or "barbaric" when seen through White eyes over 150 years ago. But it is wrong to think the Native American combatants in the Indian Territory shed cultural beliefs and traditions when they joined the Indian Home Guard or Confederate-allied Indian regiments. In fact, the Civil War was a means for members of the Five Tribes to become warriors under the same terms as those who came before (Confer 2007, 98; Warde 2013, 116; Yarbrough 2021, 151–76). Mention of cultural beliefs and traditions in the historical record is rare, but this is not a good indication that these beliefs and traditions were no longer held or acted on. Instead, their very normalcy may have made them unexceptional to most observers who also did not mention, to any significant degree, the distinctions between uniforms or weapons of different regiments of White soldiers. White soldiers did note, however, the Black soldiers' soldierly appearance, skill at drill, and bravery in combat because this countered an insidious narrative that they were incapable. For White soldiers who had been in the Trans-Mississippi West for any time, however, the differences between White and Native American combat were not surprising.

When Opothle Yahola led thousands of followers to Kansas to seek refuge, the tactics employed were defensive. His soldiers sought advantage by using landscape ("Cover and Concealment" and "Fields of Fire") to provide time for civilians to withdraw to safety. Although winter ultimately turned their exodus into a humanitarian disaster, the tactics are familiar in mid-nineteenth-century Native American warfare. The goal was not to win possession of the field of battle (the definition of victory in most regular Civil War combat) but rather to achieve victory by protecting noncombatants and with the fewest soldier casualties (Confer 2007, 61; Warde 2013, 75–78; Yarbrough 2021, 153, 176).

The Confederate-allied Muscogees and Cherokees fought four months later at Leetown in the Battle of Pea Ridge, Arkansas. They were then under the command of Brigadier General Albert Pike, commander of the Confederate Department of the Indian Territory. In his after-action report, Pike noted that his mounted Indian troops would not face artillery fire in the open, "Well aware that they would not face shells in the open ground, I directed them to dismount, take their horses to the rear, and each take to a tree, and this was done by both regiments, the men thus awaiting patiently and cooly the expected advance of the enemy" (Pike 1883, 288). Elsewhere, Pike noted, "[John Drew's mounted regiment of Cherokees] was in the field on our right, and around the taken battery was a mass of Indians and others in the utmost confusion, all talking, riding this way and that, and listening to no orders from any one" (Pike 1883, 288). It is unlikely, I believe, that the Cherokees involved would describe their action in combat to have resulted from "utmost confusion."

Of their participation, US acting assistant adjutant-general T. I. McKenney reported that "contrary to civilized warfare, many of the Federal dead . . . were tomahawked, scalped, and their bodies shamefully mangled" (McKenney 1888, 194). Third Iowa Cavalry adjutant John Noble reported, "There were Indians among the forces making said charge; and that from personal inspection of the bodies of the men of the Third Iowa Cavalry, who fell upon that part of the field, I discovered that 8 of the men of that regiment had been scalped. I also saw bodies of the same men which had been wounded in parts not vital by bullets, and also pierced through the heart and neck with knives, fully satisfying me that the men had first fallen from the gunshot wounds received and afterwards brutally murdered" (Noble 1883, 206–7).

Pike later reported on the highly controversial actions of Confederate-allied Indians at Pea Ridge, "The Indian troops are of course entirely undisciplined, mounted chiefly on ponies, and armed very indifferently with common rifles and ordinary shot-guns. When they agreed to furnish troops they invariably stipulated that they *should be allowed to fight in their own fashion. They will not face artillery and steady infantry on open ground, and are only used to fighting as skirmishers when cover can be obtained*" (Pike 1885, 819; emphasis added).

Tandy Walker's Choctaws and Chickasaws, who arrived too late to participate at Pea Ridge, rode into combat at Newtonia, Missouri, singing war songs followed by a "war whoop" (Yarbrough 2021, 127). Lieutenant Douglas Cooper wrote in May 1862 to advise Major General Earl Van Dorn that the best use of Colonel Stand Watie was to "direct the movements of guerrilla bands along the border of the Cherokee country." He added, "The Indians will make the very best guerrillas" (D. Cooper 1885, 824). Elizabeth Watts remembered that the Native Americans at Pea Ridge fought "Indian Style" (Foreman 1937a, 288). Pike's suggestion that the Cherokees should operate as guerrillas also acknowledged this Native American way of fighting. The persistence of Native traditions is finally demonstrated by descriptions of the US Indian Home Guard when leaving Kansas for the 1862 Indian Expedition. Distinctive dress, mounts, war dances, and songs were noted less than a year before the Battle of Honey Springs.

From the accounts that relate to the Indian Territory, the description of the Native American soldiers and their tradition of combat does seem to differ in expected ways from that of White US or Confederate troops. This difference has, I think, important implications for the interpretation of the archaeological findings of the Battle of Honey Springs. Also, because the status of Native American regiments allied with the Confederacy was inherently different from that of the Indian Home Guard, I suspect this difference was more pronounced among the Confederate-allied troops.[4] It must also be remembered that the goals of the Native American combatants were somewhat unique. These goals did not generally include the defeat of either the United States or the Confederacy but rather protecting their homes and way of life from outsiders: pure preservation of self, family, culture, and sovereignty.

Consideration of eight rolled-metal arrowheads has thus led to reflection on the importance of different traditions of warfare at the Battle of Honey Springs. The question becomes: are these Native American traditions evident by using archaeology as the lens with which to reexamine memory and landscape, or, said differently, do these traditions help explain the pattern of conflict at Honey Springs? Are the reported behavior and actions of Native American regiments during Opothle Yahola's exodus and at Pea Ridge—caution against being subjected to artillery without concealment and cover, preservation of individualism as warriors within the collective (regiment or battalion), and understanding combat as something other than a zero-sum game—analogous to Honey Springs?

Understanding Outcome

I return now to a question posed early on: was it poor gunpowder, lack of preparedness or even incompetence on Cooper's part, or other factors that best explain the defeat of Confederates and their allies at the Battle of Honey Springs? Grayson's opinion is perhaps the harshest, "By what I have always confidently believed to be bad management, we lost the day here when the enemy came up and engaged us, for Gen. Cooper did not even get all his men out on the firing line, or into any engagement with his adversary before he ordered his forces to retire" (Grayson and Baird 1988, 61–62). Steele also blamed Cooper for the defeat, for "having taken no steps to strengthen his position" despite having time to do so in the face of an impending attack (Steele 1888a, 32). Cooper put much of the blame for the poor performance of his troops on worthless gunpowder: "I feel confident we could have made good the defense of the position at Elk Creek but for the worthlessness of our ammunition" (D. Cooper 1888, 460).

I have shown through terrain analysis in chapter 5 that the prairie north of Elk Creek was the most advantageous place for Cooper to forestall an attack on his headquarters. Yet, although he directed his officers to clear passages through wooded areas sufficient for the movement of troops into battle, he appears to have done nothing to strengthen his position through the creation of cover or obstacles. Moreover, there is no indication that he considered preparing for the second line of defense should his line north of Elk Creek not hold. He did nevertheless say he personally directed Gillette's squadron into position to hold back the federal advance. Other than the steep slopes of Pumpkin Ridge overlooking the Elk Creek valley at the bridge, however, the terrain along the Texas Road between there and Honey Springs did not offer the same defensive advantages as those on the prairie.

Confederate-allied Indians, therefore, may have hesitated to deploy from the Elk Creek valley or moved back from the line to find cover as the US deployed their four batteries of artillery on the field. This conclusion is consistent with actions at Pea Ridge and Albert Pike's statement of a few months earlier. It is also compatible with a statement Cooper made in his after-action report that might have extended to all the Native American participants: "The Choctaws, who had skirmished with the enemy on the morning of the 17th, returned wet and disheartened by finding their guns almost useless, and there was a general feeling among the troops that with such ammunition it was useless to contend with a foe doubly superior in numbers, arms, and munitions, with artillery ten times superior to ours, weight of metal considered" (D. Cooper 1888, 460).

Native American soldiers, collectively or as individuals, may also have made decisions based on the outcome of the US artillery bombardment as to whether it was wise to join a fight they may have deemed not worth the risk. Fighting for this piece of ground at all perils against impressive odds may have been inconsistent with the traditional calculus defining success and failure in combat (Confer 2007, 97; Warde 2013, 75–78; Yarbrough 2021, 153). Reports of the carnage happening at the center on the Texas Road, where DeMorse's Texans suffered a reported 80 percent casualties, may also have informed those waiting in the valley of the unfolding battlefield inevitability. For the Cherokee regiments on the rebel right, the absence of Colonel Watie and the troops that accompanied him, as well as the illness of Colonel Adair, may have had a demoralizing effect. Cherokees still in camp whom Cooper says he order to the line may have decided otherwise, and many Muscogees may have been content with the lack of orders to engage.

In chapter 3, I also raised the possibility that Lee's battery may have been very short of ammunition going into the battle. US accounts show that this battery fired during the fight, with devastating effect against Hopkins's battery. Archaeological finds of canister and exploded cannonballs that may have come from the rebel cannon are rare in US positions. Compared to the archaeological evidence of the work of the US batteries, these small numbers may be seen as support for the shortage of ammunition for the rebel guns. Still, they may conversely simply reflect the imbalance of US versus rebel artillery. Another critical factor is that the superior US firepower probably quickly suppressed the rebel guns.

Several reports talk of federal artillery dismounting one Confederate cannon, which Britton claims caused the withdrawal of their remaining guns (Britton 1922, 278).

What is clear from both the memory and the archaeology is that US and rebel troops were heavily engaged on the prairie north of Elk Creek. The rebels may have been widely deployed early on the morning of July 17 when Blunt's scouts and troops were coming up and going into bivouac. However, the archaeological evidence shows that when the battle was joined by US and rebel artillery and then by troops with small arms, there was no perceived or actual threat and little resistance on the rebel left. This conclusion is supported but certainly not proved by memory, is consistent with Native American traditions of combat against regular troops and artillery documented in earlier fights, and flows easily from the archaeological footprint of battle.

Was Cooper correct in blaming poor gunpowder, which became useless in rain and humidity, for his loss at Honey Springs? There is certainly evidence from memory and archaeology that Cooper's troops fired on US troops with artillery and small arms. Still, it is not improbable that problems with gunpowder may have impacted morale if not the actual performance of weapons. The most quoted source for gunpowder being a problem was Cooper's reference to Walker's Choctaws and Chickasaws in the skirmish near Chimney Mountain during active rain. Confederate commissioner of Indian affairs Sutton S. Scott also questioned the quality of powder used at Honey Springs even when dry: "The powder is perfectly worthless. The mere charging of the gun grinds it into the finest dust, which is little likely to explode; and, should it do so, its power is scarcely more than sufficient to drive the ball out of the piece" (S. Scott 1888, 1097). The large number of spherical balls of variable caliber with no visible barrel damage may very well be the result of balls fired with low velocity from firearms using poorly performing gunpowder.

The archaeological finds at the Pumpkin Ridge Engagement, in which Walker's troops were involved, seem to show that they effectively engaged US troops with small arms later in the day. Our finds of arrowheads in each area of engagement may speak to problems with gunpowder or simply to shortages of firearms among the rebel soldiers. Whether or not other rebel regiments also suffered from poorly performing gunpowder is unknown. Still, demoralized members of Walker's unit may have inspired uncertainty as word spread of their early morning fight. If this was only part of why the rebel left did not engage and rebel numbers were low on the right, Cooper was not wrong.

Still, poor gunpowder and its demoralizing effects may not fully explain Cooper's loss. What of Steele's criticism of Cooper for not better preparing his defenses? In theory, Cooper could have prepared breastworks of piled rocks and felled timber or dug earthworks or rifle pits. This would have given his troops cover in addition to the concealment they already had behind brush along the rebel line. Such constructed cover would have sheltered them during the artillery bombardment, and they could have fired from behind it. This might have prevented the devastating casualties of the Twentieth Texas. Cooper could also have ordered the construction of abatis of felled trees and brush to slow the advance of Blunt's line. While there is some evidence that the rebels took advantage of existing cover, there is no evidence for any extensive preparation in the days before the battle. Blunt's chief of staff Colonel Thomas Moonlight said in his memoirs,

> Genl. Cooper had taken up a strong position in the northern edge of the timber of Elk Creek, while his headquarters and stores were some 3 miles in his rear at a place called Honey Springs, the name given to the battle. I here desire to state that the enemy never for a moment supposed that we were anything more than the cavalry and artillery force which had driven him from his entrenchments on the river the day before, and [with this in mind] had so arranged his plan of battle and stationed his regiments and batteries as to completely swallow us up as we advanced into the timber; and he instructed his commanding officers to accomplish this work in just 30 minutes. This came from the lips of commanding officer of the 20th Texas. (Lindberg, Matthews, and Moonlight 2003, 31)

So, in this respect, it seems Steele is correct that Cooper could have made better preparations for an attack he was expecting and for which he had made advance plans through his General Orders No. 25. Important in this regard is that Cooper had seen fit to protect his pickets at Arkansas River crossings opposite Fort Gibson with entrenched rifle pits in the days leading up to the fight at Honey Springs (Lindberg, Matthews, and Moonlight 2003, 30; W. A. Phillips 1888e, 355).

What Cooper lacked was artillery. His single four-gun mountain battery was certainly no match for the twelve guns, mountain and light artillery, fielded by Blunt. Lee's Confederate battery may also have been short on ammunition. It is clear from archaeology and memory that the US guns effectively focused on the rebel line at its center (on the Texas Road) and along its right. Fire from these guns dismounted one of the rebel guns and had an unknown effect on the rebel troops. The evidence is clear that the overwhelming strength of the US artillery made the work of their infantry and cavalry easier by inflicting casualties along the line. The US artillery probably also tempered individual or collective decisions of rebel Indian troops regarding whether to advance to the line or remain there if already deployed. Indeed, suppose that rebel Indians withdrew from the line during the artillery bombardment. In that case, their actions may have persuaded others still in camp along Elk Creek that this was not a winnable fight. This scenario in no way demeans the bravery of these troops, which had been many times demonstrated, but instead speaks to a different worldview about combat, victory, and sacrifice without purpose (Yarbrough 2021, 151–76).

If the artillery was overwhelming, the evidence also suggests that Cooper's troops were not an even match for Blunt's. My research strongly indicates that not all of the rebel troops Cooper intended to oppose Blunt were initially deployed into line of battle or remained there after his artillery barrage had ended. Blunt likely met a vastly smaller number of rebel soldiers when his troops advanced to engage Cooper's line. Even if the numbers of opposing armies were equal, his cavalry carried effective breech-loading carbines, and the Second Colorado and the well-disciplined and well-trained First Kansas had standard military muskets. The federals did not suffer from a lack of arms, ammunition, or deficiencies in their gunpowder. Cooper also lacked the leadership of Colonel Stand Watie, who was in Webbers Falls, and Colonel William Penn Adair, who was ill.

Lieutenant Colonel Welch's statements that "the heaviest fire was directed to the [rebel] right" and that "the enemy advanced in line of battle four deep along [the] entire front" may also speak to the issues of rebel numbers and deployment (Welch 1863).[5] An anonymous account, probably also by a member of the Twenty-Ninth Texas, is similar, stating that after the withdrawal of the Cherokees from the rebel right, the federals "converged their whole force upon Lee's artillery, Bass' and DeMorse's regiments, coming down on them perhaps eight deep" (*Standard* 1863a).

It is therefore my conclusion that Cooper lost the fight on the prairie north of Elk Creek for several compounding reasons:

- Probable numerical superiority of the engaged US troops (see final bulleted item below)
- The superiority of US artillery (twelve guns to four), possibly exacerbated by insufficient ammunition for the rebel battery
- Real or perceived problems with the quality of the gunpowder in the hands of the rebel troops
- Failure of Cooper to have breastwork, earthwork, or abatis constructed
- Failure of Cooper to order one or both of his Muscogee regiments into battle
- Individual or collective decisions by a substantial number of Confederate-allied Indians to not engage or to disengage in the fighting on the prairie, possibly due to the overwhelming advantage of the US artillery; this is compounded by the certain unavailability of Walker's First Choctaw and Chickasaw Regiment until after the rebel retreat was well underway and by the absence of Colonel Watie and a battalion of troops.

Without substantially more artillery, Cooper's chances of victory would have been difficult, even with defensive works and a full complement of troops with good-quality powder. With the convergence of some or all of these compounding issues, the outcome probably became obvious if not inevitable. At that point, the allied Indians may have reconsidered their commitment to this fight. This sentiment may have fueled what some described as a rout when the rebel line broke. Blunt's decision to send only part of his troops in pursuit is probably an indication that he believed the rebel army was a much-diminished threat.

What happened along Elk Creek during the retreat and pursuit is poorly recorded in memory and is not supported by much archaeological evidence. However, the evidence does support rebel resistance focused on the outlet of the Texas Road into the Elk Creek bottoms. It also shows the shelling of the bridge, probably by one or more guns of Hopkins's battery from the bluffs to the north. Without rebel artillery in position to challenge the federals as they occupied the bluffs and moved into the bottoms, the ability of rebels to hold any position along or south of the creek for long was minimal at best. In his 1937 interview, William Howland mentions his father's recollection that a cannon helped defend the bridge during the fighting along Elk Creek (Foreman 1937e). While no other accounts corroborate this, I have suggested that the padlocks discovered there might relate to Lee's battery. Regardless, while the fighting might have been fierce, there is no evidence that it lasted long, and a single cannon at the bridge would not have changed that eventuality, especially against the guns of Hopkins's battery firing from high ground to the north.

Fighting did not pick up again until the Texas Road crossed a broad ridge overlooking Honey Springs: the Pumpkin Ridge Engagement. Were it not for the return of Walker's troops it would have been a much briefer engagement between Gillette's squadron and federal artillery and troops of Phillips's brigade. By the time US troops engaged Gillette, the rest of the rebel army had probably passed or otherwise withdrawn, including their artillery. Archaeology, with some support from memory, suggests that the first fighting on this ridge was to dislodge a rebel line established by Gillette. US troops probably pushed Gillette's troops off the ridge and occupied their former position. Walker's First Choctaw and Chickasaw Regiment, possibly joining Gillette, then briefly demonstrated against this new US position. I think the distinct clusters of battle-related artifacts along this ridge show a brief but intense fight between mounted troops.

The southern edge of the Pumpkin Ridge Engagement was about halfway down the ridge slope toward Honey Springs and the site of Cooper's headquarters. A small cluster of artifacts, part of the larger engagement, crosses the Texas Road at this point and contains the last battle-related artifacts that we found. Due to the large numbers of artifacts from years of battle reenactments and other activity around Honey Springs itself, we paused our survey there. We picked back up on the other side of the Honey Springs monument park but at a reconnaissance level, and we then continued to the southern border of land managed by the Oklahoma Historical Society. The new Honey Springs visitor center now sits here near the town of Rentiesville. Again, we did not find any battle-related artifacts south of the Pumpkin Ridge Engagement, a finding that fits with recorded memory.

I believe the findings south of the Prairie Engagement show brave efforts, probably shouldered largely by rebel Native American combatants, to slow rather than to stop the pursuit of Blunt's army. The intent was to allow for the withdrawal of Cooper's troops and what supplies he was able to move from Honey Springs. Delaying action was certainly common during the Indian Wars, and similar actions marked Opothle Yahola's trek to Kansas in 1861 (Confer 2007, 61). There is no evidence that Cooper ever intended to do more should his plan to stop Blunt at Elk Creek fail. If he did, his General Orders No. 25 did not entertain this, and there is no other evidence for preparation other than holding troops in reserve at Honey Springs. Regardless, it is evident that any well-laid plans Cooper may have had for a concerted second line of defense would have failed. The rebel withdrawal from the Prairie Engagement followed a clear military defeat and was unorganized even by Cooper's accounting. Although Cooper's comment that he personally directed Gillette to hold the federals on Pumpkin Ridge suggests planning that today might qualify the rebel retreat as a "retrograde action," it was a rout by most accounts.

Lucinda Davis briefly described the rebel retreat to a WPA interviewer in 1937: "We can hear de guns going all day, and along in de evening here come de South side making for a getaway. Dey come riding and running by whar we is, and it don't make no difference how much de head men hollers at 'em dey can't make dat bunch slow up and stop" (Baker and Baker 1996, 113). Recorded seventy-four years after the battle, Davis's timeline is hard to reconcile with other records, and her other memories may have evolved as well.

From the long lens of history, it seems perhaps fortuitous that Colonel Tandy Walker led his entire regiment toward Prairie Springs on the morning of July 17. Had he been available to join the fray on the Prairie Engagement, the fight there might have been more brutal, but it would not likely have led to a different outcome for the reasons outlined above. However, Walker's earlier engagement in the battle might have left Gillette alone to slow the advance of Hopkins's battery and Phillips's brigade. Hopkins might have quickly occupied the crest of Pumpkin Ridge and been able to fire shell and case at retreating rebels and their supply train for well over one thousand yards—possibly reaching Honey Springs itself. Companies of the Sixth Kansas Cavalry, Second Colorado Infantry, and other mounted troops of the Indian Home Guard might also have quickly pressed the rebels, perhaps inflicting additional casualties and loss on Cooper's rebel army.

Cooper's defeat at Honey Springs had immediate consequences. His troops and those under Cabell who had attempted to join Cooper for the Battle of Honey Springs were demoralized, and desertion of allied Indians became a rampant problem. Southern-leaning residents in the Indian Territory south of the Arkansas River headed toward Texas, anticipating the victorious federal army's next move. Cooper moved south to Perryville in the Choctaw Nation, and Cabell, who had joined Cooper after the Battle of Honey Springs was ending, was called back to Fort Smith by Brigadier General Steele to aid in its defense. On August 26, a reinforced federal army under Blunt surprised Cooper at Perryville, causing his further retreat and loss of his supplies (W. Edwards n.d. b). On September 2, Blunt occupied Fort Smith after its abandonment by Steele.

Along with the surrender of Confederate forces at Vicksburg on July 4 and at Little Rock on September 10, the Arkansas River was then firmly under federal control (Castel 1968, 153–70). Although Confederates retained little hope of regaining control of the Indian Territory along and north of the Arkansas River, significant actions continued. These included rebel attacks during 1864 on Fort Smith between July 27 and August 2 and the capture on September 19 of a federal supply train at Cabin Creek (Warren 2012). Still, Yarbrough (2021, 116) shows that after Honey Springs the Choctaw interest in participating in the fighting declined significantly; a similar effect on other Confederate-allied Indians seems probable. In addition, campaigns by US troops to crush rebel resistance carried south the internecine warfare once restricted to north of the Arkansas River. At the end of the Civil War, the civilian populations of the Choctaw, Chickasaw, Seminole, Muscogee, and Cherokee Nations had suffered more per capita loss than any of the states or territories in other theaters of war. Further, because of their alliances with the Confederacy, these sovereign nations were on a course that would lead to the extinguishment of tribal governments and the loss of tribal lands. African Americans enslaved in these nations were not formally freed until

1866 but did receive lands promised—but never delivered—to people enslaved in the states in rebellion.

Conclusion

Some of the findings of a battlefield archaeology project become apparent during the project itself, and others emerge during preliminary work with project maps and found artifacts. Fieldwork stretched from 1994 to 1999, roughly progressing from north to south; we had solid insights on the boundaries of the fighting when our fieldwork ended. Then I prepared preliminary maps and artifact analyses, making it possible to speculate on how significant parts of the battle, known from recorded memory, fit the modern landscape. This preliminary insight and research informed the development of the Oklahoma Historical Society's Honey Springs Battlefield public history site. A proposal for a park access road and a series of interpretive trails presenting the story of the US bivouac and what I call in this book the Prairie, Elk Creek, and Pumpkin Ridge Engagements was the result. Recently supplemented by an impressive visitor center, the park road and trails remain the basis of the visitor experience at the site.

I do not think my conclusions in this book change the appropriateness of the placement or design of the trails. That said, I believe this analysis improves and challenges the conventional battle narrative in meaningful ways. This comes partly by adding specificity to the story. For example, Cooper's initial line of battle is now confidently anchored on the landscape, and the specific work of the US artillery to press the rebels there, at Elk Creek, and on Pumpkin Ridge is clear. Defining the location, extent, and character of the Pumpkin Ridge Engagement is another meaningful result of the fieldwork and this book. Another detail about which I am confident is that a few Native American combatants used bows in the fighting, which is ultimately less important than the broader implications of this fact. On a grander scale, the true importance of the landscape in defining how Cooper planned his defense of Honey Springs and how the battle then transpired has become evident. This finding is only possible because we now know where the actual fighting took place, as shown by the locations of artifacts found during our archaeological survey.

Still, the revealed footprint of the battle seemed to defy conventional memory-based narratives. Careful consideration and interpretation of patterns of artifacts and the related terrain in the Prairie Engagement led me to reexamine memory and the diverse cultural perspectives and knowledge of the Native American, Black, and White participants. I believe this has resulted in a nuanced interpretation of the Battle of Honey Springs that considers archaeology, recorded memory, and terrain but also acknowledges Native American cultural knowledge and practice brought to this landscape on July 17, 1863. This interpretation opens the possibility that human motives and approaches to the conflict may be at least partially responsible for the observed archaeological pattern of conflict that I have documented at Honey Springs (D. Scott and McFeaters 2011). It is my opinion that although past and present scholars fully acknowledged the diversity of the participants in this tragic day's event, the role of this cultural diversity in the progression and outcome of the event itself has never been fully embraced.

The story of the Battle of Honey Springs and the Civil War in the Indian Territory was once told as if it was just another clash between the "Blue and the Gray" that, in the final analysis, had little impact on the outcome of this great contest. To some degree, at least in my opinion, this simplified narrative was a by-product of "Lost Cause" explanations of the Civil War that swept the South during Reconstruction and later de facto and de jure segregation known as Jim Crow. First formalized in 1866 with the publication of Edward A. Pollard's *The Lost Cause: A New Southern History of the War of the Confederates*, the Lost Cause became a deliberate effort to explain southern defeat as a noble fight for honorable, constitutional goals, lost only because of the loyal northern states' overwhelming economic and industrial power (Pollard 1866). This narrative was promoted by White southerners, eventually led by the United Daughters of the Confederacy. Its ties to White supremacy were challenged with renewed energy after the 2015 murders in Charleston's Emanuel African Methodist Episcopal Church, leading to an ongoing movement to remove Confederate symbols from the public landscape (Evans and Lees 2021; Lees 2021).

What happened in the Indian Territory and at Honey Springs was, at best, an uncomfortable fit in the Lost Cause narrative and the southern history that it inspired. As seen through the work of Mary Jane Warde

(2013) on the Indian Territory and by a new generation of Civil War scholars looking at a "Greater Reconstruction" in the West, what happened in the Indian Territory during this period is now recognized as of great significance for a balanced, objective, and inclusive national story. To say that the Battle of Honey Springs had little impact on the outcome of the Civil War misses the mark, because to say this is to ignore a bigger story of which the Indian Territory and the Trans-Mississippi West is foundational. Getting the story of the Battle of Honey Springs right is crucial because it is an expression of local, regional, and national events. It is important also because the State of Oklahoma preserves this place for reflection and education. I hope that this book will move the needle a bit by adding new perspectives that will help with this public mission or at least inspire additional research and debate on the profound cultural collision that occurred at Honey Springs in 1863.

NOTES

INTRODUCTION

1. In this book "Muscogee" and "Creek" refer to the same Indian nation and people. Today the Muscogee (Creek) Nation of Oklahoma occupies what was referred to in the nineteenth century as the Creek Nation. "Muscogee" is used except when the usage is specifically historical.
2. Indian Territory: the land and waters of the modern state of Oklahoma minus the panhandle and that portion of the state southwest of the North Fork of the Red River.
3. Today the US Geological Survey shows that Honey Springs is on Honey Springs Branch, which flows into Elk Creek. Elk Creek and Wayside Creek converge and become Dirty Creek. Dirty Creek flows southeasterly to its confluence with the Arkansas River below Webbers Falls and immediately above the confluence of the Canadian River and the Arkansas. It is called Dardee Creek on an 1844 map (Gregg 1844) and Elk Creek on one published in 1866 (US Army, Corps of Topographical Engineers, 1866). In most reports of the battle and in other historical accounts, the name for this watercourse as it flows through the Honey Springs Battlefield is Elk Creek, and I retain this usage in this book.
4. It is important to note that these are not verbatim transcriptions of interviews, interviewees were responding to a loosely standardized series of questions, interviewers were both Black and White, and interviews were collected during the de jure Jim Crow era, which certainly affected responses. At the time, an attempt was made to make dialect consistent through editing, so this quote does not necessarily reflect the character of Ms. Davis's speech (Baker and Baker 1996, 8–9).
5. Field work was for three weeks in 1994: November 15–20, November 29–December 4, and December 6–11; for three weeks in 1996: February 28–March 3, March 6–10, and March 12–17; on January 24–26, 1997; and on January 23–24 and September 8, 1999.

CHAPTER ONE

1. This was a fear confirmed by Confederate brigadier general William Steele: "I think the present a favorable time, if a few more regiments can be spared, to carry the war into Kansas" (Steele 1888d, 910).

2. By the convention of the time, Gibson was renamed Fort Blunt in early May in honor of Major General Blunt. To avoid confusion, however, Fort Blunt will be referred to as Fort Gibson throughout this book.
3. On the day of battle, Watie was on detached service at Webbers Falls, and command fell to Major Joseph F. Thompson (Dale and Litton 1995, 140–41).
4. Cooper's report (1988) is published in *The War of the Rebellion: A Compilation of the Official Records of the Union and Confederate Armies*. The other report is of the Twenty-Ninth Texas Cavalry, which was published in the *Standard*, Clarksville, Texas, on September 12, 1863. This report was penned by Lieutenant Colonel Otis G. Welch because Colonel Charles DeMorse was still recovering from wounds suffered on July 17 (Welch 1863).
5. Wells's Texas Battalion was formed at Doaksville, Choctaw Nation, right after the Battle of Honey Springs, and incorporated Gillette's, Scanland's, and other Texans (Grear, n.d.).
6. "North fork": this is probably the unnamed tributary running north through the southwest quarter of Section 35, north of Elk Creek.
7. Blunt says in his report of the battle, "My forces engaged were the First, Second, and Third Indian" (Blunt 1888g, 448). Morning reports taken at Fort Gibson on July 14 record 19 officers and 604 enlisted present for the Third Regiment (Kansas Adjutant General's Office 1863b). The return of casualties printed alongside the officer after-action reports lists two enlisted wounded from this regiment (Return of Casualties 1888, 449) which matches a newspaper listing of casualties of the battle (*Daily Conservative* 1863a, 2). However, no officer after-action report for the Third Regiment exists, and none of those by other officers mention the Third. The company muster roll for July and August mention that Company L (possibly a section of mountain howitzers) came up "too late to participate in the engagement of Honey Springs" (National Archives 1964, 914).
8. This is certainly Thomas White of Company A who is on a list of federal losses from the battle published in the Leavenworth, Kansas, *Daily Conservative* on August 8 (*Daily Conservative* 1863a).
9. The rebel casualty list printed in the Clarksville, Texas, newspaper lists no killed and three wounded for Lee's Battery (*Standard* 1863c).

CHAPTER THREE

1. Although the numbers are unimpressive compared to forces fielded in the eastern theaters of war, "army" is used to describe the organization of the opponents at Honey Springs because they were each headed by a brigadier general and included regiments or battalions of infantry, cavalry and other mounted troops, and artillery.
2. The summary statement of ordnance on hand for the second quarter of 1863 for the Indian Home Guard is marginally annotated in a way that suggests that

the returns are compiled from regimental returns, including some that date after this quarter (National Archives 1983c, 40).

CHAPTER FOUR

1. It is possible, nonetheless, that land use history to the east may have affected preservation of battlefield remains. This land has been free of trees for many years, and LIDAR shows evidence for mechanized clearing of this land. Land divisions resulting from allotment clearly seen elsewhere on the modern landscape are absent here, and what may be remnants of dozer ridges run north to south through this area. Total removal of all battle-related artifacts by land clearing is, however, unlikely.
2. A single Tennessee Sabot shell, minus the sabot, and an unexploded six-pound shell or case with Bormann fuse were found in the Wooded Forty by Gary Moore. The Texas Road passes through this area, as does the rebel line on the Engagement. The Moore donation contains a larger number of specimens than our survey and tells us that, within this forty-acre parcel, twelve-pound shell was more common than twelve-pound case but that US six-pound case was the most commonly used during the cannonade on this part of the battlefield.
3. Another three firearms parts were found north of the Prairie Engagement, close to the Texas Road. These are a percussion lock, side plate, and ramrod ferrule. These were close to one another and are probably part of a civilian country rifle and thus likely associated with US Indian Home Guard or Confederate-allied Indian use. No fighting is suspected this far north, and while it may not relate to the battle, it is far more likely that it does; this is what many of the combatants certainly carried.
4. An assumption here is that the channel of Elk Creek has changed little since the Civil War. While there has been much speculation on this question, little has been resolved. The stone piers of the post-Civil War bridge, constructed in the late nineteenth century, do remain on both sides of the creek, which is testament that the channel is relatively stable. The discovery of battle-related artifacts on both sides of the creek also argues that the landscape may be little changed.
5. Due to a profusion of modern artifacts related to the once-annual battle reenactment and late nineteenth-century and early twentieth-century activity around Honey Springs itself, our metal detector survey did not extend to Honey Springs.

CHAPTER SIX

1. Based on a perimeter drawn closely around the discovered artifacts, the size of the Pumpkin Ridge Engagement is 62.5 percent larger in area than the Prairie

Engagement. The Prairie Engagement artifacts cover an area of 0.2 square miles, with a perimeter of 2 miles, whereas the Pumpkin Ridge Engagement has an area of 0.32 square miles and a perimeter measuring 2.51 miles.

2. Here I will caution that our study did not extend a full three-quarters of a mile on either side of the Texas Road, which would account for Blunt's description of a rebel line one and one-half miles in extent. Thus, although I have said it is possible, if not probable, that evidence of conflict exists beyond the limits of our survey, it is also clear that the core of the fighting did not.
3. Blunt reported that Bass had three hundred soldiers engaged at Honey Springs and that only sixty escaped death, injury, or capture. In his report for 1863, Steele reported that Bass's regiment numbered only about two hundred, although that was early in 1863.
4. Indian Home Guard regiments were regular US regiments, as opposed to being allies or partisans from an independent nation.
5. It would have been standard for troops to be in two ranks, or two deep. Increasing the number of ranks would have shortened the regiment's front, perhaps in reaction to the breadth of the rebel line.

REFERENCES

Abel, Annie Heloise. 1915. *The American Indian as Slaveholder and Secessionist: An Omitted Chapter in the Diplomatic History of the Southern Confederacy*. Cleveland, OH: Arthur H. Clark.

Abel, Annie Heloise. 1919. *The American Indian as Participant in the Civil War.* Cleveland, OH: Arthur H. Clark.

Abel, Annie Heloise. 1925. *The American Indian Under Reconstruction.* Cleveland, OH: Arthur H. Clark.

Adjutant General of the State of Kansas. 1896. *Report of the Adjutant General of the State of Kansas, 1861–1865*, vol. 1. Topeka: Kansas State Printing Company.

Agnew, Brad. 1980. *Fort Gibson: Terminal on the Trail of Tears.* Norman: University of Oklahoma Press.

Agnew, Brad. 2015. "Our Doom as a Nation Is Sealed: The Five Nations in the Civil War." In *The Civil War and Reconstruction in Indian Territory*, edited by Bradley R. Clampitt, 64–87. Lincoln: University of Nebraska Press.

Allen, A. 1888. "Report of Capt. Asaph Allen, Ninth Kansas Cavalry, July 7, 1863 [to Capt. Frank Eno, Assistant Adjutant General]." In *The War of the Rebellion: A Compilation of the Official Records of the Union and Confederate Armies*, series 1, vol. 22, pt. 1 (Reports), 444. Washington, DC: Government Printing Office.

American Battlefield Trust. n.d. "Mine Creek Battlefield." American Battlefield Trust. Accessed December 15, 2018. https://www.battlefields.org/visit/battlefields/mine-creek-battlefield.

Ashcraft, Allan C. 1963. "A Civil War Letter of General William Steele, CSA." *Arkansas Historical Quarterly Society* 22, no. 3 (Autumn): 278–81.

Bailey, Garrick. 1976. "Honey Springs: The Historical Background." In *Honey Springs, Indian Territory: Search for a Confederate Powder House: An Ethnohistorical and Archeological Report*, by Charles D. Cheek, 1–11. Series in Anthropology, no. 2. Oklahoma City: Oklahoma Historical Society.

Baker, T. Lindsay, and Julie P. Baker. 1996. *The WPA Oklahoma Slave Narratives.* Norman: University of Oklahoma Press.

Balicki, Joseph. 2010. "Watch-fires of a Hundred Circling Camps: Theoretical and Practical Approaches to Investigating Civil War Campsites." In *Historical Archaeology of Military Sites: Method and Topic*, edited by Clarence R. Geier, Lawrence E. Babits, Douglas D. Scott, and David G. Orr, 57–74. College Station: Texas A&M University Press.

Barr, Alwyn. 2011. "Confederate Field Artillery." *Handbook of Texas.* Texas State

Historical Association. Accessed July 22, 2021. https://www.tshaonline.org/handbook/entries/confederate-field-artillery.

Bell, Jack. 2003. *Civil War Heavy Explosive Ordnance: A Guide to Large Artillery Projectiles, Torpedoes, and Mines.* Denton: University of North Texas Press.

Biemeck, John F. 2013. *Encyclopedia of Black Powder Artillery Projectiles Found in North America, 1759–1865*, vol. 2. Colonial Beach, VA: Black Powder Artificer Press.

Bill, J. H. 1862. "Notes on Arrow Wounds." *American Journal of the Medical Sciences* 88 (July): 365–87.

Bleed, Peter, Douglas Scott, and Amanda Renner. 2014. "Battlespace: Archaeological Applications of a Strategist's Concept." Paper presented at the Fields of Conflict Conference, University of South Carolina, Columbia, March 12–15, 2014.

Blocki, A. 1885. "General Orders, No. 1, Headquarters Indian Expedition, Camp on Grand River, July 18, 1862." In *The War of the Rebellion: A Compilation of the Official Records of the Union and Confederate Armies*, series 1, vol. 13, 476–77. Washington, DC: Government Printing Office.

Blunt, James G. 1863. "Battle of Honey Springs, Private Letter from Maj. Gen. Blunt." *Burlington [Iowa] Weekly Hawkeye*, August 15, 1863, 3.

Blunt, James G. 1885. "Report of Brig. Gen. James G. Blunt, U.S. Army, Commanding First Division, Army of the Frontier [to Brig. Gen. John M. Schofield, October 28, 1862]." In *The War of the Rebellion: A Compilation of the Official Records of the Union and Confederate Armies*, series 1, vol. 13, 325–28. Washington, DC: Government Printing Office.

Blunt, James G. 1888a. "Jas. G. Blunt, Brigadier-General, Commanding, to Col. William A. Phillips, Commanding Indian Brigade, February 23, 1863." In *The War of the Rebellion: A Compilation of the Official Records of the Union and Confederate Armies*, series 1, vol. 22, pt. 2 (Correspondence), 121–22. Washington, DC: Government Printing Office.

Blunt, James G. 1888b. "Jas. G. Blunt, Major-General, Commanding, to Col. William A. Phillips, Fayetteville, Ark., April 11, 1863." In *The War of the Rebellion: A Compilation of the Official Records of the Union and Confederate Armies*, series 1, vol. 22, pt. 2 (Correspondence), 210. Washington, DC: Government Printing Office.

Blunt, James G. 1888c. "Jas. G. Blunt, Major-General, to Maj. Gen. John M. Schofield, July 30, 1863." In *The War of the Rebellion: A Compilation of the Official Records of the Union and Confederate Armies*, series 1, vol. 22, pt. 2 (Correspondence), 411. Washington, DC: Government Printing Office.

Blunt, James G. 1888d. "Jas. G. Blunt, Major-General, [to Major H. Z. Curtis?], July 13, 1863." In *The War of the Rebellion: A Compilation of the Official Records of the Union and Confederate Armies*, series 1, vol. 22, pt. 2 (Correspondence), 367–68. Washington, DC: Government Printing Office.

Blunt, James G. 1888e. "Major-General Jas. G. Blunt to Major-General Schofield,

June 26, 1863." In *The War of the Rebellion: A Compilation of the Official Records of the Union and Confederate Armies*, series 1, vol. 22, pt. 2 (Correspondence), 337–38. Washington, DC: Government Printing Office.

Blunt, James G. 1888f. "Report of Maj. Gen. James G. Blunt, U.S. Army, Commanding District of Kansas, June 8, 1863 [sent to Major-General Schofield, Commanding Department of the Missouri]." In *The War of the Rebellion: A Compilation of the Official Records of the Union and Confederate Armies*, series 1, vol. 22. pt. 1 (Reports), 341–42. Washington, DC: Government Printing Office.

Blunt, James G. 1888g. "Report of Maj. Gen. James G. Blunt, U.S. Army, Commanding District of the Frontier [to Maj. Gen. John M. Schofield, July 26, 1863]." In *The War of the Rebellion: A Compilation of the Official Records of the Union and Confederate Armies*, series 1, vol. 22, pt. 1 (Reports), 447–48. Washington, DC: Government Printing Office.

Blunt, James G. 1932. "General Blunt's Account of His Civil War Experiences." *Kansas Historical Quarterly* 1, no. 3 (May): 211–265. Accessed October 14, 2019. https://www.kshs.org/p/general-blunt-s-account-of-his-civil-war-experiences/12543.

Bonsall, James. 2019. "Challenges of Working with Legacy Data from Detectorists: A Case Study in the Fabrication of Evidence." In *Conference Proceedings: Fields of Conflict, 2016*, edited by T. L. Sutherland, D. Shiels, G. Hughes, and S. H. Sutherland. Dublin, Ireland: Trinity College.

Bowles, John. 1888. "Report of Lieut. Col. John Bowles, First Kansas Colored Infantry, Judson's Brigade, July 20, 1863 [to Col. William R. Judson]." In *The War of the Rebellion: A Compilation of the Official Records of the Union and Confederate Armies*, series 1, vol. 22, pt. 1 (Reports), 449–51. Washington, DC: Government Printing Office.

Bray, Robert T. 1958. "A Report of Archaeological Investigations at the Reno-Benteen Site, Custer Battlefield National Monument." Manuscript on file at Midwest Archeological Center, Lincoln, Nebraska.

Britton, Wiley. 1882. *Memoirs of the Rebellion on the Border, 1863*. Chicago: Cushing, Thomas & Co.

Britton, Wiley. 1890. *The Civil War on the Border, 1861–1862*. New York: G. P. Putnam's Sons.

Britton, Wiley. 1899. *The Civil War on the Border*, vol. 2, *1863–1865*. New York: G. P. Putnam's Sons.

Britton, Wiley. 1922. *The Union Indian Brigade in the Civil War.* Kansas City, MO: Franklin Hudson Publishing.

Buchanan, James S., and Carl Plischke. 1976. "Appendix A: Buchanan-Plischke Honey Springs Battlefield Survey, from Grant Foreman Collection, Indian Archives Division, Oklahoma Historical Society, May 8, 1938." In *Honey Springs, Indian Territory; Search for a Confederate Powder House: An Ethnohistorical and Archeological Report*, by Charles D. Cheek, 129–34. Series in Anthropology, no. 2. Oklahoma City: Oklahoma Historical Society, 1976.

Buresh, Lumir. 1978. *October 25th and the Battle of Mine Creek.* Kansas City, MO: Lowell Press.

Burrell, James. 1877a. "Second Colorado Veterans, Sixth Paper." *Colorado Transcript* 11, no. 16 (March 21, 1877).

Burrell, James. 1877b. "Second Colorado Veterans, Sixth Paper Continued." *Colorado Transcript,* 11, no.19 (April 11, 1877).

Butler Center for Arkansas Studies. n.d. a. "Earls King, 6th Kansas Cavalry." Butler Center for Arkansas Studies, Central Arkansas Library System, image bc_pho_3a_10315. https://cdm15728.contentdm.oclc.org/digital/collection/p15728coll1/id/19964/rec/2.

Butler Center for Arkansas Studies. n.d. b. "Henry Gable (on right) and unidentified man, 6th Kansas Cavalry." Butler Center for Arkansas Studies, Central Arkansas Library System, image bc_pho_3a_0288_01. https://cdm15728.contentdm.oclc.org/digital/collection/p15728coll1/id/19880/rec/1.

Campbell, William T. 1888. "Report of Lieut. Col. William T. Campbell, Sixth Kansas Cavalry, July 19, 1863 [to Colonel William R. Judson]." In *The War of the Rebellion: A Compilation of the Official Records of the Union and Confederate Armies,* series 1, vol. 22, pt. 1 (Reports), 452–53. Washington, DC: Government Printing Office.

Carman, John, and Patricia Carman. 2019. "The Wider Landscapes of Fields of Conflict." In *Conference Proceedings: Fields of Conflict, 2016,* edited by T. L. Sutherland, D. Shiels, G. Hughes, and S. H. Sutherland. Dublin, Ireland: Trinity College.

Castel, Albert. 1968. *General Sterling Price and the Civil War in the West.* Baton Rouge: Louisiana State University Press.

Checotah News. 1965. "Civil War Relics Asked for Museum." Checotah, OK. April 23, 1965

Cheek, Charles D. 1976. *Honey Springs, Indian Territory: Search for a Confederate Powder House: An Ethnohistorical and Archeological Report.* Oklahoma City: Oklahoma Historical Society, 1976. Series in Anthropology, no. 2.

Choctaw Nation of Oklahoma. n.d. "Red River Museum Arrow." Choctaw Nation Cultural Services, Choctaw Nation of Oklahoma. Accessed December 6, 2023. https://web.archive.org/web/20120114190401/http://www.choctawnationculture.com/choctaw-culture/early-choctaw-traditional-arts/bows-and-arrows/red-river-museum-arrows.aspx.

Cincinnati Daily Commercial. 1863. "The Battle of Honey Springs." August 10, 1863, 4.

Civil War Archive. n.d. "3rd Battery Light Artillery." In "Union Regimental Histories, Kansas." Civil War Archive. Accessed August 26, 2019. http://www.civilwararchive.com/Unreghst/unksarty.htm.

Coates, Earl J., and Dean S. Thomas. 1990. *An Introduction to Civil War Small Arms.* Gettysburg, PA: Thomas Publications.

Colburn, A. V. 1888. "General Orders, No. 48, Hdqrs. Department of the Missouri, Saint Louis, June 9, 1863 [by A. V. Colburn, Assistant Adjutant-General]." In *The War of the Rebellion: A Compilation of the Official Records of the Union and Confederate Armies*, series 1, vol. 22, pt. 2 (Correspondence), 315. Washington, DC: Government Printing Office.

Colorado State Archives. 1863. *Morning Reports of Major J. Nelson Smith, Battalion, Second Colorado Infantry, July 1862*. Military Records, Administrative Records, Morning Reports 1861–1865. Colorado State Archives, Denver.

Confer, Clarissa W. 2007. *The Cherokee Nation in the Civil War.* Norman: University of Oklahoma Press.

Cooper, Douglas H. 1861. "Order #23 from Col. D. H. Cooper authorizing Colonel Drew concerning arming the Cherokee Regiment." October 22, 1861. John Drew Manuscript Collection, 4026.1822, Gilcrease Museum, Tulsa, Oklahoma. Accessed September 26, 2018. https://collections.gilcrease.org/object/40261822.

Cooper, Douglas H. 1885. "Douglas H. Cooper to Maj. Gen. Earl Van Dorn, May 6, 1862." In *The War of the Rebellion: A Compilation of the Official Records of the Union and Confederate Armies*, series 1, vol. 13, 823–34. Washington, DC: Government Printing Office.

Cooper, Douglas H. 1888. "Report of Brig. Gen. Douglas H. Cooper, C.S. Army, Commanding Confederate Forces [to Brig. Gen. William Steele, August 12, 1863]." In *The War of the Rebellion: A Compilation of the Official Records of the Union and Confederate Armies*, series 2, vol. 22, pt. 1 (Reports), 457–61. Washington, DC: Government Printing Office.

Cooper, S. 1881. "S. Cooper, Adjutant and Inspector General, to Brigadier-General McCullock, Commanding, Montgomery, Ala., May 13, 1861." In *The War of the Rebellion: A Compilation of the Official Records of the Union and Confederate Armies*, series 1, vol. 3, 575–76. Washington, DC: Government Printing Office.

Corbett, Bill. n.d. "Jefferson Highway." In *The Encyclopedia of Oklahoma History and Culture.* Accessed April 16, 2020. https://www.okhistory.org/publications/enc/entry.php?entry=JE010.

Crisman, Kevin J., William B. Lees, and John Davis. 2013. "The Western River Steamboat *Heroine*, 1832–1838, Oklahoma, USA: Excavations, Summary of Finds, and History." *International Journal of Nautical Archaeology* 42, no. 2: 365–81.

Curtis, H. Z. 1885. "General Orders, No. 7, Hdqrs. Dept. of the Missouri, October 12, 1862." In *The War of the Rebellion: A Compilation of the Official Records of the Union and Confederate Armies*, series 1, vol. 13, 730. Washington, DC: Government Printing Office.

Curtis, H. Z. 1888a. "H. Z. Curtis, Assistant Adjutant-General, to Lieut. Col. C. W. Marsh, Asst. Adjt. Gen., Dept. of the Missouri, Saint Louis, Mo., July 6, 1863."

In *The War of the Rebellion: A Compilation of the Official Records of the Union and Confederate Armies*, series 1, vol. 22, pt. 2 (Correspondence), 354. Washington, DC: Government Printing Office.

Curtis, H. Z. 1888b. "Special Orders, No. 4, Hdqrs. State of Mo., Adjt. Gen.'s Office, January 13, 1863." In *The War of the Rebellion: A Compilation of the Official Records of the Union and Confederate Armies*, series 1, vol. 22, pt. 2 (Correspondence), 40. Washington, DC: Government Printing Office.

Curtis, Samuel R. 1888a. "Saml. R. Curtis, Brigadier-General, to Captain J. C. Kelton, March 13, 1862." In *The War of the Rebellion: A Compilation of the Official Records of the Union and Confederate Armies*, series 1, vo. 8, 195. Washington, DC: Government Printing Office.

Curtis, Samuel R. 1888b. "Saml. R. Curtis, Major-General, to Col. William A. Phillips, Camp John Ross, near Indian Territory, February 17, 1863." In *The War of the Rebellion: A Compilation of the Official Records of the Union and Confederate Armies*, series 1, vol. 22, pt. 2 (Correspondence), 113–14. Washington, DC: Government Printing Office.

Curtis, Samuel R. 1888c. "Saml. R. Curtis, Major-General, to Colonel Phillips, in the Field, April 20, 1863." In *The War of the Rebellion: A Compilation of the Official Records of the Union and Confederate Armies*, series 1, vol. 22, pt. 2 (Correspondence), 230. Washington, DC: Government Printing Office.

Daily Conservative. 1863a. "From Ft. Gibson & Ft. Smith, Arrival of Gen. Blunt." Leavenworth, KS. July 22, 1863, 2.

Daily Conservative. 1863b. "Honey Springs: Official List of Our Losses." Leavenworth, KS. August 8, 1863, 1.

Daily Conservative. 1863c. "Who Did the Fighting." Leavenworth, KS. August 8, 1863, 1.

Daily National Republican. 1862. "Gen Lane's Black Troops—They Fight Bravely." Washington, DC. November 10, 1862, 4.

Dale, Edward Everett, and Gaston Litton. 1995. *Cherokee Cavaliers: Forty Years of Cherokee History as Told in the Correspondence of the Ridge-Watie-Boudinot Family.* Norman: University of Oklahoma Press.

Dana, C. H., and J. P. Thayer. 1897. "Field Notes of the Survey of the Subdivision Lines of Township No. 12 North, Range 17 East of the Indian Base and Meridian in the Indian Territory." *Notes for Oklahoma*, volume 00156, survey 22288. Washington, DC: US Department of the Interior, Bureau of Land Management, General Land Office Records. https://glorecords.blm.gov/details/fieldnote/default.aspx?dm_id=85869&s_dm_id=22288&sid=4kpwoyia.oao.

Darling, Lyman A. 1976. "Appendix B: Letter of Lyman A. Darling, November 28, 1972." In *Honey Springs, Indian Territory: Search for a Confederate Powder House: An Ethnohistorical and Archeological Report*, by Charles D. Cheek, 136–37. Series in Anthropology, no. 2. Oklahoma City: Oklahoma Historical Society, 1976.

Delashaw, Corie. n.d. "Cooper, Douglas Hancock (1815–1879)." In *The*

Encyclopedia of Oklahoma History and Culture. Accessed September 23, 2020. https://www.okhistory.org/publications/enc/entry.php?entry=CO051.

DeMorse, Charles. 1863. "Letter to General Douglas H. Cooper, August 29, 1863." *Standard* (Clarksville, TX), December 5, 1863, 1.

DeMuth William E., Jr., Gary G. Nicholas, and Bryce L. Munger. 1978. "Buckshot Wounds." *Journal of Trauma: Injury, Infection, and Critical Care* 18, no. 1 (January): 53–57.

Department of the Navy. 1990. *Small Unit Leader's Guide to Weather and Terrain.* Fleet Marine Force Reference Publication 0–51 (renumbered MCRP 3–11.1B). Washington, DC: Department of the Navy, Headquarters of the United States Marine Corps.

Doran, Michael F. 1975. "Population Statistics of Nineteenth Century Indian Territory." *Chronicles of Oklahoma* 53, no. 4: 492–515.

Drass, Richard. 1980. "Oklahoma Archaeological Survey Data Record, Site Number Og-18." Record on file, Oklahoma Archaeological Survey University of Oklahoma, Norman.

Earle, Ethan. 1863a. "Articles Returned to the Quarter Master." In *1st Kansan Colored Vol. Reg't* (Account Book), 25. Mss C 4911. R. Stanton Avery Special Collections Department, New England Historic Genealogical Society, Boston.

Earle, Ethan. 1863b. "Clothing Camp & Garris, Equipage Received January, February & March 1863." In *1st Kansan Colored Vol. Reg't* (Account Book), 21. Mss C 4911. R. Stanton Avery Special Collections Department, New England Historic Genealogical Society, Boston.

Earle, Ethan. 1863c. "Clothing Issues July Fort Blunt." In *1st Kansan Colored Vol. Reg't* (Account Book), 43. Mss C 4911. R. Stanton Avery Special Collections Department, New England Historic Genealogical Society (Boston, Mass.).

Earle, Ethan. 1863d. "Equipment Issues May–October 1863." In *1st Kansan Colored Vol. Reg't* (Account Book), 48. Mss C 4911. R. Stanton Avery Special Collections Department, New England Historic Genealogical Society, Boston.

Earle, Ethan. 1873. "History of First Kansas Colored Volunteer Regiment." In *1st Kansan Colored Vol. Reg't* (Account Book), 80–132. Mss C 4911. R. Stanton Avery Special Collections Department, New England Historic Genealogical Society, Boston.

Edwards, Whit. n.d. a. "Fort Wayne, Battle of." In *The Encyclopedia of Oklahoma History and Culture.* Accessed July 29, 2021. https://www.okhistory.org/publications/enc/entry.php?entry=FO048.

Edwards, Whit. n.d. b. "Perryville, Battle of." In *The Encyclopedia of Oklahoma History and Culture.* Accessed August 12, 2021. https://www.okhistory.org/publications/enc/entry.php?entry=PE021.

Edwards, Whit. 1995. "Butternut and Blue: Confederate Uniforms in the Trans-Mississippi." *Chronicles of Oklahoma* 73, no. 4: 424–37.

Edwards, William B. 1962. *Civil War Guns: The Complete Story of Federal and*

Confederate Small Arms: Design, Manufacture, Identification, Procurement, Issue, Employment, Effectiveness, and Postwar Disposal. Harrisburg, PA: Stackpole.

Emory, William H. 1880. "Report of Lieut. Col. William H. Emory, First U.S. Cavalry, of the Abandonment of Forts Arbuckle, Cobbs, and Washita, Ind. T., May 19, 1861." In *The War of the Rebellion: A Compilation of the Official Records of the Union and Confederate Armies*, series 1, vol. 1, 648–49. Washington, DC: Government Printing Office.

Encyclopaedia Britannica. 2018. "Material culture." In *Encyclopedia Britannica.* Accessed April 23, 2021. https://www.britannica.com/topic/material-culture.

Epple, Jess C. 1964. *Honey Springs Depot: Elk Creek, Creek Nation, Indian Territory.* Muskogee, OK: Hoffman Printing Company.

Evans, Jocelyn J., and William B. Lees. 2021. Introduction to "Reframing Confederate Monuments: Memory, Power, and Identity," ed. Jocelyn J. Evans and William B. Lees, special issue, *Social Science Quarterly* 102 (3): 959–78.

Evening Star. 1868. "Sealed Proposals to Remove the Remains of Deceased United States Soldiers Lying Buried in the Vicinity of Fort Gibson." Washington, DC, May 26, 1868, 4.

Felmly, Bradford K., and John C. Grady. 1975. *Suffering to Silence: 29th Texas Calvary, CSA, Regimental History.* Quanah, TX: Nortex Press.

Foreman, Grant. 1936. *Down the Texas Road: Historic Places Along Highway 69 Through Oklahoma.* Historic Oklahoma Series, no. 2. Norman: University of Oklahoma Press.

Foreman, Grant, ed. 1937a. "Biographical Sketch of Mrs. Elizabeth Watts." Compiled by L. D. Wilson, field worker, April 27, 1937. Indian Pioneer History Collection, IPH Microfilm, roll 4, vol. 11, 278–94. Oklahoma Historical Society, American Indian Archives Division, Oklahoma City.

Foreman, Grant, ed. 1937b. "Interview with Arthur J. Cline." By Lula Austin, field worker, July 12, 1937. Indian Pioneer History Collection, IPH Microfilm, roll 1, vol. 2, 119–24. Oklahoma Historical Society, American Indian Archives Division, Oklahoma City.

Foreman, Grant, ed. 1937c. "Interview with John Chupko, Henryetta, Okla.." By Henry Day, field worker, June 3, 1937. Indian Pioneer History Collection, IPH Microfilm, roll 1, vol. 2, 91–92. Oklahoma Historical Society, American Indian Archives Division, Oklahoma City.

Foreman, Grant, ed. 1937d. "Interview with Thomas H. Graham." By Lawrence A. Williams, interviewer, July 12, 1937. Indian Pioneer History Collection, IPH Microfilm, roll 9, vol. 26, 252–56. Oklahoma Historical Society, American Indian Archives Division, Oklahoma City.

Foreman, Grant, ed. 1937e. "Interview with William Rex Howland, Cherokee Indian." By Jas. S. Buchanan, interviewer. Indian Pioneer History Collection, IPH Microfilm, roll 10, vol. 30, 33–37. Oklahoma Historical Society, American Indian Archives Division, Oklahoma City.

Foreman, Grant, ed. 1937f. "The Recollections of a Cherokee Freedman, Dennis

Vann." By Reuben Partridge, interviewer. Indian Pioneer History Collection, IPH Microfilm, roll 4, vol. 11, 62–69. Oklahoma Historical Society, American Indian Archives Division, Oklahoma City.

Fortney, Jeffrey L. 2016. "Serving the Choctaw Cause: Robert M. Jones, Sovereignty, and Pragmatic Diplomacy During the American Civil War." *American Nineteenth Century History* 17 (2): 215–33.

Frank Leslie's Illustrated Newspaper. 1863. "The War in Arkansas—the Battle of Honey Springs, July 17—Defeat of the Rebels Under General Cooper by the U. S. Troops Under Major-General James G. Blunt—from a sketch by James R. O'Neill." New York. August 29, 1863, 364. Accessed May 10, 2022. https://archive.org/details/franklesliesilluv1516lesl/page/364/mode/2up.

Franks, Kenny A. n.d. "Watie's Regiment." In *The Encyclopedia of Oklahoma History and Culture.* Accessed April 16, 2020. https://www.okhistory.org/publications/enc/entry.php?entry=WA041.

Fredriksen, John C. 2000. *Green Coats and Glory: The United States Regiment of Riflemen, 1808–1821.* Youngstown, NY: Old Fort Niagara Association.

Fremantle, Arthur James Lyon. 1864. *Three Months in the Southern States, April, June, 1863.* Mobile, AL: S. H. Goetzel. https://docsouth.unc.edu/imls/fremantle/fremantle.html.

Gibson, Arrell M. 1965. *Oklahoma: A History of Five Centuries.* Norman, OK: Harlow.

Gibson, Arrell M. 1971. *The Chickasaws.* Norman: University of Oklahoma Press.

Grayson, G. W., and W. David Baird. 1988. *A Creek Warrior for the Confederacy: The Autobiography of Chief G. W. Grayson.* Civilization of the American Indian Series. Norman: University of Oklahoma Press.

Grear, Charles D. n.d. "Wells's Texas Battalion." *Handbook of Texas Online.* Texas State Historical Association. Accessed September 24, 2021. https://www.tshaonline.org/handbook/entries/wellss-texas-battalion.

Greene, Jerome A., and Douglas D. Scott. 2004. *Finding Sand Creek: History, Archaeology, and the 1864 Massacre Site.* Norman: University of Oklahoma Press.

Greeno, H. S. 1885. "Report of Captain Harris S. Greeno, Sixth Kansas Cavalry, July 17, 1862 [to Col. William Weer, Commanding Indian Expedition]." In *The War of the Rebellion: A Compilation of the Official Records of the Union and Confederate Armies,* series 1, vol. 13, 161–62. Washington, DC: Government Printing Office.

Gregg, Josiah. 1844. *A Map of the Indian Territory, Northern Texas, and New Mexico, Showing the Great Western Prairie.* Entered according to an Act of Congress in the year 1844 by Sidney E. Morse and Samuel Breese in the Clerks Office of the Southern District of New York. Oklahoma State University Library Digital Collections. https://dc.library.okstate.edu/digital/collection/OKMaps/id/3638/rec/1.

Guttman, Jon. n.d. "Battle of Honey Springs Decided Control of Indian Territory." Accessed August 26, 2019. https://www.historynet.com/battle-of-honey-springs-decided-control-of-indian-territory.htm.

Harris, Charles. 1987. "Two Master Hunters Take On Honey Springs." *Treasure Found!* 13, no. 2: 20–24.

Hastain, E. 1910. *Hastain's Township Plats of the Creek Nation.* Muscogee, OK: Model Printing.

Hauptman, Laurence M. 1995. *Between Two Fires: American Indians in the Civil War.* New York: Free Press.

Heiston, Thornton B. 1888. "General Orders No. 25, Hdqrs. First Brig. Indian Troops, July 14, 1863, By Order of Brig. Gen. D. H. Cooper." In *The War of the Rebellion: A Compilation of the Official Records of the Union and Confederate Armies,* series 1, vol. 22, pt. 1 (Reports), 461–62. Washington, DC: Government Printing Office.

Hoagland, Bruce W. 2008. "Vegetation of Oklahoma." In *Earth Science and Mineral Resources of Oklahoma.* Edited by Kenneth S. Johnson and Kenneth V. Luza. Educational Publication 9. Norman: Oklahoma Geological Survey, University of Oklahoma. http://www.ogs.ou.edu/pubsscanned/EP9p16_19soil_veg_cl.pdf.

Hopkins, Henry. 1888. "Report of Capt. Henry Hopkins, Kansas Battery, July 21, 1863." In *The War of the Rebellion: A Compilation of the Official Records of the Union and Confederate Armies,* series 1, vol. 22, pt. 1 (Reports), 456–57. Washington, DC: Government Printing Office.

Horrell, Christopher, Della A. Scott-Ireton, Roger C. Smith, James Levy, and Joe Knetsch. 2009. "The Flintlock Site (8JA1763): An Unusual Underwater Deposit in the Apalachicola River, Florida." *Journal of Maritime Archaeology* 4, no. 1: 5–19.

Howell, Edgar M. 1982. *United States Army Headgear 1855–1902.* Catalog of United States Army Uniforms in the Collections of the Smithsonian Institution, 2. Washington, DC: Government Printing Office.

Hunt, Jeffrey William. 2018. "Palmito Ranch, Battle of." *Handbook of Texas Online.* Texas State Historical Association. Accessed May 20, 2020. http://www.tshaonline.org/handbook/online/articles/qfp01.

Huston, James L. n.d. "Civil War Era." In *The Encyclopedia of Oklahoma History and Culture.* Accessed October 22, 2019. https://www.okhistory.org/publications/enc/entry.php?entry=CI011.

Johansson, M. Jane, ed. 2016. *Albert C. Ellithorpe, the First Indian Home Guards and the Civil War on the Trans-Mississippi Frontier.* Baton Rouge: Louisiana State University Press.

Johnson, Ben. n.d. "Kings and Queens of England and Britain." *Historic UK.* Accessed September 16, 2019. https://www.historic-uk.com/HistoryUK/KingsQueensofBritain.

Johnson, David F. 1948. *Uniform Buttons: American Armed Forces, 1784–1948,* vol. 1, *Descriptions and Values.* Watkins Glen, NY: Century House.

Johnson, Howard L. 2008. "Climate." In *Earth Science and Mineral Resources of Okla-*

homa. Edited by Kenneth S. Johnson and Kenneth V. Luza. Educational Publication 9. Norman: Oklahoma Geological Survey, University of Oklahoma. http://www.ogs.ou.edu/pubsscanned/EP9p16_19soil_veg_cl.pdf.

Johnson, Kenneth S. 2008. "Topographic Map of Oklahoma." In *Earth Science and Mineral Resources of Oklahoma*. Edited by Kenneth S. Johnson and Kenneth V. Luza. Educational Publication 9. Norman: Oklahoma Geological Survey, University of Oklahoma. http://ogs.ou.edu/docs/educationalpublications/EP9.pdf.

Johnson, T. H. R., and C. H. Hickman. 1896b. "Field Notes of the Survey of the Subdivision Lines of Township No. 15 North, Range 18 East of the Indian Base and Meridian in the Indian Territory." *Notes for Oklahoma*, volume 00151, survey 22969. Washington, DC: US Department of the Interior, Bureau of Land Management, General Land Office Records. https://glorecords.blm.gov/details/fieldnote/default.aspx?dm_id=84457&s_dm_id=22969&sid=q1jwupel.an3.

Johnston, Janene W. 2018. "Overshadowed: History, Public Engagement, and Conflict Archaeology at Florida's Natural Bridge." Master's thesis, Department of Anthropology, College of Arts, Social Sciences, and Humanities, University of West Florida.

Josephy, Alvin M., Jr. 1991. *The Civil War in the American West*. New York: Alfred A. Knopf.

Kansas Adjutant General's Office. 1863a. "Consolidated Morning Report of the 1st Regiment of Indian Home Guards July 14, 1863." Consolidated Morning Reports, 1st Regiment, Indian Home Guard (1862–1865). #192333. Records of the Adjutant General's Office of the State of Kansas. Kansas Historical Society, State Archives, Topeka.

Kansas Adjutant General's Office. 1863b. "Consolidated Morning Report of the 3d Regiment of Indian Home Guard July 14, 1863." Consolidated Morning Reports, 3d Regiment, Indian Home Guards (1862 to 1865). #192333. Kansas Historical Society, State Archives, Topeka.

Kansas Adjutant General's Office. 1863c. "Consolidated Morning Report of the 6th Regiment of Kansas Cavalry July 14, 1863." Consolidated Morning Reports 6th Kansas Volunteer Cavalry Regiment for 1862 to 1865. #192333. Kansas Historical Society, State Archives, Topeka.

Kansas Historical Society. n.d. "Blunt's Sword and Accoutrements." In *Kansapedia*. Accessed September 9, 2019. https://www.kshs.org/kansapedia/blunt-s-sword-and-accoutrements/10114.

Kansas National Guard. n.d. "Civil War: The 2nd Kansas Battery." Museum of the Kansas National Guard. Accessed August 26, 2019. https://www.kansasguardmuseum.com/?page_id=2044.

Kennedy, Joseph C. G. 1864. Introduction to *Population of the United States in 1860*. Washington, DC: Government Printing Office.

King, Christopher. 2019. "Patterns in the Chaos: Battlefields Within the Landscape." In *Conference Proceedings: Fields of Conflict, 2016*, edited by T. L. Sutherland, D. Shiels, G. Hughes, and S. H. Sutherland. Dublin, Ireland: Trinity College.

Krauthamer, Barbara. n.d. "Slavery." In *The Encyclopedia of Oklahoma History and Culture*. Accessed April 19, 2020. https://www.okhistory.org/publications/enc/entry.php?entry=SL003.

Leavenworth, J. H. 1888. "J. H. Leavenworth, Colonel, Commanding Second Colorado Volunteers, to Maj. Gen. E. V. Sumner, March 22, 1863." *The War of the Rebellion: A Compilation of the Official Records of the Union and Confederate Armies*, series 1, vol. 22, pt. 2 (Correspondence), 172–73. Washington, DC: Government Printing Office.

Lees, William B. 1975. "A Report on the Ethnohistory and Archaeology of the Claremore Village Sites, Rogers County, Oklahoma." Report submitted to University of Tulsa Office of Research in fulfillment of student research grant R-311–53. Tulsa, Oklahoma.

Lees, William B. 1992. "Preservation and Interpretive Development Plan, Mine Creek Battlefield State Historic Site, Linn County, Kansas." Kansas State Historical Society, August 1, 1992.

Lees, William B. 1994. "When the Shooting Stopped, the War Began." In *Look to the Earth: Historical Archaeology and the Civil War*, edited by Clarence R. Geier and Susan Winter Frye, 39–59. Knoxville: University of Tennessee Press.

Lees, William B. 1996. "The Impact of Metal Detectors: Preservation Lessons from the Battlefield." Paper presented at the Society for Historical Archaeology Conference on Historical and Underwater Archaeology, Cincinnati, Ohio, January 2–7, 1996.

Lees, William B. 1998. "Archaeology of the Mine Creek Civil War Battlefield, Linn County, Kansas." Kansas State Historical Society, June 1998.

Lees, William B. 2002. "Earthworks and Arrowheads: Fort Blunt and Its Defenses in July 1863." Paper presented at the Society for Historical Archaeology Conference on Historical and Underwater Archaeology, Long Beach, CA, January 14–19, 2002.

Lees, William B. 2004. "A Clash of Cultures: New Finds Reveal Surprises About Who Fought Where at Honey Springs." *Dig* (Cobblestone Publishing) 6, no. 2: 16.

Lees, William B. 2016. "Closing the Loop: The Battle of Honey Springs, Creek Nation, 1863." Paper presented at the Society for Historical Archaeology Conference on Historical and Underwater Archaeology, Washington, DC, January 6–9, 2016.

Lees, William B. 2021. "The Problem with Confederate Monuments on Our Heritage Landscape." In "Reframing Confederate Monuments: Memory, Power, and Identity," ed. Jocelyn Evans and William B. Lees, special issue, *Social Science Quarterly* 102, no. 3: 979–1001.

Lees, William B., and Vergil E. Noble. 2015. "J. C. Harrington Medal in Historical Archaeology, Douglas D. Scott." *Historical Archaeology* 49, no. 2: 1–9. https://doi.org/10.1007/BF03377134.

Lindberg, Kip, Matt Matthews, and Thomas Moonlight. 2003. "The Eagle of the 11th Kansas: Wartime Reminiscences of Colonel Thomas Moonlight." *Arkansas Historical Quarterly* 62, no. 1: 1–41.

Linenthal, Edward Tabor. 1991. *Sacred Ground: Americans and Their Battlefields.* Urbana: University of Illinois Press.

Literary World. 1890. "Border History." *Literary World* 21, no. 18: 282–83.

Longo, William R. 1988. "I Led Two Lives: Archaeologist Infiltrates Treasure Club." *Treasure* 19, no. 8: 6–10, 67.

Lubbock, F. R. 1886. "F. R. Lubbock to Maj. Gen. J. B. Magruder, December 6, 1862." In *The War of the Rebellion: A Compilation of the Official Records of the Union and Confederate Armies,* series I, vol. 15, 896–97. Washington, DC: Government Printing Office.

Madaus, Howard Michael. 1995. "The Use of the Percussion Shotgun in Texas Prior to and During the American Civil War, 1861–1865." *Armax* 5, no. 1: 134–72.

Madaus, Howard Michael. 1997. "Contract Rifles of the Texas State Military Board, 1862–1864." *American Society of Arms Collector Bulletin* 77: 17–31. Accessed February 11, 2022. https://americansocietyofarmscollectors.org/wp-content/uploads/2019/06/1997-B77-Contract-Rifles-of-the-Texas-State-Milit.pdf.

Magruder, J. Bankhead. 1886a. "J. Bankhead Magruder, Major-General, to Hon. James A. Seddon, Secretary of War, December 13, 1862." In *The War of the Rebellion: A Compilation of the Official Records of the Union and Confederate Armies,* series 1, vol. 15, 897–98. Washington, DC: Government Printing Office.

Magruder, J. Bankhead. 1886b. "J. Bankhead Magruder, Major-General, to Lieut. Col. S. S. Anderson, December 9, 1862." In *The War of the Rebellion: A Compilation of the Official Records of the Union and Confederate Armies,* series 1, vol. 15, 895–96. Washington, DC: Government Printing Office.

Mahon, John K. 1967. *History of the Second Seminole War (1835–1842).* Gainesville: University of Florida Press.

Matthews, James M. 1864. "The Treaties Concluded by the Confederate States with the Indian Tribes." In *The Statutes at Large of the Provisional Government of the Confederate States of America,* 289–411. Richmond, VA: R. M. Smith.

May, Jon D. n.d. "McIntosh, Chilly (ca. 1800–1875)." In *The Encyclopedia of Oklahoma History and Culture.* Accessed November 8, 2020. https://www.okhistory.org/publications/enc/entry.php?entry=MC029.

McAlpine, R. L., and J. W. Riley. 1896. "Field Notes of the Survey of the Subdivision Lines of Township No. 13 North, Range 17 East of the Indian Base and Meridian in the Indian Territory." *Notes for Oklahoma,* volume 00151, survey 22584. Washington, DC: US Department of the Interior, Bureau of Land

Management, General Land Office Records. https://glorecords.blm.gov/details/fieldnote/default.aspx?dm_id=84457&s_dm_id=22584&sid=kopbzjl1.evw.

McAulay, John D. 1981. *Carbines of the Civil War, 1861–1865*. Union City, TN: Pioneer Press.

McBride, W. Stephen, and William E. Sharp. 1991. "Archaeological Investigations at Camp Nelson: A Union Quartermaster Depot and Hospital in Jessamine, Kentucky." University of Kentucky Program for Cultural Resource Assessment Archaeological Report 241. Lexington.

McFadden, Boyd. 1989. "The Mystery of Honey Springs: Search for Relics Leads to Civil War Puzzle." *Treasure Search* 17, no. 2 (March–April): 37–41.

McGee, David H. 2017. "Fort Pulaski." In *New Georgia Encyclopedia*. Last edited April 25, 2017. Accessed November 17, 2019. https://www.georgiaencyclopedia.org/articles/history-archaeology/fort-pulaski.

McGirt v. Oklahoma. 2020. 18–9526.

McKenney, T. I. 1888. "Acting Assistant Adjutant-General T. I. McKenney to Earl Van Dorn, Commanding Confederate Forces, March 9, 1862." In *The War of the Rebellion: A Compilation of the Official Records of the Union and Confederate Armies*, series 1, vol. 8, 194. Washington, DC: Government Printing Office.

McKinnon, Jennifer F., Madeline Roth, and Toni L. Carrell. 2020. *Submerged Battlefield Survey Manual*. Grant Agreement No. GA-2287–17–015. American Battlefield Protection Program, Ships of Exploration and Discovery Research.

Military History Collection. 1862a. "Company E. Clothing Receipt Roll[s], 1862 Dec. 15–31." Records relating to individual Kansas units, Unit ID: 455884 [MC 617: Sec. 3: Ser. K], file 17: Indian Home Guards Regiment, 3d, folder c (OV.11.03.3): Company E. Clothing Receipt Roll[s], 1862 Dec. 15–31. 7 items. Kansas Historical Society, State Archives, Topeka.

Military History Collection. 1862b. "Quarterly Return of Ordnance and Ordnance Stores." Records relating to individual Kansas units, Unit ID: 455884 [MC 617: Sec. 3: Ser. K], file 17: Indian Home Guards Regiment, 3d, folder e (OV.11.03.5): Company E. Quarterly Return[s] of Ordnance and Ordnance Stores, 1862 Dec. 31. 2 items. Kansas Historical Society, State Archives, Topeka.

Military History Collection. 1863. "Inventory of Ordnance and Ordnance Stores, April 18, 1863." Records relating to individual Kansas units, Unit ID: 455884 [MC 617: Sec. 3: Ser. K], file 17: Indian Home Guards Regiment, 3d, folder d (OV.11.03.4): Company E. Quarterly Return[s] of Clothing, Camp and Garrison Equipage. Kansas Historical Society, State Archives, Topeka.

Monaghan, Jay. 1955. *Civil War on the Western Border: 1854–1865*. New York: Bonanza Books.

National Archives. 1863. "Remarks for the Month of June 1863." Book Records of Volunteer Union Organizations, Morning Reports, Sixth Kansas Cavalry.

Record Group 94, Records of the Adjutant General's Office. National Archives and Records Administration, Washington, DC:

National Archives. 1891. "Compiled Military Service Record, Thomas White, Co. A, 6 Kansas Cav." Compiled Military Service Records. National Archives and Records Administration, Washington, DC.

National Archives. 1964. "Company Muster Roll July and August 1863, Co. L, 3 Reg't Indian Home Guards." Compiled Records Showing Service of Military Units in Volunteer Union Organizations. Microfilm Publication M594: 914. National Archives and Records Administration, Washington DC.

National Archives. 1983a. "Summary Statements of Quarterly Returns of Ordnance and Ordnance Stores on Hand in Regular and Volunteer Army Organization." Microfilm Publication M1281, roll 1, vol. 2. National Archives and Records Administration, Washington DC.

National Archives. 1983b. "Summary Statements of Quarterly Returns of Ordnance and Ordnance Stores on Hand in Regular and Volunteer Army Organization." Microfilm Publication M1281, roll 2, vol. 3. National Archives and Records Administration, Washington DC.

National Archives. 1983c. "Summary Statements of Quarterly Returns of Ordnance and Ordnance Stores on Hand in Regular and Volunteer Army Organization." Microfilm Publication M1281, roll 5, vol. 5/6. National Archives and Records Administration, Washington DC.

Noble, John W. 1883. "John W. Noble, Adjutant, Third Iowa Cavalry, to Maj. Gen. Samuel R. Curtis, Commanding, April 12, 1862." In *The War of the Rebellion: A Compilation of the Official Records of the Union and Confederate Armies*, series 1, vol. 8, 206–7. Washington, DC: Government Printing Office.

Norris, L. David, James C. Milligan, and Odie B. Faulk. 1998. *William H. Emory, Soldier-Scientist.* Tucson: University of Arizona Press.

NPS (National Park Service). n.d. "Defining Cultural Landscapes." National Park Service. Accessed September 24, 2019. https://www.nps.gov/subjects/culturallandscapes/understand-cl.htm.

NPS (National Park Service). 2015. "American Battlefield Protection Program: Programmatic Agreement Development for Grant Programs." National Park Service American Battlefield Protection Program Webinar, August 2015.

Oates, Stephen B. 1961. *Confederate Cavalry West of the River.* Austin: University of Texas Press.

Oklahoma v. Castro-Huerta. 2022. 21–429.

Perino, Gregory. 1977. "Kaskaskia Points (Metal)." In *Guide to the Identification of Certain American Indian Projectile Points.* Special Bulletin no. 4. Oklahoma City: Oklahoma Anthropological Society.

Perino, Gregory, and Mary E. Good. 1970. *A Guide to Projectile Point Types Found in Oklahoma.* Tulsa, OK: Tulsa Archaeological Society and Thomas Gilcrease Institute of American History and Art.

Phillips, Stanley S. 1971. *Bullets Used in the Civil War 1861–1865*. Laurel, MD: Wilson's Specialty Company.

Phillips, Stanley S. 1974. *Excavated Artifacts from Battlefields and Campsites of the Civil War, 1861–1865*. Ann Arbor, MI: Lithocrafters.

Phillips, William A. 1888a. "Wm. A. Phillips, Colonel, Commanding Third Brigade, to Major-General Curtis, Commanding Department of the Missouri, February 4, 1863." In *The War of the Rebellion: A Compilation of the Official Records of the Union and Confederate Armies*, series 1, vol. 22, pt. 2 (Correspondence), 96–97. Washington, DC: Government Printing Office.

Phillips, William A. 1888b. "Wm. A. Phillips, Colonel, Commanding Third Brigade, to Major-General Curtis, January 19, 1863." In *The War of the Rebellion: A Compilation of the Official Records of the Union and Confederate Armies*, series 1, vol. 22, pt. 2 (Correspondence), 56–58. Washington, DC: Government Printing Office.

Phillips, William A. 1888c. "Wm. A. Phillips, Colonel, Commanding, to Col. Harrison, Commanding Post, Fayetteville, Ark., April 18, 1863." In *The War of the Rebellion: A Compilation of the Official Records of the Union and Confederate Armies*, series 1, vol. 22, pt. 2 (Correspondence), 224–25. Washington, DC: Government Printing Office.

Phillips, William A. 1888d. "Wm. A. Phillips, Colonel, Commanding, to Col. M. La Rue Harrison, Commanding Post, Fayetteville, Ark., April 12, 1863." In *The War of the Rebellion: A Compilation of the Official Records of the Union and Confederate Armies*, series 1, vol. 22, pt. 2 (Correspondence), 212–13. Washington, DC: Government Printing Office.

Phillips, William A. 1888e. "Wm. A Phillips, Colonel Commanding, to Major-General Blunt, July 7, 1863." In *The War of the Rebellion: A Compilation of the Official Records of the Union and Confederate Armies*, series 1, vol. 22, pt. 2 (Correspondence), 355–56. Washington, DC: Government Printing Office.

Phillips, William A. 1888f. "Wm. A Phillips, Colonel Commanding, to Major-General Blunt, May 1, 1863." In *The War of the Rebellion: A Compilation of the Official Records of the Union and Confederate Armies*, series 1, vol. 22, pt. 2 (Correspondence), 266. Washington, DC: Government Printing Office.

Phillips, William A. 1888g. "Wm. A. Phillips, Colonel, Commanding, to Major-General Curtis, Commanding Department of the Missouri, February 6, 1863." In *The War of the Rebellion: A Compilation of the Official Records of the Union and Confederate Armies*, series 1, vol. 22, pt. 2 (Correspondence), 100–101. Washington, DC: Government Printing Office.

Pike, Albert. 1883. "Report of Brig. Gen. Albert Pike, C. S. Army, Commanding Department of Indian Territory, March 14, 1862." In *The War of the Rebellion: A Compilation of the Official Records of the Union and Confederate Armies*, series 1, vol. 8, 286–92. Washington, DC: Government Printing Office.

Pike, Albert. 1885. "Brig. Gen. Albert Pike, Commanding Department of the Indian Territory [to Maj. Gen. Earl Van Dorn, C. S. A.], May 4, 1862." In *The War of the Rebellion: A Compilation of the Official Records of the Union and Confederate Armies*, series 1, vol. 13, 819–23. Washington, DC: Government Printing Office.

Pike, Albert. 1900. "Albert Pike, Commissioner &c to Robert Toombs, Secretary of State, May 29, 1861." In *The War of the Rebellion: A Compilation of the Official Records of the Union and Confederate Armies*, series 4, vol. 1, section 1, 359–61. Washington, DC: Government Printing Office.

Pollard, Edward A. 1866. *The Lost Cause: A New Southern History of the War of the Confederates.* New York: E. B. Treat.

Poole, C. C. 1875. "An Interesting Letter from Texas." *Lexington Weekly Intelligencer*, December 11, 1875, 1.

Quiner, Edwin Bentley. 1866. *The Military History of Wisconsin: A Record of the Civil and Military Patriotism of the State, in the War for the Union.* Chicago: Clarke.

Randall, J. G., and David Donald. 1969. *The Civil War and Reconstruction.* Lexington, MA: D. C. Heath.

Reeves, Matt, and Eric Schweickart. 2019. "Identifying and Analyzing Agricultural Landscapes Using Metal-Detector Survey and Nail-Batch Analysis." *Historical Archaeology* 53: 412–31.

Rein, Chris. 2013. "The U.S. Army, Indian Agency, and the Path to Assimilation: The First Indian Home Guards in the American Civil War." *Kansas History: A Journal of the Central Plains* 36 (Spring): 2–21.

Rein, Christopher M. 2020. *The Second Colorado Cavalry: A Civil War Regiment on the Great Plains.* Norman: University of Oklahoma Press.

Return of Casualties. 1888. "Return of Casualties in the Union Forces in the Engagement of Elk Creek, Near Honey Springs, Ind. T., July 17, 1863." In *The War of the Rebellion: A Compilation of the Official Records of the Union and Confederate Armies*, series 1, vol. 22, pt. 1 (Reports), 449. Washington, DC: Government Printing Office.

Ringquist, John Paul. 2011. "Color No Longer a Sign of Bondage: Race, Identity and the First Kansas Colored Volunteer Infantry Regiment (1862–1865)." PhD diss., History, University of Kansas.

Ripley, Warren. 1970. *Artillery and Ammunition of the Civil War.* New York City: Promontory Press.

Ritchie, John. 1885. "John Ritchie, Colonel, Commanding Second Regiment I.H.G. to Brigadier-General Blunt, July 5, 1862." In *The War of the Rebellion: A Compilation of the Official Records of the Union and Confederate Armies*, series 1, vol. 13, 463–64. Washington, DC: Government Printing Office.

Ruane, Michael E. 2020. "Forgotten Civil War Map Shows Antietam as a Cemetery." *Washington Post*, June 17, 2020.

Rust, Albert. 1874. "A Yankee's Trip to Texas." *Nebraska State Journal*, August 7, 1874. Lincoln.

Schaumburg, W. C. 1888. "Major and Assistant Inspector-General, Trans-Mississippi Dept. W. C. Schaumburg to Brig. Gen. W. R. Boggs, October 26, 1863." In *The War of the Rebellion: A Compilation of the Official Records of the Union and Confederate Armies*, series 1, vol. 22, pt. 2 (Correspondence), 1049–53. Washington, DC: Government Printing Office.

Schaurte, Frederick W. 1888. "Report of Lieut. Col. Frederick W. Schaurte, Second Indian Home Guard, July 20, 1863 [to Acting Assistant Adjutant-General, First Brigade, Army of the Frontier]." In *The War of the Rebellion: A Compilation of the Official Records of the Union and Confederate Armies*, series 1, vol. 22, pt. 1 (Reports), 451–52. Washington, DC: Government Printing Office.

Schofield, J. M. 1888a. "J. M. Schofield, Brigadier-General, to Colonel Wm. A. Phillips, Colonel, Commanding Third Brigade, January 11, 1863." In *The War of the Rebellion: A Compilation of the Official Records of the Union and Confederate Armies*, series 1, vol. 22, pt. 2 (Correspondence), 33. Washington, DC: Government Printing Office.

Schofield, J. M. 1888b. "J. M. Schofield, Major-General, to Major-General Blunt, Fort Leavenworth, June 10, 1863." *The War of the Rebellion: A Compilation of the Official Records of the Union and Confederate Armies*, series 1, vol. 22, pt. 2 (Correspondence), 315. Washington, DC: Government Printing Office.

Schofield, J. M. 1888c. "J. M. Schofield, Major-General, to Major-General Blunt, Leavenworth, May 30, 1863." In *The War of the Rebellion: A Compilation of the Official Records of the Union and Confederate Armies*, series 1, vol. 22, pt. 2 (Correspondence), 296. Washington, DC: Government Printing Office.

Schofield, J. M. 1888d. "Troops in the Department of the Missouri, Maj. Gen. John M. Schofield, U.S. Army, Commanding, June 30, 1863." In *The War of the Rebellion: A Compilation of the Official Records of the Union and Confederate Armies*, series 1, vol. 22, pt. 2 (Correspondence), 343–47. Washington, DC: Government Printing Office.

School of Choctaw Language. 2011. "Making a Choctaw Arrow." *Iti Fabvssa*. Choctaw Nation of Oklahoma. Accessed December 8, 2024. https://web.archive.org/web/20200109160449/http://www.choctawschool.com/home-side-menu/iti-fabvssa/2011-articles/making-choctaw-arrows.aspx.

Scott, Douglas D. 2019. "Historic Rifling Data Characteristics: Using Forensic Techniques to Further Archaeological Inquiry into Firearms Use." Report for Grant P17AP00228, National Park Service, National Center for Preservation Technology and Training.

Scott, Douglas D., Joel Bohy, Nathan Boor, et al. 2019. "Firearm Bullet Performance: Phase II, Live Fire Experimental Study for Archaeological Interpretation: Colonial Pistol, Colonial Fowler, Colonial Rifle, and a Civil War Rifled Musket." Manuscript in possession of author.

Scott, Douglas D., and Richard A. Fox, Jr. 1987. *Archaeological Insights into the Custer Battlefield*. Norman: University of Oklahoma Press.

Scott, Douglas D., Richard A. Fox Jr., Melissa A. Conner, and Dick Harmon. 1989. *Archaeological Perspectives on the Battle of the Little Bighorn*. Norman: University of Oklahoma Press.

Scott, Douglas D., and A. P. McFeaters. 2011. "The Archaeology of Historic

Battlefields: A History and Theoretical Development in Conflict Archaeology." *Journal of Archaeological Research* 19: 103–132.

Scott, S. S. 1888. "S. S. Scott, Commissioner of Indian Affairs to Hon. James A. Seddon, Secretary of War, December 12, 1863." In *The War of the Rebellion: A Compilation of the Official Records of the Union and Confederate Armies*, series 1, vol. 22, pt. 2 (Correspondence), 1095–96. Washington, DC: Government Printing Office.

Scovill Fasteners (Morito Scovill Americas). n.d. "History." Accessed December 9, 2024. http://www.scovill.com/about-us/history.

Sesser, David. 2018. "Edwin Kirby Smith (1824–1893)." In *CALS Encyclopedia of Arkansas* (Central Arkansas Library System). https://encyclopediaofarkansas.net/entries/edmund-kirby-smith-9253.

Sivilich, Daniel M. 1996. "Analyzing Musket Balls to Interpret a Revolutionary War Site." *Historical Archaeology* 30, no. 2: 101–9.

Sivilich, Daniel M. 2016. *Musket Ball and Small Shot Identification: A Guide.* Norman, University of Oklahoma Press.

Smith, Edward A. 1888. "Report of Capt. Edward A. Smith, Second Kansas Battery [to Col. William R. Judson, July 19, 1863]." In *The War of the Rebellion: A Compilation of the Official Records of the Union and Confederate Armies*, series 1, vol. 22, pt. 2 (Reports), 454. Washington, DC: Government Printing Office.

Smith, J. Nelson. 1888. "Report of Maj. J. Nelson Smith, Second Colorado Infantry, Phillips' brigade [to Col. William A. Phillips, Third Indian Volunteers, Commanding, July 19, 1863]." In *The War of the Rebellion: A Compilation of the Official Records of the Union and Confederate Armies*, series 1, vol. 22, pt. 1 (Reports), 455. Washington, DC: Government Printing Office.

Smith, Stacey J. 2016. "Beyond North and South: Putting the West in the Civil War and Reconstruction." *Journal of the Civil War Era* 6, no. 4: 566–91.

Smith, Steven D. 2019. "Introduction: An Archaeology of Asymmetric Warfare." In *Partisans, Guerillas, and Irregulars: Historical Archaeology of Asymmetric Warfare*, edited by Steven D. Smith and Clarence R. Geier, 1–10. Tuscaloosa: University of Alabama Press.

Smith, Timothy B. 2017. *Altogether Fitting and Proper: Civil War Battlefield Preservation in History, Memory, and Policy, 1861–2015.* Knoxville: University of Tennessee Press.

Snow, Dean R. 1972. "1972 Saratoga Battlefield Report." The Digital Archaeological Record (tDAR). https://core.tdar.org/document/371815/1972-saratoga-battlefield-report. doi:10.6067/XCV8BP0oR9.

Sparks, Allison W. 2014. *The 3rd and 9th Texas Cavalry: The War Between the States as I Saw It.* Tyler, TX: Lee & Burnett. Amazon Kindle reprint of 1901 edition.

Spurgeon, Ian Michael. 2014. *Soldiers in the Army of Freedom: The First Kansas Colored, the Civil War's First African American Combat Unit.* Norman: University of Oklahoma Press.

Standard. 1863a. "The Battle of Elk Creek." *Standard* (Clarksville, TX), September 12, 1863, 1.

Standard. 1863b. "Letter from a Soldier of the 29th [Texas Cavalry], June 16, 1863." *Standard* (Clarksville, TX), 1.

Standard. 1863c. "List of Killed and Wounded of the 1st Brigade I. T. During the Engagement on the 17th ult. on Elk Creek, C. N." *Standard* (Clarksville, TX), September 12, 1863, Volume, 20.

Steele, William. 1888a. "Report of Brig. Gen. William Steele, C.S. Army, of operations in the Indian Territory in 1863 [to Lieut. Col. S. S. Anderson, February 15, 1864]." In *The War of the Rebellion: A Compilation of the Official Records of the Union and Confederate Armies,* series 1, vol. 22, pt. 1 (Reports), 28–36. Washington, DC: Government Printing Office.

Steele, William. 1888b. "Wm. Steele, Brigadier-General to Brig. Gen. D. H. Cooper, July 5, 1863." In *The War of the Rebellion: A Compilation of the Official Records of the Union and Confederate Armies,* series 1, vol. 22, pt. 2 (Correspondence), 906. Washington, DC: Government Printing Office.

Steele, William. 1888d. "Wm. Steele, Brigadier-General, to Maj W. B. Blair, July 1, 1863." In *The War of the Rebellion: A Compilation of the Official Records of the Union and Confederate Armies,* series 1, vol. 22, pt. 2 (Correspondence), 902. Washington, DC: Government Printing Office.

Steele, William. 1888e. "Wm. Steele, Brigadier-General, to Maj. W. B. Blair, July 10, 1863." In *The War of the Rebellion: A Compilation of the Official Records of the Union and Confederate Armies,* series 1, vol. 22, pt. 2 (Correspondence), 917. Washington, DC: Government Printing Office.

Stevens, Edward R. 1888. "Report of Capt. Edward R. Stevens, Third Wisconsin Cavalry, July 19, 1863 [to Colonel William R. Judson]." In *The War of the Rebellion: A Compilation of the Official Records of the Union and Confederate Armies,* series 1, vol. 22, pt. 2 (Reports), 453. Washington, DC: Government Printing Office.

Stewart-Abernathy, Leslie. 2019. "Cherokee." *CALS Encyclopedia of Arkansas* (Central Arkansas Library System). Revised February 11, 2019. https://web.archive.org/web/20191106192239/https://encyclopediaofarkansas.net/entries/cherokee-553.

Svenson, Peter. 1992. *Battlefield: Farming a Civil War Battleground.* New York: Ballantine Books.

Swain, Craig. 2017. "Summary Statement, 2nd Quarter, 1863—Kansas." *To the Sound of the Guns: Civil War Artillery, Battlefields and Historical Markers,* June 6, 2017. https://markerhunter.wordpress.com/2017/06/06/sum-stmt-2qtr63-ks (site discontinued).

Swain, Craig. 2018. "Summary Statement, 3rd Quarter, 1863—Kansas Artillery." *To the Sound of the Guns: Civil War Artillery, Battlefields and Historical Markers,* June 9, 2018. https://markerhunter.wordpress.com/2018/06/09/sum-stmt-3qtr63-ks (site discontinued).

TCLF (The Cultural Landscape Foundation). n.d. "About Cultural landscapes." The Cultural Landscape Foundation. Accessed September 24, 2019. https://tclf.org/places/about-cultural-landscapes.

Texas State Library and Archives Commission. n.d. "An Ordinance: To dissolve the union between the State of Texas and the other States, united under the compact styled 'The Constitution of the United States of America.' Adopted in Convention, at Austin City, the first day of February, A.D. 1861." Accessed April 20, 2020. https://www.tsl.texas.gov/ref/abouttx/secession/1feb1861.html.

Thomas, Dean S. 1997. *Round Ball to Rimfire: A History of Civil War Small Arms Ammunition*, pt. 1. Gettysburg, PA: Thomas Publications.

Thomas, Dean S. 2003. *Round Ball to Rimfire: A History of Civil War Small Arms Ammunition*, pt. 3, *Federal Pistols, Revolvers and Miscellaneous Essays*. Gettysburg, PA: Thomas Publications.

Thomas, Dean S. 2010. *Round Ball to Rimfire: A History of Civil War Small Arms Ammunition*, pt. 4, *A Contribution to the History of the Confederate Ordnance Bureau*. Gettysburg, PA: Thomas Publications.

Thomas, James E., and Dean S. Thomas. 1996. *A Handbook of Civil War Bullets and Cartridges*. Gettysburg, PA: Thomas Publications.

Townsend, E. D. 1880a. "E. D. Townsend, Assistant Adjutant-General, to Lieut. Col. W. H. Emory, First Cavalry, City of Washington, D.C., March 18, 1861." In *The War of the Rebellion: A Compilation of the Official Records of the Union and Confederate Armies*, series 1, vol. 1, 656. Washington, DC: Government Printing Office.

Townsend, E. D. 1880b. "E. D. Townsend, Assistant Adjutant-General, to Lieut. Col. W. H. Emory, First Cavalry, Commanding Fort Arbuckle, April 17, 1861." In *The War of the Rebellion: A Compilation of the Official Records of the Union and Confederate Armies*, series 1, vol. 1, 667. Washington, DC: Government Printing Office.

US Army, Corps of Topographical Engineers. 1866. *Indian Territory with Part of the Adjoining State of Kansas, &c.* Washington, DC: Engineer Bureau, War Department.

Veenendall, Augustus, Jr. n.d. "Missouri, Kansas and Texas Railway." In *The Encyclopedia of Oklahoma History and Culture*. Accessed April 16, 2020. https://www.okhistory.org/publications/enc/entry.php?entry=MI046.

Von Mueller, Karl. 1966. *The Treasure Hunter's Manual*. 7th ed. Alamo, CA: Gold Bug.

Ward, Geoffrey C., Rick Burns, and Ken Burns. 1990. *The Civil War: An Illustrated History*. New York: Alfred A. Knopf.

Warde, Mary Jane. 1993. "Now the Wolf Has Come: The Civilian Civil War in the Indian Territory." *Chronicles of Oklahoma* 71, no. 1 (Spring 1993): 64–87.

Warde, Mary Jane. 2013. *When the Wolf Came: The Civil War and the Indian Territory*. Fayetteville: University of Arkansas Press.

Warren, Steven L. n.d. "Cabin Creek, Battles of." In *The Encyclopedia of Oklahoma History and Culture*. Accessed December 13, 2018. https://www.okhistory.org/publications/enc/entry.php?entry=CA001.

Warren, Steven L. 2012. *The Second Battle of Cabin Creek: Brilliant Victory*. Civil War Sesquicentennial Series. Charleston, SC: History Press.

Wattles, Stephen H. 1888. "Report of Col. Stephen H. Wattles, First Indian Home Guard, July 18, 1863 [to Col. William A. Phillips]." In *The War of the Rebellion: A Compilation of the Official Records of the Union and Confederate Armies*, series 1, vol. 22, pt. 1 (Reports), 455–56. Washington, DC: Government Printing Office.

Weaver, Bobby D. n.d. "Texas Road." In *The Encyclopedia of Oklahoma History and Culture*. Accessed October 1, 2019. https://www.okhistory.org/publications/enc/entry.php?entry=TE023.

Weer, William. 1862. "Special Orders No. 4, Headquarters Indian Expedition, June 11, 1862." Book Records of Volunteer Union Organizations, Regimental Order Book, Second Indian Home Guard. Record Group 94, Records of the Adjutant General's Office. National Archives and Records Administration, Washington, DC.

Welch, Otis G. 1863. "Letter to Colonel T. C. Bass, July 25, 1863." *Standard* (Clarksville, TX), September 12, 1863, 2.

West, George. 1877. "Letter of July 6, 1863, reprinted in Second Colorado Veterans, Sixth Paper Continued." *Colorado Transcript* (Golden, CO), April 4, 1877.

W. H. S. 1863. "From Fort Blunt. Correspondence of the Missouri Democrat, Fort Blunt, Choctaw Nation, July 21." *Delphi (IN) Journal*, August 12, 1863.

Williams, James. M. 1888. "Report of Col. James M. Williams, First Kansas Colored Infantry, July 1863 [to Col. William A. Phillips]." In *The War of the Rebellion: A Compilation of the Official Records of the Union and Confederate Armies*, series 1, vol. 22, pt. 1 (Reports), 379–81. Washington, DC: Government Printing Office.

Wilson's Creek National Battlefield. n.d. a. "Carte-de-Visite" ["CDV (carte de visite) Image of an Osage warrior in native dress]. National Park Service Museum Collections WICR 31894. https://museum.nps.gov/ParkObjdet.aspx?rID=WICR%20%20%2031894&db=objects&dir=CR%20WICR&osearch=COMMUNICATION%20ARTIFACTS&page=3.

Wilson's Creek National Battlefield. n.d. b. "Tintype" ["Half cased tintype of an unknown federal Native American soldier"]. National Park Service Museum Collections WICR 30114. https://museum.nps.gov/ParkObjdet.aspx?rID=WICR%20%20%2030114&db=objects&dir=CR%20WICR&osearch=COMMUNICATION%20ARTIFACTS&page=6.

Wishart, David J. 2011. "The Great Plains Region." In *Encyclopedia of the Great Plains*. University of Nebraska–Lincoln. http://plainshumanities.unl.edu/encyclopedia/intro.html.

Wyant, Sharon Dixon. 1967. "Colonel William A. Phillips and the Civil War in Indian Territory." Master's thesis, Oklahoma State University.

Yarbrough, Fay A. 2021. *Choctaw Confederates: The American Civil War in Indian Country*. Chapel Hill: University of North Carolina Press.

Yeoman, R. S. 1984. *A Guide Book of United States Coins*. Racine, WI: Western Publishing.

INDEX